Come inside — take a walk along the friendly, littered highways of our land. Find out what happens when a newly-married couple sets out to discover the Real America, hidden amongst all that

Underwear
by the
Roadside

Underwear by the Roadside:

LitterWalk Coast-to-Coast
by
Glen Hanket

C A K Publishing _____

PO Box 953   Broomfield, CO   80038

Published by CAK Publishing, P.O. Box 953, Broomfield, CO 80038

Copyright © 1997 by Glen Hanket
All photographs by Glen or Susan Hanket
Cover Design by Robert Schram, Bookends Publication Design,
Boulder CO 80302
Map Designs by Chris Herron, Broomfield, CO

Publisher's Cataloging-in-Publication
    (Provided by Quality Books, Inc.)
Hanket, Glen.
    Underwear by the roadside : litterwalk coast-to-coast / by Glen Hanket
    p. cm.

    1. United States--Description and travel.   2. Hanket, Glen.   3. Walking
--United States.   4. Litter (Trash)   I. Title

E169.04.H36 1997   917.3'04929
                                          QBI97-40468

ISBN: 0-9657833-0-8

Printed in the United States of America
Printed on recycled paper

Dedicated to my beloved wife Susan . . .
without whom I would have never survived

** TABLE OF CONTENTS **

** MAPS **

A journey is a person in itself; no two are alike.   - John Steinbeck

. . . people don't take trips — trips take people.   - John Steinbeck

** FOREWORD **

Adventure is a challenge, a test, a way of stretching your potential. It can't be satisfied by dialing in a superhero on television or organized sports one afternoon every week or so. It has to be found out in the field.

- Bob Davenport, director of Wandering Wheels
(quoted in "The Long Ride" by Lloyd Sumner)

———————◆———————

I LOVE TRAVELING AND TRAVELERS. How anyone could not want to explore this incredible world is baffling to me. Those who travel are not only fascinating people, but they are also more excited about this miracle we call Life.

Whether we venture overseas or roam through our own country, we are certain to run into others who want to share their little part of the planet with us. So it was with myself, when Glen and Sue Hanket showed up at my home along the Ohio River in August 1993. Though they started out as little more than sunburnt strangers, it would not be long before I and my fiancee, Darci, eagerly vied to share with these two transamerica walkers the enchantments of the surrounding hills and villages. As Darci and I led our two guests along — to Indian graves, to a 150-year-old schoolhouse, to even the chaotic Tobacco Festival in Ripley — I couldn't help but smile. The sparkle in Glen's and Sue's eyes, the way the questions spilled off their chapped lips, the stories they exuberantly recounted from their still young odyssey . . . it reminded me so much of myself a decade earlier, when I'd also taken a long foot journey.

At that time I had been walking across the world's continents, and I had quickly realized that the world about us is a maelstrom of forces that can overwhelm some and invigorate others. Glen and Sue, it was apparent, belonged to the latter group. Their journey from the Atlantic to the Pacific was not only a journey of discovery but, incredibly, a sincere attempt to assist the earth's fragile ecology. These two ordinary Americans — one a computer software engineer, the other a paralegal — were wise enough to know that each of us has a choice to participate in either the nurturing or the destruction of the delicate balance of nature that exists on this planet. Since day one of their journey they had picked up litter along the roads they'd walked, as well as visiting schools and speaking to children of the importance of battling pollution.

Many of us mourn when we see the stupidity of mankind's callous treatment of the earth. We wonder how it is that so many others don't understand that as we destroy our environment so we destroy our own health and, possibly, even humanity's long-term survival. But then sadly we (myself included) turn away without attempting any remedy on the problem.

Glen and Sue, however, chose to take action. In a sense they became nomadic environmentalists, on a romantic journey of not only grand adventures and of lessons to be shared and learned, but also of something even more important --love. For in their actions, as well as in those of the many wonderful people across this nation who befriended them, we are reminded that in spite of society's failings, one thing, love, still exists in many individuals everywhere. And that is something we must never forget.

In an era when so many say that such noble acts as volunteerism, risk-taking, high goal-setting, and just simple compassion for strangers are being smothered by cynicism and fear, Glen and Sue's delightful odyssey serves as a true inspiration. Their story shows that we still have so much to be hopeful and thankful for.

Thus it is with much excitement that I invite you to venture further into this, the chronicle of two of the most exciting -- and noble -- persons to ever step onto my front porch.

Steven M. Newman
Author of WorldWalk

** BIRTH OF A DREAM **

October - December 1992

When I was very young and the urge to be someplace else
was on me, I was assured by mature people that maturity
would cure this itch. When years described me as mature, the
remedy prescribed was middle age. In my middle age I was
assured that greater age would calm my fever and now that
I am fifty-eight perhaps senility will do the job.
                        -- John Steinbeck, "Travels With Charley"

———————————◆————————————

*WHAT COULD POSSIBLY BE finer than spending a day walking
through a New England spring?* All around me, birds sang a tune of life.
Lawns sparkled green as they woke from a long winter's nap. Budding
trees exploded with color. Overhead, snow-white clouds danced on a stage
of blue velvet.

What could be finer, I asked myself. *Getting paid for it, maybe.* But
I had given up paychecks so my wife and I could discover America in a
way impossible from a car. By foot, we could see more than a string of
AAA-approved tourist stops ("Exit Here for the World Museum of
Buttons"), could expand our social circle beyond an eclectic mix of
convenience store clerks and motel maids. No longer would we rush place
to place, collecting "I've been there"'s like a picnic collects ants. For twelve
months, from Maine to Oregon, we would explore this great land.

I strolled alone down the wooded New Hampshire lane, the sun
warming me. This great shared trip — "an epic honeymoon," newspapers
dubbed it — had turned into a solo jaunt courtesy of Sue's latest accident.
Now I carried both our dreams, as well as a full set of camping gear in my
backpack. On a day this beautiful, I didn't notice the weight.

As I approached Brookline, I noticed a woman tending her garden. Salt
and pepper hair complemented a face that had seen its share of years. I
watched as she deftly planted a row of seedlings, never breaking her
smooth rhythm. Upon seeing me, a look of surprise turned to a smile of
recognition. She dropped her trowel, came to the sidewalk, wiped her hands
and shook mine. "I read about you in the Nashua paper, and wanted to
congratulate you." Glancing at my legs, she asked, "Did I see you

limping?"

"It's that noticeable, huh? That's what I get for playing Superhiker."
The past weekend I'd set a brutal pace, covering fifty-seven miles in three
days, and I now paid for it. One muscle after another voiced their
complaints, and I kept adjusting my gait trying to satisfy them. An 'easy'
five mile day yesterday did nothing to quell the pains.

"Is it serious?"

"I don't know. I'm taking this weekend off to visit my wife, and I hope
four days of rest cures it. If not . . ." I refused to consider that. "But first
I've got to hobble into Fitchburg, so I can catch the noon bus tomorrow."

"That's thirteen more miles!" Her smile wavered, then brightened. "If
you'd like, I can drive you to the station."

I hesitated only a moment before answering. "That's very kind of you,
but I can't accept. I set myself a goal of walking coast-to-coast, and I'm
going to give it my best shot."

She betrayed her concern with a frown. "Maybe I'll drive into Fitchburg
tomorrow morning. If it looks like you'll miss your bus, I'll give you a ride
to the station."

Thanking her, I moved on with an extra spring in my step, my spirits
further buoyed by her kind offer. *How does it happen,* I wondered, *that
every time I meet someone, my load gets lighter? Take my stop at Bagel
Haven an hour ago. The bag of fresh bagels they gave me — "for the
road," they said — acted like a helium balloon in my pack.*

The glow of the warm day spurred me forward to Highway 13 then
south toward Massachusetts. I crossed the state line and reached Townsend
shortly after classes had let out. Ahead of me, students swarmed out of the
school, running, playing, yelling.

Several houses down from the school, kids played in a fenced yard. One
girl looked up from the swing set, saw me approach, and pointed me out to
the others. They ran to the fence and called out questions. "Where you
going? Are you camping? What's in your pack?"

"I'm walking to Oregon!"

Their mouths dropped open. "WOW!" gasped the group's only boy.
"Can I have your autograph?"

When the other kids echoed his request with a chorus of "Me too!", I
took my turn at looking surprised. My John Hancock? No one had ever
asked me to sign anything more exciting than credit card slips, escrow
papers or traffic tickets. Chalk up another first for the trip. "Of course I

will."

They scampered inside and rushed back out with scraps of paper. Crowding around, they each handed me one, waiting politely as I filled them out. Asking them their names, I personalized each off-the-cuff note urging them to take chances and to live their dreams.

After all the girls had gotten their notes, the boy stepped up with his paper. "My name's Jason Scofield," he said. Though he looked only ten years old, he seemed to lead the group. When I finished his note, he pointed to the pole hanging from my pack. "What's that thing?"

"A litter stick," I replied. "With this, I can pick up trash as I walk along without bending over. See, when I pull the trigger, the jaws grab the trash." I showed them by plucking a crumpled cigarette pack from the gutter.

The girls asked questions until the novelty of the stranger faded. One by one they drifted back to the games I'd interrupted, leaving only Jason and a girl a few years younger standing near. "Go ahead, Caitlin," Jason urged, pushing her toward me.

Her auburn ponytail bobbed as she shyly looked up at me. Something glinted in her outstretched hand. "This is my lucky coin," she said, revealing an arcade token. "It's my only gold one. I want you to have it."

"Thank you, Caitlin. I promise to take good care of it." A tingle ran through my body as I carefully stashed the coin in my pack. *If only Sue could have shared this with me.*

As I waved goodbye, I smiled at the absurdity of it. Six months ago, I never imagined I would be a celebrity to kids in Townsend, Massachusetts.

Heck, six months ago I'd never *heard* of Townsend . . .

* * *

THE ADVENTURE HAD STARTED one sunny October afternoon in Orange County, as we sat in our car dealing with some freeway PTS (Permanent Traffic Syndrome — a California highway version of PMS). Seeing a pile of trash at the road's edge, I quipped, "If we want to walk across the country, why don't we pick up trash along the way? That way we could do something productive, not just do it for ourselves."

Sue glanced at me, a skeptical frown contradicting a gleam in her brown eyes. "You've been reading too many of my books."

"All those seditious adventure books you keep checking out of the library? About people who take a break from chasing a dollar to travel?"

I laughed. "I confess, guilty as charged."

Blue Highways. WorldWalk. Miles From Nowhere. The books had planted a seed. Sue started with a dog-eared copy of Peter Jenkins' *A Walk Across America* she'd found in my bookcase, and soon sought other titles. With each book read, our fascination with the notion grew. What a way to see the country, to meet people and experience folk culture! However, we'd never breathed a word of doing it ourselves — until now.

"I don't suppose the timing of this has anything to do with Dave Kunst's slide show last week?"

"Well, he didn't strike me as an athlete, and *he* walked around the world. As he said, 'If I could do it, so could you — if you have the desire'." I paused, then added, "It was just a thought."

As traffic started moving, I lapsed into silence, gazing out the car window. *It's a silly idea, walking for trash. The stuff daydreams are made of. I don't even own an orange plastic vest. No, it's just not practical . . . is it?*

Over dinner that night at a local Italian restaurant, Sue raised the topic again. "Were you serious earlier? About walking?"

"I don't know. Since college I've daydreamed about an epic trip, like bicycling through all the lower forty-eight states or kayaking the Lewis and Clark Trail."

"So why haven't you taken one?"

"Nothing ever drove me to start. I got too wrapped up in day-to-day living, thinking, maybe next year, when things settle down. Of course, every year had a 'next year.' Besides," I winked at her, "I never had anyone to do it with, and you know I hate to travel alone."

"Maybe 1993 will be our 'next year'."

I studied her from across the table. Curly brown hair reached to her shoulders, framing a face that glowed with excitement. Her tan skin appeared a shade darker in the dim light. As she leaned forward, the flickering candles reflected double off her glasses.

"I never knew anyone had done these trips until I found those books," she continued, "but now I'm hooked on the idea. No way could my hips handle sitting on a bike seat every day, but I can walk." At age thirty-five, she kept in shape, but still suffered from occasional bouts of arthritis.

As we finished our spaghetti, we discussed the hurdles involved with taking a break from the 'real world.' What would we do with the house? Or the new auto I'd leased? We had recently purchased new furniture — how much would it cost to store it? Those books didn't describe how others tied up their loose ends. Did they have all these concerns?

Most people would think us irresponsible if not insane. How could I leave a lucrative job in a recession, after working fourteen years to build up retirement and vacation benefits? What about health insurance? Would we be safe on the road?

"It's a lot of work," Sue concluded. "Maybe we're too old to have dreams like this."

That I couldn't accept; I'd always seen 'old' as an age ten years past mine. Still, at thirty-six, stiff joints and slack muscles had begun visiting me. Weekend hikes and bike rides helped, but reminded me my best years had passed. Could I leave the comforts of home and survive the rigors of life on the road?

Two nights later, Sue broached the subject again. I tried to say, "I'd like to, but . . . ," yet I couldn't dismiss the idea. Discussions dragged on for three weeks as we looked at the pros and cons. What pitfalls awaited us? Could we arrange sponsors? What other details should we consider?

Though we disagreed on some issues, one point elicited no argument: we had little time to decide. An April 1 start would let us get used to the road before hitting the dog days of summer. Shooting for 1993 would leave us only five months to prepare. If we waited until '94, any number of things could happen. Would we seize the chance or let it slip away?

Despite her concerns, Sue voted for the trip from the start. Since I would risk my job by leaving (she'd lost hers to a layoff earlier that year), she gave me the final say. For several nights I tossed and turned, agonizing over a decision that would redirect our lives. As November opened, I made our choice:

Let's walk!

SINCE MY LATE TEENS, I had proven easy prey for the siren song of adventure. My trips sounded like excerpts from *National Geographic*: Drive Jeeps to undeveloped beaches in Thailand! Rappel into vertical caves in the jungles of central Mexico! Kayak among forested islands in Alaska's Glacier Bay! It was heady stuff for someone who coasted through school as a bookworm.

After two decades, my parents had grown accustomed to my mad schemes. After only two years, my in-laws hadn't. "You're going to

WHAT?" Sue's mother exclaimed. As we laid out our plans, her silence registered her disapproval. Sue's father, along with my folks, gave us cautious support. They all voiced concerns for our safety, but offered any help they could provide.

Next we told our friends. To our surprise, many of them confessed to having similar dreams. "Could I come along?" a few joked, with a longing in their eyes. Others talked of visiting us on the road.

Despite the length of our proposed trip, no one acted surprised. Years of slide shows and travelogues of my far-flung journeys had convinced friends I'd do anything to travel. Some questioned why I'd never done this before now. A co-worker had once asked me, "Why are you wasting your time working on computers eight hours a day? How come you're not writing, taking pictures, and traveling full time?"

The more people we told, the more questions we had to answer. Some were silly — one friend asked Sue, "How will you do your nails on the road?" Others alerted us to issues we needed to address: What would we take with us? How would we protect ourselves?

Friends and family asked about the equipment we would carry, suggesting their own 'can't-live-withouts.' Though we tried to keep our load light and our lives simple, our gear list grew. Electronic frills such as a Walkman™, micro-cassettes, and a CB radio for emergencies snuck onto the list. (Time would show us how little we used or needed them.) One friend suggested a cellular phone, which we laughed off. We couldn't leave the world behind if we took it all with us!

Everyone worried about our safety. Carjackings in Pennsylvania and tourist shootings in Florida filled the TV news that fall, making the nation sound like a no-man's land for travelers. Riots and gang violence in Los Angeles kept Sue uneasy around home. How could we protect ourselves? Several friends recommended handguns, but that violated our beliefs. We were taking the walk to meet people, not shoot them!

We debated our options, assessing the risks of the road. We'd avoid most cities, sticking to quiet backwaters where crime rarely intruded. Side roads would carry less traffic, keeping us away from crowds. In the end, we settled on an arsenal of one can of mace.

FINANCES TOPPED OUR LIST of concerns. Though I had saved a sizable nest egg after fourteen years of "slaving over a hot computer," we were loath to dip into it deeply. Seven months of outflow with no income would help our savings like the Indians helped Custer. Also, I couldn't count on getting a leave of absence from work. In recession-plagued southern California, engineers faced a tight job market.

We fretted most about health insurance. Aware that one hospital stay could wipe us out, we called around for rates. Expensive! We asked several agents about sponsoring us, but most had no authority to help. Our lone hope lay with a Blue Cross agent, who passed our request to friends in upper management.

The cost of equipment also worried us. The tent and sleeping bags we owned sufficed for weekend camping trips, but would never last under daily use. Neither of us owned backpacks, and our boots were wearing out. Sturdy gear would run $2000 or more.

"Forget fund-raising," Sue said, tossing a tent brochure onto the coffee table. "No one owes us this trip. I won't hit friends up for 10¢ a mile."

"That's right; we're not charity cases," I agreed. "I don't expect people to support our dream. But if we can convince companies to donate their gear . . ."

"Why would anybody give us free equipment?"

"Because it's in their PR budget." I pointed to a picture on the tent pamphlet. "Take this Everest expedition. Do you think they paid for all their gear? No, they got sponsors." I sipped from a glass of juice, then continued. "We can give them good press while we walk, so why shouldn't we tap into that?"

"Okay," she said, still skeptical. "So how do we arrange it?"

I picked up the pamphlet and the phone. "I guess we call and ask."

The reactions to our cold-calling were consistent: "Sounds interesting; could you send us a proposal letter?" After researching how to write one, we solicited our first five companies. That was easy — waiting weeks for their answers, much harder.

A MAP OF THE U.S. covered the table before us, its network of highways both exciting and intimidating. "How can we ever hope to cross all this?" asked Sue. "Where would we start?"

I studied the map. "I think we should skip California. Yes, I'd love to

have friends see us off, but I don't want to deal with hundreds of miles of
desert our first two weeks. We couldn't carry enough supplies to last us
between towns."

"How about trying Oregon? It's beautiful up there."

"Sure, I've got cousins in Portland. Hey! Maybe we could walk from
the Portland in Oregon to the one in Maine! Like bookends of our trip." My
gaze moved up the map, checking the terrain.

Oregon, though far better than the desert, still looked forbidding. Long,
empty stretches awaited us as we headed inland. Sue pondered, then asked,
"Do we have to start on the west coast?"

Good question. "I guess not. It might even be better to start in Maine.
Towns are closer together back east, so we could carry less food and water
while we got used to the road."

Her smile grew as she studied the map. "Since we're trying to beautify
America, why don't we start and stop in America's most beautiful places
— the National Parks?" We loved the parks. Having gotten married in
Rocky Mountain National Park and honeymooned in Yellowstone, it made
sense to 'sandwich' our walk that way. We chose to start in Acadia
National Park (one of my favorites, which Sue had never seen) far north on
the Maine coastline, and finish by seeing Olympic National Park,
Washington, for the first time.

Her finger traced a path through the heart of the country. "If we drop
south to my parents' in Connecticut, then head due west, we could see my
brother in Ohio. And your relatives in Chicago, too."

I extended the line. "Trouble is, that dumps us into the Dakotas. It's
pretty country, but unpopulated. Wyoming will be enough of a challenge.
What about dropping farther south?"

"We could visit Shenandoah National Park!"

"And then turn west toward St. Louis and Colorado." I quickly added
the miles. "From Acadia to Denver is about 2600 miles. If we hit fifteen
miles a day, and took occasional days off, it would take us . . . into
October." I shivered, thinking about crossing the Rockies in the cold and
snow.

"We could spend the winter with your family in Boulder," Sue
suggested.

"Or return to California and work for six months, to earn money for the
second half. We can worry about Wyoming, Idaho, and crossing the
Rockies the next year. If we make it that far."

"DID YOU HAVE TO choose litter?" Sue ribbed me. "Why couldn't we walk across the country picking roses? Instead of *Walking* magazine, maybe we'd appear in *Better Homes and Gardens.*"

We'd just received notice that *Walking* would advertise our trip, urging their readers to join us. National publicity! Maybe we could have an impact on litter. If a thousand people heard about us, perhaps one would think twice about tossing that beer can out their car window. However, our opinions on using the media differed.

"I know you don't like it," I said, putting down a brochure on Maine, "but we need the coverage. It could help attract sponsors, and people we meet may be more open. Appearing in papers might even keep us safer on the road."

"It's still not the trip I dreamed of. I'd prefer to be anonymous, and walk across the country without people expecting things from me. I'm not doing this for glory. I just want to see the land and meet the people."

"Then let's give ourselves the best chance to do so. Would you stop and talk to a stranger walking with a pack down Beach Boulevard? I wouldn't. Would you stop if you'd read about him walking across the country? Ahhh, that's different!"

Another point bothered me. "I'm also worried about how far we'll get knowing we could quit anytime. What's to keep us going after three or four straight days of rain, if no one knows the difference?"

"What should keep us going is the desire to be out there." Sue moved about the living room, watering her ferns. "If we enjoy it, we'll keep on. If not, we don't have to worry about letting someone down."

"*WorldWalk* author Steven Newman had the desire. He planned and prepared for his walk for six years, but nearly gave up after two weeks. He knew people were counting on him, and he wouldn't let them down. We can still quit, but only after we give it our best shot."

"I still say publicity changes things. Once we have to be somewhere at a given time for an interview, or walk a certain road to meet a film crew, it's no longer our trip. It becomes a job." She sat next to me on the couch. "If you insist on getting press, I'll go along, but I don't have to like it!"

"FIRST, I WANT YOU to know that, no matter what the merits of your walk, we already have our advertising plan for next year. There's no way we can use your trip in our ad campaigns." As the phone delivered those words from Steve Gladstone, our contact person at Merrell Shoes, I girded myself for rejection. Three weeks had passed since we mailed our proposal letters. Tired of waiting, I had started calling back.

"Really, I applaud what you're doing. I think it's a great cause. What were you hoping to get from us?" he asked.

"I figured we would need at least two pairs of boots apiece, since we'll probably wear them out on the road." I heard Sue groan at my request, chastising me for being too greedy.

"You'll need at least that many. Which model were you interested in?"

I knew what we wanted, boots with GoreTex™ for waterproofing and high sides for ankle support, yet still comfortable enough to walk in. At $140/pair, would that be asking too much? "The Westwind GTX™."

"As I said, we can't fit you in our advertising, but we can send you two pairs of boots each." He chuckled a Santa Claus laugh. "In the Christmas spirit, you know." After asking about the publicity we were arranging, he requested another letter from us, detailing the shoe sizes and where to ship them.

The news exhilarated us. A major sponsor! Our initial pessimism melted away. For days the thrill lingered, convincing us our far-fetched plan could work.

Our luck with the 'litter sticks' matched that with the boots. To pick up trash, we first pictured using crude sticks with nails in one end. When our friend Ron Schrantz told us beach cleanup crews used more advanced tools, we called the Huntington Beach Parks Department, who referred us to a Colorado company. Paul Riddenmeyer at Pikes Peak Industries described his product, a lightweight rod with a trigger at one end connected to movable jaws at the other. He enthusiastically endorsed our plans, and promised to send two sticks along with a bag holder.

Those victories gave us hope, even as a string of defeats followed. One contact coldly informed us it would be "some time" before she would get to our proposal; the Glad Bags™ rep avoided our phone calls for weeks. Three more contacts politely turned us down. Our hopes for free health insurance vanished after two separate Blue Cross officials rejected our proposal.

AS THE OLD YEAR waned, our 'fame' waxed. We quickly became fixtures in the neighborhood as we trained with our litter sticks, wearing matching 'Litter Walk U.S.A.' tee shirts. People would stop and ask what we were doing. Though we didn't ask for donations, several people offered to chip in a few dollars — "for a pair of boots or something, to ease your burden a little."

These chance encounters kept our training walks fresh. To get in shape, we walked everywhere — to the bank, the grocery store, the movie theatre. On weekends we'd take longer hikes with friends, or circle a local park bagging trash. One morning, a jogger on her rounds noticed us. She quickly grabbed a piece of litter and, as she passed, added it to our bag. "Thank you," I said.

"No," she replied without slowing. "Thank YOU."

At Christmas parties we found ourselves the center of attention. Soon after we arrived, someone would announce our plans. Everyone clamored for details, taking vicarious thrills in our adventure. Many of them envied our trip or admired our ambition.

Working out details kept us busy. We solicited more sponsorships and wrote to state Highway Departments. I applied for a leave from work. As Christmas approached, we drove to Colorado to visit my family, taking a break from the growing stress.

For much of the week-long visit, we followed up with potential sponsors and surveyed Boulder stores for needed equipment. We still lacked a tent, backpacks, and sleeping bags. One backpack line, made in southwestern Colorado by Osprey Packs, impressed us. Nothing we'd seen earlier beat their construction and comfort.

As we left one store, Sue lost traction on the icy sidewalk. Her feet flew out from under her. She landed hard, her hands reaching out to absorb the impact. As she sat grimacing in pain, a crowd gathered.

"What happened?" asked a concerned passerby. "Was she running?"

No, I thought of responding. *She's just practicing to walk across the country.*

> The country, your companions, and the length of your
> journey will afford a hundred compensations for your toil.
>
> - Ovid

————➤ ◆ ◀————

SUE'S LEFT HAND REFUSED to heal. Weeks after the fall in Colorado, it continued to ache, and Sue couldn't lift so much as a glass of water with it. Ignoring the problem didn't make it go away, so in mid-January she visited the doctor.

I came home that night to find Sue wearing plaster elbow-to-wrist. "Oh, no," I sighed. "How bad is it?"

"It might heal and be fine . . . in four weeks. The bad news is, if it doesn't, I'll need bone graft surgery." She frowned as if thinking it over, then announced, "I choose option number one!"

"There's a chance it won't heal?"

She nodded slowly. "The doctor told me I broke rule number one of Hand Anatomy: never break bone in wrist called scaphoid, it can't be SuperGlued. The area has bad circulation. As he described it, blood has to pass it by then hang a U-turn to get there. If it swells, little blood gets through."

"Maybe I'm a jinx to you."

"No, you're not. You know me, only I could break a bone nobody's ever heard of."

Her words didn't ease my doubts. In the three years we had known each other, she had suffered a broken toe, five root canals, a bout of hepatitis, and a freak hiking accident. That accident, which left her leg bone exposed, took seventeen stitches to close. First, though, three other hikers had to help me carry her a mile through the woods before a search-and-rescue squad carried her out the last mile.

Now this. Sue struggled hard to stay upbeat, but frustration weighed down her smile. Trying to find a bright side, I noted, "At least it wasn't your writing hand." The timing, however, made optimism difficult. Four weeks would take us to mid-February, only three weeks before we planned to leave California. Could we still start on time — or at all, if the doctor recommended surgery? Even if her hand healed, could she use it to lift a heavy pack?

In addition, Sue's feet concerned me. Blisters plagued her during our training walks, leaving us to wonder when, or if, they would toughen. Not that I was a model of good health — my knees could give out anytime. If I kept them wrapped while hiking, I had no problems. Without kneepads, a five-mile hike would leave me limping. Would they stand up to the pounding of a dozen miles or more every day?

I wondered if either of us could handle this trek. Neither of us were expert backpackers. My half-dozen trips had lasted no more than a weekend each, and Sue's only overnight trip had come just four months earlier. We had taken countless hikes over the years, but none covered more than fifteen miles.

Was her broken wrist a warning?

THE SPONSOR SEARCH STRUCK gold again late in January. Our letter to Osprey Packs had stalled on the desk of Dave Wren, who was busy completing their 1993 catalog. Once he put that to bed, he took our proposal to the company's owner. We received our answer an hour later — YES, they would provide us backpacks!

If I floated home from work that night, I positively soared afterwards. Waiting for us was a catalog from Moss Tents, along with a letter asking which tent we wanted. "I didn't even follow up with them," I told Sue. "Why couldn't they all be this easy?"

Four days later, we landed our best-known sponsor. Following a snub by Glad Bags™, we had written Tenneco, makers of Hefty™. After weeks of weaving through the corporate maze, our proposal landed on the desk of Fady Sahhar. He lauded our project and sent us one hundred coupons redeemable for Hefty™ bags, promising more if needed. In addition, their ad agency shipped us tee shirts and sweat shirts, all adorned with the Hefty™ logo.

Our stellar month climaxed with the receipt of our hiking boots. Like kids at Christmas, we tore open the boxes. Until now everything had seemed so academic, as if we'd taken a college course on setting up a charity. With the boots in hand, the feeling changed.

As each sponsor came through, my confidence rose that the trip would happen. On top of that, I now felt obligated to give it my best. We had a contract, so to speak: the boots were the first 'paychecks' of our new litter-picking career. Now we hoped Sue's hand would heal.

"COUPLE PLAN A TRASHY VACATION" -- *Los Angeles Times* headline, Saturday, January 30, 1993

Sue hit it right: publicity *did* change things. Appearing in print gave our trip a certain cachet, an authenticity I hadn't felt before. On our training walks, people stopped to ask about our plans or wish us well. One woman called to ask about our litter sticks, and a freelance writer interviewed us for an article in *Walking* magazine. Even Sue, so opposed to seeking press, admitted to a thrill when she opened the paper and saw our pictures.

The article mentioned me taking a leave from my job at Rockwell International, a leave they had not yet approved. The story set phones ringing Monday morning, and by Friday my boss's bosses gave their okay. With approval came an unexpected benefit: the company would continue my health insurance.

We trained with new vigor, increasing our mileage as the winter wore on. Our friends Ron and Joann Schrantz kept our walks fresh, suggesting new hikes — here a beach, there the woods — to prevent boredom. The more we walked (107 miles in January, 100 in February), the more eager I grew to try my hand — er, feet — at the road.

My knees stayed strong, and Sue worked through her blisters. Only nagging doubts about Sue's hand kept my mood in check. On February 10, she went to get the cast off — and a new one replaced it. "The doctor said it was healing," she explained after dinner, "only slower than he hoped. He wanted to keep this cast on four more weeks, but I told him we'd be gone by then. He agreed to check it again in two."

"We're due to leave in twenty-five days," I reminded her as I rinsed the dishes. "We can't hedge our bets for two more weeks. There are too many details to settle, decisions we've put off in case we couldn't go."

"You're right. It's time to make our choice." She took a coin from her pocket. "Let's flip for it. Heads we go, tails we flip again."

I smiled. "Sounds good to me. How does your hand feel about it?"

"When have I ever let my body hold me back? My hand will heal — it has to. If necessary, you can start by yourself, and I'll join you on the road. One way or another, let's do it."

With the decision made, I surrendered to a dash of euphoria. The next two days floated by, the sky a shade bluer, the sun a tad warmer. Time shrunk during my lunchtime walks, and only willpower got me back to my desk by 1:00 each day.

A WALKING TRIP, FOR me, implied a simpler life. However, getting there proved anything but simple.

Our condo proved our biggest headache. Since our long-term goals included moving from California, we listed the unit in November for $165,000. With no buyers in sight by February, we panicked and looked for renters instead. (If I'd known about the Incredible Shrinking Equity virus infecting California real estate, we'd have dropped our price earlier. In 1996, after renters caused $4000 in damages, we finally sold it for $112,500. Isn't hindsight grand?) We leased the condo the week we left, almost covering our monthly payments.

Most details just took time: Sublease my truck. Shift money in bank accounts. Downgrade our auto insurance. Set up automatic payments for the mortgage. Forward mail to Colorado. My mother volunteered to handle our bills, so we gave her power-of-attorney over our accounts. "I know why you offered, Mom," I teased her. "You relish the thought of spending someone else's money!"

Good news came in February's final days. Two weeks had flown by — time for Sue's next doctor visit. This time she came out wearing a removable splint. "It's weak, but it's healed," she said. "I've got to be careful with it. He said no lifting heavy weights, like a backpack." She flashed me a toothy grin.

"Right. Let me guess — he said no pitching tents, either, or tying boots?" I gave her a hug. "You'd better behave, if you want _me_ to help you."

We celebrated Sue's cast-free limb two nights later, at a bon voyage party. Our friends gathered to say farewell, giving us addresses so we could send postcards. Several gave us supplies for the road, a medley of gifts including postage stamps, trail mix, film, sunscreen, and fast food certificates. In return, we handed out maps of our planned route and talked of areas we hoped to see. The evening flew by, and before we knew it, the party had broken up.

We spent the last week packing, getting everything ready for storage. Outlandish prices in Orange County ($120/month for a 10' by 20' locker) forced us to look forty miles away. In Riverside we found self-storage for half that cost.

To get there, we rented the 'Lemon Godzilla.' The 24' moving van sported special features such as bump-magnifying shocks, a steering wheel with one-quarter turn play, and brakes that could have stopped a locomotive. First gear sounded like a karate expert in labor, and fourth like a chain saw — shifting required an 'if you can't find it, grind it' philosophy. All this in a beautiful shade of Rental Truck Yellow!

On moving day we had the pleasure of one last southern California traffic jam. After traveling only one block in twenty-five minutes, we turned to backtrack and got stuck for fifteen more. "We could have walked to Riverside quicker," I grumbled.

A crew of friends helped us squeeze the contents of our three-bedroom house and garage into 200 square feet. It sobered me to think we could contain our material goods in such a small space, with room to spare. So long, 8-to-5 life.

"What have we done?" Sue asked as we returned to an empty house. If the enormity of our task hadn't registered before, it did now. For eight months, we would have no place to call home. Eating out would grow old, and a home-cooked meal would be something to savor. We could no longer take for granted the joy of a hot shower, or the comfort of a soft bed. Our friends' lives would continue without us there to share in their daily dramas.

We kept busy all day Sunday, delivering my truck, packing and shipping camping gear to Connecticut, cleaning the condo, and moving last minute items to storage. Finally, Monday morning dawned. We loaded the rest of our equipment in Sue's car and headed for Colorado. In the rearview mirror, familiar scenes retreated, closing a chapter in our lives. Ahead of us the open road beckoned. Together we sang along with Jerry Jeff Walker on the tape deck: "If I can just get off that L.A. freeway without getting killed or caught . . ."

WHEN I'D WORKED AS a teenage paperboy with Boulder, Colorado's *Daily Camera*, I'd always aimed for the front porch. Twenty years later, I hit their front page.

Though the Denver papers declined to cover us, the local paper ran a feature. The exposure made us instant celebrities on our hikes through

Boulder. The warm welcomes and shouted "Thanks!" encouraged us, raising our hopes for an equally warm reception in New England.

While we enjoyed the local limelight, our 'fame' spread on the coast. The _Orange County Register_ had interviewed us four days before we'd left, and printed a glowing article a week later. We had barely arrived in Boulder when friends called to tell us our faces beamed from page one of the local news.

Two mornings later, we received another call. "My name is Laura Brown," stated an unfamiliar voice, "from KABC Talk Radio in L.A. I saw your article in the paper. What are you doing in Colorado?"

"We're staying with family for ten days while we train," I replied, "then flying to the east coast to start walking."

"Well, I'm the producer for the 'Ken and Barkley Company,' on every weekday morning during rush hour. Do you listen to it?"

"Frankly, no, but I have heard of them." Both Ken and Barkley had years of hosting talk shows with different partners. Recently they'd formed a team and quickly gained a reputation for off-the-wall programming.

"They're the second most listened-to morning radio show in the area. Would you mind if they interviewed the two of you, live, on Monday's show?"

We jumped at the chance to let friends 'back home' hear us on their Monday commute. Those that tuned in heard us banter over the air:

RADIO INTERVIEWER: Why would two otherwise normal people decide to take a 4000-mile walk across America? . . . Are you guys recently wed?

GLEN: As of last July.

RI: And this is your idea of a honeymoon . . . What do you do [for work]?

GLEN: Software engineering.

RI: So you told them, "I'd like to go out and take a 4000-mile walk," and they didn't fire you?

GLEN: They sort of looked at me strangely at first . . .

RI: As you're out there walking on these lonely back roads, it can be dangerous . . . You never know who is likely to be there. Are you camping along the way?

SUE: Yes.

RI: Are you afraid?

SUE: (laughing) No more afraid than I am of living in southern California sometimes . . .

RI: Will you carry a port-a-potty along with you?

SUE: Unfortunately, no. It's called roughing it.

RI: I've hiked a little bit, and that's always a foremost concern. I know it's not one of those pleasant things to talk about, but you ARE taking a walk to reduce litter.

GLEN: We've chosen our route so we'll be in fairly populated areas. If we have an emergency, we can go to a house and ask to use their restroom.

RI: Will you, on occasion, stop somewhere and take a shower?

SUE: Oh, yes, definitely . . .

They asked about our route, our motivations, and our sponsors before asking one last question. "Could we give you a number so you could periodically check in with us? You could be, 'Sue and Glen, On the Road in America,' and every so often, call and share your experiences . . ."

That's like mixing Charles Kuralt with Mr. Clean, I mused. The offer amazed us. I'd never dreamed we'd make a stir so quickly — and we hadn't started walking yet! Within the week, our exposure spread to another L.A. station, all-news KFWB. They also asked for regular updates. Then the *Register* article hit a wire service, giving us national exposure. In Baton Rouge, Louisiana, a reporter from a German-language public radio station saw it and tracked us down.

We'd hoped to concentrate on training while in Colorado, but nettlesome problems kept us from the road. Tasks ranging from buying rain gear to writing state highway departments kept us busy. Our worst crisis arose when we checked our packs: the bulky old sleeping bags we'd planned to use wouldn't fit in them. We made urgent calls to two companies that had offered us bags at wholesale, seeing what we could work out.

With what time we had left, we hiked. Along the Boulder Creek trail, through neighborhoods dotted with Victorian homes, and into the foothills we tramped. For the first time we trained with our Osprey packs, which we'd picked up on our drive east. Since we'd shipped most of our gear to Connecticut, we couldn't load the packs, but we stuffed them with blankets to simulate the weight. I couldn't have hoped for a more comfortable fit — a dozen straps allowed me to tailor it for any load or terrain.

On our last long walk in Boulder, we ate a sack lunch on a foothill ridge overlooking the plains stretching eastward. In the sky, jet contrails crisscrossed, a symbol of the fast-paced world we had checked out of. "Hard to believe, isn't it," I said, as much to myself as to Sue. "They're moving along at more than 500 miles per hour. We won't cover that in a month."

Perched on a rock, I gazed out at the plains, trying to imagine life crossing this huge land. After a few minutes, Sue interrupted my reverie. "You know, I'm not excited about walking."

I looked at her, waiting for the punch line. "You picked a fine time to realize that."

She smiled back. "Oh, I'm excited about the trip, about traveling and meeting people. Who wouldn't get drawn up in the hoopla of it? I mean, I've never been in newspapers or on the radio before. When I think about walking every day, though . . . I'm often not a happy camper when I'm exercising. Still, I think about all the people who believe in us, and I won't let them down."

She flexed her left hand, studying it as if she could see the bones inside. "I know this trip's going to end up being a grudge match between me and my body. I don't accept limitations, and I don't like anybody or anything telling me what I can't do."

I find it hard to grasp the immensity of what we are doing. Driving to Colorado and then flying to the east coast only masks the reality of how huge a task we have undertaken — travel that took only three days by car and plane will occupy us for twelve months or more.

Now that we're ensconced in Connecticut, the trip seems a lot closer. Training in California, with its endless asphalt, perpetually pleasant weather, and hordes of people hurrying about their lives, gave us no inkling of what the road will be like. Colorado was better, but still (for me) a familiar place, a place where I grew up and not a novel setting for an adventure.

The mood enveloping us here is different. The variety in architecture, contrasted with the stucco and concrete style so prevalent in California, lends a feeling of discovery. Snow remaining from the blizzard of '93 reminds us of winter's presence, but promises a change of seasons to enliven the early days of the trip. Though we are both far less fit than

we'd hoped to start the trip, we can hardly wait to get underway.
                                                        -journal entry, March 20

CONDITIONS IN THE SNOWBOUND east threatened to delay our
April 1 start. Connecticut still bore snow dumped by the latest 'storm of
the century', promising worse conditions farther north. A second storm
greeted our arrival, adding to the drifts. For days we watched weather
reports, unhappy with prospects of holing up well into April. Luckily a
warm spell soon took over, loosening winter's hold and keeping us on
schedule.

A new state meant new papers to contact. The Danbury *News-Times*
ran a thorough article, mentioning our sponsors and getting in a dig that
Glad Bags™, made locally, had rejected us. Again, the people we met on
our training walks encouraged us. But what did they say behind our backs?
On the day the story appeared, Sue's mother overheard two women talking
about the article at the local pharmacy. They questioned both our safety
and our sanity. "I'm glad they're not my kids," one woman quipped.

"No," Mom Armstead told them. "They're mine!"

As D-day approached, the sleeping bag problem resisted solution.
Last-minute phone calls got us no closer to free bags. With only days to
spare, we accepted Sierra Designs' offer of sleeping bags below cost. "I'll
mark them 'top priority'," Leslie Kirchner said. "That way, you'll have
them in three days."

Four days later, they hadn't arrived. We called Leslie back, who found
that the 'top priority' designation had gotten lost between the stockroom
and shipping. The bags now en route would reach Connecticut after we'd
left for Maine. We filled our last afternoon at Sue's folks' house with
coast-to-coast calls, cajoling Leslie to ship two more bags, overnight
express, ahead to our hotel in Bar Harbor.

We reserved the final night to load our packs. Our gear — shorts, tee
shirts, sweatshirts, rain gear, gloves, hats, hiking socks, underwear, a
backpack stove, matches, pans, knives, the tent, maps, toiletries, cups,
water bottles, sleeping pads, litter sticks, a journal, microcassettes,
Walkman™, batteries, postcards, cameras, books, Hefty™ bags — formed
Mount Hanket on the bed. Substituting jackets for the missing bags, we
stuffed the packs to overflowing, then surveyed what didn't fit. Out it all
came, and we chose what to eliminate. When we'd made the final cut,

reloaded, and weighed the packs, mine came in over thirty-five pounds and Sue's neared thirty. *That's it for seven months*, I thought. *How can we survive on so little?*

On March 30, Sue's folks drove us to Maine through pleasant, springlike weather. We spent our last free day touring Acadia National Park, driving along the rocky coastline and hiking to Bass Head lighthouse in 60° temperatures. Mom and Dad Armstead treated us to a lobster dinner that night, though I was too nervous to savor it. The road loomed only fourteen hours ahead.

After five months of hassling sponsors, toughening the dogs, settling affairs, and whittling our immediate possessions to a minimum, the day has arrived. Our path here has been so novel, so distracting, it's been hard to focus on what awaits us tomorrow, other than nine miles of lugging packs through cold (35° predicted) weather. It will be hard saying goodbye to my in-laws — our last tie to the world we are leaving behind.   -journal entry, March 31

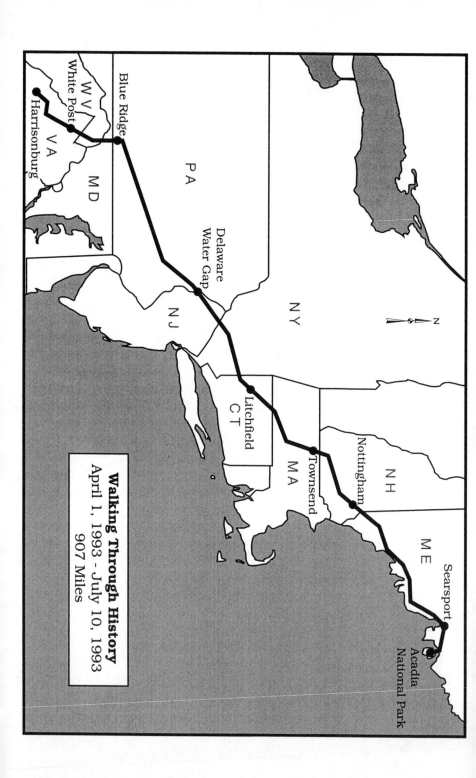

Walking Through History
April 1, 1993 - July 10, 1993
907 Miles

W V
White Post
Harrisonburg
V A
M D
Blue Ridge
P A
Delaware
Water Gap
N J
N Y
Litchfield
C T
M A
Townsend
Nottingham
N H
M E
Searsport
Acadia
National Park

N

** WALKING THE WINTER WONDERLAND **

* MAINE *

April 1 - April 15, 1993
108 miles -- 12 bags

A journey of a thousand miles begins with a single step.
- Chinese proverb

————————◆————————

It started snowing at 7 a.m. By 8, we were eating breakfast, watching as it began to stick. As we set off at 9:00, the snow swirled all about us, dropping the visibility and obscuring the road's shoulder.
What a day to start a cross-country walk.

-journal entry, April 1

GIVEN AN APRIL START in Maine, we expected to see snow fall at least once. We didn't expect six inches on the first day. April Fools!

The snow lent a special, Currier and Ives quality to the day. Pine trees bent under fresh white mantles. Smoke curled up from stone chimneys to dance with falling snowflakes. Rooftops, clear only a day before, now sparkled under a new winter coat.

Our foul weather gear proved equal to the task, keeping us warm despite temperatures several degrees shy of freezing. The icy air, scrubbed clean by the storm, powered our steps. We strolled through the winter wonderland, enjoying the feeling of freedom as we finally embarked on our great adventure. Only sporadic traffic shared Route 3 with us. As road conditions worsened, that suited us fine.

Our day ended at noon, when we reached the only open motel between Bar Harbor and Ellsworth. Though our plans called for camping most of the trip, we had budgeted for motels the first few weeks until the weather mellowed. We knew we would endure discomforts on the road, but camping in the snow exceeded our limits.

With a morning of hoofing behind us, we had joined the fraternity of

long-distance hikers. We even made their favorite mistake: packing too
much weight. Did we *really* want to lug all this equipment? Again we
analyzed our loads, weeding out items we wouldn't need our first few
weeks. Twenty-two pounds of camping gear, including tent, backpacking
stove, and — after all the hassles — sleeping bags, found its way into a
box we shipped forward to Wiscasset, farther down Maine's coastline.
That gave us two weeks with lighter loads to get used to trekking.

April Fools! Six inches of snow greet our trek

Day two dawned little better than day one. A light sleet replaced the
previous day's snow, and temperatures hovered near 30°. After calling
KABC radio in L.A. for our first road report, we embarked on the day's
seven mile trek to Ellsworth.

Despite the short mileage and no litter to slow us, we didn't reach town
until midafternoon. Boxing and mailing our gear at the grocery-store-cum-
post-office ate up an hour. A shop three miles farther promised a break
from the sleet and slush, and the owner offered us free postcards. On the
outskirts of Ellsworth, a Thai restaurant stopped us cold. Ethnic food so far
from the big city? "It must be lunch time," I told Sue. "Have you ever seen
me pass up Thai food?"

A couple at an adjacent table, intrigued by our packs, chatted with us.

When we asked about cheap motels in town, they suggested the Emmaus Center, an emergency shelter for battered women and the homeless. After all, weren't we now homeless?

In all our planning, we'd never thought about shelters. Movies and TV had shaped our image of them — graffiti-smeared buildings in inner-city slums, rooms crammed wall-to-wall with cots, a clientele you wouldn't want dating your daughter. Could we feel comfortable there? Would it be safe? Or did we simply fear Hollywood images?

"JUDI AND I HAVE been in this business for several years." Ralph Goodenough's eyes sparkled as he explained how he and his wife came to run a refuge in rural Maine. "We used to run a homeless shelter in Washington, D.C., and saw a lot of people cutting and shooting each other. Still, we really enjoyed shelter work and helping people. After six years there we stopped smelling the diesel fumes and hearing the sirens."

Sue and I sat in the common area of the Emmaus Center, listening to its director. His short, trim body was topped by a splash of red hair, and the beard he wore made me think of leprechauns. His voice carried a lilting, almost excited tone that was enchanting to listen to, like a master storyteller spinning his tales.

"Every November we came up to visit Judi's brother in New Hampshire. It was always so beautiful, with the leaves changing color. I can remember sniffing the air and thinking, 'What's that smell? Oh — it's oxygen!'

"Last year we came up this way on a visit, and were surprised to find problems here. We had grown so accustomed to urban poverty, which is so visible with homeless on every corner. Here, the poverty hides away in the woods, out of sight. When we discovered Emmaus, we applied to work and got hired on the spot."

As he continued to laud life out of the rat race, Ralph showed us the shelter. Its lifeblood, he explained, was the generosity of the town. A local grocer provided dented cans of food. The Chinese restaurant up the street supplied free dinner every Sunday. The beds, even the building itself, came from community donations.

"We love this area," he concluded. "In D.C., I could look out the window and see ten hookers and a pimp. Today I looked out the window and saw two bald eagles. We're sitting on a tidal river here, see, and when the tide goes out, the eagles come fishing."

When we'd arrived at the center, Judi recognized us from our picture in the previous day's *Bar Harbor Times*. Although the cold weather had driven people to the shelter, filling it, she squeezed us into a spare room. She and Ralph knew from hiking the Appalachian trail that a stranger's kindness always enriched a trip. Why should they let 'official capacity' keep them from enriching ours?

After Ralph's tour, we joined the shelter's guests at a communal supper. Judi served a delicious casserole, and soon we were sharing tales with the other diners. None of them fit the stereotypes we'd held, of people leeching off others' charity with no goals past their next meal. David, for instance, planned on working the fishing boats in Seattle as soon as he found passage there. Charlie would soon hitchhike across Canada to take a waiting job in Alaska. Laszlo from Hungary had stopped on his way to Washington, D.C.. Wendy sought protection from an abusive husband. Everyone had a story, and they all had hopes for a better life. Together, they formed a community, helping one another, keeping each other upbeat despite being down on their luck.

Ralph had plans for the evening; the orchestra in the local production of *Godspell* featured him on tuba. After he left, we discussed our Saturday plans with Judi. "I know Bucksport is twenty miles away," I said. "Are there any motels short of that?"

"Not open in the off-season, no." Judi thought for a moment. "But maybe I can help."

She left to make a phone call, and came back smiling. "There's a battered women's shelter a dozen or so miles from here, run by a pair of nuns. They're expecting you tomorrow afternoon."

Our first 'problem' of the road, solved. May they all be so easy!

As I relaxed last night recalling the conversation with Ralph, I thought of how much his voice emphasized he was doing something he truly loved. Suddenly it dawned on me that I was, too. As it sank in, a grin spread across my face.   -journal entry, April 3

THE NEXT TWO DAYS offered an upswing in the weather. Temperatures crept above freezing while leaden skies saved their moisture. The cool conditions kept us from overheating as we tackled the trek's first hills.

The empty miles slipped under our feet, a dreary landscape of skeletal trees, tourist cabins covered with snow, and a sprinkling of farms. Thus, when we rounded the bend and spied the store, it surprised us. The old chicken barn stretched longer than a football field and stood three stories tall. Its days of raising poultry long past, the 'Big Chicken Barn' store now advertised an eclectic mixture of antiques and over 125,000 books and magazines dating from the turn of the century. We warmed up while browsing through a collection ranging from Shakespeare to Steve Martin, from classics to comic books, and picked up two paperbacks for the road.

With three days of walking under my belt, minor aches and pains began clamoring for attention, and muscles I had never known burned from overuse. The fourteen-mile hike to the nuns' refuge reminded me I hadn't backpacked for years. My shoulders demanded I repack my load, adjusting the balance. Sue's feet swelled after the hard days, and her boots' snug fit became constricting.

On the fifth day, nature rewarded us with perfect hiking weather — clear blue skies and a forecast of 50°. Rapidly drying roads uncovered litter, and I bagged our first trash — a half eaten dinner from KFC. As we walked, I called out greetings to people lured outside by the sun.

One couple lugging five-gallon buckets to their car returned my "Hello." Ten minutes later, as I stopped to snap a photo, they drove up.

Richard Greiner had an aura of class about him, the type of person who would look well dressed in jeans and a tee shirt. "We saw you walking and wondered where you were going," he asked.

"We've just begun walking across the country," I replied.

"Across the country! Are you from around here?" asked his wife Kathleen. Like her husband, she appeared to be in her mid-forties, and she spoke with a distinct British accent.

"No, we only started here. We're from California."

"Well! We used to live in Mill Valley, near Sacramento," she said. "Are you staying around here tonight?"

"We're hoping to walk several more miles today, and look for a motel between Searsport and Belfast. Why?"

"We own the Captain Green Pendleton House, the Bed & Breakfast inn you just passed, and we'd like you to spend the night with us." Richard handed me their phone number. "Call me when you're done walking. I'll pick you up."

"CAPTAIN GREEN PENDLETON BUILT this house in the 1820's," Richard explained as he drove up to the mansion. The two-story house, gleaming in a fresh coat of white paint, presided over a lot filled with massive maple trees and an ice-covered pond. Its facade featured a symmetry we saw often in New England homes, with three evenly-spaced windows upstairs and a door flanked by windows below.

Richard and Kathleen — perfect hosts

As he showed us the house, he talked about its original owner. "Captain Peleg Pendleton, Green's father, sailed into the area in 1775 with his eldest son, Peleg Junior. Once he staked out a homestead, he left Junior to look after it while he returned to Rhode Island to fetch the rest of the family." A wry grin came to Richard's face. "Unfortunately, the Revolutionary War interrupted the captain, and he spent the next eight years fighting the British. By the time Peleg returned to Maine in 1883,

Junior had disappeared. They never found a trace of him."

He showed us through rooms filled with antique Eastlake furniture, much of it restored and refinished. Chess sets, ivory elephants, vases, chests, and other bric-a-brac from exotic ports-of-call filled odd corners and curio cases. *It's like a museum*, I thought, *except people live here.*

"Green was ten when Peleg brought him here," Richard continued. "He grew into the seafaring tradition, commanding ships for fifteen years. This was his sloop *Endeavour*," he said, pointing to a painting above the fireplace, "and a print of his schooner *Independence* is hanging in your room.

"Green had six sons in this house. He asked the youngest to stay and farm, but the other five went to sea — two of them never returning. His grandson Frank Irving became one of the last people to round Cape Horn under sail."

Richard showed us to our room and left us to get settled. After cleaning up I wandered about the house, gazing at the knickknacks, studying the paintings. I ended up downstairs, sitting by the fireplace, writing in my journal.

Later that afternoon Richard and Kathleen showed us the area, pointing out several sea captains' homes. "In the heyday of sailing ships," Richard related, "ten percent of America's sea captains called Searsport home. With Maine's second largest deepwater harbor, the town thrived on shipbuilding. Through the 1880s, the town produced over a hundred schooners and fourteen full sail ships, including the massive 'Downeasters.' When steam power sounded the death knell for the sailing era, the area lost most of its jobs, and today this region is riddled with poverty."

On our way back to the B&B, they stopped at their friends' house where we had seen them lugging buckets earlier. "Those pails? They were full of maple sap," Kathleen revealed. "The sap just started running, and we have to collect it several times a day."

We helped them empty the sap buckets as Richard taught us about maple syrup. During the winter, he explained, sap collects in the maple roots and the sugar concentrates. Once spring hits and the cold nights mix with days above freezing, the sap rises. 'Mapling' season lasts at most a month before the flow of sap dwindles.

When I saw my first bucket of sap, I mistook it for water. The transparent liquid contained no hint of amber color, and it poured rather than oozed. The sap escaped from each tree via a metal straw (called a 'spile') stuck through the bark. It flowed like a leaky faucet (a drop a second or faster for many trees) into a bucket hooked onto the spile.

In the Greiner's side yard, they boiled the sap over a small fire. The steam billowing from the black pot conjured up images of black cats, broomsticks, and witches stirring their cauldrons. Rather than adding 'eye of newt' or 'wing of bat,' we added more sap, stirring the mixture occasionally to keep it from burning. The 'broth' would boil all day, reducing volume by over 95%, until all that remained was the sticky brown translucent goop that drove my tastebuds wild.

While sap contains only 2-4% sugar, syrup consists of 85%. At a 30-to-1 sap-to-syrup reduction, it takes two gallons of sap to produce one cup of syrup. Since the sap only runs for a few weeks, I could see why pure maple syrup costs so much.

We tasted the fruits of our labor this morning at breakfast. With no preservatives, syrup reaches peak freshness immediately and slowly deteriorates. With one-day-old maple syrup enhancing our waffles . . . well, forget Aunt Jemima!   -journal entry, April 6

WE SPENT AN EXTRA day with the Greiners, helping them maple while we waited for another pair of boots. Sue's swollen feet barely fit into the pair she'd been wearing, and the pressure on her blisters shot pain through her legs. Her mother agreed to express mail us the boots, one-half size larger, Sue had started training in.

It took only four miles the next day to realize they didn't solve the problem. By the time we hit Belfast, new blisters tortured her feet, and the weight on her back made it worse. "If only I had a wagon to haul my pack . . ." she sighed.

Minutes later, we walked by Hall's Antiques and noticed a broken-down little red wagon out front. The price was right, and the shop owners rigged a rope handle for Sue. They also called motels for us, and found that the next open lodging was the Northport House, six miles distant.

As we ambled through Belfast with the wagon in tow, a rust-covered pickup truck stopped and a farmer decked out in coveralls emerged. "I was driving by and thought I saw 'LITTER' written on your tee shirts, so I came back to see for sure. I had to stop to thank you and say, 'God bless you.' I figured you need the support of people dressed like me."

"Well, thank you for stopping," answered Sue. "It's nice to know what we're doing is appreciated."

"I try to do my part," he said, beaming. "I live out in the boonies, and people say there's no problem out there, it's clean; but I'm there, and I know it isn't. So I'll let you get on your way, and again, God bless you! And remember one thing — never give up!"

For the next several miles, my pack didn't seem quite as heavy. My steps stayed light until we reached the Northport House, which had yet to open for the season. After trudging another quarter-mile to a pay phone, we called them to explain our predicament, and Pete, the owner, agreed to rent us a room. The promise of finally taking her boots off drove Sue the long quarter-mile back to the inn.

That evening we visited with our host. After a long winter, he eagerly welcomed his guests, and it took little prodding to get him talking. He quickly had us laughing with his reflections on life and people in Maine:

"You can always tell a real Mainer. He's got a wife that weighs more than his truck, he's got five or six broken down appliances sitting on his porch, and the sign on his front lawn says, 'Forget the dog, beware of owner.'

"I've got a friend, a real Mainer. He looks like he's eighty, but he's only forty-seven. Used to work in Belfast at the chicken factory, hanging up chickens. He had to hang two thousand chickens a day. Can you imagine?

"You know how Route 1 goes through all the cities on the coast, but takes a wide swing around Belfast? Know why? Because it stunk! Belfast used to call itself 'Chicken Capital of the World', and during the summer the whole town reeked. The people didn't care about tourists then. If a tourist had strayed into town, they probably would have thrown a chicken at 'em."

ALL AROUND US, HINTS of spring grew stronger. Temperatures neared 60°. The sun dried the roads and attacked the snow on the shoulders. We saw the season's first robins in the yard of the Northport House.

While the weather improved, Sue's feet worsened. Further swelling made her new boots too tight, leaving her feet blistered and sprained. Merrell Boots came to our rescue, agreeing to ship us boots a full size larger and at a cost under wholesale. It would take two days for them to reach us in Camden, fifteen miles away. For Sue, that meant two more days of pain and frustration, of willing her body through the miles.

We covered barely three miles that morning before a cotter pin broke on Sue's wagon. "Steering assembly," I reported, looking at the undercarriage. "It's gone from 'low-tech' to 'no-tech'." With help from a big rock, I performed emergency surgery and got us back on the road. When the wagon went into remission two miles later, we looked around for other help. Luckily, it broke within sight of 'Check With Chuck' Classic Car Repair and Restoration.

As we strode up his driveway, Chuck eyed us with curiosity. "We've got a classic for you!" said Sue. "Want to put it on the hoist and check it?"

While Chuck bolted the offending pieces together, Pete from Northport House drove up in his truck. "Do you need a lift?" he asked. I persuaded a limping Sue to accept his offer, getting a ride to the next open motel in Lincolnville Beach.

The following day we struggled for three miles, Sue's limp growing worse with every step. Two miles outside Camden, we agreed to hitchhike into town for a couple of days rest. It took only five minutes of waving our thumbs before an elderly couple stopped. Again, Sue rode ahead while I walked the last miles.

In town, we followed lunch with a stop at the local paper, then checked into a motel. While Sue rested, I picked up her boots and visited our sponsors at Moss Tents. Ted Dishner gave me the factory tour, and then introduced me to Marilyn Moss, company president. "A lot of us in the company have a question about your trip," she said. "After you collect the trash, what do you do with it?"

I chuckled. "Everyone asks that. We look for a business with a dumpster we can use. Since we haven't found much trash so far, we haven't had a problem dropping bags before they get too heavy."

With an afternoon to kill, I decided to hike up Mt. Battie. This hill overlooking Camden rose three hundred feet above the town. I chose the direct route, a steep trail still choked with snow and ice. At the summit, I caught my breath, admiring the vista looking over Penobscot Bay. Islands studded the bay, anchored in the crystal blue water. Fingers of fog clung to the far shoreline. Jutting above the horizon, nearly lost in the mist, lay Mt.

Desert Island, where we'd started eight days before.

Energized by the short rest, I half-jogged, half-skied down a snow-covered road heading out of the park. Partway down, I overtook a trio of retirees returning from the summit. Sonia Spaulding and Mary and Bob Eddy walked there daily to stay in shape, enjoying the solitude of a world blanketed in white. When I mentioned my crusade, Mary flaunted a beer can she'd retrieved only minutes earlier.

I accepted Sonia's offer of a ride back into town. In the car, I described the plight with Sue's feet, telling her we planned to hole up for the weekend. "If you want to save money," she said, "Camden's not the place to stay. Let me drive you to Rockland, seven miles south of here. Rooms there run 20% less."

When Ralph and Judi Goodenough of the Emmaus Center talked of hiking the Appalachian trail, they spoke of 'trail angels' — locals who helped them or urged them on, expecting nothing in return. Sometimes only the trail angels kept them going. Well, we're meeting our share of 'road angels.'   -journal entry, April 10

"SONIA COULDN'T MAKE IT," Mary Eddy greeted us. "Bob and I will drive you to Rockland instead."

Rather than zipping down U.S. 1, the Eddys treated us to a tour of the area. Just south of Camden, Rockport embraced one of Maine's most beautiful harbors. This cozy little town nestled away from the main road had escaped the commercialization of its neighbor. Outside town, we passed a farm raising Belted Galloway cattle, black cows with a large white band across the center. _Since when have cows dressed up as zebras?_

In Rockland, I faced a dilemma: Would we make a true cross-country walk, or must we admit we skipped sections? Not yet willing to settle for the latter, I thumbed a ride back to Camden to walk those seven miles. Dan Bourkas, a slim man a few years shy of thirty, went out of his way to ferry me back to Camden. As he dropped me off, he invited us to dinner, rescuing us from a lonely motel room. "I'll pick you up at five!"

The evening passed too quickly. Dan and his wife Kristie barbecued steaks on the back porch, and topped dinner off with chocolate cake. We talked for hours. They both worked for FMC-Marine Colloids, the company that turns seaweed into McDonalds' McLean™ burgers. Dan, however, had more enterprising plans. "We own several acres, and I want to open a campground and miniature golf course. There's nothing for kids to do here except rent videos, so there's definite market potential."

For now, health insurance kept them tied to 'real' jobs. "Our son was born fifteen weeks premature," Kristie explained. "He only weighed one-and-a-half pounds. Last week we finally took him off oxygen. We still take him to Portland every other week for a checkup."

Doing laundry topped our exciting plans for Easter Sunday. The rainy weather encouraged us to rest Sue's feet another day. Monday we returned to the road, trekking six miles through a light drizzle.

Harold "Cap'n" Frost and his wife Arlene, proprietors of Cap'n Frost B&B, hosted us that night. We had grown accustomed to quiet nights visiting with innkeepers, and the Frosts continued the tradition. Reclining by the fire in a sitting room filled with antiques, Harold resembled a grandfather in a Norman Rockwell painting. As he rocked back and forth, he reminisced about the lodging business.

"We owned property in southern Maine when I retired, and I didn't know what I'd do. Sit in a rocking chair and watch cars pass by, something active like that? My wife wouldn't have none of it. She said, 'Why don't we buy a B&B?' So we came up here, and this starts our eighth year.

"Running a B&B is a good way to open your mind if you've got a negative attitude toward people. It doesn't take long to find out that — like Ivory soap — 99 44/100% of the people around are good. We rent about 230 rooms each year, and I can say we've only had two or three guests we'd just as soon not see again."

"THEY HAVEN'T YET FOUND any treasure in the trash itself. But when Sue says, 'Somewhere on this trip I'll find something of value,' you get the feeling that she already has."
                         - Sarah Goodyear, Camden _Herald_, Apr. 15, 1993

So far, most of the litter was mundane. Fast food debris, cigarette packs, milk cartons — use it up and throw it out. Still, some items left us thinking. Who lost the blade from a table saw — a carpenter on the lam? How about the surgical mask — do surgeons make road calls? And don't forget the dirty men's undies! ("Hmm. I'll never clean these brown stains.

Let's jettison!")

We finished our second week with two eleven-mile days. Though Sue suffered the final mile or two each day, her feet were toughening up. Or was she only getting used to the pain? Her hand now concerned us more, since pulling the wagon aggravated the recent break.

As temperatures settled into the 50s, we found ourselves enjoying the countryside. A state ban on billboards reduced the visual pollution, and only small informational signs let travelers know what vendors lurked down side roads. Signs on businesses generated chuckles: "You should see what we saw" advertised a cabinet maker; a realty company pondered, "If at first you don't succeed, so much for skydiving."

The quaint Maine towns filled with 19th century mansions, boomtowns in the days of sailing ships, now lived as quiet backwaters. Waldoboro, for example, had gained renown for making five-masted schooners. Today, it had traded that reputation for jobs making light bulb filaments for GTE Sylvania. A customer in the Laundromat informed us that the last 'celebrity' (or weirdo, take your pick) to pass through town was a man walking across the country, dragging a large wooden cross emblazoned with a "Jesus saves" banner.

And on the fifteenth day, Sue fell.   -journal entry, April 15

** SHIFT TO SOLITUDE **

* MAINE - NEW HAMPSHIRE - MASSACHUSETTS *

April 15 - April 29, 1993
182 miles -- 16 bags
TOTAL, 290 miles -- 28 bags

The one who goes is happier
Than those he leaves behind.   - Edward Pollack

———————◆————

THE PORCH HAD ONE step too many.

As Sue carried her pack to the yard, she didn't notice the extra step. Her heel caught its edge, twisting as Sue fell.

"Oh my ankle!" she cried as I rushed to her. Her hands shot to her feet as she tried to stop the pain. "Ow! It hurts! It hurts!"

I touched her ankle gingerly, trying to gauge the damage. She winced from the pressure, so I untied her boot and slipped it off. A neighbor who saw the fall hurried over and asked if she could help. "If we could get her inside," I answered, "we can ice it."

"I think I sprained it," Sue stated as we helped her to the couch. "I'm not going to be walking anytime soon. What do we do now?"

I thought as I filled her ice pack, then replied, "We have no choice. We'll have to call your folks and tell them we'll be back."

She fought to hold back tears. "I can't do that, not on my mother's birthday. She didn't want me to take this trip anyway . . ." She shook her head and looked away.

"We have no choice," I repeated. "You can't walk with a sprain, and we have no home to go to." I waited for her to calm down, then made the call she dreaded.

That solved one problem, but another remained. How would we get to Connecticut? The closest public transportation, the bus, stopped twenty-six miles away in Brunswick. Newcastle had no airports, trains, taxis, or rental cars. All they had was U.S. 1, so I helped Sue limp a half-mile to the road and we stuck out our thumbs.

We quickly hitched a ride to Brunswick. The day's bus had already left, so we rented a motel room and spent the afternoon watching Sue's ankle swell. When her foot turned into a flesh-colored grapefruit with toes, we taxied to the hospital to have it checked.

Sue disappeared into the emergency room as I paced outside, waiting for the results of the X-ray. After what seemed like hours her doctor emerged, smiling as he quipped, "Looks like we'll have to amputate." (Of all the doctors on staff, she had to get the comedian.)

Sue had underestimated the damage. Instead of a sprain, the fibula had broken at the ankle, and the swelling kept them from casting it. The doctor told her to keep it elevated, and not travel for forty-eight hours.

No words could ease our despair. Sue slumped into depression, mourning the loss of her dream trip. At least six weeks of infirmity faced her, robbing her of walking while spring burst forth. Should we bother continuing?

"You know I'm not a quitter," she emphasized, "but how much can I take? Sometimes I feel like I'm nineteen, and trapped in a ninety-year-old body." Her frown relayed her despair.

"It would be a shame to quit, after all our work." If we gave up now, I knew we'd never try again. "And just when we were getting used to the road."

She murmured agreement. "I was starting to enjoy the trip, being outdoors and meeting people. Now I'm off my feet until it gets hot and muggy."

I looked out the motel window, trying to devise a Plan B. "I know you wanted to walk through New England. Maybe we should break until June, then try —"

"I can't ask you to do that! I've already ruined your trip—" she cut off my protests "—yes, I have ruined it. I can't see you sitting around my folks' for two months. You'd go bananas! Watching you look miserable would make me even more miserable." She saw she hadn't convinced me. "My mother can care for me. Besides, if you lose six weeks, we'll never make Colorado by winter."

"Do you want me to keep walking until you can rejoin me?" The thought brought me little joy. Single traveling meant long days and lonely nights. And would Sue resent me if I abandoned her to pain and boredom while living out our dream?

She looked away as I mentioned leaving. "I'd worry about you. After all," she added with half a smile, "I'll have to do something to pass the time."

I knelt by the bed and grasped her hand. "I don't know what's best. What do you think we should do?"

"We? Right now, I have no options. You have them all. I can't tell you to leave me, and I won't make you give up your dream. You have to choose. Remember," she concluded, "if you're coming with me, my bus leaves in two days."

WHETHER WE QUIT OR NOT, I still needed to return up the coast. Sue broke her leg one town shy of Wiscasset, where our camping gear awaited us. Again, I hit the road.

An hour of waving my thumb got no results; two minutes of waving a dollar bill got me a ride to Wiscasset (then the driver refused my money). After reclaiming our gear, I quickly hitched a ride to Newcastle. From the site of Sue's disaster, I struck out solo, seeing how the road felt now. Dingy gray skies mirrored my mood as I shuffled south on U.S. 1.

Memories of Europe flooded back. That 1989 trip, a planned seven-week bicycle tour of the continent with a college buddy, turned solo when my friend broke his shoulder a week before our departure. Having never vacationed alone before (and having never taken a trip longer than two weeks), I set off with equal parts fear and anticipation.

Often I struggled with loneliness. However, people always rescued me when my mood got darkest, buying me coffee among the Amsterdam canals, inviting me to teach English classes in Belgium, or pouring out their hearts over a beer in Bavaria. Where my travel plans left off, life stepped in.

Life had stepped in again. I knew I couldn't give up our dream. I also couldn't help Sue heal, and a layover would only make us late reaching Colorado. By the time I reached Bath, ready to hitch a ride back to our motel, I'd made my choice:

The walk would go on!

I finally discovered the fury of the Downeaster. I thought attaching 'down' to a description of Maine seemed contradictory, since it lies in the upper corner of U.S. maps. However, the Maine nickname of "Downeast" developed during the days of sailing ships, when prevailing

winds blew clippers from Boston toward this area. Sea captains thus
spoke of sailing "downwind to the east," or shortened, downeast.
     That wind, the Downeaster, blew today, trying to push me off a bridge
into the Merrymeeting Bay.   -journal entry, April 17

RATHER THAN GIVE THE local drivers another chance to snub me,
I returned to Bath by taxi the next morning. Minutes after I began walking
back to Brunswick, the raindrops joined me. Five minutes of drizzle would
rinse my pants, followed by the Downeaster blowing them dry. Once I
dried, the rain started again, repeating the cycle. (If I had soap, I could have
done laundry!) The main event came after lunch, when the skies opened.
Was this my trial by water, my last chance to change my mind?

Stuck in the motel room, Sue had sunk deeper into depression, and our
last night together passed in silence. Sunday morning I helped her hobble
aboard the bus and hugged her goodbye before hurrying off. In a daze I
walked away, seeing the passing cityscape through a veil of tears.

The pack on my back felt heavier than ever.

Perhaps the hardest thing I've ever done was putting Sue on the bus
today. We had no other choice — we couldn't continue to hitch rides and
have me backpedal to walk the miles. The tough decision was to
continue.
     So I trudge on. My only hope is to find more 'road angels,' and soon.
If I find myself truly alone up here, I doubt I will make it.
                                        -journal entry, April 18

THE DAYS DRAGGED. With no one to pace me, I pushed myself.
Sixteen miles a day, eighteen, twenty — my dogs devoured the distances.

The coastline slipped past as I adjusted to my solitude. In Freeport,
home of countless factory outlets tucked into 19th century storefronts, I
lost myself in the weekend crowds milling through L.L. Bean. Portland
impressed me with its small-town heart beating under a big city disguise,
as people called out greetings to this lanky stranger. I roamed its downtown
streets that evening, envying the families still out after dark.

In Portland, I parted company with the coast. After 150 miles of following U.S. 1, I turned inland. No more ocean breezes and island-studded bays awaited me. No more quaint harbors and sea captains' mansions would pose for my camera. Instead, farms and forests surrounded me.

The land has slipped from the white calming glove of winter. Though a few patches of snow remain in the shelter of thick shade or hidden under roadside grit, the familiar white expanses have vanished. Ponds that weeks ago wore mantles of ice have opened their waters to the new season. Yes, Maine has entered the season known to the locals as 'Mud,' between Winter and Tourist.   -journal entry, April 20

ONCE OFF THE COASTAL tourist track, I faced a new challenge — camping. Thirty-three miles separated me from the next motel, so despite a forecast of rain, I got ready to rough it.

As the sun sank to the horizon, I searched for a camping spot. The area boasted no parks or campgrounds, and woods filled with leafless trees offered no spots to hide. I finally struck a conversation with a man tending his yard, and asked permission to camp. Hesitantly he agreed. "But could you use the woods on the edge of my property?" he asked. "If my wife sees you, she'll have my hide."

The night stayed dry, and I woke with the dawn. I stayed inside my sleeping bag until the sun warmed the air from 'frigid' to 'bearable,' then hurried to the highway diner to warm up over breakfast. Once full, I set off south on U.S. 202.

Waterboro served as my lunch stop. The town featured only one restaurant, and locals filled the tables. From conversations swirling about me, I quickly identified what passed for news in this hamlet:

"That truck's from Modena, N.Y. I'll bet he's lost."

"There goes another refrigerated unit. That must be the third one I've seen today."

"Lot of truckers today been asking me if the scales are open."

Oh, the excitement of small town living!

"You'll never make it to Californ-ee-yay!"
The old man called to me as I shuffled down U.S. 202. Even as I told
him I was aiming for Seattle, I wondered if maybe he was correct. Unless
I can change this walk from a grudge match to a journey of discovery,
my chances of finishing are nil.   -journal entry, April 21

A PORTLAND REPORTER HAD told me the tale of 'Weston the Pedestrian.' Weston, he said, had taken a few cross-country, New York-to-San Francisco walks around the turn of the century. He walked with no packs slowing him, relying on support crews to carry his equipment. His fastest transit took only ninety-one days. He thought nothing of walking from 3:00 a.m. until midnight, some days covering over eighty miles.

To which I replied: "Why bother?"

Far from reaching eighty miles daily, my body revolted at eighteen. The days of pounding pavement took their toll, and minor aches graduated to major pains. As I neared Sanford, Maine, sore muscles forced me to hobble, and I dragged into town only minutes ahead of a storm.

The next day I aimed for New Hampshire, twelve miles away. Two miles shy of the state line, I pulled up lame. A sharp pain in my thighs forced me to rest every fifteen minutes as I struggled the last four miles into Rochester.

"Are you Railroad Willie?"
That's the question asked me by six kids sitting under trees along the
side of the highway. When I described my journey, they were shocked.
"Are you crazy?" asked one boy. I nodded.
                                          -journal entry, April 23

THE PEOPLE I MET gave me the strength to continue. One woman offered me lunch, and arranged a phone interview with Maine Public Radio. The motel clerk in Sanford dropped the price on my room, mentioning how he, too, dreamed of walking coast-to-coast. Many people greeted me as I passed, and more honked and waved as they drove by.

Response from early news articles also inspired me. A couple from

Danbury, CT called Sue's folks to ask if we wanted donations (we didn't). An elderly woman living near the Canadian border saw us in the *Bangor Daily News*, and tracked us down. She asked us to call her collect every month and keep her informed of our/my progress.

The papers had become the brightest spot of my trip. Thus, as I limped through the late afternoon drizzle into Rochester, I headed straight for the offices of *Foster's Daily Democrat*. After I introduced myself, John, Allen, and Mark (the self-named JAM crew) took over. They greeted me, took my picture, interviewed me, recommended a restaurant for dinner, reserved me a motel room, gave me a New Hampshire map, and suggested a walking route. "Anything else we can do for you?" asked Allen.

"Sure. Do you know any masseuses?"

I had to do without a rubdown. Still, a solid night's sleep erased the leg pains of the long day. The next morning I set off under clear skies, anxious to try my luck at camping a second time.

What appeared on my map as 'South Lee' was nothing more than a highway intersection with a woodworking shop on one corner. I stopped to ask a girl raking leaves for info, and she referred me to her father. Billy confirmed I could find dinner down the right fork, and asked if I would help him load an old rabbit hutch into his pickup. He paid me with a Coke (diet — gotta count them calories!) and a sandwich, and we chatted for a few minutes until his wife yelled at him to get busy. With a sheepish grin, he bade me goodbye, and I continued into the beautiful countryside.   -journal entry, April 24

"LOVELY DAY FOR A camping trip, isn't it?" The lady raking her lawn outside Nottingham greeted me as I walked amongst the evening's lengthening shadows.

"If only they could all be this nice, my trip would be easy," I replied.

Her gray hair framed a face which gave no hint of her age. "Oh? Where are you going?" she asked.

"Eventually across the country. Right now, I'm just looking for a spot to pitch my tent for the night."

"Really? Why don't you pitch it on my lawn?"

"Are you sure?" I tried not to pressure her. "That would be great. My feet are aching."

Joy introduced herself as I dropped my pack and began assembling the tent. Concerned about the moist ground, she disappeared inside to search for a ground cloth. She came back, not with a tarp, but with a glass of cold apple juice. "You looked thirsty. When you're through with the tent, would you care for a shower?"

"Oh, that would be too much to ask."

"Not at all. Just knock on the door when you're ready." She mentioned she had called her daughter, her son, and neighbors to tell them about the 'celebrity' camping on her lawn, and that her son might drop by to meet me.

After building camp, I wrote my day's journal entry, making special note of the state's hospitality. As I finished the entry, I glanced through the tent window and saw a woman in blue uniform, one of Nottingham's finest, approaching.

"Can you come out of there? I'd like to talk to you."

"Of course, officer. What can I do for you?"

"Do you have some ID?" I showed her my driver's license, and she began an interview that would have done a reporter proud. What's the purpose of your trip? How far have you come? Where was your wife's accident? What do you do with the trash? What spurred you to do this?

"Let me tell you what's going on. The people who live here, they're elderly, and they're a bit nervous about having you camp here. If you'll pack up your things, you can camp at the school. That's back up the road a mile."

What caused Joy to change her mind? Did someone she called about the 'celebrity' scare her, poisoning her friendly nature with a fear of strangers? Had an unseen husband nixed the deal?

Under the watchful eye of the police, I broke camp as the light failed. _What's the sense in asking permission,_ I thought, _if they'll roust me anyway?_

The road started out like a roller coaster, undulating through forests until ending at Raymond. As Route 102 took over, the road bobbed and weaved like a punch-drunk fighter. It finally straightened out in Chester, and rather than hiding the hills behind curves, it displayed them in full foot-agonizing splendor.   -journal entry, April 25

RATS DON'T RACE IN hiking boots.

That thought consoled me as I trudged along the wooded lane. True, I faced twenty-two miles for the day, since I'd made plans to meet the *Walking* photographer in Derry. True, I had to walk past Joy's house, a reminder of the previous night's eviction. Still, it beat the alternative: eight hours in a windowless cubicle, writing software no one cared about or understood.

The long day started cool. Morning fog crept through the forests beside the road. Little traffic shared the lane, though two drivers stopped: one asked directions, the other offered me a ride. Funny, but he turned down an offer to walk with me.

After a mid-morning nap, I strolled into Chester. A loose dog charged me at the town limits, providing the morning's adrenaline rush, but it had only a warm, slobbery welcome on its mind. The excitement wore me out, so I followed my power lunch with another nap on the town commons.

By 3:30 my steps were dragging. As I passed another cluster of houses, a middle-aged couple gardening in their yard saw me. "Nice day for a walk, isn't it?" they called out.

Within minutes they poured me a cold juice, let me use their restrooms, and stocked me with several stamped, self-addressed envelopes. "We'd have you stay the night," Judy Hamer said, "but we won't be here. I wish we hadn't made plans."

Their friendliness chased away lingering bitter taste of Nottingham. *Maybe I can't win 'em all,* I thought. *Just let me win my share.*

Cookie's & Carol's Variety Store and Diner was a bit of Americana in Nashua, NH. Squeezed into a back street storefront barely wide enough for a serving counter and a rack of junk food, it was hardly as long as its name. Posters and historic pictures, some labeled "What year is this?" or "Who is this businessman?", lined the walls. Behind the counter, amidst the other clutter, hung a New York Times front-page photo of one of their regular patrons having coffee with President Clinton.

William Least Heat Moon, in "Blue Highways," rated diners by the number of calendars adorning the walls. The more calendars, he stated, the better the food. Cookie's had only two, but they had ten clocks, ranging from California and Rocky Mountain times (Camel cigarettes clock and Coors clock), through local time (Coca Cola clock), to Moscow time (a clock turned on its side), with Rock'n'Roll time and cooking time (a clock constructed from an old skillet) thrown in for good measure.

The 'high' point of the decor was the "Been There — Done That" collection of postcards hanging from the ceiling. Cards sent from their customers hung from hooks representing all fifty states plus foreign countries such as India, Taiwan, and Egypt. People sending a postcard earned a free cup of coffee when they returned.

The food was honest, straight-off-the-grill Yankee grub. My hamburger was fat and juicy, the home fries perfect with onions. I chatted with Cookie, who encouraged me to return the next day to autograph my pending newspaper article.

-journal entry, April 27

* * *

"... AND WHEN SHE HANDED me her coin, I could hardly speak." I finally found an audience for my story of the Townsend schoolkids: Richard Medeiras, the reporter for the Fitchburg, Massachusetts *Sentinel/Enterprise*. As low reporter on the newspaper's totem pole, he got assigned to write about the trash trekker.

He shook his head in amazement. With his boyish looks and his wiry body, he more resembled an athlete than a reporter. In fact, he would soon canoe the Nashua River to research an environmental piece.

"So tell me about the trash," he asked between bites of lunch. With two hours before my bus left, he had invited me to join him at a downtown deli. "What strange things have you seen?"

"How about a live Christmas tree, sales tag still attached? Or a pink papier-mache ballerina slipper? Near new houses, I found a pamphlet on 'scaffolding safety instructions.' But nothing is more disgusting —" I crinkled my nose "— than the daily quota of disposable diapers."

"You even pick up diapers?!" he asked.

"Not usually. I can't pick up everything — if I tried, I'd still be in Maine. I don't grab heavy things, like bottles, metal — or diapers — unless I'm about to dump a bag."

He scribbled more notes. "So now you're taking a break?"

I nodded. "I haven't seen my wife in two weeks, so I'll bus down for the weekend. Maybe the time off will help my leg. I guess I wasn't built for twenty-mile days!"

As he finished the interview, he remarked, "Your story reminds me of a local folk-hero. John Chapman was born in this area, before he headed west with his bag of seeds. You've probably heard of him — Johnny Appleseed?" He grinned. "Maybe I'll call you 'Johnny Litterseed'."

** HOMETOWNS I'VE NEVER KNOWN **

* MASSACHUSETTS – CONNECTICUT *

May 3 – May 14, 1993
153 miles -- 23 bags
TOTAL, 443 miles -- 51 bags

The soul of a journey is liberty, perfect liberty, to think, feel,
and do just as one pleases. We go on a journey chiefly to be
free of all impediments and of all inconveniences; to leave
ourselves behind, much more get rid of others.
 - William Hazlett, "On Going On a Journey"

━━━━━▶ ◆ ◀━━━━━

*As the miles drop away on the bus ride to Connecticut, it strikes me
how this is such an antiseptic way to travel. Watching scenery from a
glass-and-steel cocoon rather than breathing it, smelling it, living it,
leaves me yearning to walk again.*   -journal entry, April 30

SUE STRUGGLED TO STAY upbeat. She spent her days in a
wheelchair, sentenced there by her doctor. "Besides the broken leg," she
reported, "hiking with too-small boots sprained my right foot. Then pulling
the wagon strained the hand I broke. Maybe I should will this body to
science and buy a new one."

Her moods swung wildly, fueled by her frustration. At times she talked
eagerly of the walk, guessing how soon she might join me on the road.
Other times she would sit in a trance, staring blankly at the TV set, reacting
to nothing. I felt powerless to help her, unsure what to say that might make
a difference.

The four days passed too quickly, and again we worked through
awkward goodbyes at a bus station. "I'll be back in two weekends," I
promised, giving myself time to walk from Fitchburg. "If my legs hold up."
I fought back tears as I boarded the bus. As I pulled away, she waved, a sad
smile on her face.

From the Fitchburg bus station, my route traversed the gritty side of town. The road held little traffic, and gray skies added to my subdued mood. The few people who passed honked and waved, but they couldn't penetrate my gloom. At least the time off had done wonders for my legs, and my only twinge of pain fled quickly under an attack by Ben-Gay™.

I hoped a friendly face could pull me from my funk. Near Rutland, Massachusetts, lived the brother of the friend who had hosted our 'bon voyage' party. She had insisted we look up Addison and his wife, and called ahead to warn him. When I called them for directions, though, his wife's surprised silence told me she'd heard nothing of me.

Virginia still welcomed me, awaiting my arrival with cold orange juice. Her grandson Jason joined us, and we chatted for an hour about the walk and the area. Soon we ran low on conversation.

"So, what are your plans for the rest of the day?" she asked as my stomach began gurgling, asking about lunch.

"I don't have any. On the road, I keep my days open so if I feel like stopping someplace, I can."

"I sure wish you could meet Addison, but he won't return until 9:00 tonight. I'll have to tell him what he missed."

"Nanna, maybe he could stay here tonight," Jason suggested.

She glanced his way. "It's early, Jason. I'm sure he wants to move on."

Getting the hint, I rose and headed for my pack. Virginia thanked me for stopping, and gave me a dozen granola bars for the road. After a last glass of water, I hurried the two miles into Rutland, anxious to appease my rumbling stomach.

After lunch I settled down on the commons to write in my journal and fritter away the afternoon. Jason bumped into me in the general store later as he ran errands for his grandma. When Virginia arrived to pick him up, he ran to the truck, spoke to her, then ran back to me. "Nanna says if you want to walk back to her house, you can set up your tent on her lawn."

I thanked Jason, but told him I wasn't up to walking back from where I'd just come. Disappointed, he trudged away.

Lying in my tent that evening, I reflected on the last two days. Earlier in the trip, whenever our spirits flagged, we'd meet someone who would give us a boost. I needed that someone now.

Talking about North Brookfield in his "Historical Discourse" of 1850, Dr. Snell states that prior to 1810, "the people of this town . . .

*were making next to no progress in anything profitable, or calculated to
elevate their character and promote the cause of morality or civilization.
They had no productive employment, and did but little else through the
winter months, but to get their fuel, sit by the kitchen fire, drink their
cider, and tend their cattle."*

*The North Brookfield I walked through today bears no resemblance
to that dreary picture. Instead, I found a delightful New England village
of picturesque churches, well-kept houses and lawns, and extra-
ordinarily friendly people.*   -journal entry, May 5

OH, WHAT A DIFFERENCE a day makes!

The crisp, clear morning filled me with a new energy, and I struck off
through the wilds of central Massachusetts. Few cars passed as I made my
way down the pike, hemmed in by thick forests. An occasional cabin, store
or farm claimed a foothold in the woods; otherwise I shared the land with
brooks and birds.

Late in the morning, I entered North Brookfield. From the first
restaurant I passed I heard an ice cream cone calling my name. While I
indulged, a couple seated nearby asked about my backpack. I passed fifteen
minutes chatting with them, glad for the company.

Another half-mile took me to the town center. A small downtown lined
the main street, and (typical for New England) a First Congregational
Church anchored the square. After window shopping, I read on the church
lawn for an hour.

At noon I headed for a cafe I'd spotted earlier, two doors off the main
drag. It was closed. I looked around, wondering where to try next, when a
car pulled up and a silver-haired gentleman rolled down his window. "Can
I help you find something?"

"I was hoping to get lunch, but all the cafes look closed. Is there
anyplace open nearby?"

"There's a brand new restaurant, opened last week, on the edge of town.
If you'd like, I can drive you there."

Of course, he meant the eatery where I'd bought ice cream. On the ride
there, David Libby mentioned he had first seen me outside town. "I
wondered what you were up to."

As we walked through the restaurant, he stopped to greet people at
every table, introducing me. Those he missed dropped by our table to say

hello. Was he the town's most popular person? No, I found out, just the minister of the First Congregational Church.

It refreshed me to talk with someone about their travels, not mine. David had recently returned from Russia, where he'd visited large cities and small towns. Our discussion touched on many topics, and I hated having it end.

As I strolled through town later, the couple I had met over ice cream saw me and waved a greeting. A few blocks farther, an elderly gent on crutches flagged me down to ask where I was headed.

Ahhh, small town life. I felt like I belonged, returning home to friends.

The bank sign in Ware claimed 70° at 11 a.m. As I climbed the first of two hills beyond town, sweating like a warthog, I felt every degree. Thank heavens for the clouds scuttling across the sky, keeping the sun from beating down unchallenged.   -journal entry, May 6

I MISSED LAKE CHARGOGGAGOGMANCHAUGGAGOGG- CHAUBUNAGUNGAMAUG.

While planning the trip, I'd heard about the lake with the longest place name in America. "It sounds like a must-see," I'd told Sue. "In the native tongue, it means, 'you fish on your side of the lake, I fish on my side of the lake, and no one fishes in the middle.' How could we not stop there?"

"Char-googa-what? How could they fit that on a map?"

"They shortened it to Webster Lake, that's how."

However, it was not to be. The stop in Rutland pushed my course further west, and then Virginia and Jason urged me to see Massachusetts's largest lake instead. Always looking for local input, I changed my path and struck west at West Brookfield.

As I crested a rise, Quabbin Reservoir stretched northward out of sight. Dense forests marched to the shoreline, and wooded islands peeked out from the calm blue water. The lake's surface was as flat as glass — as designated wilderness, boating was prohibited. Permitted uses included only hiking, picnicking, and fishing (both sides, but not in the middle).

A visitor center near the dam lured me with the promise of a cold drink, and exhibits inside caught my attention. The reservoir, they explained, resulted from an ever-expanding Boston that demanded fresh drinking water. When the reservoir first reached capacity in 1946, it ranked as the largest manmade water supply system in the world. Even after slaking my thirst, they still had 300 million gallons to spare.

The center showed before-and-after photos of the four towns disincorporated when they flooded the Swift River Valley. The state uprooted 2500 people from Enfield, Dana, Prescott, and Greenwich, razed their empty houses, demolished their factories, clear cut their land. Not even cemeteries escaped the purge — the state exhumed 7500 bodies from thirty-four sites, reinterring them outside the park.

I have come to terms with the road. I drifted through the first two days following my weekend off, nursing a cheerless attitude and hoping for handouts. Since the disappointment of Rutland, my mindset has changed. I now appreciate the days for whatever they offer, whether I get a free lunch, outlast a thunderstorm in the tent, chat with a Vietnam vet whose army buddy just died, soak in the beauty of Quabbin Park, tell a local deli they have the best fast food I've yet tasted, or simply exchange a few sentences with people I come across. Even long stretches with no people don't bother me, as I enjoy the weather and scenery.
                                                        -journal entry, May 7

I DIDN'T EXPECT ANY impact from the article in the Springfield *Union-News.* They spent only five minutes interviewing me over the phone, and declined to send out a photographer.

My first hint to the contrary arrived at 7:30 a.m., when the desk clerk rang my room. "Someone from WGGB-TV, the local ABC affiliate, called. They want you to call them after 9:00, when their reporter gets in." *Me? On TV? Here come those fifteen minutes of fame!*

By nine I was walking U.S. 202 through Holyoke, frantically looking for a phone booth. Several blocks of businesses passed without one, and ahead the road turned residential. Finally I spied a Friendly's Restaurant and decided to see if they measured up to their name.

They did! They let me use their phone and treated me to breakfast. While I ate, several patrons noticed my backpack and 'Litterwalk USA' shirt, and stopped to encourage me.

The TV crew filmed a spot aimed for the 6:00 news, working around the passers-by who kept stopping to wish me luck. As I headed out of town afterwards, drivers blew their horns, waved, or yelled, "Thanks, Glen!" A clerk in a pizza shop hurried to his door as I walked past. "The paper said you'd be walking south on this highway, so I hoped I'd see you. Here — have a pepperoni!"

In Westfield early that evening, a woman on her front porch asked if I wanted a juice. Within moments she and her husband raised the ante to include a shower and spaghetti. Having eaten, I turned down the dinner, but took advantage of the shower. Once clean, I paused long enough to catch the 6:00 news, hoping to see my TV debut. No such luck — they must have saved the footage for the late news.

I headed south on a side road along a quiet stream, enjoying the cool evening air, smiling as I thought about the day's encounters. As shadows lengthened and the sun prepared its goodbyes, a car pulled up and interrupted my reverie. The driver asked, "Looking for a place to camp?"

"I sure am."

"I run a wilderness camp down the road a half mile. It's not open for the season yet, but that doesn't matter. You can spend the night in my tepee."

Here I am, ready for a nap under a tree in East Nowhere, New England. If I thought I was in the wilds around Nottingham, NH, or Rutland, MA, I didn't know the half of it. Highway 179 from Granville, MA, into Connecticut goes fifteen miles or more without a single store selling food -- only an occasional orchard, greenhouse, or liquor store.

The countryside bursts with beauty. Bubbling brooks weave through forests on both sides of the road, and flowers accent the green of the leaves. This is hill country, though. In Connecticut, route 179 straightens out, and roller-coasters all the way to the nearest village.

-journal entry, May 9

THE BICYCLISTS IN GRANVILLE assured me the next town had a store where I could pick up dinner supplies. They had stopped there during a tour two years ago, and remembered it well.

The townspeople remembered it well, too, especially the fire that claimed it last year. At least the town hosted a tavern, so I wouldn't go hungry. If I wanted a meal that night, though, I would have to eat there.

With a whole afternoon to pass, I took the pack off and got comfortable.

Relaxing under a massive oak, watching families scurry about in their Sunday best, I pondered my latest lesson. On the road, things constantly change; always prepare for the worst. I could have lugged groceries from Granville, and been on my way after lunch.

To travel is to learn — about the land, about others, about oneself. With the time I had to reflect on life's lessons, I fancied myself a 'Roads Scholar.' My course of study covered many fields:

American History. Fifth-grade textbooks could never bring the past alive like walking through it. Stories of early settlements along the coast segued into tales of Revolutionary War battles. Red brick buildings in Massachusetts towns spoke proudly of the Industrial Revolution. Next month would come the Mason-Dixon line and battlefields of the Civil War, followed by traces of our westward expansion.

Biology and Health. Backpacking introduced me to muscles I'd never known. My legs, I learned, could handle an occasional twenty-mile day. They balked, however, at averaging over fifteen.

Real Estate. In housing, the top three concerns are location, location, location. The same goes for free camping. With woods filling the countryside, I easily found spots to slip off the road and pitch a tent out of sight. Contrary to the fears voiced by the deejays at L.A.'s KABC radio, I had no problems with anyone bothering me.

Business and Advertising. Advertising can be as simple as a hand-lettered sign in a window or a wood carved sign out front, if it attracts attention. Several signs and shingles attracted mine. I grinned at the irony of the TLC Pet Shop running a sale on ferrets. On a rural stretch in Connecticut, I did a double-take when I saw an alchemist's shingle. Down the same road, proprietors Reid and Wright ran their antiquarian bookstore.

Garbology. More questions than answers came from my scrutiny of roadside trash. Did a tourist fresh from the Bahamas leave the foreign 25¢ coin on the highway? Which driving diner (or galloping gourmet) lost his salt and pepper shakers? Who dropped the keyring with keys on it miles from town, and how did they drive home without them? And the month's burning question — why did I find so many pairs of dirty underwear, panties, and bras?

Life. Most importantly, I learned to value simple pleasures. One day, for instance, as I walked a barren stretch of road toting a nearly full bag of litter, a garbage truck pulled up and took it. Half an hour later, a passing motorist handed me $5 to "buy yourself something at McDonalds." Following a lunch stop, I took a long break with a reporter, swapping my stories with his tales of summer jobs in Alaska.

Now, I faced only three more days of 'school' before reaching Susan.

Can this be real life? If not, when does it set in?
                                                -journal entry, May 11

LITCHFIELD, CONNECTICUT SAT ATOP the steep hills outside Torrington. During the heyday of the Industrial Revolution, the town served as home for wealthy mill owners, who built their mansions above the heat and bustle of the river town below. Today, these glorious mansions attract tourists from afar, who wander its quaint streets and frequent its eclectic shops.

The first thing I attracted upon entering town was a wad of gum, which I brushed against tossing away my latest bag of trash. As I cleaned the sticky gunk from my fingers, I heard the question, "So where's your next stop?" I glanced up to see a man, a bit younger than I, eyeing my pack with a wistful look.

"Well, here for lunch and a break, then who knows? Eventually, I'm going all the way across the country. Can you recommend a cafe in town?"

On his way to lunch himself, Walter invited me along. Over the meal, he gave me a nutshell history of the town, and encouraged me to see the estates on the side roads. After paying our tab he showed me the school where he worked. Sandy, a co-worker who had founded the Litchfield Walking Club, overheard us and stopped by. Together they raptly listened to my stories.

I received an enthusiastic reception at the *Litchfield Enquirer* offices. The editor interviewed me, asking the usual battery of questions: "How old are you? How long have you been married? How far do you walk each day? What inspired you?" After the obligatory staged photo of me picking up garbage, she gave me a county map and helped me find a shortcut to my in-laws' house.

Hoping to trade in old books for new reading material, I visited the Cobble Court Bookshop. The owner quickly sized me up, curious about what stranger had entered her domain. Noticing the 'Don't Litter' sign hung to my backpack, Anne Talcott sprang to her feet.

"I've got your book! I've . . . got . . . your . . . book!" Her eyes lit with delight as she bustled to a far corner of the cramped store, leafing through stacks of children's readers.

"Here it is!" She returned with a thin book titled _The Wartville Wizard_. "I have children's hour here every week, and this is a book I read to them." She read several pages aloud, talking about a wizard with "the power over trash." He could point to a piece of litter and send it back to stick to the person who threw it. _Hmm. Could he teach me that trick?_

Before I moved on, she donated a dog-eared copy of Steinbeck's _Travels With Charley (In Search of America)_ to my traveling library. It seemed an appropriate addition to my pack.

I wandered down the mansion-lined streets, enthralled by the stately homes. Gables, bay windows, front porches — the buildings had character. Very different, I thought, from the concrete-and-stucco cancer overwhelming southern California.

While I ambled along the lanes, more residents came up, intrigued by my backpack. One gent told me of a shortcut out of town, bypassing the main highway for a stroll through a nature center and past a civil war era cemetery.

Though I finally left Litchfield behind, its hospitality followed me to the next town. As I passed a gas station in Bantam, a man filling his tank asked my destination. Five minutes later he drove up, asking if he could do anything to help. I assured him he just had.

As evening bore down, I looked for a secluded spot. Rounding a bend, I saw the sign for a campground, and noticed a truck pulling out of the entrance. I approached them as they strung a chain across the driveway.

The burly truck driver looked at me skeptically. "I hope you're not planning on staying here tonight. We're not open."

"I'm walking across the country, and was looking for a spot in the woods." I watched his expression change from surly to surprised. "Any chance I could sneak in here and pitch a tent?"

"Across the country, huh?" He glanced at his partner. "Well, we're leaving for the night in two minutes. Once I'm gone, I don't have any control over what might happen . . . Get my drift?"

THE BICYCLIST RODE UP as I sat on the grass, slathering on my morning ration of sunscreen. As he came close, his features revealed an American Indian ancestry. Sitting several feet away, he started, "I saw you back there, and I wanted to say I think it's great, what you're doing with trash."

"Thank you."

"It's a shame so many people don't care." He appeared ill at ease talking to a stranger, and I had to strain to hear his soft voice. His eyes stared off into the distance, or studied the grass at his feet.

"I agree, it's terrible so many people don't care. But on this walk, I'm finding a lot of people DO care. People I meet thank me, and tell me they do their part. Still, there's a large group of people who litter, and they ruin it for the rest of us."

"Some people just don't think about the land. Maybe we need to go back to the old ways."

"You mean the Indian philosophy?" I asked. "Using instead of abusing our resources?"

"Yes. Years ago, the elders would judge what they did by how it would affect their children's children's children, seven times over. If people could be that way again . . ."

"I don't know if our society could ever change that much. Trouble is, our history has seen centuries of a 'use it up and move on' ethic, and now there's nowhere else to move on to."

He sat in silence for a moment before changing topics. "Did you see the spot up the road, where they're going to build houses?"

"The site with 111 plots planned? Yes, I saw it."

"It's so beautiful the way it is, so peaceful and free. I walked through there a few days back, and found an arrowhead." After pausing to sigh, his voice quieted even more. "I can't believe they're going to ruin it."

"I can believe it, I'm from California. But I do think it's a shame." Our conversation lasted a few more minutes, until he excused himself to go to work. "Thanks for stopping by and talking," I said.

"Thank YOU for helping Mother Nature."

** ON AND OFF THE "A" TRAIL **

* NEW YORK - NEW JERSEY *

May 17 - May 27, 1993
132 miles -- 15 bags
TOTAL, 575 miles -- 66 bags

Two roads diverged in a wood, and I -
I took the one less traveled by,
And that has made all the difference.
                    - Robert Frost, "The Road Not Taken"

Depart not from the path which fate has you assigned.
                    - fortune cookie, received May 19

I'D LOST MY WIFE.

I returned to New Fairfield expecting a warm welcome. Instead, I found a stranger. Gone was Sue's laughter, her easy smile, her zest for life. The spark had left her eyes, replaced by a dull indifference. The stranger who'd taken her place greeted me coolly with a peck on the cheek.

I quickly saw the toll four weeks of infirmity had taken. Sue had healed enough to leave the wheelchair for crutches, but took no joy in it. The lingering pain, the boredom, and the loneliness had turned her mood black. What little she said came out caustic and biting.

Leaving was hard, especially doing it twice. As I walked away from her parent's house, Sue offered to pick me up at the end of the day. The next morning she drove me back to the same point. As we sat in her mother's van, I wondered whether the trip should finally end. "We need to talk, hon."

"It's too late to talk." A solitary tear ran down her cheek as she stared straight ahead. "Just go walk."

I made no move to leave. "If I go walk, it will be too late. Too late to save 'us'."

"There is no 'us'," she said acidly. "There's 'me', a cripple, and 'you', a walker. That's all."

"Bull!" I shot back. "When we recited our vows, we did so as a couple. We've got a future that —"

"My future? What a laugh! My life's dream has been taken from me. You can't possibly know how much that hurts. It's like a friend dying." Her eyes flared with a mix of anger and sorrow.

Shocked by her intensity, I paused. "You're right, I can't know how you hurt. I've never had such a loss."

"Damn right you haven't. I'm angry and I'm jealous. You wake up every day in perfect health, just raring to go. All I want to do is walk, simply *walk*, and I can't." She turned and stared me down. "How do you think it feels to sit there, day after day, with your body rotting away? For two years, it's been one thing after another."

"So now you give up? Call it quits? I've never known you to prefer sympathy to fighting back."

"What do you want me to do, smile? I'm sorry, but happy Susan left the day I broke my ankle. I can't be cheery and say, 'Today's going to be rosy,' because it isn't. I sit there every day with no home, no job, no friends, and no husband." She looked away as tears battled for control of her eyes.

I reached for her hand. "Why don't we go home? I've been gone too long, and a break would be nice. In a week or two, we'll decide what to do."

"Then what? I know you want me to drive a car while you walk, Glen, but that would kill me. That isn't the trip I wanted. I'm sorry, but I haven't reconciled myself to that yet."

I sighed. "Maybe it's time I gave up this farce. Maybe it wasn't destined, and we should go back to the 'real world.' You're far more important to me than any trip."

"I wish you'd get out and walk. There's no sense in us both being miserable. Besides, I can't make any choices until I hear what the doctor says, if he ever takes my cast off."

I closed my eyes, fighting my own tears. "Let's go back to your folks' and ---"

"Please." she interrupted me. "Walk."

I walked.

What a day of contrasts. From 18-wheelers roaring down the asphalt arteries to the pine and elm forests of Bear Mountain Park, from the crowds on the streets of Peekskill, NY, to the white-tailed deer silently watching me pass on the Appalachian Trail, I marched west. A gray day accompanied me, with the clouds that missed last night's rain keeping the sun at bay.   -journal entry, May 19

"I HAVE TWO QUESTIONS," stated the photographer from the Peekskill *Herald*. "What are you doing, and WHAT are you DOING?"

The second question I couldn't answer. For the first time, my steps carried me away from Susan, down heavily-traveled U.S. 6. I barely noticed the Greek Orthodox churches hidden in the trees, or the construction traffic kicking up dust. In a daze I walked on, struggling with the choice I'd made.

One young woman shook me from my funk. As the afternoon wound down, she passed me on the sidewalk and noticed my 'People Against Litter' shirt. "How can I join?" she asked. "I already pick trash in my neighborhood. I'd love to meet others like us."

I smiled. "If you pick up litter, you're already a PAL."

Mostly, I feel alone, with a touch of lonely thrown in. I miss the companionship -- and security -- of another person, and I know how much Sue would adore this place. Still, I feel peaceful, at one with the world.   -journal entry, May 19

PACKING EXTRA FOOD AND water to handle two nights on the Appalachian Trail, my load increased to fifty pounds. I noticed the extra weight, though it didn't slow me. Five hundred miles of trekking had toughened me.

What caught me unaware was the rigor of this part of the Trail. After crossing the Hudson River into Bear Mountain State Park, it climbs directly *up* Bear Mountain. As night approached, I struck camp two-thirds of the way to the top, surrounded by mists.

Another hiker wandered up minutes later, and stopped to chat. This Tennessee native had come for a talk with God, something he did whenever life wore on him. A certified trail guide, he often led backpackers on week-long outings along the A.T.

He quickly humbled me. Fifty pound pack? His weighed seventy, which was light for him. "If the going gets too easy, I'll add rocks to bring it to ninety pounds. That's what I carry when I lead trips."

Today had a bit of everything:

WORRY — would I injure myself, alone in the wilds? Would my water hold out until I reached Lake Tiorati?

FEAR — when I slipped and fell on a rock. Luckily, I was unhurt.

AWE — at the beauty from the overlooks, one toward the Hudson River and one toward Tiorati.

DISAPPOINTMENT — when the overcast skies started dumping their load as I ate lunch, pelting hard for forty minutes and raining intermittently the rest of the day.

ANGER — when I kept losing my way on the trail, before I learned how to read the blazes.

RELIEF — upon reaching the ranger station at Lake Tiorati, where I refilled my water bottles and got my bearings.

PLEASURE — that despite the damp, cool day, I was not suffering in the 80° heat of the previous week.

DISBELIEF — that a 37-year-old man would risk a high-paying job in a recession so he could slog through the rain and pick up garbage across the country.

SURPRISE — that I didn't think of it before.

-journal entry, May 20

IT TOOK ME NO time to discover that the Appalachian Trail differed greatly from trails I'd hiked in the Rockies and Sierras. The A.T. often led straight up slopes, rather than conquering them through switchbacks. At times, it forced me to my hands and knees, scrambling down boulders and up rock faces.

While some A.T. stretches followed well-cut paths, others looked untouched by man — except for white paint marks on the trees. Without the constant reassurance provided by these trail markers (known as 'blazes'), I couldn't have said whether I was on course or wandering lost. If the trail veered, I searched the woods for the next mark to direct me.

After twice losing my way and backing up to the last blaze, I finally broke the code: a double white mark meant the trail turned, and the mark on top leaned in the new direction.

Eighteen miles of climbing hills, fifty pounds on my back, and four hours of drizzle combined to wear me out. Exhausted, I ended my long day at a shelter hut. These three-sided stone hovels, spaced an easy day's hike apart along much of the A.T., provided simple refuge from the elements — a roof overhead, a wooden floor beneath. I threw my sleeping bag down, thankful I didn't have to pitch a tent in the rain.

I shared the shelter with one other hiker, a twenty-year-old whose beard added years to his face. He had his own tales to share. "I'm finishing the thru-hike [walking the length of the A.T.] I started last year. I did over sixteen hundred miles, and have five hundred more to go."

"So now you're heading to Maine?"

"No, I'm what's called a 'flip-flopper.' I started in Georgia and walked to Virginia, then flew to Maine and headed south. I'll finish in Shenandoah."

"After one day on the trail, I have loads of respect for you. By the way, my name's Glen."

"I'm Purple Pilgrim." Seeing my confused expression, he continued, "Thru-hikers always go by their trail names. It makes sense, leaving your name behind with the rest of the world."

I pondered that for a moment. "You can call me Litterman."

I spent the morning hiking the A.T. with Purple Pilgrim. I enjoyed again having company.

After leaving the trail and Purple Pilgrim, it was lonesome time in the boonies. The A.T. had served as a vacation from pavement, and I quickly lost my vacation glow. My dedication to this epic is waning again, and is not helped by the thought (after a cold phone call) that Sue is once more losing spirit. This great journey of American discovery (and self-discovery) may soon end.   -journal entry, May 21

"WANT A RIDE?" THE blonde in the sports car pulled up minutes after I left the trail.

In this area, my backpack turned into a giant signal beacon. It seemed every other driver stopped, offering to take me back to the A.T. — even if they were going the other direction. "No thanks, I'm enjoying the walk." I saw her smile as she drove away.

A half mile away, a store beckoned with lunch. As I approached, I saw her eating a sandwich. "I thought you might stop," she said. "My name's Surefoot — er, Becky. I thru-hiked last year."

"I'm Glen, or Litterman. Take your pick."

The conversation presaged others I would have in the coming week. "Are you doing the whole trail, or just pieces?" became the question *du jour* as I paralleled the A.T..

Becky gave me a contact at the *New Jersey Herald* before driving on, leaving me with the unending pavement. I struck off through the forested countryside, anticipating my first-ever look at New Jersey.

The land turned more rural as I crossed the state line. My first impression was far from the urban sprawl I envisioned. The distinctive aroma of cattle farms laced the air, and I passed my first quicklimed carcasses, road kill rotting by the road side.

Only four days remained before Sue saw the doctor. When I called, she had regained her enthusiasm. She excitedly talked of rejoining me, urging me to slow down and save Pennsylvania to do together.

WITH TWO LONG DAYS behind me, I planned a leisurely Sunday. Entering Hamburg at 10:00, I bought the bulging weekend paper and settled under a tree to read it. At noon I crossed to a deli, where the employees had been watching me. My tale won their interest and a 20% discount on lunch. When I finished, the manager gave me his address. "Send me a card when you get to Oregon," he asked, "so I won't lose sleep worrying about you."

Outside Hamburg, houses lined the road. I waved to families in their yards, enjoying the beautiful day. Within a mile, I returned the wave of a retired couple sitting on their porch. "Are you in a hurry?" he called out. "We're getting ready for our Sunday dinner. There's room for one more."

Remember the first commandment of trekking, I told myself. *Thou shalt not turn down home-cooked meals.* "Well, maybe just a bite."

'A bite' turned into a full meal and two hours of visiting. The conversation flowed easily, as if I'd known the Wiltons for years. Eileen talked of the area from an insider's angle, having lived her whole life within five miles of her current house.

the Wiltons

"Thank you so much for dinner," I said as my feet began itching. "Can I help with the dishes before I go?"

"Nonsense," Bill cut me off. "Eileen's got a sixty-year-old dish-washer that never gives her a lick of problems. She knows I'll get 'em clean."

"Why don't you stay the night?" Eileen asked. "Our guest room's all made up. If you want, you can keep walking and call us when you're done. We'll come get you."

I accepted, and set off whistling. One hour of strolling took me to the next town, and I stopped in a bar to use the phone.

"Take your pack off and siddown, you're makin' me nervous," commanded a girl sitting at the bar. "Now, you wanna beer? It's on us. My name's Debbie; this is Jim."

I answered their questions over the beer. They struck me as an odd couple — she was outgoing, he seemed reserved; he envied my journey, she hated hiking; she wrote poetry, he worked with computers.

"Barmaid! Another beer for our friend." Before I could object, she told me, "Don't worry. *We'll* drive you back to those other people's house.

Hey — do you wanna explore a deserted church? It's locked, but we know how to get in."

I passed on the church, and returned to the Wiltons. As we watched the farewell episode of "Cheers," I thought how much they — and other people I'd met — passed for family. I'd never dreamed people would so easily open their lives and houses to me.

After a morning phone interview with a local radio station, I headed to Newton. At the *Herald* offices, I uncovered more of the hospitality I had come to expect. The staff took my story and my picture, but didn't stop there. They directed me to the best deli, then invited me back to eat with them. When I asked about supplies, they called every sports shop in town trying to find fuel for my backpacking stove, and offered to drive me to the next town to look for it.

They finally bade me goodbye at 3:00. Was it a coincidence that their rival paper now had too little time to photograph me? I didn't care; they'd earned the scoop. I made an appointment with the *Star-Ledger* photographer for the next morning in Middleville, then headed to Swartswood Lake to camp. Maybe tomorrow I could make up the miles.

I made only three miles, getting no farther than the Middleville P.O./ Robbins General Store. The photographer had beaten me there, and when I arrived, everyone asked about my trip. He posed me for several photos while I chatted with folks from the store, then he set up shots of them waving "Goodbye" to the crusader.

Trouble is, I never said goodbye.   -journal entry, May 25

AT THIS RATE, I'D never get across New Jersey.

The Robbins General Store crew peppered me with questions as I posed for the newsman's camera. They offered me muffins and oatmeal when I finished, and soon added a dinner invitation. "You can camp on my ranch," Ann Esses said.

The offer tore me. My mileage had suffered in this state, and the day was perfect for hiking. But wasn't mixing with people and slowing the pace of life the goal of this trip?

Brother John, a Franciscan posted there, volunteered to show me the ranch, around the corner from the store. He showed me barns filled with stray dogs and cats. We stopped and dangled our feet in the stream bisecting the ranch. He led me through a meadow bursting with flowers.

Brother John and Ann Esses

At his cabin John and I sat on the porch and talked. He had joined the church in '85, as part of the Charismatic Revival (similar to the Protestant 'born again' ethic). "My most memorable experiences have been with faith healing," he confided. "I have served as God's conduit twice. Once a woman had broken her arm in seven places, and doctors told her she would need a cast for six months. I prayed with her, and after only two months she went back to the doctor. They couldn't believe it — no trace remained of the breaks.

"Another time, an accident victim was not expected to last the night. If he did live, he faced reconstructive jaw surgery. I prayed with him that night. By the next afternoon, his condition had improved. Days later the doctors x-rayed his jaw again, and the results shocked them. The damage had healed itself!

"When I did this work, a calm came over me, and I asked the Father what was happening. 'He is filling you with the Holy Spirit,' he told me. 'Just let it happen, and God will take you where he wants you.'

"After seventeen months at the church, I came up here, and fell in love with the area. When I go back to Newark now, I can't breathe the air. It's so fresh and pure here. My life will be so different in a few days, when I go to New Haven and enter the seminary for the Legionaries." This order, he explained, works as a guerrilla band for Christ, aggressively spreading the Word. He had been accepted into the order, and saw it as his calling.

As he talked, I noticed the same peace of mind and clarity of mission I had seen in the Goodenoughs. At thirty-six, he was my age, but had a tranquility I rarely saw.

John summarized his mood. "My life used to be humdrum, going nowhere, with no meaning. Then I felt that calm, and it was tangible. Now I make sure to have those quiet times, when I can step back and say, 'Lord, I'm available for you,' and that peace runs through me again."

I decided to stay. As I helped John feed the strays, he told me about Ann Esses's financial straits. Unless she could raise $14,000 in the next two months, the bank would foreclose on her store. *She's losing her store,* I thought, *but she still invites me, a stranger, to dinner? These people are special.*

I passed the afternoon sitting by the brook, soaking my feet in the too-cold water, pondering life on the road. Two more days of hiking would take me to Memorial Day, when I would return to Sue and hear the final word on her leg. Yes, this trip had taken unexpected turns, and I knew more awaited us. Despite the disasters, despite the hassles, I didn't regret taking it.

The Appalachian Trail challenges me in so many ways -- struggling with loneliness (a problem I haven't often dealt with in New Jersey); staying aware of trail markers and not missing a junction while daydreaming; even seeing the blazes at times; and of course the physical demands. Though miles and miles of tramping down asphalt and other ungiving surfaces does torment the feet, the trail spreads its pain among the feet (when crossing hard rock), the ankles (stepping through uneven footing amid jutting rocks), the knees (especially on steep downhills), the balls of the feet (hopping rock-to-rock and pushing off from tight spots), the neck (from constantly looking down to check footing), and the upper legs (hauling myself up steep slopes). Plus, my backpack weighs more, filled with additional water and supplies of food.

-journal entry, May 27

RUDE TOWN ROAD. SLATE Pencil Hill Road.

The names jumped off the map, conjuring images, posing questions. What drove someone to name a road Wits End? Does Mt. Benevolence Road lead to a charitable peak? Was there once a Mudtown, now brought to mind only by its namesake avenue?

I stayed on Highway 521, heading for the edge of the state. In Stillwater I stopped for supplies, picking through the meager selection of the one-aisle general store. I grabbed a paper to read later, glancing at my cover story. As I waited for the clerk to make my sandwich, I fielded question from customers who had noticed the photo of me waving goodbye to the Middleville folks.

From there I left the main road to climb steeply over the Kittatinny Ridge into the Delaware Water Gap. I promptly ran across a group of high schoolers from inner-city Newark. The eight boys I met were one team of a large, multiethnic group from St. Benedict Prep School, out on their annual one-week wilderness expedition. I tagged along with them until dinner time, talking with a teacher who resembled Richard Dreyfuss.

The hike along Kittatinny Ridge rewarded us with long views over the countryside seven hundred feet below us. On one side, forested hills and reservoirs covered the New Jersey landscape; on the other, the Delaware River wound through the valley, separating us from Pennsylvania. Below our feet, rattlesnakes twice barred our way, and the troop backed up waiting for them to leave the trail.

What a way to finish my solo journey.

The hospitality of New Jerseyites continues unabated, as the group from St. Benedict Prep invited me to ride in their bus back to Newark. Once at the school, Gus (not the Richard Dreyfuss-looking teacher -- this one came closer to Wilford Brimley) drove me through downtown Newark to Penn Station, where I had the (hopefully) once-in-a-lifetime experience of bussing through the heart of NYC.

-journal entry, May 27

** LOST AND FOUND **

* PENNSYLVANIA *

June 10 - June 24, 1993
186 miles -- 67 bags
TOTAL, 761 miles -- 133 bags

A good traveler is one who does not know where he is going to, and a perfect traveler does not know where he came from.
- Lin Yutang

Halfway through our two-week hiatus, I'm amazed at how remote the trip seems. Once away from the day-to-day pavement pounding, it feels less real, like a dream that ended too soon. What feels even more remote is the work-a-day world, the forty hours per week madness that saps people of the best years of their lives. As the reporter from Torrington, CT, mentioned, I have never felt freer or been freer my whole life, and will likely never again be as free.   -journal entry, June 3

HER LEG WAS FREE of its plaster prison.

The doctor had removed the cast the day before I returned. In its place he'd fitted Sue with the latest fashion in plastic splints, a chic Pepto-Bismol-pink low-cut model. He'd also given her an attitude.

"He told me I should think about a more sedentary lifestyle — like being a librarian!" Her eyes flared as she recalled his words. "He said there were plenty of highway crews to pick up litter, and I didn't need to. That lit a fire under your wifely one!"

He'd scheduled her for another checkup two weeks hence, which gave us time to plot our strategy. If Sue had a car, she could pull ahead and park it, then walk back to meet me. Together we'd return to the car, and she could pull ahead again and walk until her legs tired. Once she'd fully recovered (which the doctor warned would take eight-to-twelve weeks), we'd store the car and get back to the trip we'd planned.

Sue did have a car . . . in Colorado. With two weeks to wait, we used the return half of our plane tickets to fly west. We spent a week with my folks, resting, taking short hikes, and enjoying a vacation from our 'vacation.' Our break ended with a long three-day drive to Connecticut to get the 'all-clear' from her doctor. Then we motored back to the Pennsylvania/New Jersey border where I had left off.

Three days to drive across the Great Plains, the Midwest, and the Appalachians. Now we had four and a half months to walk back.

"On the road again . . ."
Maybe I unconsciously planned today as punishment for taking time off. Choosing a three-mile climb with a one-thousand-foot gain to cross Kittatinny Ridge, instead of following the river past it, would surely whip me into shape. Mix that with a humid 90° day, our first taste of the summer to come, and I knew my easy days were over.
-journal entry, June 10

IT FELT WONDERFUL TO walk again. Good to stretch the legs, to fill the lungs with fresh Poconos air, to smell the forest on the breeze. Most of all, it felt good to share the trip with Sue again.

Standing atop the Kittatinny Ridge, we looked over Pennsylvania. Hills shrunk and disappeared. Forests faded into farmland. In the distance haze from factories marked the skies over Bethlehem. "That's where we're headed," I pointed out. "Easy, flat walking as we parallel this ridge."

On our second morning, Sue walked her first mile since Maine. Driving ahead, she found a wooded stretch of road and waited for me to arrive. Together we strolled south, ending at Pinocchio's Cafe. A fortysomething man tending the grounds leaned on his rake, watching as we approached. Wearing a stylish sweater and slacks, Paul Beahn looked too well groomed for a gardener. As we took out our water bottles, he asked if we'd like something colder.

Paul owned the cafe, and he returned with huge iced lemonades. While we sipped our drinks, he told us about the area. "You've got miles to go before the next town . . . or restaurant, either. Why don't you eat lunch here? It's on me."

I glanced at my watch: 11:00. "The *Express-Times* reporter said she'd find us on the road before noon. What if we come back after that?" *Maybe having the car wouldn't be so bad . . .*

. . . which was good, because we sorely needed it. By day's end, Sue had walked three miles. A good start, but it had a downside: her ankle ballooned that night. "I guess I overdid it," she admitted. "You'll be walking alone for a few days."

So I again soloed the side roads while Sue waited at pullouts. The temperatures rose as the week wore on, slowing me as I stopped more often for water. After one dry stretch, as I focused on the drink break soon to come, I saw the front door of the next house open. The man who came out strode down his walk carrying an iced tea. He caught me at the sidewalk and handed me the drink. *Service like this could spoil me!*

Bethlehem marked our return to big cities, and with it a return to heavy traffic. While I walked along, collecting yet another Burger King wrapper, I felt a tug on the bag. I whipped my head around in time to see a Cadillac pass only inches away.

Sideswiped! Though it hadn't hit me, the shock shot adrenaline through my veins. I stood stunned, my heart racing, staring at the car moving away. Behind me another motorist stopped. "Are you all right?" he asked.

"I'm fine. Thank heavens he only hit my bag."

He shook his head. "I can't believe he didn't even slow down."

"Amazing." I noticed a hole in my trash bag where the litter stick had poked through. "Well, he now has a scratch down the side of his car. Just desserts, I guess."

I continued on shaky legs and with a quickened step to meet Sue for lunch. My news alarmed her, and she urged me to stick to the sidewalks until we left the city.

By the time I reached downtown, I'd changed my mind about Bethlehem. The streets were clean (for a city) and the pedestrians friendly. Well-kept mansions anchored the streets, and horse-drawn carriages ambled by. "I'm no big fan of cities," I reminded Sue, "but I could live here."

As we left town, we had our first trouble with maps. As I rounded a bend, highway signs blared out 'no-pedestrians.' Luckily, Sue had stopped behind me for gas. When she came by I flagged her down, and we chose a new road. I got only a quarter-mile down that road before Sue drove up again. "Guess what? This one dead-ends. Shall we try a third route?"

At least we hadn't lost each other — this time.

Outside Israel, where could you leave Nazareth, walk through Bethlehem, and then turn toward New Jerusalem? Outside Maine, where could you head south from Bangor toward Belfast, knowing that Portland is not far away? And where in the world could you walk from Denver to Oregon in half a day?
Only in Pennsylvania.   -journal entry, June 13

AFTER TWO MONTHS OF avoiding big cities, our route now strung them together like a connect-the-dots puzzle. Bethlehem to Reading to Lancaster to York marked our passage through eastern Pennsylvania. After the quiet back roads of New England and the solitude of the Appalachian Trail, the crush of people and traffic kept me on edge.

Our car and the crowds conspired to make free camping difficult. Alone I'd had no problems tenting. The rural areas always had forests I could hide in, many with 'No Trespassing' signs to keep people from bothering me. Hiding a car, though, presented new problems. We hit campgrounds when we could, but few towns had them.

Our first night we got lucky. A Volunteer Fire Department lay on our route, and a fireman wandered by as we checked the grounds. He traded us a campsite for a signed liability disclaimer. That night we picked wild strawberries, watched a turtle amble by on his way to turtle business, and lay under a sky bursting with stars. Fireflies flitted around us, reminding me of childhood nights spent chasing them.

Rather than the norm, that night became the exception. We filled most afternoons driving back and forth, checking this city park, that churchyard, or poring over maps in the library. One night we camped in a tree farm, a half-mile from railroad tracks that hosted trains every hour. Another found us at a roadside park, with highway noise to keep sleep at bay. The night we happened on an abandoned religious retreat, a Tudor-style mansion backed by twenty acres of wooded hills, we thought we'd hit paydirt. We didn't notice the truck entrance to the PH Glatfelter paper mills across the road.

When we weren't struggling with free camping, we struggled with the growing piles of trash. With two of us collecting castoffs we doubled our rate to four-to-six Heftys™ per day, roughly one every three miles. Soon even that rate fell, and we set a high mark of eleven bags filled in one thirteen-mile day.

Some trash raised questions. At the base of one driveway I passed a pile of rainbow-colored aquarium gravel. Did the fish get a proper, commode burial? On another road pieces of a Canon copier dotted the shoulder. Was it simply a poor packing job, or had the unit gone on the fritz once too often?

As always clothing spiced up the haul. I could understand tossing *that* necktie, but the 'Cashtown Fire/Police' baseball cap and the Mickey Mouse bib looked brand new. A continuing parade of underwear kept us laughing, especially the hot-pink G-string.

We haven't yet found the right combination. Sue resents needing a car, and the time spent in it wears on her. We have yet to minimize the back and forth driving or the side trips. The last two days have been especially bad, as our attempts to skirt Reading have taken us onto poorly marked and confusing side roads.

-journal entry, June 16

PENNSYLVANIA WAS NO NEW JERSEY.

In late May I couldn't go two days without getting an invitation — for a drink, a dinner, a night inside. Now we'd gone a week in a new state, and few folks even said "Hi." Paul Beahn at Pinocchio's had welcomed us to the state, filling us with hope. Since then we'd met no one, and I wondered why.

Did the heat make people aloof? If so, we faced a long summer as the heat got worse. Maybe the car scared people away. "What sort of weirdos drive around wearing backpacks?" they might think. Whatever the reason, I missed making new friends.

With our moods down, we chose to bypass Reading. The 'Outlet Capital of the World,' as it billed itself, held no allure for us. Traffic, malls, and endless concrete would not likely brighten our day. Instead I studied the county map to find a way around the town. "Here's your directions," I said as I handed Sue a detailed routing. "We've got six left turns, five dead-end roads, four that change names, three right turns, two streets named Leesport, and a partridge in a pear tree. Okay, okay — how about a pigeon on a wheat stalk?"

The detour took us from the flat farmland into rolling hills dotted with woods, lakes, and horse farms. A cloudy day dropped the temperatures below 80°, giving us a break from the heat. Sue, tired of sitting in the car, pushed herself for five miles. By day's end, the ankle had again ballooned.

At least we had nights indoors to look forward to. David Kurfman, a close friend of mine since grade school, shared a converted one-room schoolhouse outside Reinholds with his wife Cindy and their four- and six-year-old daughters. For three days we used their home as a base while we hiked through the area.

One evening, while Dave trounced me in another game of chess, we reminisced about our school days. "Remember junior high," he said, "when they called you the 'Human Computer'?"

"When they banned me from the math bees so the other kids would have a chance?" I smiled at the memory. "So I was a bit bookish. If not for bowling, three legged races, and goofy golf, I'd never have gotten any exercise at all."

"You always had a way with windmills and schoolhouses." He pondered the board, then checked me with his rook. "You used to chase me around the chessboard . . . now you're chasing around the country. Back then, who woulda guessed."

"Not me. I didn't even get interested in traveling until college." I hid my king behind a pawn. "Maybe I got it reversed. You did the vagabond thing in your teens, drifting across the country while you were still young. Years later you got your degree and settled down. Me, I spent my best years behind a desk. Then I get married, and three months later we start packing for the road."

"You may be the Human Computer, Glen," he joked, "but I always said you had a head crash!"

So far it hasn't failed - when we write off an area as unfriendly, someone proves us wrong.

We had ducked inside a Turkey Hill Mini Mart for a juice break. As Sue pulled out her money, a man walked in and shouted, "I'll pay for those!" He had seen the article in the Reading paper, and saw us entering the store. As we chatted, he introduced us to other customers, most of whom he didn't know.

Earlier, as I waited outside Denver, PA for Sue to catch up, a police car approached. One of Denver's finest asked, "Excuse me, but have you

seen a steer go by?" I hadn't -- though Sue thought I should have told
them there was a cow in a purple 'Litterwalk' tee shirt down the road.
                                              -journal entry, June 17

THOUGH THE CALENDAR PROMISED three more days of spring,
the weather didn't oblige. The temperature shot over 90° by noon, slowing
our steps on a road with little shade. By 12:30, a couple miles shy of our
downtown Lancaster goal, Sue declared we had finished hiking for the day.
We drove east of town, pitched camp in a commercial campground, and
spent the day seeking air-conditioned refuge.

Leaving the movie theater at seven o'clock, I noticed it had cooled
down. "Maybe I should go back and finish walking into Lancaster," I
remarked.

"Now? What are you, crazy? It'll be dark soon."

"I thought I'd get through downtown today, so you wouldn't have to
walk in the city tomorrow," I said defensively. "Besides, the TV station
promised they'd have a crew available to film us."

"Yeah, they promised you that yesterday too, and again this morning."
She shook her head. "That's sure my first choice, getting back in the car
and driving twenty more miles."

"Fine, then I won't go." I got in the car and folded my arms, staring out
the window.

My playing the martyr irritated Sue further. "It's getting late. Just tell
me what you want to do!"

Losing patience, I barked, "I told you! I'd like to walk."

"Fine. You can go walk in the dark."

Rising tempers on both sides killed any chance for compromise. Riding
back to where we'd stopped, I halfheartedly offered to forego walking, but
she rebuffed me. Dropping me off outside town, she sped away to wait at
the downtown Turkey Hill Mini-Mart.

I called the newsman at the TV station, who gave me another lame
excuse. "Maybe if you called back tomorrow morning . . ." Angry, I hung
up and walked briskly — nearly running — into Lancaster.

I reached the Turkey Hill in only thirty minutes, but found no Sue
waiting. Panic struck me. *She should have beaten me here. Did something
happen?* This wasn't the best section of town, and on a Friday night it
seemed worse.

I asked inside the store — the clerk had not seen her.

I walked another block down Prince Street, then two blocks back. No Sue.

I flagged down the cop on the foot beat. He'd heard of nothing amiss.

I called the campground. She hadn't returned.

Another thirty minutes had passed, and I grew frantic as the city grew dark. I again stopped the beat cop, wondering what to do next. "She's not in these four blocks, no one's seen her, and — wait! Is that her?" Sure enough, she drove by as I stood there, panic on her face. "Sue! Sue!"

After calming down, we pieced together what had happened. When she left me, she had driven to the Turkey Hill. Within twenty minutes, homeless people had approached her twice, begging cigarettes. Uncomfortable sitting there, she decided to drive back along my route, and stop me before downtown.

Normally she would have caught me. Since I'd rushed, though, I was already walking south on Prince, a one-way street, while she drove north one block over. She parked three blocks from the mini-mart and waited for me until dusk fell, when worry got the best of her.

"We need an emergency plan," Sue said. "We're apart too often, and anything could go wrong."

I nodded, thinking. "Let's name my folks a contact point. If we get lost, we can call them, and they can relay our positions."

"That sounds good. If this happens again, we'll be prepared."

After ten weeks and seven hundred miles of results from car-animal interactions (also known as road kill), I knew someday I must actually see a critter get hit. The victim this time was a chipmunk darting across the road and zigging when a zag would have saved him. As his body slid to a halt, only one paw still quivered. I averted my eyes, feeling helpless as I passed.

Another first was a miniature golf course with real grass on the greens.   -journal entry, June 20

WALKING THROUGH MOUNTVILLE, I heard a call from behind me. "How far are you going?"

I turned to see a bicyclist ride up. A short, lean man with a tanned face, he looked in his forties. "All the way across the country," I answered.

His eyes grew wide. "My name's Ron Ettelman. My wife and I own the frame shop you just passed, and we'd love to have you stay for lunch."

I promised to return after getting Sue, who had parked ahead and was walking back to meet me. With an extra bounce in my step, I set off to find her.

Ron and Virginia — fellow dreamers

Together we returned to the Dream Framer, where Ron's wife, Virginia, waited. "When we saw you walk by, I told Ron to fetch you," she said with a lilting Spanish accent. "You see, we have a son who tried a cross-country bike trip, so we empathize with bikers and hikers."

That piqued my interest. "Your son does a lot of biking?"

She shook her head, her reddish-brown hair sweeping across her shoulders. "He never did before he got this notion to bike to California. After buying a bike, he rode seven miles a day to prepare for the trip. He got as far as Richmond, Virginia, before he gave up and bought a train ticket."

When Ron returned with sandwiches, we sat down to eat. The fan circulated the warm air, and we were grateful to be out of the 95° heat. As we ate, Ron talked about his business, pointing out pictures he needed to frame. He explained, "I think I've done well because I'm not greedy and I have a background in art. My prices are 20% lower than anyone else's, and I do good work. Of course, my modesty helps too."

Twenty-one years earlier they had escaped Philadelphia, leaving behind big-city stresses for the pleasures of small-town life. Eight years ago he moved into this shop, replacing a cafe closed by the mafia. "It was right after the _20/20_ show on the mafia-pizza connection," he said, "and I was buying a pizza when these two mafia guys walked in. One didn't even speak English. I mentioned I'd love to have a shop here, and the other one asked, 'Ya ain't gonna sell pizza, are ya? Then it's alright'."

They asked about the trip, and we talked of our adventures. "Meeting people makes the trip worth the hassles," I said. "Sometimes they'll see us in the paper, and stop to talk. Unfortunately we haven't met as many people here. Even worse, nobody's hearing about us now. The Lancaster TV crew never did film us, and the newspaper turned us down cold. It's the only paper so far to snub us." (It would remain the only one, too, until Boise, Idaho.)

Ron nodded with a stern look on his face. "Is that so? Looks like I'll have to write a letter to the editor."

The Ettelmans insisted we stay for the night, letting us bivouac in their yard. With that settled, we let them go back to work as we lazed away the afternoon in the city park, dangling our feet in the cool water of a brook.

Ron had warned us of the night train, but assured us it went by only once. With that good news, I ignored the train tracks lying down a gully only fifty feet from our tent. Ignored them, that is, until early the next morning. The 4:30 a.m. express must have registered 8.0 on the Richter scale.

As we crept closer to summer's opening, the days grew hotter and the clouds more ominous. For several days we suffered through Pennsylvania tempests, cloudbursts accompanied by thirty mph winds. We took to hiding in cafes or libraries during the afternoon, then walking again in the evening's cool.

In Hanover we stopped for supplies in Meyer's Market. While we shopped, a manager came up to us. "I read about you in the _York Dispatch_ today. I think it's great, and I wanted to donate these trash bags."

Anxious to keep the publicity flowing, I called the _Hanover Evening Sun_, arranging an interview. When the reporter arrived, he had a smile on his youthful face. "Would you believe that less than a minute after I talked with you, my editor asked, 'Have you heard from that couple walking across the U.S.A. picking up litter?' Talk about timing!"

My timing didn't last. When the reporter got his story, he produced a camera and asked me to "Pick away." I set off through McSherrystown, looking for a burger wrapper, a Bud can, cigarettes, anything. I found nothing. McSherrystown, I quickly decided, topped our list of clean towns. Finally I found a straw wrapper to snag, hoping it would show on film.

Sue, who sometimes declined to 'meet the press', waited for me up the road. We spent the afternoon in a Brushtown park, playing on the swings, taking naps, writing, letting the day drift away. With night pending, we set up the tent at 8:00, then began a game of cards on the picnic table. By 8:30 a man strode up, looking very official despite wearing shorts and a tee shirt. "Do you have permission to camp here?"

Trying to appear cooperative, I asked, "Who do we need to ask?"

"Where are you from?" Though his tone was businesslike, his face showed no hostility.

"Right now, nowhere. We're walking across the country, picking up litter. We have a car only because my wife's recovering from a broken ankle." I added, "We appeared in today's York papers, and will be in the *Evening Sun* tomorrow."

He paused for a moment. "How late will you stay here tomorrow?"

"6:30, 7 a.m. at the latest."

"Well, that's okay then. See, this is a private club. I just got back from a softball game to find my answering machine lit up with seventeen messages asking if we were running a campground."

Sue apologized, "We're sorry. We didn't see any signs, or we wouldn't have stopped. We would've asked somebody if we knew."

"As long as I know what's going on, it's all right. If anyone else comes by, tell them Herb said it was okay." He left then, going home to pacify the seventeen people worried about the homeless couple that had taken over their park.

Sue smiled at me as she picked up her cards. "You know, we'll probably end up as the biggest story of the year here in Brushtown."

NOTES FROM SUE'S JOURNAL:

Walked five miles today — foot still sore. Don't know if I'll ever walk

normal.   _- June 19_
Foot very sore. I want to walk but am afraid of long-term effects.
                                               - June 21
It's killing me riding in a car. I JUST WANT TO BE ABLE TO WALK
AGAIN!   _- June 23_

THIRTY-FIVE YEARS AGO, MY family passed through Gettysburg on vacation. Hearing that President Eisenhower was in the area, my folks took us to his hotel one evening, hoping to see him. As the time passed, a Secret Service agent took pity on the woman holding the baby, allowing her to sit in the lobby. When I nodded off, a local reporter saw a human interest story. The next day I made headlines as "the baby who fell asleep waiting for the president."

Funny, but no one rolled out a red carpet for my return.

We entered town early, hit the newspaper, and passed the rest of the day playing tourist. Gettysburg's history had intrigued me since grade school, and I spent hours touring the battlefield. Cannons still aimed over fields where so many had died. Pickett's Charge. Little Round Top. Cemetery Hill. The names resonated in memory.

That night I dreamt of Litter's Charge and Hefty™ Bag Hill.

The next morning we plotted an attack on our eighth state, Maryland. "If we stay on State 116 through Fairfield," I said, "south of town there's a side road that goes our way — let's see, Jack's Mountain Road."

"I don't know, Glen. That's not a numbered route, and it could be real steep. With a name like that ..."

"But the 116 veers south before heading west. That means another four or five miles." As I studied the map, other towns caught my eye. "Pennsylvania has the most unique town names. How about 'Rough and Ready'? And over here, 'Bird in Hand' is on the way to 'Intercourse'."

Sue pointed to two nearby villages. "How about 'Two Taverns' and 'Seven Stars?'"

"There's another 'Seven Stars' fifty miles north of here. Shouldn't that be 'Seven More Stars'?" We shared a laugh, then set off toward Fairfield.

The day was eventful, as far as days on the road go. One motorist handed me $10, and gave Sue another $2. We picked up golf, rubber, and whiffle balls, tossing them back and forth before bagging them. While soloing a stretch, I declined a ride offered by a woman in an open-air Jeep.

(She passed me again later, her long blonde hair flowing in the wind.) Entering Fairfield, I walked past 'Randy's Pre-owned Cars and Trucks,' whose selections included two trucks first owned over sixty years ago.

We stopped for a long lunch and afternoon nap in Fairfield, waiting for the day's heat to subside. Soon afternoon wore into evening, and Sue drove ahead to park and start walking back. As the car disappeared around a bend, my stomach took an unpleasant turn.

Did we ever agree about taking Jack's Mountain Road?

** DERELICTS AND DINOSAURS **

The more I traveled, the more I realized that fear makes
strangers of people who should be friends.

- Shirley MacLaine

———————◆———————

JACK'S MOUNTAIN ROAD CAME far too quickly. I took only ten
minutes to reach the junction, all the while worrying what to do.

Should I wait there for Sue? I knew she'd drive three miles ahead as
usual before walking back. She'd expect me to catch up well before she got
this far.

I could stay put until she hightailed it back to the car and came looking
for me. Of course, that would cost us ninety minutes of walking, or four
miles we'd have to make up the next day. Worse, we'd be stuck searching
for a tent site at dusk. We had enough trouble finding them in broad
daylight!

Should I keep walking and hope she found me? At least I could look
for places to tent.

I looked at my watch: 5:15.

I paced the road shoulder, trying to decide. To the left, traffic whizzed
by on highway 116. To the right, Jack's Mountain Road narrowed to a one-
lane bridge, then promptly climbed over a hill. Which to take, which to
take.

Certain whichever road I chose would be the wrong one, I took the right
fork. Half an hour passed, then forty-five minutes with no sign of Sue.
Despite my hopes, she must have stayed on the highway. *What do I do
now?*

It's not time to panic. We HAD agreed to finish the day in Fountain
Dale. Sue's road dumped into state highway 16, and the map showed the

town right at PA16 and JM Road. If I could make it there, she'd surely find me.

I reached PA16 at 7:00, and found a cluster of houses. To the east a forest flanked the road; to the west I saw farms and hills. Across the road, a farmer pulled into his driveway. I flagged him down and showed him my map. "How far to Fountain Dale?"

He stared at the map, then slowly shook his head. "Sorry. No such town around here."

Now it's time to panic. By now Sue would certainly be looking for me. If I stayed visible, she'd have to drive by soon. Wouldn't she?

Unless she stopped to call my folks.

I needed to find a phone. To the east on PA16 I saw nothing but trees, to the west mostly the same. However, she wouldn't expect me to head east, so I turned west.

The time flew — 7:15, 7:30, 7:45. Every mile I grew more concerned, afraid she wouldn't drive that far. Still, I needed a pay phone, a business, something.

At 8:00 the Blue Ridge Sportsman's Association caught my attention. The nondescript cinder-block building had a 'Private Club' sign in the window, with archery fields and a fishing pond across the road. For five minutes I waited outside, hoping she would pass, but finally decided to check in. As I entered the lounge, all eyes turned to me.

"I've lost my wife!" I blurted. "Can I use your phone?"

With trembling fingers I dialed my father. No, he said, Sue hasn't called. I left him the number and location of the bar and stepped back outside.

Five minutes had gone by, giving me a new worry: had she driven by while I was inside? Would she come by again? As the sun inched toward the horizon, I paced . . . and waited . . . and fretted . . . and finally saw her white Mirage pull up.

She jumped from the car, relief washing over her face. "Oh, God, I'm glad I found you! I was frantic!"

"I'm so sorry," I said. "We never decided . . ."

"I forgot too! I drove by here fifteen minutes ago, and a man up the road said no backpacker had been by. I've never been so worried!" We hugged each other, and still held each other tight as two Association members left the clubhouse.

"I take it you found your wife," the taller man remarked.

"Yes, I did. Thanks so much for letting me use the phone."

"Glad to help." He smiled, then asked, "Are you staying around here?"

"I hope so. We need to find a spot to camp." Hesitating, I added, "Can you recommend someplace?"

"Right across the road is the Association's fishing pond. No one'll mind if you stay there." As he walked away, he added, "If someone asks, tell them Gary gave you permission."

What more can be said for a day which begins with the songs of birds, wisps of fog rising from a lake glassy still, and two ducks posted by the tent flap waiting for breakfast?

-journal entry, June 25

Duck! He's having a bad hair day!

IN OUR LITTER OLYMPICS, we kept turning in gold medal performances. Our eleven-bag record fell to a twelve-bag day, and soon the mark jumped to fourteen — seventy pounds of debris in one day's stroll. We guessed the extra trash came from vacation traffic, piling up faster than crews could clean it. *Faster than I can clean it,* I thought as one passing motorist barely missed me with a half-full McDonald's drink cup.

Between the unending beer cans and the walk's fiftieth pair of dirty underwear, we found treasures. Near the Blue Ridge Sportsman's Association I unearthed a Casio Digital Diary, a hand-held computer worth $250 new (worth much less with a shattered screen). Fresh from a box of kid's cereal, a plastic Fred Flintstone hitched a ride on my backpack. As we crossed into Maryland, we played catch with a reclaimed baseball. Our biggest surprise came when I opened an L.A. Gear shoe box, and found a butterfly collection pinned and labeled inside.

As we entered state eight, the growing trash forced us to regroup. No longer could we count on finding dumpsters; we filled bags too quickly. For the first time, I called the Department of Highways. Our contact greeted us warmly, setting a tone echoed in states to come. We gave him our route, and he promised to have crews collect the bags we dropped.

One muggy Maryland afternoon I ran a 'trash derby', counting the most common litter along a two-and-a-half-mile stretch. "Cigarette packs jump to an early lead, and they're pushed hard by aluminum cans. It's neck-and-neck, packs — cans — packs, and here comes fast-food drink cups on the inside. What a three-way race! Cans — cups — and now packs are making their move!" The results, no photo finish, had cigarette packs winning with one hundred eleven, followed by cups placing with ninety-seven, and cans showing with seventy-seven.

Over live L.A. radio the next day, I talked about our taxing days, running trash derbies and writing 'wish you were here' postcards. One deejay warned me, "One of these days, Glen, you'll have to get a real job."

As we 'streaked' down our Maryland route, I reflected on the contrasts the state offered. The highways have shoulders the width of a full traffic lane, while country lanes are too narrow for two cars to pass. Some people take vicarious thrills in our walk, and others tell us to move on. A reporter gives us the most in-depth interview of the trip, and her editors hold the story for days. Farms and houses pack in so tightly that we can't find free camping, but miles and miles of main highways pass with no businesses.

The scenery in Pleasant Valley is, well, pleasant — Appalachian ridges on either side, thickly forested, with farms speckling the hillside. On the valley floor, farms share the land with villages, with a few *schools and churches thrown in for good measure. As we headed south, the ridge lines squeezed the road, directing its course toward Harper's Ferry.*   -journal entry, June 27

"FACE IT, WE'RE NOT going to find a spot." We had crisscrossed the county, and Sue despaired of finding a tent site. "There are no parks, no country churches, no farms for sale here."

"We haven't tried this road yet." I turned up the lane, hoping our luck would change. "If only this wasn't Saturday night, the state park wouldn't have been full. We could have camped AND had a shower."

Sue gazed out the window, watching more houses slide past. "I really hate this, looking for a place to hide. Like last night, driving behind that abandoned barn while no neighbors were looking. I feel like a fugitive, like I'm doing something criminal."

I agreed with her. We never expected to find campgrounds spaced fifteen miles apart along our route, and knew motels were a luxury. However, we never anticipated a land so festooned with 'No Trespassing' signs that we couldn't stop for a well-deserved rest. The clouds darkening above mirrored our mood.

As we entered Keedysville, MD, Sue eyed a 'Community Center' sign. "Let's check it. Otherwise, I give up."

The driveway led behind the center to a small park surrounded by trees. At the far end, a baseball diamond sat unused, waiting for sunnier days. The center itself had closed for the night. "It looks good to me," I said. "No one can see back here, and once it starts raining, I doubt any kids will come by."

"Speaking of rain, we'd better get set up before it starts." We didn't quite beat it, but finished most of our two-minute drill before the drops arrived.

A steady drizzle ensued. We watched the liquid sunshine from inside the tent for five minutes, until a truck drove up. A burly man got out to throw his household trash in the dumpster, and then approached our tent, scowling.

"Who gave you permission to camp here?" he growled.

"We weren't sure who to call," I began, taking the tack that had worked in Brushtown. "There was no —"

"This is corporation-owned land, and it's clearly marked out front," he stated, though we had looked carefully and seen no signs. "It's private property."

"So who do we call for permission?"

"I can tell you, you're not going to get any. My wife's on the board, and our liability won't allow it. Pack up your stuff and get out of here." He terminated the discussion by stomping back to his truck. From the dryness of the cab, he watched to make sure we packed.

With the light rain moistening us, we threw our gear in the back of the car. A few miles away, we checked into a cheap motel, downhearted from the encounter.

There had to be a better way . . .

We spent last night at the Harper's Ferry Youth Hostel, which was run by an authentic Appalachian Trail legend — Harry the Indian. This Winnebago Indian had lived on the A.T. for years, hunting and fishing and working side jobs. We visited with him and his wife, and read posted articles about his life. Later they showed a video about Bill Irwin, a blind man who thru-hiked the A.T.. After the video, one woman asked me, "Didn't I just read about you in Walking magazine?"

-journal entry, June 28

IN 1859 SLAVERY THREATENED to tear the United States apart. Hoping to capitalize on the crisis, abolitionist John Brown led a raid on the federal arsenal at Harper's Ferry. His dream, of confiscating arms and leading an army of slaves on a march to liberate the south, failed when government troops surrounded his band and captured him following a shootout.

In 1993 we used Harper's Ferry to kick off our own march into the south, liberating litter. After touring the battlefields at Gettysburg and Antietam, I looked forward to tackling the only Confederate territory on our route. However, concern over being separated amongst 'rednecks' tempered Sue's enthusiasm. "Suppose one of these hillbillies with a gun rack on his pickup sees a female walking alone, and gets ideas?"

We followed the Shenandoah River south as it cut through the 'spout' of West Virginia. We met no rednecks, though we wondered if they were responsible for the new trend in trash: household appliances. In pullouts along the river, mixed in with other litter, we found a microwave oven, a washing machine, and a TV. One person left a blue plastic wading pool, and in a field sat two abandoned school buses.

Not all the trash was too large to bag. Outside Harper's Ferry I found a new wool sweater drenched with dew. A powder-blue negligee caught my eye on the river road, but it unfortunately wasn't Sue's size. Sue saved the foam pillow I picked up; we threw the pillowcase away, but slept on the pillow the rest of the year. (Living without an income meant waste not, want not!)

As we passed fishing hole after fishing hole, finding each choked with garbage, I understood why we saw so many 'No Trespassing' signs. _I wouldn't want my property used as a garbage dump, either. If people abuse the land, they lose the land. Why can't litterers figure that out?_

The litter went hand-in-hand with decay. We had seen signs of small-town blight earlier in the trip, but it worsened as we plunged south. Our route passed through several towns which withered away in today's fast-paced world, towns such as Kabletown, West Virginia. The last business, a general store, had closed that spring when its elderly owner died. It stood silently on the main drag, shelves still stocked, waiting for a new owner who never came.

White Post, VA, still struggled to survive. The town's history dated to 1750, when George Washington lay a white survey marker to direct travelers to Lord Halifax's estate. In its heyday, trains stopped regularly and businesses boomed. Now only a convenience store and a post office, both on the highway skirting the town, kept it alive.

We began the first day of July in the center of White Post, sitting in front of a long-closed gas station. As we geared up for the day's walk, an elderly black man across the street stepped onto his porch. Seeing us, he jumped up, yelled something unintelligible, and disappeared inside. Moments later he popped back out and hurried in our direction. He looked a sight, gray hair topping his lean, stooped frame, wearing homemade pants held together with patches and a shirt of like style. As he neared, we saw him waving a copy of the morning's paper. "Is this you? This has to be you!" he said, pointing to our latest headline.

He wanted to hear about our trip, and how things were going for us in the south. We chatted with him for ten minutes, happy to meet our first Virginian. His enthusiasm kicked off our day on positive note.

It went downhill from there. As the heat raced the humidity to 100, we slogged along. Sue found a baby rabbit moments after a car hit it, lying on the shoulder. Still alive, its eyes stared at her, begging for help. Powerless to save it, Sue cried.

By day's end, we had found no camping site, and took off on another driving tour of the area. This time luck visited us. Right on U.S. 340, a state recycling center — a highway pullout with bins for cans, papers, plastic, and bottles — featured a grassy area flanked with a copse of trees. Since the center was under nearly constant use, we drove down the road and waited until dark.

At dusk we pulled the car to one side, and quickly pitched camp before anyone drove up. Lying in the tent, we heard several more cars stop, but the trees kept us safely out of sight.

Sue noticed the flashing red lights first. From our tent, we could barely make out the police car parked behind the Mirage. "Time to get dressed and see what's up," she lamented.

As we entered the pool of light around his car, the sheriff looked up, surprise on his face. "Is there a problem, officer?" I asked.

"Could I see your IDs?" He took our licenses, and as he looked them over, the plate check came over his radio. "California license plate 2GVC071, registered to . . . " preceded our name and (former) address.

As we explained our situation, a wry grin came to his face. "That sounds great. Personally, I wouldn't care if you stayed here. But you see that fence?" He pointed past our tent. "On the other side is the Virginia State Penal Institute, Camp Number Seven. You've got some guards very nervous."

Sue gasped, her eyes wide with shock. "You're kidding!"

"No, this isn't a good place to spend the night. Back up the road twelve miles is a motel, or you can park two miles back at the traffic lights. Did you see it earlier, the lot for Dinosaur Land?"

We spent the night sleeping in the car under the watchful eye of a concrete brontosaurus. The next day we drove to the suburbs of Washington, D.C. to spend Independence Day with cousins, certain we must find a solution to our camping travails.

The everyday kindness of the back roads more than makes up
for the acts of greed in the headlines.
  - Charles Kuralt, "On the Road With Charles Kuralt"

THE TIME OFF HELPED. For three days we relaxed in Fairfax,
enjoying picnics and fireworks, forgetting litter. My cousins welcomed us
without doting on us, giving us space yet including us in their plans. The
much-needed break let us unwind and regain our zeal for the road.
However, we still faced a big problem.

"I came out here to meet people," Sue reminded me as we spent an
afternoon at the Great Falls Tavern on the Potomac. "I'm getting great
exercise, and the roads sure need cleaning, but people make the trip."

I watched the river cascade over the Great Falls, frothing as they fell.
"And we're not meeting them, are we?" Sue slowly shook her head to
answer my question. "Instead, we're spending too much time in that damn
car, getting on each other's nerves. I know I've been short with you lately,
and I apologize."

"It's not your fault. I've felt it too." She sat on a rock and dangled her
feet in the water. "Maybe the car is to blame. We met more people when
we both walked."

The notion had troubled me also. Did the car make us look like dime-a-
dozen tourists, stopping for a gallon of gas and a six-pack of Coors before
hitting the road? Did people see us as self-sufficient, in no need of kindness
from strangers? "Maybe we rely on the car too much, driving around to
scout campsites. Driving someplace to get out of the rain. Without a car,
we couldn't do that. Are we getting spoiled?"

"Maybe we did get spoiled — not by the car, but by Maine," Sue countered. "We met so many wonderful people there — the Greiners, the Goodenoughs, the Bourkases — that we got used to it. Perhaps Maine is more friendly than most states. Who knows? Two or three 'road angels' a month might be average for the rest of the trip." She looked away, unhappy at the thought.

Sounds of kids upstream, climbing over rocks, infiltrated our silence. I reflected on the last three weeks, wondering where — or if — we had gone wrong. After several minutes it dawned on me. "Ever since I got rousted in New Hampshire, I've been leery of asking people for permission. Still, we have to stop playing fugitive. Hiding away every night doesn't help us meet anybody." I paused before adding, "Besides, it ain't much fun."

"I second that idea." She dried off her feet and reclaimed her shoes. "This 'grand adventure' is starting to feel like a job."

"Yeah — and someone's garnishing our paychecks."

WE SPLASHED THROUGH the rain into Bill's Sporting Goods. The cloudburst had welcomed us as we returned to our stopping point, killing our chances to squeeze in a few miles after the long drive. Instead we decided to shop. What better place to find camping supplies than Front Royal, Virginia, the gateway to Shenandoah National Park?

Still dripping, I stepped to the counter where an elderly man stood at the register. "Do you carry Bleuet fuel?" I asked. "It's in a metal canister, for a backpacking stove."

He turned to us, looking us over. "That French stuff, B-L-E-U?" he drawled. "I used to sell it. It's made in France, you know, and shipped over here." He moved about behind the counter, his slow movements matching the cadence of his speech. "Last one I knew who sold it in town was Martin. You seen him yet?"

No, we confessed. We didn't know any Martin.

"He's over at Top of the Line Sports, by K-Mart. Do you know where K-Mart is?" Seeing our blank looks, he continued, "Maybe the best thing is, I call Martin and ask if he has any."

He turned and rummaged around the counter. After several minutes of this, I thought he'd forgotten us. Finally the other clerk asked, "Whatcha lookin' fer, Bill?"

"Martin's number." He savored every syllable. "I had his card in here somewhere."

"He's in the phone book. Why dontcha just look it up?"

After a second eternity looking through the directory, he got Martin on the line. Pleasantries followed before he finally asked, "You got any of that B-L-E-U, that perfumy stuff?" When we realized Martin didn't, we thanked Bill and buttoned up our rain gear.

We dashed across the street to the pharmacy, looking for Fujichrome slide film. The pharmacist apologized, but they didn't stock it. When we asked who in town might, he shrugged, then replied, "Probably everybody else. You might check the mall."

"We're new in town. How do we get there?"

He pointed to the right. "You go down the street we're on. Are you parked on this side?" We shook our heads. "Well, first you go down there," he pointed the other way, "and turn around, then take this street to the end . . . "

Getting used to the south promised to challenge us.

Another sweltering day in the Shenandoah Valley, with the 'humerature' (like 'wind chill', but for humidity and temperature) soaring to 110°. We found few people, fewer still places to free-camp. Luckily, the post office clerk directed us to a cheap campground right on the river. Now I'm enviously eying canoers, wishing I could trade places with them.   -journal entry, July 6

SUMMER ATTACKED WITH A VENGEANCE.

· For seven days across the Shenandoah Valley we struggled through a heat wave. Humeratures climbed to 120° and beyond, melting the asphalt, frying the air. Haze steamed up from the lush fields, obscuring the nearby mountains. In the afternoons, storm clouds rolled through, hurling hail and flooding our campsites.

The nights offered little respite. Hot, still air kept us tossing and turning, and air conditioners filled our few dreams. When we fled to Mount Massanutten in a vain attempt at a full night's sleep, we traded the heat for a new problem: whippoorwills. We'd heard that these nocturnal birds could call "WHIP-poor-will" four hundred times without pausing.

The one perched above our tent proved that from midnight to dawn.

Down the valley we plodded, rising early and walking before the day's
worst heat. As we pushed south, we grimaced at the growing mountains of
trash. A Christmas card made us wonder whether someone mixed up their
holidays, or if the state hadn't cleaned the roads for six months. The squirt
gun seemed more fitting, providing a slight antidote to the heat. A slighter
antidote to our trip finances occurred when, after 850 miles of walking, I
found our first dollar bill.

Our litter campaign received a mixed welcome in the valley. One
morning all eight people in an aging VW bus waved and gave us thumbs-
up. Before they passed from sight, the driver of a Buick shouted, "Get off
the road!"

In the Rileyville general store where we stopped for a cold drink, the
owner asked what brought us to his area. When Sue mentioned picking up
trash, he sneered. "Lady, I pay the state of Virginia twenty-five bucks a
year to pick up the litter. So does every other shopkeeper. I'll be damned
if I'd go and pick up *their* litter!"

*We shall call it 'the WorldWalker's Law': "When you reach a low
point and think of quitting, kind people will lift your spirits."*

*Yesterday we reached a nadir. As a storm raged, we holed up in a
Burger King, playing cards for four hours and trying to stave off
boredom. A pit deep in my stomach told me this wasn't working —
hiding, meeting nobody, snapping at each other. That night we discussed
our frustrations, trying to clear the air.*

Today the dark cloud lifted.   -journal entry, July 9

THE FIRST BREEZE IN a week ruffled the air, taking a bite from the
searing heat. The valley carved by the Shenandoah River's North Fork
swam in beauty, with hills cloaked in green, farms checker-boarding the
land, and a sprinkling of southern mansions anchoring the slopes of Mt.
Massanutten. Along the flanks of the hill ran U.S. 11, once a major artery,
now a quiet country road perfect for walking.

We ambled south, taking our time. Our day's booty included a set of
baseball cards and a stuffed dog with a cockeyed ear. While I bagged trash,
Sue chalked up the trip's first rescue. A turtle crossing the road faced a
certain future as *tortoise terribly-flat-us* before Sue carried it to safety.

The towns along the byway put me in mind of *Petticoat Junction*. Lacey Springs, for example, we reached at noon, stopping at the general store for lunch. A slim gray-haired man in overalls and a straw hat guarded the bench outside, watching all who passed, chatting with customers. Inside, another old man sat at the only table, reading a paper and puffing on a cigar. When we drove back that evening for dinner fixings, Mr. Overalls still sat checking out the world, and Mr. Cigar continued to fill the store with smoke.

The afternoon heat drove us to the shade of an elm tree in Tenth Legion, where we frittered away time playing Travel Scrabble™. A reporter from the Harrisonburg, VA, *News-Record* found us there, rescuing me from an unusable 'Z'. Janine Gatesman took her time interviewing us, showing no desire to rush back to the office late on a Friday afternoon. By the time she finally left, she'd offered to put us up the following night. (Unfortunately the plan fell through, but the offer lifted our spirits.)

After the interview, we visited Tenth Legion's leading retail establishment (in fact, their only one), Haun's Store and Gas. Over ice cream we met the owners, who told us of the area's (and store's) history. Mr. Haun had started the store in 1928, when U.S. 11 was the spanking new road paralleling the Appalachians. He ran it for better than half a century, even after a stroke in '77. When he finally sold out in 1981, he had a ready buyer — John, the lad who began working for him thirty-three years earlier.

Unlike the Rileyville storekeeper, John lauded our effort. When we apologized for pestering him with questions, he laughed and asked what else he could do for us. He offered us cold drinks, opened his restrooms to us, and allowed us to camp at the abandoned Tenth Legion school. His quiet enthusiasm dispelled the last traces of the funk that had gripped us.

"HOW ABOUT WORKING WITH an Adopt-A-Highway family?" Chuck Hansen, our contact at Virginia's Department of Transportation, had raved about our venture when we first wrote him. In the months since, he had wondered how he could best help, and landed on a great idea. "It's a natural. Let me know your route, and I'll find a group to join you. I'll arrange TV coverage to give both you and the Adopt-A-Highway program publicity."

He scheduled us for Monday west of Hinton, our last town in Virginia.

We could camp the night before in the yard of Herman and JoAnn Simmons, our AAH family, and be ready for the media in the morning. "But let's not get there too early," warned Sue. "They may have Sunday plans. We shouldn't barge in."

Their only plans were welcoming us. When we arrived at 4:00, the visiting granddaughters (ages nine and five) quickly abducted us. The little people showed us the Simmons' horses (Tennessee Walkers — how appropriate!), helped us pitch camp, played with our litter sticks, and peppered us with questions. When JoAnn promised Rachel, the elder girl, that she could pick trash "with the adults" in the morning, she beamed with delight.

By five, the girls had settled down, and we visited with our hosts. Herman, a barber by trade, looked trim and fit, his age betrayed only by his vanishing grey hair. JoAnn also looked too young to be a grandparent, matching Herman's fit appearance.

They knew the area well. "See that house next door?" From the window, JoAnn pointed across the field. "That's where I grew up. My family built it in 1878, and my mother still lived there a few years ago. When we finally sold it, we took so many memories out of there . . ."

"I grew up in a big town," I said. "What's it like living in the country?"

"Everybody knows you," JoAnn offered, "and everybody looks out for you. I'm sure that sounds cliche."

"Even so, it's true," Herman added. "For instance, we don't worry about crime. For years, I'd always left my keys sitting on the seat in my truck, so I'd know where to find them in the morning." He leaned back in his chair, remembering. "Never had a problem until a couple years ago, when a local kid got drunk, saw the keys and took it. Everyone knew who'd taken it, and we got it right back."

When Herman asked if we'd like a grilled burger, we accepted. Minutes later he sat us down to a spread that included potato salad, zucchini, Jell-O, tomatoes, and corn — enough food for a family of six. "We ate earlier this afternoon," he said. "We'll leave you to eat in peace."

Monday dawned early. Herman bowed out of our litter army in favor of an exciting day of cutting hair, but a neighbor took his place. When Chuck showed up with a supply of orange plastic vests, we were set for the cameras. The TV crew caught our act as we headed toward the hills.

Though we missed seeing our first TV appearance, JoAnn told us later the spot included filmed interviews with Rachel and with Sue. Rachel soared after seeing herself on the idiot box — what a story to tell her friends! The news also buoyed our spirits as we faced our next challenge: the Appalachians.

Yes, after tacking southwesterly for nine hundred miles, we finally headed west. All the stops I had looked forward to — Sue's folks, the Kurfmans, Gettysburg, Harper's Ferry, Shenandoah — now lay behind us. The milestones ahead — logging one thousand miles, reaching the Ohio River — merely marked progress.

Would we have the inner fire to survive this year's toughest terrain?

NOTES FROM SUE'S JOURNAL:
Walked along beautiful quiet forest road. Found unbelievably perfect campsite: pine trees — needles for bed — bubbling stream (cold!). Soaked feet sitting on rocks. Had campfire. The stars were incredible! I just listened to music and stared at stars for hours. So perfect and peaceful — that's why we're doing this.   *- July 12*

THE HEAT WAVE FINALLY broke. Lazy clouds played in the sky, dropping the mercury ten degrees. Route 33 wove through the national forest, treating us to a shady, tree-lined lane. At night secluded campsites abounded, and we traded the roar of traffic for the relaxing purr of rushing streams.

The cool spell arrived in time for our hill work. Virginia's last miles climbed up Mount Washington to the ridge separating it from its daughter state. According to Herman Simmons, this began the string of seven mountains stretching over the next ninety miles.

As the roads grew steeper, the volume of trash soared. ("We're losing power on this climb, Spock. Quick — jettison those beer bottles and potato chips or we'll never make it!") We picked twelve, seventeen (a new record), and fifteen bags of trash on consecutive days, and hit sixteen bags twice later. Ninety-four bags of litter (almost a quarter ton) in one week set a mark tough to challenge.

Our luck picked up as we headed west. For the second time in four days, I spotted 'clean green' by the roadside — another dollar bill. A decorator pillow embroidered, 'I Love You, Mother' (price tag still attached) caught my eye on our descent into West Virginia; we sent it to

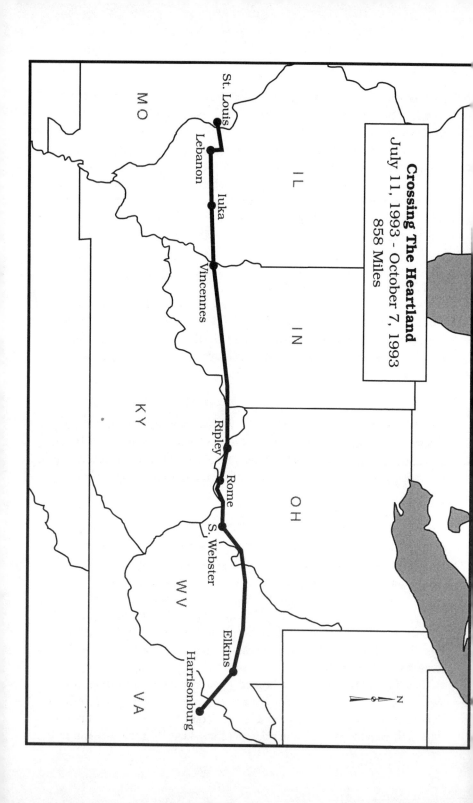

Crossing The Heartland
July 11, 1993 - October 7, 1993
858 Miles

St. Louis
Lebanon
Iuka
Vincennes
Ripley
Rome
S. Webster
Elkins
Harrisonburg

MO
IL
IN
KY
OH
WV
VA

N

my mother for her birthday.

Other oddities were less valuable. A beach ball and a baby bottle livened the haul one day, and the next we found original legal documents dated April 1939. Sue eagerly studied the probate statement and bad check warrant. (A year after her layoff, she still craved her paralegal fix!)

Stepping into Franklin, West Virginia, county seat of Pendleton County, we stepped back thirty years — or so we thought. $1.95 bought a filling lunch of spaghetti and garlic bread. Five cents in the parking meter -- a nickel! -- gave us an hour on the street. The town boasted no traffic light; ditto for all of Pendleton county. Signs on buildings got right to the point: 'CAFE', 'HARDWARE', 'SNACK BAR'. The Pendleton Times *offices, with aged printing machines filling the room and mail bags stacked against one wall, reminded us of a set for '*The Front Page*'.*
     -journal entry, July 14

"THE MAYOR SAID YOU could camp by the swimming pool." Franklin's city clerk relayed that message when we returned to city hall after lunch. If only we'd known a month ago that asking goes a long way.

However, hizzoner's okay didn't appease the weather gods. They brewed up a raging storm as we dined in the park pavilion, interrupting our picnic with sideways sheets of rain. Within an hour the clouds dispersed, and we slept that night under a sky saturated with stars.

Despite Franklin's ferocious rain, the state suffered from a drought. Storm clouds hopscotched over the region, soaking one hollow while leaving its neighbors parched. As we crossed another pass and dropped into the Germany Valley, dry hillsides and brown lawns bore testimony to nature's caprice. We soon crossed areas which had seen nary a sprinkle for weeks.

In the valley, we passed a Ruritan Club park near the hamlet of Judy Rock. Our search for permission to camp led us to Debra Judy, a vivacious blonde more suited to a southern California beach than to rural Appalachia. She recognized us from the Harrisonburg paper, and wanted to hear about our trip. "I'd invite you to dinner tonight, but we've been on vacation and there's no food in the house. If you're still in the area, why don't you come by for dinner tomorrow? I'll whip up something simple."

A day off, especially on the heels of eleven hard, hot days, sounded good. In the morning we moved camp down the valley to a campground looking onto Seneca Rocks. The Rocks, a knife's-edge ridge of granite six feet wide and hundreds of feet high, dominated this isolated valley. With free time to kill, I joined the droves of tourists and — what else? — hiked to the top. Afterwards we drove to Dolly Sods, a wilderness area perched on a bluff high above the Potomac basin, and picked wild blueberries to go with our picnic lunch.

At six we returned to the Judys' house. While Debra busied herself with dinner, her husband Gary showed us around their log cabin. He took great pride in its construction, having built it himself. The home, fair-sized for a family of four, impressed us with its open, airy feeling. Antiques filled the corners, lending a relaxing aura of rustic life.

Debra soon called us to her 'simple country dinner': haddock and flounder, corn on the cob, spinach, apple sauce, potatoes, cornbread, salad — all delicious and all abundant. "Now you've spoiled us," I told her. "How will we ever top this?"

Debra, who worked as a welfare case worker, shocked us with stories of Appalachian squalor worse than any we could imagine. "In my first week on the job, one of my charges held me at gunpoint. The woman thought I was from Child Protective Services, coming to take her child. It took me ages to convince her I had come to help — of course, time passes real slow when you're looking down the barrel of a gun." She closed her eyes and shuddered.

"It was a hell of a first week," she continued. "Two days later I called on a family living in a shack. When I walked in, I noticed a grayish lump on the kitchen floor, and another in the hallway. I finally got a good look at one of four piles in the living room. They were the decomposing bodies of dead cats!"

She shook her head as more memories popped up. "I had one client whose scalp was infected. When I took him to the doctors, they found three hundred maggots. Three hundred! The next week I gave a lady a washing machine. Two months later she had a room full of dirty clothes. When I asked her why she kept buying new clothes, she said she didn't know how to use the washer. Of course, people like that you'd never see, since they live down dirt lanes away from the main roads."

"We've seen some pretty ramshackle places," I said. "We passed one yard stacked so full of beer cans, tires, and other garbage, we could hardly see his trailer."

"Oh, yes, that man's one of mine, too. You wouldn't believe how much he's improved. The first time I visited him, the stench was so strong I couldn't step into his trailer. I had to talk to him from the yard." She sighed. "They just don't know any better. Their parents raised them that way, so it's natural to them."

"I suppose if they live that way," Sue added, "it's no wonder the roads are so filthy."

"Is it that," I asked, warming to my favorite topic, "or laziness? Too much trouble to carry a trash bag in their car and empty it when they get home? Take the last pass we climbed — I picked up Burger King and Wendy's wrappers at the top. From there, the nearest fast food backwards is Harrisonburg, and forward is what, Elkins?" I saw Gary nod. "That's fifty miles either way, on mountain roads. They had to hold on to that wrapper for over an hour. They couldn't hold on to it until they got home, or stopped at a gas station?"

Gary nodded. "We pick up a stretch with the Ruritan Club. At one spot we always find a pile of 7-11 coffee cups. The day after we come through, there'll be another cup. Since the nearest 7-11 is in Franklin, you can tell how long it takes the guy to drink his java."

"Sometimes they don't know what they're losing." Debra paused from cleaning the table. "Did you notice the guardrail on the summit of North Fork Mountain?"

I nodded. "I stopped there for a picture. It's a gorgeous view over the Germany Valley."

"There used to be a table there, and no rail. People could pull over for a picnic. Instead, people would dump bags of household trash. Eventually the state got tired of cleaning it, ripped out the table and put in the guardrail. Now you can't stop there."

We chatted more, letting the dinner digest. As the sun dove to the horizon, Gary offered to give us the grand Judy tour of Judy Rock. "My family was one of the earliest settlers here, and they named the town after them." We climbed into his Jeep and set off.

After clearing the gates, Gary crossed a field which gradually tilted to a 50% slope. At the ridge top, we stopped and spied several deer grazing nearby. "Our property once extended over to that next ridge," Gary pointed to the east, "and back south to the highway. Down in this hollow is the one-room schoolhouse my father attended."

With dusk setting in, we descended the hill, then drove to the hollow. Up the dirt road, silhouetted in the setting sun, stood the rock pinnacles of Judy Rock. We sat in silence as the skies slowly faded from blood-red to dark purple. As the light faded, I felt a kinship to the hills and to the new friends we'd made.

Here again was the America we'd come looking for.

West Virginia continues to amaze us with its scenery, weather, and people. Mountains cloaked in mist, rolling farmland, elegant houses side-by-side with broken-down shanties, and occasional herds of cattle combine to create a picture of remote, times-past life. Beautiful, yes, and quite similar in parts to what we expected. The weather steals in quickly, changing a brilliant blue sky speckled with clouds into a wind-driven lightning storm within an hour.

The area is fertile ground for people-watching. An ancient woman in the Franklin cafe looked old enough to have known dinosaurs. One trailer-dweller bustled about heaps of junk in his yard, as if flaunting a 'waste not, want not' ethic. Many people we passed on the road bade us "Good morning!" and sometimes added "How far ya goin'?", but few offered as much as a drink. On the flip side are people like the Judys, people who warm our hearts with their kindness. It's our favorite recipe: take two lonely travelers, add special people and — voila! — instant family.   -journal entry, July 15

SENECA ROCKS REALLY ATTRACTS sports nuts. As we packed our tent in the morning, I glanced to the picnic pavilion where rock climbers had made camp. Though a couple of them had tents, most had rigged harnesses from the pavilion roof and slept suspended above the tables. As I hit the road, a roller-blader schussed past down the center of U.S. 33, vainly trying to plant his ski poles in the pavement.

Four more passes separated us from our rendezvous with West Virginia media. Anna Shahan and Mary Perry from the state matched Chuck Hansen in enthusiasm, and arranged for an AAH group near Elkins to join us three days hence. This time, though, Anna hinted at bigger things.

Mama said there'd be days like this!

The trash kept piling up, and the arrogance of the litterers dismayed us. A truckload of garbage crowned one pass, a mountain of refuse composed of a couch, TV, truck parts, and over twenty bags of assorted trash. Half-buried under the load, the "No Littering -- $1000 Fine" sign lay where the litterer had bowled it over.

Sometimes subplots crept into the trash. One day began with the discovery of bedroom slippers. A mile later the pajamas expanded on the theme, and the bath towel formed a troika. So how could we be surprised an hour later when I passed the dregs of the milk-soaked Fruit Loops?

The following morning, we met our first highway workers. They flirted with Sue, asking, "Forget Adopt-A-Highway, why don't you adopt us?" One worker followed me as I topped off a bag. All of them thanked us.

As we neared the one-thousand-mile mark, we continued to trek through verdant National Forests. The camping cost nothing, and rewarded us with crisp, pine-scented air and quiet nights. We ended our final day B.M. (Before Media) in a forested campground bordered by a stream. Though signs warned of bears in the area, we saw no wildlife save a stray white mutt whose gaunt figure earned him the nickname 'Ghost.'

"You're sure there are no bears here?" Sue asked the ranger. "I've never seen one, and don't want to camp with one." The ranger dismissed the danger, so we pitched camp and spent the evening roasting marshmallows. By 9:30 we doused the fire and retired, nervous about the next day's media binge.

The next morning, as I lie half-awake at 6:00, Sue's scream split the air. "It licked me!" she cried as she leapt up. "Through the flap, it licked me! It's a bear!"

I peeked out the tent flap and looked into the jaws — of Ghost, happily wagging his tail.

We're ready for the TV cameras now!

July 21 - July 25, 1993
82 miles -- 80 bags
TOTAL, 1054 miles -- 380 bags

Long voyages, great lies.   - Italian proverb

————————◆———————

IT APPEARED AN UNLIKELY spot for our springboard into fame. On one side of the dirt field trucks hurtled past on U.S. 33, heading downhill to Elkins; on the other, wildflowers blanketed the slopes. The field itself resembled the staging grounds for a tent revival, or maybe an ad hoc meeting place for Overdresser's Anonymous. A dozen or more men and women milled about in suits and ties, sweating in the summer sun. A photographer kept busy checking his exposures, and one man checked names off a list.

As we approached the group, decked out in our best 'Litterwalk U.S.A.' tees and shorts, one casually-dressed man greeted us. "I'm Fred Clark," he said, "district honcho for the Department of Highways." He introduced us to several others: Tom Staud, District DOH Engineer; the Randolph County Commissioner; a local AAH rep; the Randolph County Litter Chairman.

"How'd you like that title on your resume?" I whispered to Sue.

While waiting, we talked with a few people; others kept their distance as if afraid our insanity was contagious. I looked forward to meeting Mary Perry and Anna Shahan; their lilting voices and southern drawls had me picturing Scarlett O'Hara and hoop skirts. At 9:50 the car from the capital finally arrived, carrying my contacts along with Anna's boss, the head of the Division of Natural Resources (DNR), Ed Hamrick. My mental picture of the ladies quickly evaporated; Scarlett O'Hara became Bette Midler in a power suit.

With the officials now assembled, we awaited only the TV crews. At 10:10 Fred Clark spotted two trucks from WBOY-TV. They turned onto the road where everyone had parked, waved at us, and drove up the hill.

"Where the devil are they going?" wondered Fred. "That's a dead end road. There's nothing up there but a gravel quarry."

"Maybe they're turning around," guessed Ed Hamrick. He exuded an air of authority, and others deferred to him. "We'll give them a minute to regroup."

Fifteen minutes later, they had not returned. (Who knows? Maybe the quarry workers had uncovered a body.) With the morning stealing away, Ed brought the group together. A wave of his hand quieted the crowd. He removed his suit coat and began.

"I had prepared a speech," he began, pulling a paper from his shirt pocket. Then he crumpled it and stuffed it back inside. "But we're running a bit late, so I'm going to wing it.

"We're here today to honor Glen and Susan Hanket for their adventure, this coast-to-coast litter walk they're taking. We're glad they included West Virginia on their route."

He turned to face us. "I talked with Governor Caperton yesterday. He said he'd love to be here, but his schedule wouldn't allow it. However, he did sign this plaque and asked me to give it to you." With a flourish, he handed us a 'West Virginia — Make It Shine' award thanking us for our efforts.

Award time in the Appalachians

"We at the DNR also want to show our appreciation." He turned to Anna Shahan, who handed him a bundle. "We brought you each two tee shirts." He unfurled the shirts, one having an AAH slogan and one with the 'Make It Shine' emblem.

"That's all I have to say, but I believe the District Engineer wanted to add something." With that, Ed stepped back, and Tom Staud sidled up.

Tom, looking less comfortable than his predecessor, left his jacket on. He gave a short spiel on the importance of volunteering, then he got into the giveaway business. "We'd like to present you with litter sticks," he began, handing us two poles with plastic nails in one end. "We also have gloves, so you won't dirty your hands, and a pair of orange vests so you're visible on the road." He handed us the gifts and the spotlight, melting back into the crowd.

All eyes turned to us. "Thank you very, very much," I said, shocked by the gifts. "We hardly feel worthy of this. We can't clean the roads we walk — we don't have time to get it all. No, the people who deserve the thanks are the Adopt-A-Highway crews who come out three or four times a year, and clean — really clean — the road." I paused, then held up the two nail sticks. "In fact, since we already have litter sticks, we'll donate these to the AAH crew we're helping today."

I handed them the new sticks, then grabbed my well-worn picker. As a group we moved down the road, picking trash as the photographer snapped away. A hundred yards later I glanced up to see the WBOY trucks come down the hill. They passed us, smiling and waving as they headed toward Elkins.

The suits and ties straggled back to their cars, eager to escape the morning heat. Before he left, Fred Clark came up and pressed a scrap of paper into my hand. "This is the area AP correspondent," he explained. "He wants you to call him, collect."

Maybe we could yet salvage some publicity.

Our heartiest laughs in this state come from the businesses. In Brandywine, "Fat Boy's Pork Palace" left us salivating, and Norton's "Chat'N'Chew" advertised sandwiches, beer, music, and a pig roast. In Jimtown, "Met Motors" had four cars lined up in front of a pint-sized shack. Outside Elkins, "Bob's Truck and Auto Sales" boasted one hundred yards of highway frontage festooned with cars missing windows, truck beds, doors, or even engines.

                                        -journal entry, July 22

OUR FAME WAS SECURE. From here on, people would remember us as 'the couple who spent their honeymoon picking up dirty underwear.'

The AP wire spread like a cold virus in a crowded office. Every paper in the state ran it, as did papers from coast to coast. In Connecticut, Sue's sister heard our names over WEBE radio while stuck in traffic; she nearly hit a wall. Friends in California reported hearing about us over several stations.

When we reached Ellamore, we got the first taste of our new fame. The burly man behind the counter of the general store asked, "Are you Glen and Sue? I just read about you!" Butch Roberts covered our ice cream — a priority that hot day — and directed us to a camping spot. When we returned for dinner, he again refused our money. "You've got a long haul ahead. Save it."

That afternoon I called Anna Shahan to report another sixteen bags dropped. An air of excitement permeated her southern twang. "I've good news for you!" she said.

"What?" I asked. "Have they made littering a capital offense?"

"Not that good," she chuckled. "I just got a call from *CBS This Morning.* They're trying to get ahold of you." She gave me the phone number of the show's producer, Kathryn Davis.

Kathryn had seen us on the AP wire and wondered if we'd celebrate our anniversary on her show. "It's too late to slot you in for tomorrow, since Fridays are always busy. We can do a remote with you Monday. How does that sound?"

"Wonderful!" What an opportunity to spread our litter gospel. "We're available at any time."

"We'll shoot for Monday. I'll bring it up at tomorrow's planning meeting, and iron out details. Now, have you had any TV coverage by a CBS affiliate we can look at?"

Of course, neither station that filmed us so far was CBS. Kathryn signed off with a promise to arrange our appearance, and asked me to call back the next day for details.

National TV. Here come our fifteen minutes!

"I'M LESTER BOOTH AND I've been waiting to meet you."

The elderly gentleman had come out as we passed his home. He wore a broad smile under a mane of short gray hair, and stepped sprightly for his age. "I've adopted this stretch of highway. In fact, I've adopted more road than anyone else in this state — nine miles of U.S. 33, and more on the back roads."

He and I checked out each other's litter sticks as avidly as high schoolers admiring each other's hot rod. "Sleek lines," I admired. "How's it handle?"

"It's great on bottles. How's your pick-up?"

"Zero to sixty cans in under five minutes."

"Mine can stop on a dime and grab it."

I snatched a scrap of colored paper at my feet. "Ahhh, but I got the pink slip!"

Before we moved on, Lester amused us with a story of litter justice. "I came out one morning and found some jerk had tossed two bags of trash on my property. After I got done swearing at the long-gone fool, I opened those bags. Well, the idiot forgot to separate his junk mail from his pizza boxes. I gave his name and address to the DNR, and they sent him a nice, expensive ticket."

A mile later another local greeted me. "Are you that cross-country walker I heard about?"

"In yesterday's paper? Yep, that's me."

"No, I don't get the paper. I saw you on the channel five news yesterday."

"The TV?" Had WBOY given new meaning to the term 'live remote'? But they weren't channel five, anyway. "Did they show film of us?"

"Of you and your wife picking up litter."

I left the encounter deep in thought, wondering how a Clarksburg station could have gotten footage. Ten minutes later, a car pulled over to interrupt my reverie.

"You talked to my brother a bit ago," the middle-aged woman began. "Lester Booth? He called to tell me where you were walking, and I wanted to come and commend you and your wife. I think it's great."

With this much attention, my hat started feeling tight. "Thank you very much."

"Before I left, I called channel five to tell them about you. They said they already had plans to interview you Sunday."

Great, I thought. *I sure hoped they'd invite us to take part.* Of course, since they had already created footage of us, maybe we weren't required.

As Sue and I finished walking the stretch, we found an officer checking her car. "Oh, no," Sue muttered, "here comes a parking ticket."

"Is this your car?" he asked. Our nods prompted another question: "You're the two litter walkers, aren't you?"

He smiled widely when we nodded again. "I'm Sergeant Jim Vance of the DNR. I cover this county and the next one. If there's anything we can do for you" — he handed us his card — "anything at all, we're here to help." He asked about our trip and our impressions of the state, then a sheepish grin crept across his face.

"Would you mind if I took a picture of you?" He pulled out his camera and took several shots. Before leaving, he gave us directions to Stonecoal Campground, the only one in the area.

Soon lunch called, and we found a secluded oak to picnic under. In the heat of the afternoon we returned to knock off the final miles to Buckhannon. As the country road turned to freeway, Sergeant Vance drove up. "I thought you two disappeared off the face of the earth! I've driven up and down this road looking for you."

"I'm sorry, we stopped for lunch," I said. "Is anything wrong?"

"Have you talked to the people at Stonecoal? I called the owner, and he knows you're coming. There'll be no charge. Now, what are your plans for tomorrow night?"

Sue shrugged. "My husband promised me a hotel room and a fancy dinner to celebrate our first anniversary."

"Good! Have you heard of a lake south of Weston, Stonewall Jackson Lake?" He unfolded a brochure as he spoke. "A paddlewheel boat there runs nightly dinner cruises. I talked to the couple who own it, John and Joyce Griffith, and they've invited you to be their guests. They do a great prime rib."

Today we walked one of the prettiest (and least-trafficked) stretches of freeway we're likely to see. Lush green hills, well-kept houses, and whitewashed churches surrounded us.

Besides having our pictures taken by the Upshur County Solid Waste Committee, we chatted with Charles Hall of the 'How Come Tree Farm'. His land included the old valley chapel dating from the 1880s. "I've

been here forty-three years," he told us. "In that time, they've put in a four-lane and driven away all my neighbors. We love it here, though. Several people have tried to buy the old church, but we aren't selling."
                                                        -journal entry, July 24

GIANT FLYING CAT TERRORIZES STATE!
Tabloid headlines never failed to amuse me. I always looked for them while biding time in checkout lines, wondering what startling stories they had scooped the *L.A. Times* and *Washington Post* on that week.
REPAIRED HUBBLE TELESCOPE TAKES PICTURES OF HEAVEN!
Though I knew some stories contained seeds of truth, most had no passing acquaintance with reality. The cheaper the rag, the more incredible the stories — and the worst came from the weeklies which couldn't afford color printing.
ELVIS SECRETLY RUNNING RWANDAN MASSACRE!
So when I saw the black-and-white front page of the current *Weekly World News* blowing across the highway, I snagged it and scanned the stories. The top headline jumped off the page: WIFE SLICES OFF HUBBY'S PRIVATES AND TOSSES IT OUT CAR WINDOW! *Geez,* I thought, *I hope I never see that piece of trash.* Several more days passed before I found out the Bobbit case actually happened.

Despite no private parts by the roadside, the haul implied them. The pile of discarded condoms didn't surprise me; I had seen others. A used home pregnancy kit two miles later, though, got me wondering about possible connections.

If the day's litter had a theme, it was food. The diet parade started with a bologna and cheese sandwich, still fresh in a ziploc baggie. Soon I longed for tortilla chips to go with the whole can of bean dip. By the time I reached the French fries, my stomach growled for lunch.

My day's haul did contain one treasure. A pair of Ray-Ban sunglasses proved a timely find, since my generic pair was falling apart. The new specs would last me the whole trip and several years after.

The parade of business signs kept us laughing. Linda's Rustic Corner advertised 'crafts, gifts, and concrete' — one stop shopping for even the pickiest people. In Buckhannon, Sparkey's West End Grocery and Wholesale Tire won our award for most imaginative motto. In red paint wrapping around the front of the building, it cajoled the shopper, "If you go to bed when you ought to, you'll never see us closed."

In 1790, the roadside sign stated, Indian Scout Jacob Reger saved the pioneer community near Buckhannon, WV, from certain destruction when he ran 125 miles in twenty-four hours from present-day Parkersburg to warn them of a planned Indian attack.

Would that make him America's first ultra-marathoner?
- excerpt from a series of articles written from the road

IT RANKED AS A major Hooda Everthawt.

"You know," I told Sue, "as in, 'Hooda Everthawt we'd celebrate our first anniversary cruising an unknown lake in West Virginia?' I'd never have believed it."

She nodded. "Me neither. Of course, I was too stressed with the weddings to think of anniversaries. I can hardly believe only one year has passed."

"It does seem a lifetime ago, doesn't it?" *Or a different life entirely* . . . which in a way, it was. A life without litter sticks, media events, and living from a pack. One full of close friends, favorite restaurants, and yuppie toys. A life which had already started changing.

Sue's layoff early in 1992 started the chain of events. By the time the law firm let her go, she'd had enough of the legal world, and of southern California. We sent resumes throughout the west, hoping to move, but no one had room for another Californian.

February '92 marked two years of our dating and fifteen months of 'shacking up.' The prospects for marriage had dimmed that past fall, courtesy of an impassioned and eloquent "I'll never settle down" speech by Sue. Within weeks she told friends she regretted speaking out, but the topic stayed closed.

Until Memorial Day. On a long solo kayak ride, it hit me. "Air fares are low, so — we should get married!" When I proposed that night, Sue missed the logic but didn't miss her chance. Afraid I might regain my senses, she suggested a wedding date of late July.

Plan a wedding in under two months? Piece o' cake, let's plan two! For our families we chose Rocky Mountain National Park with no frills, no church, no rings, not even a minister or judge. We wrote the ceremony and delivered it in front of our parents, siblings, aunts, uncles, and a host of visiting gophers. Our fathers (as planned) each gave a heartfelt speech, and a horse pack train (unplanned) wandered by to add a rustic touch. Following our vows and an exchange of roses, we pedaled away on a tandem bike to the strains of "Daisy (A Bicycle Built for Two)."

One week later it was "Son of THE WEDDING." The California beach replaced the mountain meadow, palms replaced pines, and friends replaced family. This time no horse trains interrupted the ceremony, though an anonymous bongo player furnished a background beat for our wedding march.

Two months later a pile of freeway trash showed us our escape route from California. That route had now taken us a thousand miles, on foot, to this unknown lake. Beyond the railings of the ship, green hills threw shadows onto sandy beaches. The waters of the lake, cutting through the forested knolls of the state park, reflected the rose glow of the setting sun.

After serving the last of the prime rib, Joyce Griffith sat with us. She talked about the cruise business, and being her own boss. "John always wanted to charter boats and I wanted to run a restaurant, so here we are."

The Griffiths (center) and crew of the Stonewall Jackson

In the two years they've been doing cruises, she told us, they've had one engagement and a triple wedding with a mother, her son, and her daughter. "But you're our only cross-country walkers."

As darkness spelled an end to a memorable anniversary, all seemed right with the trip. We had only one nagging question: Whence CBS? Brian Jones of WDTV-5 had shot footage of us early that Sunday as we trekked into Weston. Brian had last heard from New York on Friday, when someone told him we would appear on Monday's *This Morning*.

It sure didn't look that way to us.

❈ APPALACHIAN SUMMER ❈

✦ WEST VIRGINIA - OHIO ✦

July 26 - August 9, 1993
163 miles -- 127 bags
TOTAL, 1217 miles -- 507 bags

Every walk is a sort of crusade.
- Henry David Thoreau, *Walking*

Into the wilderness . . . of western West Virginia.

Our fame lasted one more day. As we left Weston, we passed road crews busy tearing up U.S. 33. The workers called out greetings, thanking us. One told me, "I saw you on the news! You're a movie star!" I laughed and waved.

"How far do you walk each day?" asked another.

"Twelve to fifteen miles, average."

"Geez! Do you have sponsors to help you with expenses?"

"Just for our equipment. Sometimes, though, people treat us to a meal. Especially here -- we've found lots of friendly people in West Virginia."

"Well, you may find folks a bit cranky today. We've got them sort of bottled up." - journal entry, July 26

OUR NATIONAL EXPOSURE GOT bottled up, too. Kathryn Davis had not yet squeezed us in — "Could you call back next week?" she asked. With no interview to wait for, we set off.

Rural, of course, is relative. In some states, a town of ten thousand qualified as a backwater; here, five thousand counted as a big city. We had traversed three 'big cities' in the last four days, tolerating traffic and detouring around road construction. Now wilderness sounded good.

West of Weston the land grew wild. We would see no freeways, no road crews, not even a stop light for over one hundred miles. The highways sliced through scenic countryside, following streams down forested valleys, snaking along ridges with far-flung vistas.

Names on the map hinted at the history of the hollows. Burnt Bridge referred to a crossing on U.S. 33 damaged by a fire; the state moved the bridge to a side road when they widened the highway. (Why they bothered moving a burned bridge, no one could tell me.) Pickle Street honored an old-time resident who pickled beans in town.

While most towns boasted a history, few held much promise for the future. City lights lured many young people away; lack of jobs forced others to move on. Abandoned homes and decaying shops became a common sight. In some places, only the general store kept the village alive, providing locals with beer, snacks, videos, and a place to gather.

What the area lacked in people, it made up for in satellite dishes. Rarely did we pass a home, whether a broken-down shanty or a palatial estate, without seeing one in the yard. We also noted an abundance of churches, all with a unique West Virginia touch: 'Adam' and 'Eve' outhouses.

With less people came less trash, and our fifteen-bag days dropped to single digits. To keep entertained, I invented a new trash game: Connections. We played by blaming one person for the oddities we found. One morning we wondered who would throw away twelve bags of potato chips, three bottles of Lemon Pledge™, and a flashlight. A couch potato who dusted his furniture in the dark? A fairy godmother with bad night vision and a weakness for junk food?

The next day, Sue unearthed a full box of tampons. Unfortunately, moisture had invaded the package, exploding the devices. While she looked for any units to salvage, I longingly checked a brown bag filled with donuts and a sandwich.

As we moved west, brown patches in the fields spoke of the stifling drought. Well water had dropped to the lowest level in years. Farmers, faced with no grass for their cattle, were already feeding them winter hay. What they would do come winter, no one knew.

Though we sympathized, we enjoyed the dry weather. At night we watched storms fill the sky with dry lightning. During the day cool breezes kept the edge off the heat, and I pushed my miles to make up for lost time. We finished with three hundred miles for July, our best month but still well shy of my initial, optimistic projections.

Sue's recovery had far exceeded her doctor's prediction. He'd warned us it would take three months before she could walk without pain. Now, after only two months, she walked a dozen miles daily, many with a pack.

Though her feet still suffered from blisters, she was anxious to ditch the car. We planned to do so in two weeks, when a good friend would visit us.

NOTES FROM SUE'S JOURNAL:
Perfect walking day! Spectacular wispy clouds — 80° — lonely country road — flowers blooming. Saw deer near creek. Had picnic at cemetery on hill. Walked thirteen miles — feel OK except feet hurt.
- July 31

WE MARKED PROGRESS ONE town at a time: Alum Bridge, Coxs Mills, Burnt House, Smithville. The days flowed together, a pastiche of forested highways, coal trucks, hot afternoons, and colorful locals. We collected trip memories as we plodded west. Memories . . .

. . . of spending our laundry quarters playing pool in Coxs Mills. The store owner kept us company (or vice-versa) as we stretched out several games of eightball. "Don't worry about the shims under the table legs," she told us. "They keep the table level. Just be glad it's not raining outside. Then the rain runs in from the high side, under the pool table, and out this side over here." She rapped the wall behind her for emphasis. "We've asked the landlord to fix it, but he never has . . ."

. . . of the mailwoman stopping to find out about us. "I've passed you three times since yesterday," she said, "and my curiosity is killing me. Where *are* you going?" . . .

. . . of the old man tending his garden. Pushing eighty years as sure as he was pushing a wooden plow (very slowly, to be precise), he sweated and strained to turn the soil. As we played cards in the park, he kept glancing in our direction. A neighbor explained his nervousness to us. "You see how much effort he puts into his garden? Even after the three strokes he's had. Well, last summer someone stole his pole beans."

"Stole his pole beans?" Sue was astonished.

"Oh, we all felt terrible about it, too. Everyone knows who did it — one of the local kids. But his parents won't admit it, so what can we do?" . . .

. . . of the general store in PeeWee, a cinder block box with little sign of life. Inside, an ancient woman rocked behind the counter, her sharp eyes following our every step. She had little to say about the present, but opened up when we asked about the past. "The interstate highway killed this town," she said, "back who knows how many years ago. Just another change — Lord knows, I've seen enough of 'em." She looked beyond us, focusing on better times. "Shoot, I remember when they built this road you're walking. It was just a mud path when my husband and I got married, sixty-two years ago . . ."

. . . of the persistently helpful driver. As I neared the top of a long hill, he barreled over the crest in a beat-up Pontiac. Seeing me, he skidded to a stop, staring at me with glazed eyes. After half a minute waiting for him to speak, I broke the silence. "Can I help you?"

"Sure," he woke up. "Need a ride?"

I passed on his offer, and after another long stare, he drove off. On the far side of the hill, I caught up with Sue and told her the story of the out-of-it local. Before I could finish, the beat-up Pontiac crested the hill again and stopped alongside us.

"You two need a ride?"

When I again declined, a hint of awareness dawned on his face. "Saaaay. Didn't I see you a few minutes ago?"

Characters. Appalachia was full of them.

Our day began with beautiful ridge-line views in the early morning mists. Once past Palestine, we cut west on Route 7 and left traffic behind. Sue startled a doe and fawn drinking water from a roadside stream at one point, scaring them into the woods. Later, while walking without me, she picked her way past one house when a woman stepped out, saw her, and asked haughtily, "Are you looking for someone?" (Yeah, I lost my husband in the weeds somewhere!)   -journal entry, July 31

AFTER 240 MILES AND 208 bags of trash — both state-high marks for 1993 — we finally left West Virginia. Behind us lay three weeks of trekking up and down mountains, ahead, the promise of flat walking along the wide and lazy Ohio River.

We welcomed the flat terrain, but not the ticks. The minute pests, only a minor irritant to this point, would plague us through Ohio. A rare day passed in which we didn't each pull three to five of the bloodsucking buggers off our legs. Worried about catching Lyme disease or spotted fever, we checked each other at every break, anxious to keep them from invading our equipment. For the rest of the year, when anyone asked us the biggest problem we faced, we replied, "Ticks."

If West Virginians treated discarding beer cans as a hobby, then Ohioans regarded it as a calling from God. The plethora of empty cans first surprised, then disgusted us. One worker mowing the cemetery warned us, "You'll see a lot more, too. People around here are alcoholics, and it's the first of the month — payday!"

To our roadside lost-and-found, we added an 'Official U.S. Taxpayer' keyring with three keys still dangling — maybe the IRS repossessed the car. Nearby we found a tow-rope reel; sorry, tow rope sold separately. 'Roadside Farmer's Market' took on a new meaning when we found the produce spill — over thirty pounds of ripe peppers and tomatoes strewn along the road. "What a waste," I noted. "Why couldn't it be okra or Brussels sprouts?"

Sue finally joined the money parade, finding her first greenback. We wondered if we hadn't hit paydirt, though, when she found the roll of S&H green stamps. How much can you get with one thousand stamps?

It took two days of walking to reach our first burg in Ohio. Pomeroy, population 2300 and seat of Meigs County, earned a listing in Ripley's _Believe It Or Not_ as the only town in America with no four-way intersections. Squeezed between the placid river and soaring bluffs, the city is only two streets wide. However, the region was known for more than a quirk of geography. Meigs County Green, a potent marijuana strain developed at Ohio State University, was renowned across the country (so the Pomeroy _Sentinel_ reporter told us). _High Times_ gave the area high marks.

Locals knew the county best for one thing: a crippling depression. Statistics painted a bleak picture: unemployment at 14%; 23% of the people on assistance. The numbers alone, though, couldn't tell the whole story. We discovered that as we crossed Leading Creek.

Below us the stream ran a dark orange, steadily adding its noxious waters to the Ohio River. Upstream a mine had flooded, submerging needed mining equipment. Officials faced a Hobson's choice: pump poisoned water from the mine to retrieve the machines, or lose those jobs and put more families on welfare. The day's score read Economy 1, Environment 0.

The next morning our moods matched the weather — gray and drizzly

— as we got turned down by *This Morning*. "We dropped the ball by not having you on for your anniversary," Kathryn Davis apologized. "We really need a 'hook' when you appear. Try us again when you've been on the road for a year . . ."

Adding to our woes, Sue's feet took a downturn. Blisters plagued her, keeping her from training with a full pack. In only a week we would ditch the car. Would she be ready?

By noon, the sun and the *Sentinel* had come out, and the day started looking up. Drivers gave us thumbs-up. A fleet of dump trucks laid on their horns. One couple drove ten miles to find us and take our picture.

We camped that night at the Cheshire-Kyger school. Driving behind the school left us out of sight of the road and nearby houses. We settled in, looking forward to a good night's rest.

A Jeep passing next to the tent roused us at 6:30 the next morning. We executed our best quick-dress drill, and I popped out of the tent as two workmen rounded the corner of the school. "How are you this morning?" called out one of them.

"Probably as surprised as you, seeing a tent here!"

He beamed a smile from under his 'International Harvester' cap. "Sorry to wake you so rudely. California, huh?" he said, looking at our license plates. "What are you doing in Cheshire?"

We gave him the condensed version. Afterwards, he unlocked the school and invited us to use the showers. It was our first hint of Ohio hospitality.

In the evening cool we strolled through Gallipolis. When we stopped at Tawney Jewelers to get my pocket knife lubed, we met a kindred soul. Once I mentioned travel, he started reciting place names, and soon he ushered us into the back room. The walls were filled with photographs of him holding weapons with Chinese and Israeli soldiers, talking with Saudi sheiks, attending Bali funerals, at Burmese temples and Rio de Janeiro hot spots, on African savannas and in Swiss Alps, in Sarajevo before the revolution and Prague and Warsaw after.

-journal entry, August 6

THAT SATURDAY OUR LITTER army numbered five. For the first time, company joined us on the road: Tim Klepaczyk, a longtime friend from Detroit; and Margie Hill and her teen-age daughter, Heather. The Hills had read about us in _Walking_ magazine, and accepted our open invitation for readers to join us.

We covered four miles that morning, taking turns with the litter sticks. Our troop must have presented an unusual sight, strung out along the country lane. Sue and Margie, chatting like old friends out for a stroll, set the pace. Tim and I, our lean frames loaded down with packs, trailed behind. In the rear, her black hair blowing as she scoured the ditches, Heather bagged the litter we missed.

The company made the morning fly by. We shared a common disgust for litter — the Hills had adopted a road near their home. Heather set the day's tone with her zeal for leaving nothing behind, rooting out trash with her hands when the stick wouldn't do. When they left at noon, we knew we'd miss them.

Sunday Tim, Sue and I hiked into Rio Grande — not "ree-oh" as in Texas, but "rye-oh" to rhyme with Ohio. As we hit the town limits, a car with four teenagers approached. I braced myself for a sarcastic comment as they slowed.

"I see your bag's full," the driver said. "Do you want us to throw it away for you?"

The question caught me off guard. I had seen too many teens tossing empty Coors cans, too many chucking Marlboro packs. Could I reopen my mind and accept that youth, like adults, come in all varieties? "Thanks a lot. That really helps."

At the Raccoon Creek campground that night, we jury-rigged a shower. Next to the office, a three-sided fence flanked a faucet mounted five feet above the ground. With no campers nearby to disturb, we draped a sheet across the fourth side. As I stood under the tepid water, shampoo-crowned head towering over the sheet, two other hikers walked by. After doing a double-take, one smiled and asked, "Just keep sticking quarters in, hey?"

Sue, standing outside waiting her turn, piped in, "Sometimes you've got to make do!"

"Oh, but those hot showers feel good when you get home."

I added, "They sure will, three months from now!"

WE HAD ONE LAST day with Tim, one more day before he would drive off with our car. Another day Sue could practice with her pack on —

but she wouldn't take advantage of it.

"My knee really hurts today," she confessed. "It feels like mush. Why don't you and Tim walk?"

"Are you going to be all right? Maybe we shouldn't get rid of the car."

She shook her head emphatically. "No, I'm fine. Besides, this is our only chance to ditch it."

She hadn't convinced me. "Let's not risk it. We can always park the car somewhere later. I don't want to push you before you're ready."

"I'm ready, trust me," she insisted. "I feel — I don't know, hesitant, like I'm not all there today. I'm more likely to twist something when I'm like this." She paused, then added, "Besides, it's your last chance to spend time with Tim."

So Tim and I strolled down country lanes, talking about engineering, about women, about life, solving the world's problems as we collected paper cups, newspapers, and discarded shoes. Along the way, I taught him all I'd learned about lawn decorations. "See, Tim, different states specialize in different ornaments. I first noticed it in Pennsylvania, when I saw throngs of those plastic pink flamingos. They must have had a population explosion. What they need to do is introduce a flamingo predator — maybe fiberglass crocodiles?

"The Virginias went for the rumps in a big way. Those plywood grandmas leaning over in the garden, so all you can see is two legs and polka-dotted underwear? Nearly every yard had one.

"Jackson County, our last in West Virginia, had some rumps but far more pissers. That's the wooden profile of the blue-jeaned boy with hands near his waist and a thin wire arcing out. What that says about those locals, I wouldn't guess.

"But Ohio has something I've never seen anywhere else: shadowy characters. The plywood figures, painted black like silhouettes, range from dogs and bears to golfers and dancers. However, most — 90% or more — are like that one." I pointed to a standee next to a fence. Backlit by the sun, it almost looked real -- a man leaning against a pole, wearing a cowboy hat and smoking a pipe. In the midst of all the black, one dash of color leapt out. "They *all* wear the same red bandana."

Tim smiled. "I remember working with you, watching you make sense of computer gibberish. Now here you are, analyzing lawn decorations."

I nodded. "When you're in the middle of nowhere, you'll do anything to keep entertained."

** HOSPITALITY REDUX **

* OHIO *

August 10 - August 16, 1993
33 miles -- 16 bags
TOTAL, 1250 miles -- 523 bags

Even disasters — there are always disasters when you travel
— can be turned into adventures.   - Marilyn French

———————◆———————

The first day of backpacking was typical -- after an hour, we started wondering what we could mail home to lighten Sue's load. The second sleeping bag, the extra bath towel, Sue's boots that inflicted another huge heel blister.   -journal entry, August 10

NINE MILES, AND SUE felt every inch. Her left knee tightened up in the first hour, shooting needles through her leg which grew worse with every mile. To balance the pain, four new blisters bloomed on her right foot. By the time we entered Scioto County, only sheer willpower kept her moving.

We stopped for our third break in the town of Eifort — rather, what was left of it. Four houses still stood at the bend in the road. Three slowly crumbled against the ravages of time, while a lone worker diligently painted the fourth. We headed for the nearest vacant house and dropped our packs in the shade of an elm.

We'd barely sat when the painter vanished inside his house. By the time I fished candy bars from our packs, he emerged and headed in our direction. As he got close, I noticed the beaming smile on his face and three cans in his hands.

"I think you two could use a cold drink," he offered, handing us a Pepsi and a 7-Up. "Sorry about the lack of selection."

He introduced himself as Charlie Horner. "I lived in this area all my sixty-seven years. Believe me, this town used to be a lot livelier than it is nowadays."

He plunked himself down on the grass, taking a break from the midmorning sun. With his large but not awkward frame, he resembled a giant gray-haired teddy bear. His smile grew as he talked about the area's history.

"Take this house behind us." Ivy clung to its sides, and bricks fell from one corner. "It was made of sun-dried bricks by the man they named the town for. He had two kids who lived here after he died. I can remember helping brother and sister Eifort with chores, until they passed on, too.

"Most of the town I grew up in has disappeared. Across the road," he pointed to where he had been working, "stood an office building and more houses. Down in the hollow, a clay dig employed the town's men. Up the road in Firebrick — you walked through Firebrick, didn't you?"

On our map, it lay one mile back. "Supposedly," I said, "but I sure didn't see it."

"That's 'cause nothing's there anymore. In 1910, they built a Methodist church, and every other Sunday a circuit rider came in. That's where one preacher works in several towns, and schedules sermons in each of them on alternate weekends."

His words took us to a simpler time, before superhighways and cellular phones. When living in a remote town meant sometimes doing without. A time when people respected others' property . . . "Well, the church closed several years ago, and it really attracted vandalism," he continued. "Last year, the Methodists burned it down and returned the land to the family that donated it eighty-three years ago."

Before returning to his painting, Charlie gave us a contact. "When you get to South Webster, check with Todd Gates, the town's new Methodist pastor. He'll tell you where to camp. He's 'good people'."

For Sue, the last three miles seemed like thirty. Her coterie of blisters made every step a challenge. By the time we reached town, she was ready to collapse.

Again, we lost the game of 'what will he look like.' For Todd Gates, we pictured a bookish young man fresh out of the seminary. Answering the door of the parsonage instead was a man who could have played pro football. We found out later he had, as defensive tackle on the Philadelphia Eagles training squad and, later, coaching high school ball before turning to the ministry.

He gave us a warm welcome. "You can camp in the churchyard, you can camp in our backyard, you can even sleep inside on our floor. Do you have plans for dinner? My wife's not here, but I'm sure she'll insist you join us and the kids."

After we pitched our tent, Todd showed us the church. "The town's original church burned to the ground in 1932, and they rebuilt this on the old foundations. The fire burned everything but one picture," he said, guiding us to a side wall. "Though buried in ashes, it suffered no fire or water damage."

He pointed to a picture of Jesus tacked to the wall. Yellowed edges spoke of its age, but nowhere had fire left a mark. As I looked at it, my eyes focused on the weathered caption at the bottom: "People need faith in times like these."

WE MADE IT TO Ohio
           and we love the people we meet
After hard miles on the road
           Such hospitality can't be beat
Your kindness keeps us going
           Until we meet some family new
So, when like the wind we're blowing
           We leave our thanks to you.
     - our entry in Todd & Ginny Gates' guest book, August 11

LED BY HER KNEES, Sue's body staged a rebellion against walking. Faced with the revolt, we took the day off, hoping twenty-four hours rest would convince most of her anatomy to rejoin us.

We ate breakfast with Todd and his wife Ginny. Her young face, framed by beautiful black tresses, looked harried from dealing with three small children. Their youngest, Clayton, had entered his 'terrible twos,' and three-year-old Mitchell suffered from an unknown malady. "Last year doctors diagnosed him as autistic," she explained. "We couldn't believe that, though, since he does respond to things. Now they suspect he has Landau-Kleffner syndrome, so next week we take him to Chicago for more tests."

As Ginny cleared the table, Sue hit upon a way to repay their kindness. "The other kids are still sleeping. Why don't we take Lucas outside to play and give you a break?" Ginny's look of pleased surprise gave us our answer, and we ushered their son out the door.

"Where do four-year-olds get so much energy?" I asked Sue as we watched Lucas scamper through our tent for the three hundredth time. "If only I could bottle it and sell it, we'd make a fortune."

"Sell it?" she replied. "I'd use it to get through our fifteen-mile days!"

Thirty minutes of play wore me out, but Lucas still bubbled with energy. My rescue came from next door, when a neighbor wandered over. As the older woman neared, she waved a newspaper. "Would you happen to be these people?" she asked.

She handed me a week-old *Sentinel*, folded to our pictures. "My sister-in-law lives in Pomeroy, and she sent us this. My husband recognized you right away, but I wasn't sure."

I returned the paper. "It's us," I confirmed, "though it's a terrible picture."

"My name's Jean Hamm. Oh, you've got to meet my husband. Do you have a minute?" She waited for us to take Lucas inside, then showed us through the alley. "I left him puttering in his workshop. He'll be so excited to meet you!"

She led us into a garage that had been converted into a woodworking shop. Handmade candelabra filled boxes scattered about the floor. Toy cars and wagons crowded the shelves. On the workbench, a dollhouse stood above a sea of tools and wood chips. In the center of it all sat Delmer Hamm, tall, thin, and bespectacled.

He apologized for not coming next door. "Isn't getting old a crime? I just can't zip around like I used to. I can't even go to all the craft shows I used to frequent, because it's too hard to load and unload the truck by myself."

He showed us around his shop, pointing out details in this votive candle handler, spinning the wheels in that wooden car. The pride he took in his work echoed in the quality of his craft.

We stepped outside and chatted about woodworking for twenty minutes, until I noticed a young woman drive up to the Gateses' house and look around, puzzled. "I hate to cut you short," I apologized, "but that must be the reporter from the *Portsmouth Times*. Maybe we could stop by and visit later?"

"As long as you're staying here today," Jean said, "let us treat you to dinner. I don't cook much anymore, but there's a great restaurant in the next town."

We accepted her offer, then flagged down Susan Schwartz. For the rest of the morning we entertained her with tales of our offal adventure. By noon, she had her facts, and we had an open offer for help when we reached Portsmouth.

When Susan Schwartz left, our thoughts turned to lunch. In this town of 840 people, we had two choices: microwaved sandwiches and junk food at the convenience store, or order off the menu at Jeep's Den, the local hangout. We chose the hangout, splurging on spaghetti and salad, ignoring the furtive glances thrown our way. After months on the road, we had grown used to the stares and the lulls in conversation as the locals checked us out. The gossip after we left, we heard later, centered on 'the strangers in town.' At least one person figured us as members of a motorcycle gang.

The afternoon passed like so many others, as we caught up on postcards, updated our journals, tried to lose to each other in the endless series of card games. We visited the library, researching the road ahead, and visited both of the town's grocery stores. With such a busy day, we hardly had time for a nap.

Following a filling dinner at a smorgasbord (the best part of walking was not worrying about calories), the Hamms drove us around the area. "South Webster turned one hundred in 1987," Delmer said, "and I served as chairman for the Centennial Celebration. By the time the year was over, I knew everything you could want to know about the town, and more."

He filled us in on the history Charlie had missed. "This area was known for bricks. They fired them here from 1871 until 1902. When people first settled here, they called the town Iron Furnace. The name didn't change until they incorporated."

Delmer drove us around town, telling us about the old homes we drove by, and about others long since vanished. "Like most towns, we've lost a lot the past few decades. The train quit coming through in 1950, after almost a century. They had a movie theatre here, started in 1923, before talkies. TV finally killed it in 1957."

"Did you walk through Firebrick?" Jean asked.

"Yes, Charlie Horner told us about it. The old church with the circuit rider."

She nodded knowingly. "They opened it in 1913. My father gave the first sermon in that church."

By the time we returned 'home,' Todd had already started his Wednesday night prayer service. Jean joined Sue and me as we quietly took seats in the back of the church, trying not to disturb the small group.

As the meeting wound down, Todd asked us to introduce ourselves. We did, and answered questions from his parishioners. Several shook our hands and wished us luck as they filed out. When the crowd thinned, a man who had held back came up to us.

"I'm so glad I could meet you. You talked to my brother yesterday, and he told me about you. I'm Bob Horner."

I could see the resemblance. Like Charlie, he was sturdily built yet far from heavy. Like Charlie, he had a genial smile which put us at ease.

"Charlie gave us a great welcome to the area," Sue said. "In fact, everyone in town's been incredible. Except for my feet, this ranks as one of the best days of the trip."

the Gates family

"Your feet?"

"Blisters," I answered for her. "Her feet are prone to them. It's the one big problem we've yet to solve."

"I've given up on hiking boots," Sue added. "I know they're great for ankle support, but they have no give. I'm hoping to find a store in Portsmouth, and buy a large pair of sneakers. Maybe that'll help."

"Tell you what," he said. "There's a big shoe store in Sciotoville, before you reach Portsmouth. I buy my shoes there. When I'm in town tomorrow, I'll talk to the manager. I'll make sure they treat you right."

We wandered back to the parsonage, where we found Todd loading the car with drinks and blankets. "A bit late for a picnic, isn't it?" I asked.

"Tonight's the Perseids!" he said. "I promised Lucas we'd drive out to see them. Why don't you join us?"

The Perseids. This swarm of meteorites, left over from an asteroid long since destroyed, crossed the earth's path early every August. Several heavenly rocks met a fiery fate each year, blazing across the sky — the proverbial 'shooting stars.' In the city, excess light made seeing them difficult; here, we would have a front-row seat.

Armed with cold snacks and hot drinks, Todd drove us to Simmering Ridge, far from the lights of town. Above us stretched an inky black sky, speckled with billions of stars. Though a fine mist softened the stars with a gauzy haze, no clouds ruined our views.

Experts had predicted the best asteroid showers in years, and they guessed right. In previous Perseids showers, I'd rarely seen a 'shooter.' This night I spied over a dozen streaking across the heavens. Sue saw even more, the first shooting stars she'd ever seen.

What a magical night. What a wonderful day.

ONE DAY'S REPRIEVE HADN'T softened the sentence. Even after lightening her load, Sue still struggled with the weight. If possible, her knee hurt worse than the day before, and she soon had blisters on her blisters.

Three miles into our day's trek, Bob Horner caught up to us. "Thought I'd stop and say 'Hi'," he said from his pickup. He again gave us directions to the shoe store in Sciotoville, and asked if we needed anything.

"Maybe you could answer a question," I asked. "Charlie mentioned a motel in Sciotoville, but someone else said it had closed. Do you know anything about it?"

"Sorry, I sure don't." After a handshake and another "Best of luck," he sped off to town. We shouldered our packs and followed at a much slower pace.

In Scioto Furnace, another one-horse, one-store town, we stopped at Bob's Grocery for a juice. The woman mopping the floor, unkempt with dirty brown hair, struck up a conversation. "Walking across the country? Aren't you scared?"

"Not really," Sue said. "We haven't had any problems."

"Do you camp out? Oh, I'd be so afraid someone would come along and hurt or kill me."

Sue glanced at me, rolling her eyes. "People were worried when we started," she told her, "but we've only come across great people."

She shook her head, pushing her mop vigorously across the floor. "Why would you want to walk? That's a long way, even driving."

"You can't meet the people driving by at fifty-five miles an hour," I emphasized. "And we've met some wonderful people."

"Not too many of those left, are there?"

I could read Sue's thoughts through her eyes. *You think I'm cynical?* she responded. *She sounds like a New Yorker!*

The woman's relentless gloom beat us down. We left Bob's Grocery, subdued after her tirade. We trudged along, Sue's pain growing with every step. After three more miles we found a church, and stopped for a lunch break.

Bob Horner found us picnicking on the lawn. He popped out of his truck, bubbling with good news. "I talked to the manager of the shoe store, and they're expecting you. They'll discount any shoes you want."

His smile grew even wider. "The Scioto Motel is open. Turn right at the first light you come to, and go a quarter mile — you can't miss it. I've paid for your room tonight."

Was this a dream? We thought ourselves lucky when someone let us camp in their yard! For a stranger — a man we'd exchanged maybe a dozen sentences with — to treat us to a motel room amazed us. *Ohio,* I thought, *must be the 'heartland' we'd heard of.*

However, five miles of heartland still lay between us and the motel. As we walked, the heat crept higher, dragging the humidity with it. The weather and the blisters turned the green rolling hills into Sue's private torture chamber. She spoke less and less as her pain grew. By the time she dropped her litter stick and bag and walked away, she'd ceased speaking altogether.

Halfway to Sciotoville, we entered Slocum. This time, the sole business was Charlie and Mary's Place, a cinder-block shelter adorned by one small blinking sign. A plastic 'Closed' sign stood in the building's sole window. We passed it before noticing people inside.

Above us the clouds massed, threatening to add rain to the day's miseries. However, our parched throats posed a more immediate threat, and a cold drink wouldn't delay us long. Ignoring the 'Closed' sign, I tried the door. Open.

We stepped inside to a sparsely furnished room. An empty counter stretched away from the door, five video games (four of them poker) lined the unpainted walls, and a pool table sat in the middle of the cement floor. One patron sat plugging quarters into a poker machine, a blank stare on his face. A large grizzled man — presumably Charlie — watched it all from behind the counter.

I turned to him. "Do you have any soft drinks?"

He looked at me, sizing me up. "We have Pepsi."

"That sounds good — one Pepsi, we'll split it." As he reached into his private refrigerator, I added, "Looks like those clouds are going to bring rain."

"We need it, Lord knows." He handed Sue the Pepsi. "We haven't seen any rain here, seems like months."

Sue sipped the Pepsi, then handed it to me. I took a slug and, handing it back to her, glanced out the door. "Well, you're getting some now."

In the thirty seconds since we had entered, the heavens had opened. Sheets of rain pelted down, running off the road and turning the shoulders to mud. I gaped at the sudden storm. What perfect timing for a break!

"No sense in rushing back out," I told Sue. "How about a game of pool?" I racked the balls, and she broke.

We hadn't pocketed two balls before a drop of water splashed on the table. From a spot directly above the rack point, a steady drip ensued. Within minutes the trickle became a steady stream, joined by two smaller leaks at the far end of the table. Waterfall pool! The rain puddled on the felt, creating obstacles to shoot around. Wet spots on the balls caused them to curve unpredictably. With the cue ball veering wildly on every shot, the game dragged on.

By the time we finished, so had the rain. We paid for the Pepsi and stepped out of the bar into a sauna. The rain had not budged the heat, but cranked up the humidity. Our last three miles to Sciotoville proved three too many for Sue as she staggered the distance. She completed the day under her own steam, but collapsed in the motel room.

"I can't do this anymore," she admitted, tears streaming down her face. "Today put me past my limit. I'm sorry I let you down, but I can't bear the pain. I'm done. You'll have to decide what you want to do."

One hall at the Scioto County Fair contained antique farm equipment. What an array of devices! From a hog-scalding barrel to a windmill seed cleaner, and gadgets to plant, cut, husk, shell, crack, and shred corn. The shredder resembled a supermarket checkout belt with the optical scanner replaced by a spike bracelet surrounded by seven buzz saws.

Churns, washtubs, hundred-year-old school desks, and moonshine stills from the 1970's crowded the shelves. One sign by a boy's wooden bat claimed it once belonged to a teen-aged Babe Ruth; another claimed an ancient saw was used by Noah to build the ark. We couldn't miss the Kentucky chain saw -- a standard rip saw with the blade replaced by a chain.   -journal entry, August 14

SCIOTO COUNTY'S FAIR REMINDED me how far we'd come. The last county fair we'd visited had been three years before, early in our courtship. In Orange County, that fair reflected the surreal atmosphere of the big city: dozens of thrill rides clogged the grounds, relegating livestock exhibits to a forgotten corner. Food merchants hawked wares from around the world. Jugglers and acrobats provided daytime entertainment, while stars like Johnny Cash and the Gatlin Brothers headlined at night. The frantic pace and endless crowds lent a Hollywood aura to the affair, a set-piece not grounded in the real world.

The Scioto County version bore little in common with its west coast cousin. Thrill rides ran only to four or five carnival favorites — Ferris wheel, haunted house, and others. Livestock auctions drew a big crowd. Instead of walls of photos vying for prizes, we found displays of prize winning vegetables. The flower arranging competition paid tribute to nature, with themes such as Severe Storms, Parched Earth, Rain Dance, Summer Sunshine, and Still Waters.

We had gone to the fair with Susan Schwartz, the reporter from the *Portsmouth Times*. After a second night in the Scioto Motel hiding from our problems, we took her up on her offer of help. She found us a camp site behind a church in Portsmouth, then ferried Sue there while I hoofed the five-mile stretch.

Sue's knee still threatened the trip. One day of rest hadn't cured it; if anything, the long haul to Sciotoville had made it worse. I bought a wire luggage cart in which to drag her backpack, but that ranked more as a 'lock the barn after the horse is gone' solution. Dr. Glen prescribed two more days off Sue's feet, praying her luck would change.

Susan Schwartz had volunteered to man a booth at the fair, and invited us along. Anything beat another day twiddling our thumbs in camp, so we jumped at her offer. While she worked, I toured the halls and Sue caught up on her people watching. Later, we dropped in on the auction.

We grabbed seats as the 4-H'ers started selling their lambs. First up: the Grand Champion, raised by a teenage girl with long blonde hair and a cheerleader smile. She showed the crowd she knew how to raise more than just animals. When bidding on her ewe mired at $19, she ran into the audience and sat on the losing bidder's lap. "$19.50!" quickly followed. Visits to other bidders drove the price to $20, then $20.50 before topping out at $21.

At five o'clock we returned to Susan's booth, catching her as she packed up. Behind the table with her sat a heavyset woman, who rose to greet us. "I'm Trudy Bostick. I missed you when you came through South Webster, but I think it's great what you're doing. Do you take donations?"

I shook her extended hand. "We're not out here to raise funds," I admitted.

"Well, I'd like to do something for you. Could I treat you to a meal tomorrow? Breakfast, lunch, dinner — whichever one's best."

Was there no end to the town's hospitality? "Thanks for the offer, but we don't have any way to get back to South Webster. That's over twenty miles, and we're walking the other way."

She waved away our objection. "Oh, I'll drive in. Tell me where and when to pick you up, and I'll take you someplace in Portsmouth. It'll only take me forty minutes."

For the first time since the homeless shelter in Maine, I found myself face-to-face with a personal prejudice: portly people. Nature had blessed me with a high metabolism, and I never worried about my weight. Hiking, biking, and other sports kept me in good shape. I held little sympathy for those who let their bodies go, and the bigger the person, the less I felt at ease.

Trudy was *big*. Still, she had the generous heart we'd seen everywhere in South Webster, and we weren't in a position to refuse anyone's help. Besides, it was only a meal. "Okay, let's do lunch!"

We left with Susan Schwartz, ready for dinner. She took us to a rib joint, and spent the meal regaling us with tales of her career in journalism.

"I grew up on the east coast," she said, "and I love the slower pace here. I've met so many wonderful people. Of course, I've also met my share of eccentrics."

"Such as?" Sue asked.

Her eyes twinkled. "Oh, the mayor, for instance. We call him the Sash Man, because he wears sashes proclaiming, 'Mayor of Portsmouth.' He even color coordinates them with his ties!"

We made it an early night, anxious to rest for Sunday's noble experiment. Would the luggage cart work? Could Sue even walk, given two more days off?

No, and no. Three miles emphatically answered both questions. She gave it a game try, but hurt from the first step. "We can't do this," she conceded. "I have to stay off my feet for several days, maybe a week. And we can't just stay here, either."

I couldn't deny it. Without real time off, her knee would never heal. We had no place to hole up, and couldn't afford to even if we did. As much as we hated it, we needed the car. "Portsmouth must have bus or train service to Detroit," I suggested. "We'll have to check after lunch."

Trudy picked us up as planned, and drove us back into town. After the meal, we piled back into her truck. "Now, should I take you back to where I picked you up?" she asked.

I shook my head. "We need to find a train or bus station. Sue's knee is shot, and we have to pick up her car in Detroit."

"Detroit, huh?" She considered that. "If you can wait until tomorrow, I'll drive you."

We thought she was joking. "It's nice of you to offer," Sue said, "but we couldn't ask you to do that. That's three hundred miles away."

"It's no problem," she said. "My sister and cousin live up north, and they've been pestering me to visit. This gives me a reason."

We declined again, but she insisted. As I listened to her plan the trip, I realized she was serious. Neither of us felt comfortable imposing such a long drive on her, but Trudy's smile spread wider as she talked about it. "I'll have to call my sister tonight. She'll be so excited!"

It was settled. She drove us back to South Webster for the night, our curtain call for that friendly burgh. Trudy lived across the highway from the church, sharing a ranch house with her brother, five cats, a Dalmatian, and a bundle of memories. Eifort blood ran in her veins, and she counted Jean Hamm among her cousins.

"That ink drawing is of a Dalmatian I had — Jake," she said, noticing me admire it. "I sketched him last year for Christmas presents. He was our family dog, and all my siblings loved him. I'm so glad I did, since he died this past spring."

"Is that what you teach at the college, art?" I asked.

"Oh, no. That's a sideline. I teach math and statistics. Before my illness, I had a computer supply store in Portsmouth, but I had to close it. I still sell supplies to my former customers." A Jill-of-all-trades, she'd also freelanced for American Greeting cards, won prizes for cartooning, and sold TV scripts.

For such an accomplished person, she didn't boast. We heard of her talents as we chatted with her that evening. We talked of many things, but when the subject turned to sports, she surprised both of us. "I used to compete in equestrian events," she said. "That ended a few years back, when I severely injured both legs. The accident laid me up for months, and the drugs the doctors gave me slowed my metabolism to a crawl." She struggled for words, her frustration evident.

In hushed voice, she continued. "Depression really hit me hard. My parents died around then, and I had doctors telling me I'd never be out of a wheelchair. When I couldn't exercise, my weight ballooned.

"I'm still not over it. Sure, I can walk, but not much else. Just when I start making headway, something happens — I hurt myself, or different drugs throw my system off. Sometimes I wonder if I'll ever get back to normal."

Inside, I lashed myself for my perverse fears. To think I'd nearly passed on the chance to know this fascinating woman, all because of a stupid stereotype. Yes, she was big, for good reasons. Maybe she needed a body that large to hold her enormous heart.

We received another gift from her. As we talked about the road ahead of us, we mentioned one inspiration for our trip. "We read Steven Newman's book," I said, "about his walk around the world. We planned our walk to start ten years to the day after he started his."

"His book said he lived in Ripley, Ohio," Sue added, "a couple towns past Portsmouth. If he's listed in the phone book, we're going to call him next week."

"Hold on," she said, "let me get you his number." She had hired him a few years before to speak at the college, and still had his home phone.

As we lay in bed that night, my mind kept replaying the past several days. I could never have guessed, before starting on this venture, to find so much peace in one town. For me, a poem hanging on the wall above our bed summed up the place:

> I've never seen God but I know how I feel
> It's people like you who make him so real
> It seems that I pass him so often each day
> in the faces of people I meet on the way
> He's the stars in the heavens, a smile on some face
> a leaf on the tree or a rose in the vase
> He's winter and autumn and summer and spring . . .
> In short, God is every real wonderful thing
> I wish I might meet Him more often than I do
> I would if there were more people like you

August 17 - August 28, 1993
86 miles -- 44 bags
TOTAL, 1336 miles -- 567 bags

I think that whatever I shall meet on the road I shall like,
   and whoever beholds me shall like me,
I think whoever I see must be happy.
         - Walt Whitman, "Song of the Open Road"

———————➤ ✦ ◄———————

On the drive to Columbus, we saw a series of modern Burma Shave-
type signs: *"Roses are red*
                  Violets are blue
                  Cows eat corn
                  Cars can too."
Can we say 'ethanol'?   - journal entry, August 18

ONLY SUE COULD INJURE a rhyming body part.

"My lateral collateral ligament is sprained due to hyper-exertion," she reported. Seeing our blank stares, she added, "In other words, my knee's messed up."

"You're the original bad luck kid, aren't you?" joked her brother Jim. "Maybe walking 'cross the country's not your forte."

"Not at all," I teased. "She only does these things so we can visit you." For the second time this trip, reclaiming Sue's car had taken us near Jim and his family. Again we'd spent the night, and in the morning I'd prevailed on Sue to have their family doctor check her.

"So what's the cure?" Jim asked. "Amputation?" ✲

Sue smiled. "Yeah, and start over with a new leg. I'm about ready for that."

I thought back to the comment Sue had made in March, before leaving for the east coast. "It's going to be a fight between me and my body," she'd predicted, not knowing her body would get in the best punches. Still she kept fighting, setback after setback.

"The doctor said it needs rest," she said. "I've got to stay off it a week, maybe two."

"Why don't you hole up here?" Jim's wife Melinda offered. "We'd love to have you stay."

Sue hesitated, considering it. "I'd really like that . . ." She glanced at me and gave a small sigh. "We can't, though. I've already cost us too much time. We're way behind, so I've got to get Glen back on the road."

I thought of objecting, but knew it would do no good. I knew she blamed herself for our setbacks, and a week off would make her feel worse. We'd already given up thoughts of reaching Colorado this year; we now hoped for Kansas.

So we bade Jim and Melinda goodbye and headed south. The drive back dragged as we stayed lost in thought. The specter of more lonely miles — and for Sue, the prospect of sitting in the car — weighed heavy, dragging our smiles into frowns. I didn't realize how sorry we must have looked until the waitress in another greasy spoon served our breakfast the next morning. On my strawberry pancakes, she added a whipped-cream happy face.

As we crossed a land long on farms and short on people, the trek fell into its old pattern — Sue sat, I walked. After walking with Sue, doing so alone rang hollow. Gone were the spontaneous laughs and jokes we shared. Gone was the friendly banter that made empty miles slip past. Now the mileposts stretched further apart, and my watch ran at three-quarter speed. Somewhere ahead, sitting in the car, Sue grew bored.

The litter still piled up on the shoulders, with the area's theme centering on sports and games. The mirror from a bike helmet, the badminton shuttlecock, and the dart formed a troika, leftovers from an Ohio Triathlon. I also found a pile of Playmate playing cards laying in a ditch. *Someone somewhere*, I mused, *must be playing without a full deck!*

To pass the endless hours, I ran more litter derbies, pitting beer cans against soft drinks. The first day, beer won convincingly with 56%; the next day soft drinks outnumbered them three-to-two. On both days, people tossed out cans in front of me, laughing as they drove by. *Am I crazy to care?*

THE OHIO MAP CALLED it 'Rome,' while the Kentucky map listed it as 'Stout.' When we reached the bend in the highway, it didn't look like a town at all: an abandoned store and a house stood on opposite corners of the intersection, and a narrow lane led toward the river. Disappointed, we laid our blanket next to the deserted shop and pulled our picnic food from the car.

As we ate, steady traffic came out from the lane. "Must be something down there," I noted. "It's getting too hot to walk. I say we check it out."

Sure enough, the town was hidden a mile back, on the banks of the Ohio River. It wasn't large (only one hundred people), but did support a store and a pair of churches. We headed for the post office, our favorite place to get the scoop on a town. Postmasters, we'd found, knew what was going on.

The woman behind the counter, blonde-haired and fiftyish, looked up as we came in. The name plate identified her as Barb Jackson; her smile identified her as friendly. "What can I help you with?"

When we mentioned our trek, she called her husband Wayne out from the back room. Her counterpart, stocky, graying, and also pushing fifty, greeted us, and asked about the trip. After a few minutes, Barb moved to a desk in the corner and dialed the phone.

Walt peppered us with questions, but I did squeeze one in for him. "How come one map calls this town Rome, and the other says Stout?"

He chuckled. "That throws everybody off. The town's named Rome, but don't try to send a letter here — it'll never arrive. Back when they set up the country's mail system, they named this branch after the first postmaster, Mr. Stout. Mail addressed to Stout now gets delivered to Rome — go figure! And people have been mailing to Stout for a long time. This is the first place ever to use a return address on an envelope." While he talked, I noticed Barb make a second, then a third phone call. Finally, she hung up and returned to the counter.

"I called Bill Simmers, the head of the church board," she said. "You can camp at the Methodist Church. He'll meet you there in a few minutes to unlock it."

We thanked them and hurried to the other end of town, all of three blocks away. As we started looking around the church, a burly man crossed the street, heading our way. "What can I do for you?" he asked, suspicion in his eyes.

Behind us another voice rang out. "It's okay, Joey," said a thin, white-haired man. "These folks are walking across the country, and are going to camp here tonight."

Joey nodded, placated. "Sounds good." To us, he added, "If you want to hear about the town later, drop by the store. I'll be open till six."

Bill showed us through the church, then unlocked the outhouse. "You're not the first walkers to come through Rome," he said. "Roy Hancock stayed here three years ago. He carried a cross from coast to coast and back again." *Could it be,* I wondered, *the same person we'd heard about in Maine? After all, how many people walk across the U.S. toting a cross?*

We pitched camp behind the church as a neighbor watched from her garden. Though she moved about like a younger woman, her face betrayed more years. Soon she dropped her hoe and strolled over. "Barb Jackson told me about your trip," she began. "My name's Lena Fenner." Minutes later we had an offer for dinner.

We wandered about town to pass the afternoon. From the bluffs over the river to the fields four blocks to the north, we checked out our night's home. We ended up in Joey's store, receiving a much warmer welcome. "I'm sorry if I scared you earlier. We look out after each other here, and there's been some vandalism lately. When I saw you nosing around the church, I figured I'd check it out."

After a little girl buying ice cream left, he talked about Rome. "This town was settled by immigrants from the 'real' Rome, in Italy," he proudly stated. "Our biggest claim to fame is the Rome Beauty apple. They developed it here."

This sleepy backwater had a lively past. "In the 1800s this was the county seat. Back then the river carried all the frontier traffic, and the town boomed. It had seven grocers, a millinery making women's hats, a livery stable, and two hotels. One of them, right on the waterfront, was known up and down the Ohio as *the* place to stay."

His family dated to the town's early years. "I can trace my grandparents back to the early settlers, and to the Indians they displaced. Tecumseh was one of my grandfathers."

Joey kept us entertained between customers, spinning yarns of frontier life, until dinner called us. We returned to Lena's trailer to find a card table set up on her front lawn, overlooking the river. After seating us, Lena brought out a light meal, perfect for the warm day. Fresh vegetable soup complemented a platter of sandwiches, and corn on the cob, still steaming from the boiler, completed the dinner.

We sat with her for hours, watching the river flow, letting the evening drift away. A litter of kittens frolicked on the edge of the bluff, providing a side show. A breeze ruffled the air, easing the heat. As we unwound, the sun dropped to the horizon, painting the sky with orange and red hues.

At Lena's insistence, we returned for breakfast the next morning. The aroma of frying bacon and scrambled eggs got my mouth watering before my eyes fully opened. I downed a double order, then we sat as the sun burned off the last of the morning fog. As we began our goodbyes, a knock sounded on the door and Lena's neighbor, also a widow, came in.

"Sorry I didn't come over yesterday, but Lena told me you'd be here for breakfast. I baked these for you," she said, handing us an ice chest. Inside, two loaves of bread lay warm from the oven. "Something for you to snack on while you walk."

What *was* it about this state?

Heat and humidity takes its toll. We're short with each other, quick to flare to anger. It must be so much worse on Sue, unable to walk and on highways with no spots to pull off and wait.

-journal entry, August 23

"CHEW MAIL POUCH TOBACCO!"

That phrase, urging us to "Treat Yourself to the Best," shouted from numerous barns. The ads, paint fading as the years took their toll, kept us company on our final Ohio miles. Though newspaper articles claimed the barn ads were a vanishing art, we had seen the huge yellow letters on black backgrounds since entering West Virginia, and kept seeing them through Kentucky.

One old farmer explained them to us. "Sure, Mail Pouch could use billboards. Trouble is, kids with a rifle and a little spare time tend to use signs like that for target practice. Now you put an ad on a barn, and kids'll think twice before shootin' holes in it. They don't want to chance killin' some farmer's animal."

Like our friends, the 'Boviners'. Sue had developed a special affinity for cattle, amused by how raptly they watched us pass. After so many months on the road, we had begun talking to the indifferent critters, asking them about upcoming towns, chiding them for littering, and discussing the weather. ("Hot today, eh, Bossie? You sure found some nice shade there. Oh, been dipping into the Twinkies again, huh?") At times I felt like a bit player in a *Far Side* cartoon.

By the time we hit Aberdeen, I had amazed every cow along the way with tales of Ohio generosity. Not yet ready to cross the bridge and leave the state behind, we chose to spend one last night north of the river. No churches looked inviting, so we checked the city park. The sign stated the park closed at dark, but to ask at the city building to get permission for after-hours use.

We hadn't seen such a place. Stopping a man out walking his dog, I asked, "Where's the city building?"

The man looked at us skeptically, frowning. He looked rough, as if he dared someone to cross him. "What do you need?"

We explained, and his frown barely changed. "I'm the police chief," he told us. He thought for a second, then said, "You can pitch your tent on the waterfront, right next to the park. No one will bother you."

What an appropriate finish to our stint in Ohio. *Why shouldn't the area be friendly to foot traffic?* I asked myself. *This must be the Mecca for long-distance hikers.* Roy Hancock carried his cross through here. Steven Newman, WorldWalker, lived only ten miles downriver. We made three and four. And at the store, a clerk told us that yesterday's Cincinnati TV news featured another man hiking around the world.

Before we left Ohio, we had one last task: calling Steve Newman. His answering machine picked up the phone promptly. "Hi, this is Steve. I'm on vacation right now, and will return on August 25. Please leave a message . . ."

Five more days. By then, we'd be sixty miles into Kentucky — too far to backtrack. It bothered me to come so close, yet not meet him.

The missed connection dampened our moods as we entered the Bluegrass State. Our route dove into a countryside of rolling green hills and whitewashed mansions. Despite the hilly terrain, Sue walked a short stretch, testing the knee after a week of rest.

We kicked off Kentucky with another newspaper story. The Maysville *Ledger-Independent* sent Terry Prather to cover our walk. Middle-aged with a thick beard fuller than my road whiskers, Terry shot a roll of film as we bypassed the town of Washington. Afterwards, he briefed us on the road ahead. "If you reach May's Lick today, you'll pass right by our house. Why don't you camp in our yard?"

Always eager to connect with local families, we accepted. The morning flew by, and we reached May's Lick by noon. We spent the afternoon lolling in the shade of the Prather's maples, immersed in the Sunday paper. That evening Terry and his wife Vicki took us to an ice cream social, introducing us to their neighbors. People asked about our trek, and thanked us for taking on a job that sorely needed doing. Later, we relaxed at the Prathers' house, reading _The Wartville Wizard_ ('my book' from Litchfield, CT) to their two-year-old daughter, Deanna.

They sent us off with a big breakfast, fueling us for the road. "We're so happy you came," Terry said. "I'm sorry our teenage son Josh couldn't meet you. He spent last night at a friend's house. He'll be so disappointed." Unfortunately he wasn't due home for hours, and the forecast called for a blistering day. We needed to get our hours in early.

That afternoon (so they wrote us) they drove along our planned route, bringing Josh to meet the LitterWalkers. However, their trip was for naught. The heat had done us in, and after walking eight miles, we drove to Tennessee for a quick two-day break visiting Sue's grandparents.

NOTES FROM SUE'S JOURNAL:
The pain in my leg isn't going away! I'll probably never walk and that thought scares me. My body is falling apart and I don't look forward to sitting in the car this whole trip.   _- August 25_

THE BREAK DID LITTLE to recharge our batteries. The six-hour drives to and from Tennessee, coming so soon after the trip to Detroit, tired us. Though we enjoyed seeing Sue's grandparents, guilt pangs kept me from relaxing. _Am I wimping out, looking for reasons not to walk? Have I lost my edge?_

We returned to Kentucky hills suffering the throes of a heat wave. In an encore of the weather we'd hit in Virginia, the humeratures soared to 110° and beyond. We could see the heat rippling up from the valleys.

After a late afternoon hike, we chose Mt. Olivet's Baptist church for our campground. Pastor Lynn Bertram proved as genial a host as the other pastors and deacons we'd met. "You can sleep in the church," he offered. "Throw your bags on the carpet if you want to escape the heat outside."

He told us about a unique program taking place in Robertson County.

"Lately I've wondered about the moral breakdown of America," he began, "with kids into drugs and gangs and vandalism. Even here, in Kentucky's least populous county, we have problems."

Though we hadn't seen any problems (other than litter) ourselves, I knew they were out there. "It seems no one teaches responsibility any more."

"Exactly. But the state just started a new program in rural districts, one that lets children leave school for one hour each week to take religious instruction. Since our church is next door to the school, we've signed up 75% of the students. I'm hoping this will pull them back into the community."

Not enough time had passed to judge results. We agreed on the program's merits, trying to fill a moral void in our 'instant pleasure' world. "Doesn't it come back to the Golden Rule?" I asked. "Treat other people and their property with respect, and maybe they'll respect you and yours."

Later that night we tried the WorldWalker again. Our unplanned break had kept us nearby, giving us another chance to connect. This time, he was home. "Cross-country walkers? You've got to come by! Do you want me to pick you up?" He gave us directions, and we promised to drive up the next day.

We knocked off another dozen miles in the morning, then returned to Ohio. Steve's home lay three miles south of Ripley, according to his directions. "Turn off the dirt road after the mobile home. Go over the rise. My driveway's next to the one-room schoolhouse."

This must be the WorldWalker's, I thought as we approached the log house. On the porch, six pairs of shoes were lined up — boots, loafers, tennis shoes and more. The house itself stood in a stand of trees, the unpainted wood blending into its surroundings. Behind it the woods thickened, giving the place a wilderness feel.

From the moment he answered our knock, Steve Newman charmed us. He struck us as down-to-earth, as if he couldn't understand anyone making a fuss over him. Sparkling eyes perched over a beaming smile, and a splash of red hair topped his lean frame. Though he had done his walk ten years before, he was only two years older than us.

"Let me show you around," he said. "I know how it is to be on the road, and I want you to stay as long as you want — a couple days, a week, whatever, make yourself at home." He had plans the next few days, but since he never locked up, we could come and go.

"My uncle and I built this house ourselves," he said, leading us inside. "It's a real retreat for me, a place to escape from the world, to connect with nature after spending my weeks on the road." Currently, he made a handsome living as an inspirational speaker, but spent most of his time driving to engagements.

After stowing our packs, we headed outside. "Gotta have comfortable shoes," he said, slipping on a waiting pair before leading us into the woods. "I've got twenty-five acres here. The dirt road you drove in on? That was the old stagecoach route down the Ohio River."

He took us up a rise behind the house, his cat Billy leading the way. "This hill was a sacred Indian burial ground, and Tecumseh visited it often. The local Indians communed with the spirits here." He knelt down and brushed away dirt at the base of a tree. "Someone's been digging. They've disturbed some bones."

After showing them to us, he placed the bones back in the small hole and covered them. "In October a medicine man will re-consecrate this ground. I won't be here for the ceremony, but I've told them to come right in."

We passed the night swapping road tales and learning about

two LitterWalkers and a WorldWalker

Steve. He had gotten married after his walk, but it fell apart after a few years. "I spent all my time traveling from convention to convention, giving speeches. She finally had enough of it and left." He sighed. "Lately I've wondered if I should settle down and get a regular job, teaching maybe. A few schools have said they might have room for me."

Not since leaving California had I felt so peaceful, so at home. For once I had no one to impress, no one to hold me in awe. Steve didn't dote, or make us feel as if we were imposing. As I watched Sue play with Billy, teasing the black-and-white kitten with string, I could see she felt the same way. She rocked in a chair, her bad knee up and a relaxed smile on her face.

The next day, as Steve ran errands, we played tourist. On his urging we returned to Washington, KY. This quaint town could have passed for a snapshot of the booming Midwest 150 years ago. Most buildings on Main Street dated to 1850 or before; those that didn't were replicas of original structures. The settlement boasted the first post office, first theatre, and first paved road west of the Alleghenies. Harriet Beecher Stowe had seen a slave auction here, and the incident helped inspire *Uncle Tom's Cabin*.

At the Rankin House in Ripley, the docent told us more about Stowe. "She stayed here before the Civil War, when this was a stop on the underground railroad. She heard first-hand stories from people coming through, and used those as background in her book. *Uncle Tom's Cabin* made Rankin House famous as the spot where Eliza left the South, crossing the frozen Ohio River."

That night we double-dated with Steve and his girlfriend Darci at the Ripley Tobacco Festival. The evening passed quickly, a blur of Ferris wheels, hot dogs, and carnival games. Twice people approached Steve, recognizing him as the WorldWalker; one gave him a lead for a speaking gig.

What a pleasant change for someone else to get the attention!

THIS TIME I COULD have stayed. The comfort of Steve's home had lulled me, and I spent the morning looking through his bookcase. As I read, Sue collected apples from his trees and baked him two pies. "It's my pleasure," she told him. "I loved cooking and baking at home, and I really miss it on the road."

Though the heat outside discouraged me, I knew we had to move on. Steve understood. As we packed, he gave Sue an Ohio memento: a buckeye. It resembled a chestnut, reddish-brown with a white spot, the size of a creme-filled chocolate. "According to legend," he said, "if you keep it in your pocket, you'll never suffer from arthritis."

"Do you have anything that prevents strained ligaments or broken bones?" she asked.

Steve chuckled, and hugged us goodbye. As we climbed in the car, he gave us parting words of wisdom. "The key is patience. You'll find you can't hurry things. You can only go the speed of life."

** GRINDING OUT THE MILES **

* KENTUCKY - INDIANA *

August 29 - September 16, 1993
224 miles -- 148 bags
TOTAL, 1560 miles -- 715 bags

Most travel is best of all in the anticipation or the remembering; the reality has more to do with losing your luggage.
- Regina Nadelson, *European Travel and Life*

————◆————

Newman's place had cast a spell we found hard to overcome. For two days, we'd felt at home, insulated from everything (especially the torrid weather) outside. The pull of the road had faded. When we finally dragged ourselves away, though, the thrill of the trip came right back.
-journal entry, August 29

"IF IT'S RAINING WHILE the sun is shining, it means the devil is spanking his wife."

Or so we heard as we slogged through Kentucky. Not that we saw much rain; the devil kept too busy exporting his weather to spank anybody. Temperatures stuck in the high 90s, with a matching humidity. The misery index approached 100%.

August began its swan song, and that meant tobacco harvest time. Everywhere we looked, we saw crews in the fields, cutting the leaves and loading them on trucks. From there, the leaves went to the barns, where the farmers hung them to dry. The barns bulged with leaves fading to yellow, and the aroma of tobacco filled the air.

In this area farms outnumbered cities and trees outnumbered people. Our route ran over a plateau scooped out with gentle valleys and hillocks. One minute, we'd be on top of the land, looking for miles over the heat waves radiating off the greenery. The next, we'd dip into the valley, surrounded by farms and woods.

The heat kept us from enjoying the scenery. By noon it drove us from the road, and we battled boredom through the long afternoons. At night it hindered our sleep, making us toss and turn. We even blamed it for our strange dreams: in one of Sue's, she saw Bozo the Clown open the tent flap and point a gun at her.

Again, we found ourselves using the car as a crutch. Hot afternoon? Let's drive to Cincinnati and take in a movie. No place to camp? The next town'll probably have a church, or there's a state park ten miles further south. Not meeting people? Blame it on the humidity.

Despite the unending summer, I felt the days of the trip dwindling. Five months had passed, and less than two remained. Our hopes of reaching Kansas dimmed with each hot day. We'd have to shoot for Missouri, barely 40% of the way across the land. If we couldn't get at least that far, we'd have to consider whether we had a chance to finish in '94 — and whether it was worth trying.

Faced with our poor performance in August — 244 miles, a trip low — I set an ambitious goal. "Let's try for St. Louis by October 1," I told Sue. "It may be our only chance to get on CBS _This Morning_. After all, the producer said they needed a hook, like an anniversary. That marks six months on the road, and they could tie us in to a story on the Mississippi's Great Flood."

"Do you think we can make it?" she asked.

"Well, we have to cover 340 miles this month. That's forty miles better than our best month so far." I thought, _The numbers don't look good_. "But we don't have any reasons to stop, any more people to see. If summer finally breaks and the weather cools off, we have a chance."

At least we did if the litter didn't slow us. For roads with so little traffic, the amount of debris amazed us. We filled seventy-five Heftys™ in only five days, and left nearly as much trash behind. September opened with us smashing our old one-day record of seventeen bags. By day's end we filled twenty-two, over one hundred pounds of society's jetsam. It would take another two thousand miles to find a road as filthy as U.S. 127.

The numbers didn't lie: Kentucky quickly passed West Virginia as the trashiest state. Perhaps it fit, then, that the trash here raised more questions. Where did the hundreds of ropes in a two-mile stretch come from? Why were they all cut into lengths under two feet? Did they have a connection to the sudden abundance of chocolate milk cartons?

Our 'collector's item' for the week was the Tennessee personalized license plate reading "1 ELVIS." Later that day, I found a plastic bag with six cassettes inside. Checking them, I recognized the names of rap artists. "If they'd been in my car," I told Sue, "I'd have thrown them out, too!"

Having stolen West Virginia's trash title, the state also made a play for the funniest business signs. Several small towns had a branch of the area's favorite business, the Fifth Third Bank. "Sounds like a good place for a second mortgage," I noted. Later, as we inched down U.S. 127, we took shelter from a rain squall in the S&M Restaurant.

The miles dragged. By day we sweltered in the heat; at night we camped alone, stymied when we tried to meet people. The frustrations grew until our tempers boiled over. A sudden rainstorm lit the fuse one day, catching us a quarter mile from the car. For Sue, adding rain to a new set of blisters proved more than she cared to deal with. When I insisted on finishing the last two miles into town, hot words were exchanged. The rest of the day we spent in stony silence before cooling off after sundown.

We did manage to finish Kentucky on a high note. For the first time in weeks if not months, we enjoyed a sunny day with a cool breeze and a temperature under 80°. To the east lush green farms blanketed the land. To the west, the sternwheeler *Mississippi Queen* floated down the Ohio. When we reached Milton, we sought out the Methodist church for the night. The pastor, Ron Master, gave us the typical warm greeting, opening the church, asking about our adventures. Though he and his wife had plans for the evening, they invited us to breakfast the next morning.

Over pancakes, we swapped stories with our host. "I'm related to Mark Twain," Ron told us matter-of-factly. "He was my mother's mother's mother's sister's son."

He looked in his late 40's, and had a soft voice well suited to telling tales. Listening to him, I thought he must have received Twain's storytelling genes. I raptly listened as he told us of life off the beaten track . . .

"I had a rural parish a few years back," he said, his eyes dancing. "This one farmer regularly fell asleep during my sermons. One morning, after sleeping through another sermon, he invited me to dinner. That night, as we sat talking after the meal, he asked me, 'I suppose you've noticed how I always fall asleep in church?' I nodded. 'Well, I want you to know,' he said, 'if I didn't trust you, I wouldn't go to sleep on you.'"

Sue now complains of boredom with our trek. "I'm tired of America, of people going to church and going to work, of a 7-11 on every corner. I find nothing exciting here.

"I want to experience a different culture, to see castles not K-Marts, foreign lands not farm silos. Instead, I pick up litter and have trucks whiz by me every day. I feel like I have a job, like I'm on a Winnebago vacation. I set up camp. I grocery shop. I do laundry. I cook. I wash dishes. I go to bed. On my good days I see a movie, or watch TV in a motel room."   - journal entry, September 5

"DID YOU SEE THAT big black Brahma back there?" Sue asked as I caught up to her.

We thought of the Brahma bulls as the 'royalty' of the cattle kingdom. Huge, hulking, and with a hump on their backsides, they stood out from the rest of the herd. "I'm not sure. Was he standing in a barn?"

"No, he was 'pasture-ized'."

Cows dominated our conversation as we strode through the Midwest. In Indiana, the lay of the land had changed, with large (over three thousand people) towns popping up every other day, and fertile — and flat — farmlands between. And LOTS of cows. "I must have missed him. But that's quite the party group you've stopped next to."

I pointed at the herd milling to our side. For the first time, we noticed a bull making little bulls. A couple others tried to follow his lead, with little success. "Hey! You!" Sue called to them. "Try mounting the other end!"

We watched while taking a water break, amused by their antics. "I can't help it," Sue said. "They get to me. They stand there looking vacantly at us and swatting their tails, like they're saying, 'I'm stupid, can you help me?' and my heart melts."

I smiled as I stowed my bottle and shouldered my pack. Our pace has grown more relaxed in Indiana, now that summer's heat had finally broken. High temperatures no longer forced us off the road at noon. The trash volume also dropped by half after the record-setting miles in Kentucky.

After two weeks in the 'wilderness,' we returned to newspapers. Cecil Smith, the editor of the _Salem Democrat-Leader_, caught us at the outskirts of his town. He took our facts and photos, asked about our route, and told us of the last cross-country walker he'd interviewed. "This man did a solo walk, without a backpack but with two cars. He'd drive one several miles ahead, then walk back to the other. He'd then drive forward with that car and walk back to the first one. He crossed the country from east-to-west while walking west-to-east."

When Cecil asked about our plans for Salem, I mentioned an unmet goal. "We really want to stop at a school and talk to the kids about our walk, now that classes are back in session."

He wrote down a phone number and handed it to us. "Dan's a science teacher at the high school. I'll bet he'd love to have you talk to his classes."

We called him after lunch, only to have our hopes dashed. "I'm sorry," Dan said, "but I've already got tomorrow planned. I'd need more notice to bring you in."

In Campbellsburg we gave them a two-day notice, cold calling to an elementary school. The principal turned us down flat. Later schools rejected us as well. "Didn't Steve talk to schools?" Sue wondered. "What are we doing wrong?"

The rejections mirrored our problems in meeting locals. Pastors let us camp, but spent little time chatting. No one in stores or cafes gave us a second look. On the road, few people honked and waved, and none stopped to talk. We began feeling like pariahs.

One small country church illustrated our problems. When we drove up, four parishioners had just finished work on a new pavilion. Before leaving they invited us to stay there, and use the new lights to read, play cards, or whatever. Later one man brought his wife by to see the lights. Eager for the company, we put away our books.

After chatting for five minutes, his wife rose. "Well, we don't want to bother you, so we'll be going."

What if we WANT to be bothered?

Running on empty, looking for a way to rekindle our flagging enthusiasm.   -journal entry, September 9

We're fighting a losing battle against time, trying to make the trip work before we lose all interest in it.

Today did not help. First, Sue had another large heel blister, causing her pain and frustration almost to tears. Second, the weather reminded me of autumns growing up, making me homesick: temps near 70°, a light breeze, and a hint of changing seasons in the air.

                              -journal entry, September 10

THE MILES SLIPPED AWAY as we rushed across Indiana. We left behind our daily rut as we looked for new diversions, trying to regain the spirit of adventure we'd lost hundreds of miles ago. The state was a blur, a melange of memories. Memories of . . .

. . . *the smell of fresh baked bread.* As I wandered past a restored home in Spring Mill Village, a living-history hamlet, the aroma drew me inside. There a volunteer decked out in a pioneer's gingham dress talked to visitors about life in the 1850's mill town. On the table bread sat steaming, waiting for Sunday brunch.

. . . *Gothic spires jutting from the Indiana countryside.* The forests of the Midwest looked more like the forest of Bavaria when we visited the Benedictine Abbey. Here monks had built a campus more European than American. Spires soared to the sky, red-tiled roofs topped castle-like buildings, and flowers blanketed the immaculate gardens.

. . . *the taste of genuine apfelstrudel.* Returning from the abbey, we stopped in Jasper to sample "the best German food in the state." The knockwurst and kraut at The Schnitzelbank tickled my stomach, but it was the strudel that sent my taste buds back to Oktoberfest in Munich.

. . . *cheerleaders rousing the crowd.* A chill in the air, hot dogs on the grill, and the home team on the field — ahhh, fall is the time for high school football. We sat with the Mitchell fans, cheering their team in their homecoming game. A late score had the crowd on their feet, but the team fell short at the final gun.

. . . *an ocean of yellow.* Detouring around Mitchell, we crossed a rise and saw them — hundreds, no, thousands of school buses. Behind fences, parked on lots, small squat carriages side-by-side with full length models, they sat, waiting for spitwads, chewing gum, and carved initials.

"Carpenter is the biggest bus maker in the country," one wizened man told us at lunch. "They started a hundred years ago with horse-drawn buses. When Henry Ford hit it big, they built wooden buses around his model T. Yep, they got a history."

He talked slowly, in no hurry to move on. "I retired from there a few months back. Installed heaters when I started, kept it up for years. Finally graduated to upholstery."

Did the lines on his face come from worrying about the abuse his handiwork took? "New York City has the worst record for bus seats getting cut up. Shoot, we'd send them trucks full of replacement cushions."

. . . *headlining the Sunday service.* We hit Shoals Sunday afternoon, ready for company. After pitching camp in the riverside park, we headed for the Methodist church to take in the evening services. With less than a dozen people there, our presence attracted quick attention. The minister, a stocky man gracefully entering middle age, detached himself from a conversation and headed our way. "Hi, I'm Howard Bell. Are you new in town?"

He chatted for a moment, then parted to start the service. "I'd like to thank everyone for coming tonight," he said, stepping to the lectern. "Unfortunately, our organist is on vacation tonight." Turning to us, he asked, "Do either of you play?"

We shook our heads. "I guess, then, we'll do without accompaniment." He asked for requests, then led the congregation in *a cappella* song. After a half-dozen tunes, he closed his hymnal.

"I have a sermon I'd planned on giving, if you want to hear it. However, we have guests tonight, and if you'd prefer, maybe one of them would speak about their novel journey." A show of hands nixed the sermon, so Howard beckoned me to the podium.

For twenty minutes, I talked about our trek, focusing on the spirit we'd seen in the people across the land. From 'instant family' in Maine, through schoolkids bearing gifts, to small towns which couldn't stop giving, I wove a picture at odds with the nightly news. "I never imagined we would find so much caring, so much heart in the land."

They received my message warmly, asking more about the voyage. Even Sue, tired and ill at ease earlier, relaxed and took part in the questions and answers. After the service Howard invited us to stay at his house, but since Sue was exhausted, we declined.

Sue hit the sack early, while I stayed up to read. At 9:30 I put down the book, turned off the flashlight, and relaxed to the murmur of the White River. As I collected the energy to move to the tent and my waiting sleeping bag, I realized I had company. In the half-light of the starlit night, I could see he was well dressed, wearing pressed pants and a print shirt. He was near forty, and looked deep in thought, neither smiling nor frowning. "Didn't mean to startle you," he said. "Just out for my evening stroll."

He sat at the picnic table with me and began to talk. I listened, too tired to contribute much, but interested in hearing of his Amish life.

"I don't always get along with my neighbors here," he confided. "Sometimes they don't care for how we do things. For example, on an Amish farm, we always leave a field wild for the birds and insects to have a place to feed. If I tried that in town, they'd have a fit. Call it an eyesore and probably fine me.

"Nature has a way of taking care of things, if we'd let it. If you have an infestation of insects one year, you'll probably get more birds to balance them out. Used to be, when you had too much tall grass, you'd have extra bison to eat it."

He rambled on, his voice sometimes flowing softly like the river just out of sight, other times turning strident. "People shouldn't have more kids than they can support. The Amish, we take care of our own. We run benefits for widows and orphans, because they're part of our lives. Me, I had a son at age fourteen, and I had to take care of him and his mother. I did, too, for eighteen years."

He paused, and I turned to see him with his eyes closed, his face lined with sadness. "When my son left to go among the English — that's what we call anyone not an Amish, Mennonite, or Quaker, the 'English' — I warned him he'd lose his way, he wouldn't make it. After four years out there, he took poison and killed himself." His voice grew softer. "He kept saying, 'I can't find the answers.' I tried to tell him, 'There aren't any answers to find because there are no questions.' By twenty-one or twenty-two, you should know the path you are on in life. If you stray from that path, you're going to get confused, and look for ever more answers to which there are no questions."

He lapsed into silence, the white noise of flowing water surrounding us. When he spoke again, his voice had regained its strength. "The trouble is, people always need a thrill, they always need to feel good. They don't realize life isn't all 'feel good,' there's pain involved, and 'feel good' is relative. If I have a bad toothache, I feel good when the ache is cured."

After nearly an hour he left, vanishing into the night much as he had appeared, leaving behind not even a name. Subdued but fascinated, I joined Sue in our nylon castle, drifting off with his words replaying in my head.

"THANKS FOR THOSE DIRECTIONS, you idiot! That turnoff doesn't exist."

Sue's harsh words grated on me. She had driven ahead only five minutes before, ready to walk, and now she'd returned. Seeing her standing by the car, arms folded and body rigid, I knew she didn't have good news.

"Well, don't yell at me! I didn't write the damn street map." The city map of Washington had clearly shown a left turn on the side street, one which should have routed us onto a back road to Wheatland.

"If you wouldn't go overboard, trying to find every out-of-the-way road in the country, we wouldn't have this problem." Her eyes, normally filled with laughter, instead flamed with anger. "Why don't you spend a day in the car, driving around looking for roads that don't exist, and see how much you like it!"

"Oh, buzz off," I growled. "You know if I hadn't found a back route, you'd have bitched about walking on the freeway." Though we usually had good luck with country highways, here U.S. 50 widened to four lanes.

She muttered something under her breath, and turned to get back in the car. "Wait a second," I said. "I'll check the route with you. I'll find where the —"

"Just go walk!" She jumped in the car, gunning the engine. "I need some time alone. I'll be up ahead, at the freeway."

As she sped away, I shook my head. The fights were growing more bitter, and coming more often. Anything could provoke a fight, and usually did. The stresses piling up kept us at each other's throats.

Not that I saw any solution. The car wore on us both, a symbol of our failure to do the trip we'd wanted. Continued difficulties in meeting people kept us on edge. Questions about the end of this year's walk, now only a month away, weighed heavily on our minds. Where will we stay? Will my job be waiting? What will Sue do?

The rejections from schools made our moods worse. After several more attempts, giving two or even three days advance notice, I thought of giving up. Sue tried her luck with one school, phoning the woman principal. "Do you have references?" she asked Sue. "We can't let just anyone walk off the streets and talk to our kids."

And now fights, really, about nothing. Or, more correctly, about everything left unsaid and unresolved, about too much time spent together, about our habits that grated on each other. All these issues simmered below the surface, whittling our tempers razor-thin.

By the time I reached the freeway, we had both calmed down. Following a light lunch by the roadside, I tackled the dreaded highway. Heavy truck traffic buffeted me, worsening when the road narrowed back to two lanes. I welcomed reaching Wheatland, population 440.

Sue had already scouted the town. "This convenience store is the only business. Looks like microwaved burritos or chili dogs for dinner. For camping, there's a Methodist church three blocks away."

We drove to the church, then walked around it. Though spotlights glared on several sides, we staked out two good tent spots. No one was home at the parsonage, so we sat in the car and read, hoping the pastor would return soon. At 4:30, we noticed him and his wife drive into the garage. Fifteen minutes later, we knocked on his door.

Hugh Reynolds answered, a middle-aged man with graying hair. "Can I help you?"

"My wife and I have been walking across the country," I said, "picking up litter —"

"And you're looking for a place to stay for the night."

"We have a tent, and wondered if we could camp in the church yard."

"You could, but it's going to be pretty nippy tonight. You'd be much more comfortable inside." He opened the screen door. "Come in, come in. Louise! We have company!"

His wife emerged from the kitchen, a slight woman with sparkling eyes. She listened to our introduction, then greeted us as warmly as Hugh had. "The guest bedroom's all set up. I'll put out extra towels and washcloths for the shower. You haven't eaten yet, have you? I'll whip us up something for dinner."

Before we knew it, she had prepared a wonderful Midwest meal: pork chops, fried potatoes, peas, and rolls. Hugh entertained us with tales of his pre-pastor days, of army assignments in Korea, Germany, the Azores, Hawaii, Japan and more. Between his military and his ministry stints, he battled alcoholism, finally beating the disease. He also delighted us with stories of their family pet, a friendly dachshund named Chopper.

"Let me tell you about Chopper," he said, sitting back after dinner. "To look at him, you wouldn't think he's anything special, would you? Two years ago, I didn't either. My old dog had just died, and a woman I knew had this dog she had to get rid of. 'Take him fishing with you,' she told me. Since I love fishing, I planned a trip, and took Chopper along."

His smile grew as he warmed to the tale. "This little dog, he has own style of fishing. We'll get in the boat, and Chopper will perch himself in the front and point to where he wants the boat to go. You understand, he has a lot better eyesight than you or I, and from his low vantage point, he can see where those catfish are hiding.

"Well, he directs the boat to the side of the river, to the shallow water where he knows the fish like to hide. Once I position the boat so it's between the fish and the open water, Chopper lets out a bark. In fact, it's a bark that's known up and down the Wabash River as 'Chopper's Catfish Catching Bark'."

He drew out the last phrase, giving the words impact. "Well, the fish gets pretty scared by this bark, and it wants to get back to the safety of deeper water, but the boat — and that scary bark — is in the way. It can't go the other way, since that's dry land, and all fish know they can't swim on dry land. Now you've got to remember the catfish is a very strong fish, and this strong fish doesn't know which way to go. Panicking, it gives its tail a big kick and goes the only way open to it — straight up. The kick is strong enough to lift that fish clean out of the water.

"Now, catfish have a spiny sort of horn coming out from around the gills — you probably know this if you've ever fished for catfish. Well, near the banks of the river, the tree branches hang real low, and this fish gets its horns snagged in the branches, and it stays stuck long enough for me to reach over, shake the branch, and the fish goes plop! Right into the boat."

That produced a chuckle from us, but Hugh wasn't finished. "Amazing, huh? I wouldn't have believed it if I hadn't seen it myself. Which reminds me, have I told you about Chopper's squirrel hunting technique?" He proceeded to tell us how Chopper helped him tree the critters, and 'Chopper's famous Squirrel Catching Bark' startled them into falling. The evening flew by as Hugh spun more yarns, each more fantastic than the last.

In the morning Hugh asked for help loading WordPerfect© onto his PC. "I haven't touched a computer since March," I warned him as I sat at his desk. Within minutes I warmed to the task, my fingers dancing over the keyboard. Five minutes later I had him up and running, typing sermons.

The day's good deed done, we bid Hugh and Louise a fond 'goodbye.' Outside the road waited — as did the maelstrom we had left.

We almost lost it — the trip, the marriage, everything — yesterday.
                                        -journal entry, September 19

THE TIFF IN WASHINGTON paled in comparison, a mere dress rehearsal for the blowup in Vincennes. The glow from the night with the Reynoldses lasted less than a day, doing nothing to ease the tensions besetting us. We finished our Indiana miles under these unseen clouds, a psychic sky filled with emotional thunderheads. After setting camp in a state park a few miles into Illinois, we backtracked to Vincennes for dinner and an early movie. At 8:30 we returned to the park, eager to check out the advertised square dance.

This time, the fuse was ambiguous directions to the dance, given to us by an RV camper. Not clear on which 'main road' she meant, I asked her a second, then a third time.

That was all it took. Sue lit into me, deriding me in tones steadily gaining in volume. I dove into the fray, screaming back insults that reverberated inside the closed car. We drove across the park to the tenting area, the car powered as much by invective as by gas.

I sentenced myself to the car, resigned to a night chasing elusive sleep. We spoke no words as Sue retired to the tent, and talked even less as we broke camp in the morning. Breakfast passed silently, and I took to the road with nary a farewell.

I prayed the exercise would do us both good, working out our aggressions in vigorous walking. However, Sue refused to take part, instead sitting in the car doing needlepoint. After ninety minutes passed, I confronted her.

She sat impassively, working her needle magic. I asked her questions, I cajoled her, I yelled at her, but she wouldn't respond. Finally I gave up. "I'm sorry, but I can't deal with it any longer. You do what you want, and I'll see you in a few weeks."

I moved to the hatchback and repacked my pack. What did I need to get to St. Louis? We kept the tent in the car; I'd need that. Take the stove from my backpack, get rid of the extra weight. Sleeping bag? Check. Pillow? Raincoat? All there.

As I made one last check, she broke the silence. "Now maybe you know how I feel, when you won't open up and talk to me." Those words began an earnest discussion of the crisis we faced. Forty-five minutes later, we hadn't solved all our problems, but we had agreed to tackle them — together.

Our walk would go on.

** SMALL TOWN SONNET **

* ILLINOIS *

September 17 - September 30, 1993
157 miles -- 49 bags
TOTAL, 1717 miles -- 764 bags

One may go a long way after one is tired. - French proverb

'TWAS THE CALM AFTER the storm. We both took pains to be more attentive, trying to ease each other's way on the endless road. The perfect weather helped, letting us relax, healing our open wounds. Illinois natives gave us a boost, too, welcoming us and showing an interest in our journey.

Three days of walking took us to Clay City, another of the once-bustling villages that dotted the Midwest. The downtown, all of one block, had seen better decades. Aged brick buildings lined the street. A tavern filled one storefront in the middle of the block; across the street the Youth's Club looked unused. Next door, a hand-letter sign advertised 'Auction Tonight.' The only signs of life came from the Laundromat on the corner.

Dirty clothes called, so I got Sue started at the Laundromat before scouting the town. I quickly found the post office, which sat across from the city park and next to the Methodist church. *Looks like one-stop shopping!*

I entered the post office, where a woman manned the counter. Introducing myself, I described our needs. "Just a place to pitch a tent for the night. Usually we use churches or parks."

She nodded. "Tell you what — the pastor lives across the street . . . " She pointed to the white frame house next to the park. "That house there. Why don't you ask him?"

First I checked the park, looking for a hidden corner. Satisfied, I wandered to the pastor's house for permission. His inner door was open, and inside I saw the cleric on the phone. Before I could knock, he waved me in.

"Are you the cross-country walker?" he asked, his hand covering the phone. "The postmistress called me, so I called the mayor. He wasn't there, but his wife got hold of him and he's on the line now. Hold on."

He turned back to the phone. "Okay," he replied. "Okay. Okay." When he hung up, he turned to me, smiling. "You can camp in the park by the softball fields — did you see them on your way into town? That'll work better, since the park next door has no restrooms. The mayor will call the sheriff, to let him know you'll be there."

He asked about the trip. "I'd love to hear more about it. I just started Peter Jenkins' book — have you read it?" I nodded, and he continued, "Maybe I'll stop by and chat later. All the way from Maine, huh?" His eyes reflected awe.

As the sun sunk low, Sue and I headed to the town's sole cafe. We lingered over dinner, ignoring the curious stares of the other diners. When the cafe closed, we returned downtown, hoping to find nightlife.

I stuck my head into the tavern, checking the action. Three people sat at the bar, and a juke box in the corner belted out a country tune. *No pool table here, may as well move on.* As I withdrew, I heard one barfly call out, "You can come in, we don't bite." Across the street, lights blazed in an open storefront, and people milled about outside. As we got closer, I remembered — the Auction!

Forty people crowded into the narrow room, and in front the auctioneer ran through his spiel. We took a seat in back, trying not to attract attention.

Quite an assortment of odds and ends came up on the auction block. If one item wasn't enough to bid on (as often happened), the pitchman would offer three or four items together as a package. For a dollar or two, people bid for a basket full of sponges; a doll with a leg falling off; heat lamp bulbs; a crate of Halloween masks; a tube of caulking; and a box of belts. In the hour we sat there, the high bid we heard was $3 for a TV with a very purple tint. The auctioneer hyped it, "Works great if you're color-blind!"

Our walk the next morning took us through the heart of town. As we passed the post office, a van tooted its horn and rolled to a stop. "Excuse me," the driver asked. "You've got the whole town talking. I'm as curious as anyone, so I volunteered to ask: What *are* you two doing?"

Last night's camping in the county park was free, courtesy of a sympathetic ranger. When he came for our three dollars, he asked if we

were traveling through. Our reply surprised him, and he gave us our
money back. "I can't charge you. If the boss wants the cash," he said,
"I'll pay it out of my own pocket."   -journal entry, September 22

IN ILLINOIS, OLD HIGHWAYS never die, they just get bypassed.

At least, that was the case with U.S. 50. The new road ran straight west through flat terrain filled with corn fields. Ten yards to the north, shadowing the main track, lay the old concrete path. Some stretches carried local traffic, others succumbed to weeds. For us, it provided a welcome buffer from the trucks whizzing by.

Having been born in Illinois (outside Chicago), I took pride in the relative cleanliness of the state. Like Indiana before it, we found less and less trash, though (as always) some amused us. The roadside shower cap surprised me — was it required outerwear this season of the Great Floods? Near a cemetery, I collected four bouquets of plastic flowers. "I know they can't replace the roses I grew in California," I told Sue, "but they're real low maintenance. A little something to brighten the tent our last month on the road."

Reminding me of the break soon to come, a yellow balloon floated by while I walked Salem's main street. "Twentieth anniversary celebration," its logo stated, "Centralia facility, June 1991." Had it spent two years drifting from the factory fifteen miles to the southwest? I did a double-take, though, when I noticed the company celebrating their years: the corporation I'd left in March, Rockwell International.

Thoughts of leaving the road kept cropping up. How far past St. Louis could we get? Jefferson City? Sedalia? How late could we walk before weather — or fatigue — forced us to quit?

And what of next year? What could we learn from this year's lessons to ease our way next year? "The car is out," Sue declared as we ate lunch in Olney's city park. "I want to be an equal partner on this trek. Besides, I've logged enough hours in a car to last two lifetimes."

"I can't argue that. But what options do we have?" I threw a crumb to a white squirrel (found only in Olney) which had crept close. "We've proven your body won't let you walk, no matter what you set your mind to."

She nodded, watching the squirrel scurry off with his treasure. "I don't know. Maybe if I bicycled really slow . . ."

As always, we found time to stop and talk to the Boviners. After one long chat with a heifer 'in the family way.' I turned and saw an old farmer standing twenty yards ahead, emptying his mailbox. He warily watched as I approached.

I greeted him as if talking to his cattle had been perfectly normal. His suspicious glare quickly melted into a smile, and we traded stories of travel. He had crisscrossed the country from Oklahoma to the east coast, competing in checkers tournaments. Now retired from farming, he spent his time studying the game.

My trek impressed him. "That's one heck of a trip! Are you going to write a book?"

"I'd sure like to."

"You won't write about me, will you?"

As the days dropped away, our St. Louis-in-September goal looked more and more certain. The weather cooperated, staying cool and dry — a far cry from the torrential rains behind the Great Flood of '93. We lost only one day to rain, a wet and cold Wednesday we greeted from a motel room. Fortunately, we already had plans — we would finally talk to school kids.

Persistence had paid off on our sixth attempt. Two days earlier I'd seen a phone listing for the Iuka, Illinois, grade school. My call had found a receptive principal, who invited us to talk to grades kindergarten through fourth.

Iuka was a tiny village, barely a hundred souls. A few businesses lined the railroad track, and a diner down the road hosted a crowd this rainy morning. The school stood another block down the main drag, a two-story brick building towering over its residential neighbors.

I honed my speech on the kindergartners. To involve the kids, I made it short and asked them questions: "What kinds of trash do you think we found?" "What animals do you think we've seen?" Their answers gave new meaning to the term 'stream of consciousness:'

"Did you see — a deer?"

"How about a cow?"

"My uncle has cows on his farm."

"We went on vacation to a farm in Vermont!"

The first and third graders stayed more focused, and we finished them early. Since fourth grade was still in gym class, we waited for them in the cafeteria. Soon, fifth-graders passed us on their way to gym, and seeing my backpack, asked what we were doing. "Wow! Are you going to talk to our class, too?"

After repeating our 'lesson' for the fourth- and second-grade, we returned to the principal's office. Before we could thank him, he asked, "What are your plans for the rest of the day?"

I looked out the window to see the rain still pelting down. No walking today, I knew. "Trying to stay dry."

He followed my gaze. "Not letting up, is it. As long as you're stuck inside . . . I know you've talked to all the classes I set up, but the fifth graders heard about you. They asked if you could visit their class, too."

So we went back upstairs for an encore performance. This class, if possible, showed more enthusiasm than the others, peppering us with questions. "What do you carry in your backpack?" (Clothes, rain jacket, sleeping bag, toiletries, news clippings, camera, journal, book, towel, and the coin from Caitlin in Massachusetts.) "Where do you eat?" (Convenience stores, cafes, or we cook at our camp.) "Are you going to hit all the states?" (No, only twenty-three.) "What do you do with your free time?"

"We try to do things particular to the region. In Maine, for instance, we learned how to make maple syrup." I hesitated, then added, "One thing I want to do in Illinois is milk a cow."

Several hands shot up. "There's a dairy farm near here," one girl said, "where second grade goes every year on a field trip. You could try there!"

The teacher, Patricia Timm, promised to give us the phone number. The class then finished with two requests: "Can you leave us an address, so we can write you?" and "Will you have lunch with us?"

We did and we did. The hot lunch — turkey, mashed potatoes, Jell-O, and milk — surprised me. Though the portions were tiny, it tasted far better than I remembered from my school days. It must have been the atmosphere.

Late that afternoon, we visited the Beer Family Dairy Farm. Mr. Beer himself, a fit-looking man in his fifties, greeted us. "You're just in time for the evening milking."

He led us to the milking shed, a marvel of high-tech. Computers had taken over! Two rows of four milking machines divided the room into thirds: the cows filed through on either side, and the farmers worked in the middle. From each machine a hose emerged, then separated into four tentacles which attached to the udder. This half-octopus device, once attached, vacuumed the milk out of the heifer, automatically detaching itself when a lack of pressure signaled 'empty'.

The cows lined up outside, waiting for servicing, so Mr. Beer and his son let the first eight enter. "First, we clean the udders," he explained, "then disinfect them." With an experienced grace he swabbed them clean, then touched each nipple with a small vial, leaving a yellowish residue. "That's iodine, to keep bacteria off."

He punched a number for each cow into the matching machine, then made sure they started drawing milk. "After the milk is extracted, it runs through this ductwork to drop the temperature ten degrees." He pointed to stainless steel tubing coiled like an old radiator. "It then stays in the holding tank until the processor picks it up."

Leaving his son to milk, Mr. Beer took us into the main yard. "The numbers I punched into the machines? Each cow has its own. That number, along with how much milk the cow produces, is sent to the central computer, which keeps track of production."

"Sort of a bovine 'Big Brother'," I said.

He smiled and nodded. "The computer then decides how much a given cow gets fed based on how much it's producing. Each cow wears a medallion with its number encoded on it. When a cow walks into a feeding stall, the medallion hits a sending plate, which transmits the number. The computer calculates this cow's ration of special feed, and sends it into the stall."

We heard more facts, such as a cow gives milk for about ten months, each is worth $1000, several died in the heat wave, production goes down in hot weather since they don't eat, the farm uses artificial insemination. Nothing, though, thrilled me as much as finally milking a cow. With Holsteins as full as these, I had no problem in making it flow. Just squeeze and pull, and out it squirted!

- journal entry, September 23

"HERE'S A SHOVEL, AND the bags are over there." The park manager, Dan, pointed to a pile of canvas sacks. "If one of you will shovel and the other hold the bag, I'll tie them for you."

He looked as if he belonged outdoors. In his 40s, he had no paunch from long hours sitting staring at a computer screen. Today, though, I noticed a weariness in his face, dark lines brought on by nonstop hours on the sandbagging line. "Yesterday's rains really filled the lake," he said. "If they get the two or three inches tonight they're predicting, it'll flood for sure. We've been sandbagging since yesterday afternoon, trying to keep ahead of it."

I grabbed the shovel and stepped to the mountain of sand. One — two — three shovelfuls into the bag Sue held open, and she strained to lift it to the waiting manager. "That's too heavy," she said. "Two scoops should do it." We quickly fell into a rhythm — scoop, scoop, lift — and our pile of bags grew.

To keep our muscles fresh, Sue and I switched chores every twenty bags. As I held the bags open, I watched the activity around the sandpile. Four other three-man teams had staked out positions, chipping away at their portion of the hill. Many wore orange vests, identifying them as city workers, but a few looked like volunteers. "Last night the high school football team pitched in. Their muscle power really helped." Dan paused, glancing at our car, then asked, "California, huh? How did you end up on the flood detail in Salem, Illinois?"

I mentioned our walk, and of how we always found ourselves on the receiving end of kindness. "We wanted to repay the help we've been getting. Last night, we stayed with the fifth grade teacher from Iuka and her family. When she mentioned this was going on, we checked at city hall and they sent us over."

An hour's work sufficed to build the emergency levee. In the end, the torrential rains did not return — the predicted overnight storm turned into an all-morning drizzle the next day. By early afternoon, the storm system had passed, leaving us with walker's weather for the rest of the state. Temperatures hovered near 70°, and towering clouds raced across the skies.

The storms had left their mark. We walked by fields covered with water, lines of withered cornstalks marking furrows planted with great hopes months earlier. Woods had turned into swamps, and side roads into stream beds. One three-mile stretch of U.S. 50 near Breese threaded its way through a scene more Louisiana bayou than Illinois heartland.

As we entered the shorter days of autumn, our afternoons and evenings fell into a rut. Upon entering a town we'd check in with the police, then retire to the library to read. (On the better days, we'd even find a comfortable chair.) When the sun set we went to dinner, lingering to write postcards. We ended days at pool halls or bowling alleys, sometimes playing eightball, at other times sitting at the bar watching TV. After six months of travel, ennui had set in, and keeping entertained became our biggest challenge.

Summer has ended. The weather forecast told of an arctic front pummeling us with chilly winds all week, followed by another rainy weekend. We woke to sub-50° temperatures this morning, accompanied by a brisk breeze. Brrr!   -journal entry, September 27

"ARE YOU THE TWO wanting to camp in the city park?" The question came from a woman standing in the doorway of the newspaper office, silhouetted by the late afternoon sun. "I'm JoAnn Gray, and my husband's on the park board. The rules don't allow camping in the park, but we've got a large yard you can use."

Again, the city clerk had come through for us. We had stopped there a half hour earlier, asking to camp in Lebanon. When the clerk could find no board members at home, she promised to track someone down. "While I'm calling," she'd suggested, "why don't you stop at the _Lebanon Advertiser_? I'm sure they'd love to talk to you." That's where JoAnn found us, wrapping up an interview with Harriet Church.

"Or you can stay at our place," Harriet offered. The newspaper woman rose from her chair, her curly brown hair bouncing. "That way you can meet my husband Harrison. He'll want to interview you himself when he gets back. He usually handles that sort of thing."

What a first — dueling invitations! We considered it a good week when we got one offer from a local family. Now we had to decide between two.

"Whichever works best for you is fine," JoAnn said as she stepped inside. She looked our age, with dark hair and a warm smile. "But I've got to get home, so if you want me to take you out there . . ."

If we'd learned anything from the road, it was the one key to camping: location! The Church's home bordered the highway, while the Grays lived on a quiet cul-de-sac. That swung us to JoAnn's offer, and word of her menagerie — a veritable zoo with dogs, cats, hens, and a Vietnamese potbellied pig — clinched it. "We'll come back in an hour," I told Harriet, "and talk to Harrison."

The Grays' spread impressed us, fourteen acres and a house leased for $165 per month. In one corner of the yard guinea fowl and peacocks shared a shack. A couple of cats lolled in front of the house, and a Rottweiler wandered about barking at the intruders. When Hamlet waddled out, though, he won my heart.

He looked like a miniature rhinoceros without the horns. Short, stubby hair covered his squat body. He waddled over to sniff out the new guests, but came promptly when Jason, the Grays' teenaged son, called him.

"They don't sweat at all," Jason told us, showing off his knowledge, "so they don't attract flies. Of course, during the summer he wants to stay in the air conditioning all the time. They're easy to housebreak, too. Hammy can hold it in for more than twenty-four hours. Of course, when we let him out, he can whiz for fifteen minutes." He got down on the floor next to the pig. "He can even do tricks. Watch this — shake, Hammy!" The pig offered its right — foot? paw? hoof? to Jason.

We played with the pig, then shared a beer with JoAnn and her husband Jim. I could have sat for hours, letting the world rush by outside, but we'd promised Harriet. Reluctantly we said goodbye and drove back downtown.

Harrison greeted us warmly. Six feet tall with graying hair hidden under a hat, he radiated energy. His eyes sparkled behind his glasses, taking everything in. After getting our facts, he took us outside and pointed out downtown sights.

"This town was built on the main Vincennes-to-St. Louis trail," he said. A spokesman for the local historical society, he knew the area's history. "See the bricks used to pave St. Louis Street? Trolleys ran down this street, carrying commuters into the city." We looked at the buildings lining the main drag, some stretching to three stories, many over a hundred years old.

Harrison stepped back inside to turn off the lights. "Harriet told me you were camping at the Grays' tonight. How about if we treat you to dinner?" We quickly accepted, and he called his wife to say he'd pick her up.

On the way home, Harrison pointed out other landmarks. "That building is the Mermaid House, built in 1830. When Charles Dickens visited this area in 1842, he stayed there and wrote about it in his book, *American Notes*. That's Lebanon's biggest claim to fame." He hesitated, as if debating whether to continue. "Not everyone was impressed with him. My great-grandparents owned the inn where Dickens had stopped the previous day, and they thought him rather rude. Of course, it didn't help matters when he wrote very disparagingly about their inn."

The Church's house could have passed for a museum. (What more could I expect from a historian?) A collection of oil lamps, each with a unique leaded glass shade, filled the shelves. Their lights shone on a score of antique clocks. Dozens of gavels on display had been carved by Harrison from wood salvaged around the town. "This one came from a church they tore down years ago, this was from a tree which stood in the town park, this one came from a bell tower . . . "

For dinner they took us to a tavern in the neighboring town of Summerfield, where we feasted on chili dogs and hamburgers. They asked more about the trip, and Harrison jotted down an occasional note. After the meal, they suggested another stop. "Would you like to see a deer farm?"

Joe and Shauna Crabtree greeted us as we drove up, and readily agreed to give us a tour. "We have thirty-five deer here, but most are in the fields tonight. Only a few are in the barn."

I had never seen a deer farm before. "Do you raise them for venison?"

Joe winced for a second. Thin and wiry, he looked too young to own his own 'ranch.' "Oh, no, we don't slaughter our animals," he explained. "We offer stud service, rent reindeer for Santa displays, and sell bottle-raised fawns. Our biggest customers, though, are hunters. We sell them deer lure made from doe urine."

He showed us around the barn, where several animals were penned. "This doubles as our hospital. Since the vets here aren't too familiar with deer, we've got to try different approaches. One doe had trouble delivering, so we did a C-section on it. Another one had a broken leg which we set with pins and screws." Between him and his brother (who raised elk) they kept the vets hopping.

We found it hard to leave Lebanon the next morning, the friendliest town we'd seen since Ohio. St. Louis, the only metropolis on our route, loomed ahead. We didn't fear hitting a big city, but East St. Louis we'd heard too many horror stories about. To avoid it, we jogged north. By 3:00 we reached Troy, and headed for the city clerk's office. As in Lebanon, the clerk's phone calls netted us two possibilities for camping: the city park and the Methodist church.

No sense in setting the tent up this early, we figured. The library beckoned, so we went to check on our route into the city. The maps showed three bridges over the Mighty Mississippi, but they left out one important fact.

"Can you tell me if any of these bridges allow pedestrians?" I asked the librarian. She asked someone else, who asked a third person. By the time the library quieted down again, we had three different opinions about which bridge we could walk, and one invitation for a night inside.

We accepted Judy Little's offer, eager to avoid another cool night in the tent. I spent the evening playing with her husband's computer, while Sue relaxed in front of the TV set. The sofas we slept on sure beat the hard ground.

Before leaving town the next morning, we stopped to thank the city clerk for her help. "Where did you end up last night?" she asked.

We told her about the librarian. "I'm glad you found a place," she said. "I got worried last night that it would be cold, so I stopped by the park and the church looking for you."

I was proud to be an Illinois native son.

** SOGGY CITY **

* ST. LOUIS, MISSOURI *

October 1 - October 8, 1993
48 miles -- 1 bag
TOTAL, 1765 miles -- 765 bags

No city should be too large for a man to walk out of in a morning.   - Cyril Connolly

———————➤ ◆ ◄———————

From Forest Park in the heart of St. Louis, we rode the new Metro Link to Laclede's Landing (the historic riverfront district), had lunch, and walked back to the park. Wonderful city! Besides the arch, it is adorned with massive buildings lining the streets: colonnaded court buildings, ivy-covered university halls, dominating cathedrals and shrines, and an impressive Union Station, all interspersed with parks to lend an open feeling.

Forest Park is a real credit to the city. It has waterfalls, a free zoo, a spacious Omnimax theatre, and a Science Center which far outshine those in Los Angeles and San Diego.

We could spend a month here!   -journal entry, October 1

FINALLY — THE MIGHTY MISSISSIPPI. To me, it seemed a miracle we'd made it this far.

That didn't mean I could walk on water.

We didn't actually *walk* into St. Louis. No one could tell us if bridges allowed foot traffic, and the attendants at the toll booths didn't look accommodating. Instead, we walked to the water's edge, then drove across the McKinley Bridge.

The region surprised me, not at all the urban sprawl I expected. In southern California, the city extends endlessly into the hinterlands, mile after mile of cookie-cutter condos, convenience stores, and strip malls. Here we found farmland less than ten miles from downtown.

We had reached our goal, entering St. Louis on October 1. Unfortunately, our success did not carry over to the media. None of the local TV stations considered us important enough to cover, and we barely rated a photo and caption in the _St. Louis Post-Dispatch. CBS This Morning_ passed on us, instead asking us to "keep in touch."

After our 'rush' across the Midwest, we took time to explore. Though we normally avoided cities, St. Louis had sounded worth visiting. It did not disappoint us. Our two days as tourists passed far too quickly, and we rushed trying to catch all the sights.

The old federal courthouse, where justices handed down the 1854 Dred Scott decision which hastened the Civil War, looked as if trials could begin tomorrow. From atop the famed arch, we gazed out on the swollen Mississippi River, seeing stop signs on the flooded riverside drive peeking above the water. On the Anheuser Busch factory tour, we saw the machinery that cranks out ten thousand cans and seven thousand bottles of beer every minute of every day. "Scary thought, isn't it?" I told Sue. "All the cans we've picked up this year, they could have filled in three to four minutes."

We lodged ourselves at the city's Youth Hostel, where owner Tom Cochran covered our two-night stay. On our second morning, I glanced at the notices on the bulletin board. One caught my eye. "Did you see this, Sue? The Salvation Army is looking for volunteers to help with flood relief."

An hour later, we walked into the Salvation Army headquarters. Twenty to thirty volunteers milled about, waiting for assignments, while a handful of officers organized the group. "Start with these waivers," one man told us. "Then read the instructions for volunteers. Do you need shots? Sit in this room, and someone will be right with you."

Fill out forms. Get a tetanus booster. Root through boxes of boots and gloves, search for pairs which fit. Grab a smock and a tee shirt. Now we're ready for the dirty work!

Before leaving to slog in the mud, we attended an orientation class. "We're just helpers here," the lecturer emphasized. "The people out there are the bosses. They're dealing with a big loss in the best way they can. They'll tell us how we can help them, and that's what we'll do. It's not our job to decide what needs to be done, even if it's obvious. Don't tell them their new carpeting needs to be torn out, or that the family heirloom dresser is a total loss. They've got to deal with that in their own way, on their own terms, at their own pace. When they're ready to accept it, they'll tell us."

The group split into teams, and each team piled into an RV for the hour-long drive to the day's work site. Our team numbered six. The other helpers were all from St. Louis: a college professor, one of his students, a father and his twenty-year-old son.

We spent four hours shoveling mud out of homes, pulling up waterlogged carpeting, packing china, hauling out mattresses, prying open cabinet doors which had swelled shut, and moving boxes. The damage sobered us: paneling warped and pulling off the walls; water stains four feet high on a china cabinet; mud everywhere.

Sue saw first hand the denial implied in the orientation class. She followed the victim, a short stocky lady in her early 50s, as she told Sue to box up ruined goods. "Save these shoes," she said, pointing to a closet full of muddy footwear, "and this basket of yarn. I'll look through those pictures later — box them too. And these cosmetics."

In no hurry to hit the road, we volunteered for a second day. The work Monday, if possible, was more demanding. We tore up more carpeting, shoveled inches of mud out of a basement, and cleaned walls with a high-pressure hose. When lunch break came (the Salvation Army provided sandwiches, apples, and soda for the helpers and the helped), we chatted with the other volunteers. This time, our teammates were Southerners.

on the flood relief detail

"Eight of us drove up from Montgomery, Alabama, yesterday," said Sandy, a young blonde-haired woman. "We all belong to the same church group. We've come up for five days because we'd thought that, this long after the floods, maybe fewer people volunteered. We heard they still needed workers."

Julio, our team leader, agreed. "It's true," he said, "on the weekdays — like today, with only a dozen people — we don't get many folks. But weekends are entirely different. Saturday we had over three hundred volunteers. They weren't all local, either. We had groups drive down from as far away as Detroit and Milwaukee, to work for one day."

People drive five hundred miles to help for a few hours? Now, THAT'S the sort of story they should put on the six o'clock news.

Today's walk took us through Forest Park (very peaceful walking) and Washington University (like a castle in the midst of the city — how I'd imagine Oxford must look). Chatted with friendly people everywhere we went — very congenial city.   -journal entry, October 5

THANK HEAVENS FOR INDIAN SUMMER.
Walker's weather had returned. Temperatures climbed into the low 80s, a burst of heat after three weeks in the 60s and 70s. Lazy clouds drifted by, fluffy cotton anchoring the blue sky. The season's last butterflies fluttered by as we trod through the city.

The flood forced changes in our route. Our original plans called for taking the shortest path out of the city, heading due west toward the old Spirit of St. Louis airport, the Daniel Boone bridge over the Missouri River, and open country. However, the authorities had closed the area except to residents, diverting us north to St. Charles. We walked through neighborhoods ranging from ritzy to middle-class, by country clubs and past industrial sites.

To stay together, we parked the car, and shuttled back and forth by bus. That plan worked for one day, until another huge blister slowed Sue. When her toe began bleeding, she almost gave up. "I don't know how much more of this I can take," she confided.

Two weeks of sunny weather had done little to dry the area. Near the Missouri River, hundreds of acres still lay under water. For one house, a rise of land had become an island. Elsewhere, in fields where the waters had receded, dead crops gave testimony to the flood.

As we walked along a trail paralleling the river, the drama took on a more personal tone. I passed one house while people dismantled it, throwing the planks onto a fire — a life going up in smoke. Another house, surrounded by sandbags stacked four feet high, sported a seven-foot-high waterline.

Mingled in with the scenes of disaster were the first stirrings of fall's colors. Dark red, yellow, and orange joined the greens of summer, giving hints of colder weather — and the trip's hiatus — soon to come.
-journal entry, October 7

ON THE 7TH, WE finally left the city behind. Houses thinned out, and we hit our first hills since Indiana. Warm temperatures almost felt hot with the sun beating down. Away from the city's grime, I picked up Missouri's first bag of trash. The collection included a can of hoof dressing (for cattle, not salads) and a box of 'edible undies'.

After logging our twelve miles, we faced again our biggest burden. Inquiries at the ball field and the Catholic church earned us rejections, and we couldn't find a Lions club member to ask. We nearly quit before a call to the Baptist church won us permission to camp.

"This is really getting old," Sue sighed. "I'm so damn tired of begging for a place to pitch our tent. I feel like I have to justify myself to total strangers."

"I couldn't agree more. If I could only think of a better way . . ."

With lodging solved once more, we turned our attention to the night's entertainment. Sit at the Burger King and play cards? Please, not again. A movie? We did that yesterday. How about checking the action at the ball fields?

When we pulled in, over a hundred cars already packed the lot. We parked in a corner near left field of one diamond, and joined the locals in the bleachers. While Sue did crosswords, I watched the game in progress, taking my cues on cheering from the people sitting near us.

As the first game neared its end, a power hitter stepped to the plate. Earlier, he'd hit a home run. Now he took a strong swing, fouling the ball on a high loop into the parking lot. It landed with a crunch somewhere in the dark. "Someone ain't gonna be happy," I heard a teenage girl remark as she went with a friend to inspect the damage.

Minutes later the girls returned. "It hit a Honda or something," they remarked to a woman sitting in front of us. "California plates."

Sue dropped her puzzle, shot me a petrified look, and headed for the lot. I followed.

The ball had hit dead center on the windshield. Spiderwebs now decorated the glass, stretching door-to-door. Looking behind the car, I reread the sign we had ignored earlier. Its black letters mocked us, stating, "Park and play at your own risk."

Enough was enough. The next day we fixed the windshield, then took off for Denver — driving.

So much for Litterwalk '93!

** LIVING IN LIMBO **

October 1993 - April 1994

Allons! The road is before us
It is safe - I have tried it - my own feet have tried it well -
be not detained!
Let the paper remain on the desk unwritten, and the book
on the shelf unopened!
Let the tools remain in the workshop! Let the money
remain unearned!
- Walt Whitman, "Song of the Open Road"

———————◆—————

*The first change I noticed was realizing how little we needed.
Coming home to boxes of winter clothes, Hefty™ sweatshirts, and hiking
socks, we quickly donated much of it to charity.*

*Though we decided to come home for the wrong reasons, we still
made the right decision. We ended at a place we could easily return to
next year; we lacked clothing for the predicted cold temperatures; and
Sue couldn't walk with a bleeding toe. The hard part was letting events
control us, not vice versa.*   -journal entry, October 11

WE DROVE STRAIGHT FROM St. Charles to Boulder, through an
autumn night cold outside and in. Few words lit the darkness. Sleep eluded
me, and I passed hours struggling to cope with the sudden end of the trip.
If only I'd . . . What if we'd . . . I should have . . . By the time the rising
sun overtook us, I had accepted it as destined.

We scheduled seven days in Boulder, a treat after the rigors of the road.
Culture shock! Six months of bare-bones travel had given me a new
appreciation of things we used to take for granted: A soft bed every night.
A kitchen where we could cook. Bathrooms when we needed them.
However, I missed the sense of purpose the trek had given me, the feeling
of working toward a goal. The walks I took every day around Boulder
lacked the same spirit.

The week off did little to relax us. On the road, we had control of our life. We chose what route to take, how far to go, and had a good idea what we'd find there. Now we'd traded that in for questions. Would I have a job? What would Sue do? Where would we live? In Colorado, we could do nothing to answer those, only wait and fret. The rising stresses whittled our tempers thin.

What lit the fuse, I can't remember. Some slight, real or imagined, sparked a spat on our fifth morning in Boulder. That afternoon we traded barbs again. Five o'clock rolled around, and we were barely on speaking terms — but we had a dinner date with Sue's aunt and uncle, an hour's drive away.

In the tight confines of the car, heated words flowed anew. Insults and angry charges replaced conversation. Within ten minutes, we reached new heights of bitterness. "Why don't you shut up," I snarled. "You're so full of crap."

"Oh, bullshit!" she shot back, tromping on the gas pedal as the traffic light turned green. "You're a lazy slob who never lifts a finger to help anyone. You just refuse to admit it, while you go right on using people."

"At least I don't walk in and try to run everyone's life. You should take responsibility for THAT once in a while. That'd be a novelty." I clamped my eyes shut, trying to keep my anger in rein.

"You're really useless, you know that?" Her voice rose as she slowed for another red light. "I've got to wonder whether it's worth staying married to you. Right about now, I doubt it."

"Fine. I may just give you that chance." I got out of the car, slamming the door convincingly behind me. Without looking back, I headed home, too numb to notice the traffic passing by.

The steam had left my stride by the time I got home, and a cold dread filled me. Had we pushed our marriage too hard for too long? We'd had our share of fights before, but never had they grown so bitter — and so frequent. How high a cost would this trip exact?

Again, anger had gotten in the way, blinding us to what really mattered: each other. Why did it take fights to remind us of our special bond? For three-and-a-half years we'd grown together, gaining strength from each other, merging our lives. My thoughts turned back to the quirk of fate that had thrown us together . . .

. . . on that Movie Night sponsored by the Sierra Club singles group early in 1990. Twenty-three men had come looking for love or hoping for luck. With only five women present, neither seemed likely.

Before the shows, we gathered for dinner at the mall's fast food court. With my plate of Cajun food, I grabbed a seat next to one of those few women. Lisa, a bubbly blonde with a button nose, attracted me immediately, and we chatted while eating. When she mentioned French films, I made my move. "If you liked 'Jean de Florette,' have you seen the second part, 'Manon of the Spring'?" She shook her head. "Why don't you come over to watch it on VCR next week?"

She jotted her phone number on a scrap of paper, then passed it to the woman sitting on her other side. "Glen wants to have us over for a French film," Lisa stated to this woman she had met only minutes before. "Write your number under mine." With the second phone number in place, Lisa handed me the paper.

I had high hopes for Lisa. (For bachelors in southern California, unceasing optimism was a job requirement.) Three nights of hearing, "This is Lisa's answering machine. I'm not home, but if you leave your number . . ." dimmed those hopes. Of course, I did have that other number. It belonged to one Susan Armstead.

We hit it off over the phone. Her love of the outdoors surfaced at once, combined with a love of travel. Of course, she had grown up 'on the move:' in her childhood she called six states from Connecticut to Texas 'home.' "No, I'm not an army brat. It's the family life for a traveling soap salesman."

When suggesting a bike ride for our first date didn't scare her off, I knew great things would follow. Hikes and more bike rides highlighted our mating dance, a perverse courtship ritual involving leather boots and silly-looking helmets. Within the month I had sworn off other women.

Before long, I tested her adventure quotient. "Let's spend the weekend canoeing the Colorado River," I proposed in late March. That led to a Memorial Day hike seventeen miles into Arizona's Havasu Canyon. To kick off the summer, I introduced her to Rocky Mountain National Park.

She proved a perfect foil for me, giving as good as she got. When she returned from a business trip, I met her at the airport in mime makeup, toting a sign saying, "Help me welcome Susan home!" (Several strangers did.) For my Feb. 29 unbirthday the next week, she showed up at my door wearing a trenchcoat and clutching a note stating that Boppity from the planet Leap had taken over her body.

Seven months after meeting, we ran across Lisa at another Movie

Night. We both thanked her profusely . . .

   . . . *and I still thank her,* I thought. For the good years we'd had, and those still to come. We *would* get through this.

I STAYED UP LATE that night, waiting for Sue's safe return. Wordlessly we went to bed. Neither of us mentioned the angry words we'd spoken, then or later. Had the outburst relieved the tension, or did it wake us up to our real priorities? Whichever, we made an extra effort to get along. As we focused our energies on California, our moods improved.

Thank heavens.

Our first week in Orange County may have finished us otherwise. We spent seven nights in a friend's camper, cramped conditions sure to reignite tempers. However, good news on the job front eased our stress. Sue quickly found contracting work, and my job at Rockwell waited. "We'll need to reactivate your clearance," my boss said. "It shouldn't take more than two weeks."

Eager for a real home, we scoured the area for an apartment. When we found one within walking distance (for me that meant five miles) of work, we signed a six-month lease. Within two days Sue had it ready for company. Ron and Joann Schrantz were our first guests, kicking off a parade of friends. "We're glad you're back," said Ron, "and working like the rest of us, not out enjoying yourselves."

Eight months before, we'd had a normal life — now we hardly knew what that meant. We relished seeing friends again, catching up on their lives, spending time with them. However, Lotus Land no longer felt like home. After half a year walking through the heart of the country — "the real world," we insisted — southern California struck us more like Mars. Vignettes of the urban life reminded us of what we hadn't missed: Eight people in In'N'Out Burger talking on cellular phones while eating (or ordering) lunch. The blonde-haired Adonis rollerblading down the beach trail, pushing a stroller with his collie in it. The beggar on the street corner with a sign reading, "I'll take your wife please!" And who could forget the brown cloud, the ever-present smog which shrouded the surrounding hills and made the air taste bitter.

Even off the road, the walk dominated my life. The *L.A. Times* ran a follow-up story our first week back. Two Sierra Club chapters invited me to speak, asking to see my slides. People everywhere asked about the trip, curious about this great land — or about people who'd try to walk across it. "What is inside you," asked our auto mechanic Zack, "that would drive you to do that?"

What indeed? Was it the enjoyment of doing something we believed in? A stubborn pride which refused to let the road beat us? The satisfaction of seeing a difficult job to completion?

That is, if we managed to finish. Worries we'd tried to dismiss still lingered. The soles of my feet ached daily, never getting better — would they survive another summer of pounding? Sue wanted to try a bike, but had never ridden one loaded with panniers — could she handle it? We'd pushed our marriage to its breaking point — would it survive a second summer? Could we afford to return?

The finances loomed as our largest problem. October segued into November, and November into December, and I still waited to return to work. In the top-secret world, the customer had the final say on clearances, and they balked at renewing mine. Who knows what Commie spies lurked on those back roads!

Sue's salary covered our bills, but left little for savings. One week after leasing the apartment, we also lost the tenants in our condo, saddling us with a mortgage. Thanksgiving came and went with no renters and no job, and our hopes of finishing grew dim.

I spent the days half-heartedly looking for work amidst the ruins of California's economy, or listlessly walking to keep in shape. Even showing slides to our friends failed to excite me . . .

I can't believe how the time has flown — five months down, and only one more to go. As our departure date nears, that calm again overtakes me on my lunchtime walks, tempting me to stay outside and forego work.

Still, the exhilaration of last year is missing. Then, the unknown loomed ahead, a life's dream about to unfold. Now, we know we face a lot of boredom and a lot of hard work. Last year we also looked forward to visiting friends and family, and seeing the beautiful Maine coastline. This year our contacts are limited, and our 'scenery' starts with 500-600 miles of plains.   -journal entry, March 15

". . . AND GLEN SWEARS WE can afford to go out again," Sue said to Joann Schrantz as they dodged a skateboarder. The Huntington Beach promenade was, as usual, filled with skateboarders, bicyclists, and surfers on this Saturday morning. "I don't see how," she continued, "since Rockwell didn't take him back until a couple days before Christmas."

"It's only because of your job," I said over my shoulder without breaking stride. "The extra money adds up. That, and refinancing the condo." The lower interest rate meant we could clear almost $200 a month renting it — very different from 1993, when we lost money.

"I'll bet you were glad to finally get tenants in there," Ron said.

"Especially on a one-year lease. Now we don't have to worry about it until next December. We'll be done by then."

"You still think you can finish this year?" he asked. "Didn't you stop short of halfway?"

I nodded. "We still hope to finish in a National Park, but we've ruled out Olympic. If we shoot for Redwood, in California, we can save 150 miles. I know, that still leaves twenty-four to twenty-five hundred miles."

"And we're not doing this a third year," Sue added. "Two years of having my possessions in storage is enough. I'm so used to moving, I could work for Bekins."

The four of us continued down the path, talking about what lay ahead as Sue and I tackled the prairies and the Rockies. My backpack set us apart from the bicyclists and joggers passing by. Lightly loaded as I worked to get back into road shape, it provoked stares. The bright yellow 'Don't Litter' banner tied to the pack drew the most attention, and people gave us 'thumbs up'.

On the bluff west of the pier, we took a break before heading back. Below us, waves crashed on the shore, and surfers crashed in the waves. I dropped my pack on the grass and stretched my muscles.

Ron stepped over to look at it. "You sure can't tell this thing has had six months of use."

"All our equipment held up well," I agreed. "Of course, the boots don't have much tread left, as expected. Merrell sent me another pair for this summer. Pikes Peak also sent us new litter sticks."

"And we still have oodles of Hefty™ coupons," Sue added. "They've really saved us money."

"How about your other gear?" Joann asked.

"We're getting a lighter tent from Garuda at half-price," Sue said.

"Ours is still in great shape, but it's so heavy, and we don't need anything that large." She poked me playfully. "*He* doesn't have to carry it. It'll be on my bike, and I'm counting every ounce."

Her bike, I thought, *the one she still hasn't ridden with panniers. I hope we don't regret this . . .*

I took a long break this morning, standing on the third-floor landing and gazing at the world below. Outside, the business of life carried on silently: traffic whizzed by on its way to important events; gardeners rearranged nature's castoffs with leaf blowers; workers took their cigarette breaks. Inside, the only sound was the hum of the air conditioner.

An old friend came up. "Bet it's hard to be inside, isn't it?" he asked.

As we chatted, he asked if I thought my litter mission had made an impact. Another co-worker heard the question and responded, "He sure has. He's inspired me to clean up a local park every month."

-journal entry, March 21

"SO I BET YOUR feet hurt very bad. If not, you have some heavy duty feet, and I mean heavy duty."

Thus wrote Roger, from the fifth-grade class at Iuka Elementary. We got a package of letters from them in November, chatty notes thanking us for stopping at their school. "We have been snowed on — dum-da-da-dum — twice! (Keep your fingers and toes crossed we don't freeze to death!)" penned Ashley. Kayla wrote, "Me and my brother pick up cans along the road too. We can't stand trash either." Jimmy, guessing we wrote many letters, taped a present to his note: "If you run out of pencils, I'll give you one. P.S. I sharpened it for you."

These letters, and others from the new friends we'd made, kept us focused on the walk. The Greiners in Maine wrote that they missed our help mapling. The Gateses updated us on young Mitchell's condition. Hugh and Louise Reynolds entertained us with more tales of Chopper the Wonder Dog.

As April approached, we took every opportunity to work out. Every weekend we hiked, and the weight on my back grew. I bicycled to work most mornings, and Thursday afternoons I walked the five miles home.

The Thursday walks brought back the excitement of the road. The first time I set out for home, I dreaded walking the two miles through the Seal Beach Naval Weapons Reserve. This stretch took me down a four-lane highway fenced in by chain link and barbed wire. While I walked along the shoulder, warily eyeing the weapons bunkers beyond the fence, I heard a car pull up alongside me. "Do you need a ride?" asked the well-dressed businessman inside.

"Thanks, but I'll walk." *It's a fluke*, I thought. *No one else would stop for a person who wasn't even thumbing.* Then I saw a woman heading the other way pull into the center lane.

"Do you need a ride? I can turn around."

More cases in the following weeks, always along the same stretch, reminded me of the heart of the road. Soon we'd live it again.

In early April, I gave my final farewell to Rockwell. A declining project budget ruled out another leave. Instead, I volunteered for an upcoming layoff, a move which gave me severance pay and a year of paid health insurance. We'd worry about jobs after the trek.

As in 1993, departure week caught us scrambling. With three days left we finally overhauled Sue's bike, readying it for the road. We loaded the panniers and sent her on a spin around the block. She handled it with little difficulty, a fine trial run for a cross-country epic.

Who needs more practice than that?

As Joann Schrantz observed, "You two don't seem as enthusiastic as last year."

So true. Last winter we were filled with anticipation of the Great Unknown, like a child's Christmas Eve frenzy to get through the night and see what Santa left. We lived the trip every day, arranging sponsors, basking in publicity, second-guessing problems we might face.   This year the novelty has worn off. We had much less organizing to do, letting us forget about the road. Our giddy anticipation has grown into a solid desire to meet America at its roots.

Now again we're heading to Colorado, our lives on hold for the duration . . .   -journal entry, April 17

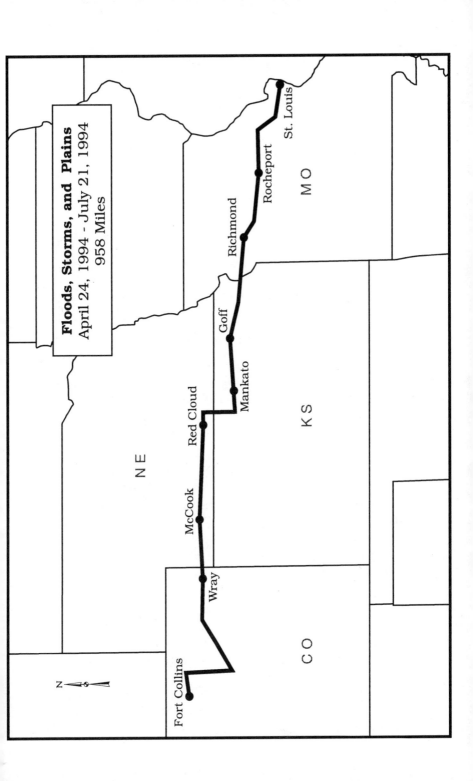

Floods, Storms, and Plains
April 24, 1994 - July 21, 1994
958 Miles

N

Fort Collins

CO

Wray

McCook

Red Cloud

Mankato

Goff

Richmond

Rocheport

St. Louis

NE

KS

MO

** AND THE STORMS RAGE ON **

* MISSOURI *

April 24 - May 7, 1994
146 miles -- 15 bags
TOTAL, 1911 miles -- 780 bags

They made up their minds that they would see
and learn about geography
And with bags on back and sticks in hand
They started their tramp across the land
- from "The Roosevelt Bears,"
quoted in "Foot By Foot" by Francis Line

"Did you see that? Two hawks floating above the valley, playing in the breezes!" Sue waited for me at the turnout, excited about seeing the first wildlife of half two.   -journal entry, April 25

AHHH, TO BE BACK on the road. No more packing boxes, no more letters to Highway Departments, no more twenty-hour bus rides. Ahead of us stretched six months of freedom and fresh air, of plains, mountains, and deserts.

I watched the bus pull away from St. Charles, taking my weariness with it. The tingling in my legs, a product of the cramped overnight ride, quickly faded as I stretched them. The Missouri sun blazed overhead, warming the spring day.

We unboxed the bike and started assembling it. One problem quickly surfaced — the 'thumbnail,' a tiny piece that secured the handlebars, had disappeared. Luckily a bike store one-half mile away was open on Sundays. They had the part, and we added a kickstand, and bungee cords to strap the tent to the panniers.

After a quick lunch, we took a taxi to Weldon Springs, site of last fall's disaster. Jane Giles, secretary of the Baptist Church, had again offered the church grounds for camping. She drove up as Sue made practice circuits of the parking lot, getting used to the loaded bike.

"Welcome back to Missouri!" she greeted us, a broad smile lighting her face. "You all ready to hit the road?"

"We sure hope so," I replied. "Tomorrow will tell!"

"Let me unlock the church, so you can use the restrooms. We have a service here tonight, and we'd love to have you come. Oh — if you need any help before you start tomorrow, let me know."

We appreciated her offer later, when I discovered my flashlight bulb had burned out. Like the bungees, I should have caught it before leaving Colorado. Jane ran us to WalMart the next morning, where we also bought a pad for the bike seat. *What else did we forget,* I wondered.

"Good luck!" Jane said as Sue mounted the bike and I shouldered the

pack. "Call if you have problems!" With that, we were off. Cool breezes and a smattering of clouds kept high temperatures at bay as we climbed the rolling hills. Sue rode slowly ahead as I bagged trash, or walked the bike beside me. My senses worked overtime, drinking in everything around me.

It took little time for the real world to intrude. As Sue crested her second hill, heavy traffic forced her to the shoulder. She put her foot down to stop, but

Let's get this show on the road!

couldn't control the weighted bike and toppled. By the time I reached her, she sat massaging her knee. "I think I pulled a ligament," she said, shaking her head.

"Oh, no. How bad does it hurt?"

"Not *that* much. Of course, it'll probably swell like a basketball tonight."

NOT a promising start. At least we had finished most of the day's climbing, and Defiance lay a downhill run away. Sue took it easy, coasting much of the way.

As we rolled down State Highway 94, the land presented contrasts. Close by, the trees heralded the coming of spring, with barren branches hiding under budding cloaks of green. Vistas overlooking the Missouri River, however, revealed a grim scene of flooded fields and waterlogged woods. We'd never dreamed that, nine months after last summer's floods, the land would still suffer.

At the bottom of the hill, we hopped on the Katy Trail. This well-graded dirt-and-gravel path shadowed the highway, giving us a welcome break from the cars racing by. We hurried the last miles into town, uneasily watching the clouds gather.

Defiance consisted of a sprinkling of houses, a pair of shops, and a tavern at the west end. We chose the Defiance Trading Post to shop for a juice and postcards. The tinkling bell on the door signaled 'customers', and the owner hurried from the back room. When she saw my pack, she looked surprised. "More backpackers?" she asked. "Are you with that other pair?"

I glanced at Sue, who looked as confused as I. "What other pair?"

"Another couple with packs, a guy and a girl, came through — oh, two weeks ago. How far are you traveling?"

"All the way across the country," Sue said.

"That's what they said, too."

"That's incredible. And they chose the same route as us!"

I shook my head, amazed at the coincidence. "They must be following the Katy Trail too."

The Katy had interested me when we first planned the trip. Formerly the route of the Missouri-Kansas-Texas — MKT, shortened to KT — Railroad, the state converted it to a linear park when the railroad abandoned the line. It now stretched over two hundred miles, with nearly half open to public use.

We talked with the woman — she introduced herself as Yvonne — for several minutes as we looked through postcards. While we made our purchase, I asked about camping.

She hesitated, then said, "I wouldn't normally mention this, but you're a special case. See the barn on the postcard you just bought? It's right on the trail two miles from here. The owner plans to open a campground there next year. The barns are vacant. You could hole up there."

We thanked her and headed to the tavern for an early dinner. Over burgers we watched a light sprinkle start and then stop. However, the skies threatened worse weather, so we didn't linger. We found the barn as Yvonne had described it, in bad need of red paint, but solid and dry. Dried mud caked the floors, and flood waters had left a waterline five feet above the ground.

The loft offered the cleanest accommodations, so we climbed the stairs and spread our bags on the wood floor. We took a good look at Sue's knee — no swelling! "It doesn't really hurt. At least, no more than I'd expect after riding twelve miles."

As the darkness crept in the wind picked up, and the whole barn creaked. Soon the rain played a lively tune on the tin roof. We cuddled together, happy to be dry and warm. Our first night spent in a barn — what a wonderful start to the year's trek!

"FORGET IT! I CAN'T do this, I'm going home."

Sue cursed as she pushed the bike up the steep hill. Flood damage to the Katy Trail, which stays flat as it follows the river, had forced us back onto MO 94. Leaving the bottomlands, it climbed the long hill on the way to Augusta. Pedaling had soon become impossible; now she struggled to keep the bike rolling.

I came up behind her and helped push. She quickly waved me off, saying, "Get away from me! You've got your own pack! I'll handle the bike!"

Why are uphill miles so much longer than those downhill? We fought for every yard, and finally bested the hill. I dropped my pack and grabbed my water bottle. Sue reached the crest moments later, parking the bike and sitting several yards away.

After a long drink of water, she apologized for snapping at me. "No matter how fit I get, I'll never be able to ride hills that steep. But I *will* get up them!" She smiled. "I'll threaten to quit at least a hundred times before this trip is over. You'd better get used to it!"

I made a mental note. *One down, ninety-nine to go!*

We caught our breath before heading downhill to Augusta. From there we again left the road for six quiet miles along the Katy. By late afternoon we reached Dutzow, and stopped at the Dutzow Deli for cold drinks. Three workers drank coffee at the next table, so I asked them about churches or parks in town.

"No park," replied one. "There is a church. If you take this main road east two miles, on top of the hill . . ."

I shook my head. "Too far. I've already walked thirteen miles today, and that's backtracking. There's no other public place?"

All three shrugged and returned to their conversation. A few minutes later one of them turned back to us. "You might check with Chick. He owns the house out back, and he'd probably let you camp in the yard." He pointed across the street, where an ancient-looking man sat on the front porch of a small home.

We finished our lemonades and went to meet Chick. Though his body looked frail, his sharp eyes followed us as we approached. We explained our plight, and he broke into a smile. "Of course you can. No one will bother you there."

"Except the storm clouds." I glanced up to see dark thunderheads gathering forces. "Haven't they had enough rain here?"

Chick nodded. "Too much. Last year's floods were the worst I've ever seen, and I've been here since 1917. Not that it doesn't flood here every few years — it does. Still, last year's were the worst."

With little prodding, he told us about life in the bygone years. "I can remember the KT rolling through twice a day in the '20s and '30s. It'd come at five a.m., the post express. They'd throw out the bag of local mail and grab the outgoing mail bag from a hook without slowing."

For half a century his barbershop had kept the town groomed. "Cut a lot of heads of hair in fifty-two years, even a few famous ones. George Bush, for instance. He worked with my brother in the State Department, and I gave him a trim years before he became President."

We finally tore ourselves away, anxious to pitch the tent before the imminent deluge. By the time we finished, Chick had crossed the road with his walker, camera in hand, to get a picture of the town's celebrities *du jour*. We snapped one of him, too, and asked where we could send a copy.

"Just send it to Grandpa Berg, Dutzow, and I'll get it."

That night our new tent received its official christening, getting battered by a Missouri storm. Lightning lit the sky in all directions. Rain pelted down and eased up, then pelted down again. The wind gusted, shaking the tent and testing the stakes. Through it all, we stayed dry.

The next morning we started late, held up by a wagon train. "It's the Boys and Girls Town of Missouri Wagon Train," Chick told us as the string of Conestogas entered town. "They come through every spring. It's a special trip for the kids. They take nine days to travel from St. James to St. Louis, camping along the way."

The procession stretched for a half mile along the highway. Behind the thirteen covered wagons, over one hundred youths followed on horseback. One leader gave me the stats: 132 kids aged nine to sixteen, eighty adults, two hundred horses and mules.

I'm glad we weren't on dung patrol!

"Grandpa" Chick Berg, Dutzow

As we ate dinner at Our Place in Treloar, we kept hearing metallic "clangs" coming from a back room, out of sight. The noises sounded like a carnival strongman contest, with revelers trying to ring the bell.

Curiosity finally got the better of us, and we peeked into the back room to discover — WASHERS! Not the Laundromat kind, but a game akin to indoor horseshoes. The equipment consists of two metal coffee cans, centered in wooden boxes placed twenty feet apart. Teams of two people, one at each box, compete by tossing heavy metal washers toward the opposite target. They score one point for each disc landing in the box, two in the can, and play to twenty-one. One player explained the game to us, his tee shirt (with a '1984-1994 Washer Leagues' logo) identifying him as a pro.   -journal entry, April 27

How nice of Mother Nature, lulling us into complacency with three days of good weather. We saw her other side last night, with driving rain till morning, lightning bright enough to read by, and thunder which rolled like dams bursting. The storm left pools in the tent, and we woke up surrounded by standing water.   -journal entry, April 28

THE NIGHT PASSED SLOWLY as I tossed and turned, fretting about the rain. I knew the ground was saturated, and levees breached upstream in last year's flooding had not yet been plugged. Treloar, though a country mile from the banks of the Muddy Missouri, still lay in the bottomlands. Every hour, I stuck my hand outside the tent, checking for rising waters. Still safe.

While the thunder and lightning eased with the dawn, the rain kept falling. We ducked inside Our Place to dry out over breakfast, and watch the soggy world through rain-smeared windows. Leroy White, the stout man working the counter, kept Sue primed with coffee. As he filled her cup for the third time, he asked, "You two passing through? I saw you here last night."

I recounted our saga. "We hoped to reach Hermann today, but the weather's not cooperating."

"It's supposed to keep raining, too." A look of concern stole across his face. "The way it's going, this area could flood again. I'd recommend you grab a ride into town. You don't want to get stuck out there."

I looked to Sue, who nodded. Turning back to Leroy, I said, "I guess you're right. Do you know anyone who's heading into town today?"

"You'd need a pickup for the bike, wouldn't you? Hold on a sec." He retreated to the kitchen to confer with his wife. In a moment, he returned.

"If you can wait an hour, I'll drive you."

On the twenty-mile ride to Hermann, I asked Leroy about the Katy Trail. "A lot of it's still closed. When is the state supposed to open the rest?"

"They'd planned on last summer, but the floods set them back. That, and there's still a lot of opposition to it in some towns."

"Why?" Sue asked. "The towns with the trail had businesses — cafes, bike shops. The other towns, like Treloar, seem to barely hang on."

He nodded. "Trouble is, the trail cuts through private property. Folks resent the state grabbing what they consider their land. Also, some hikers and bikers leave the trail and trespass, maybe harass the livestock or leave gates open." Chuckling, he continued, "I knew one farmer who found people from South St. Louis picnicking on his land. He introduced himself and asked their names. When he asked for their addresses, they asked why he wanted to know. 'Well, I'm going to St. Louis next week, and need a place for a picnic. I'm sure your lawn would be perfect.'"

By the time we reached Hermann, the sun had broken through the clouds. We checked into a motel, rolled out our tent and sleeping bags to dry, and set off to explore the town. This region, with its lush forests and rolling hills reminiscent of the Rhineland, had attracted German settlers in the mid-1800s. The German influence was easily seen, with soaring cathedral spires and a Gothic train station. Even better, the restaurants dished up hearty German food: spætzle, wurst, schnitzel, and strudel to die for. A plate of that gave us the energy to tramp up and down the town's hills.

The next day dawned dry, with no rain forecast. Leaving our heavy gear at the motel, we crossed the Hermann bridge to Loutre and route 94, and stuck our thumbs out. *Someone has to head east*, I reasoned. *Then we can walk the miles we skipped yesterday.*

However, Treloar and points east attracted little traffic. The few cars which passed didn't stop, and we lost three hours waiting for a ride to Treloar. We stayed only long enough to thank Leroy again, and pay him for the coffee we'd forgotten to cover. The surprise on his face almost made the trip back worth it.

Almost, but not quite. "What a pain, hitching a ride," I said as we strode out of town. "It cost us half a day."

"You're right. We can't keep doing that." Sue matched my pace down the nearly deserted road. "We're supposed to head forward, not backtrack."

"Maybe we wimped out yesterday. Our first rainstorm, and we run and hide." I lapsed into silence as I mulled that over. "Maybe," I concluded, "we should make a vow. No more backtracking. And no more skipping stretches, except for real emergencies."

With that rule adopted, we followed MO 94 inland. Climbing the lush green hills, we found the sparse west bound traffic much friendlier. Within minutes a motorist offered us a lift, but we had hardly begun. After we'd covered fifteen miles and Sue's feet cried 'Uncle,' our extended thumbs brought the next auto — a pickup — to a stop. We climbed in the bed and rode to Loutre, our hair blowing in the breeze. For the two miles from Loutre into Hermann, our thumbs went out, and the fourth car by pulled over. The elderly driver quipped, "I stopped because you had a nice smile. You can concentrate on your hairdo another time."

The sheriff waved me over in the Loutre lot, asking me, "Did you just walk over the bridge from Hermann?"

"Yes, sir. We're walking across the country." Looking up at the clouds, I added, "Picking up litter when it's not so blasted wet."

He made to leave. "I guess we're looking for someone else."

                                                        -journal entry, April 30

A SECOND DAY WITH no rain forecast raised our spirits. Maybe Mizzou would start drying out! However, those hopes dried up as I left the sheriff's car and eyed a barricade where Route 94 continued west: 'Road Closed.' "Watch my pack," I told Sue. "I'll bike ahead and check it out."

A hundred yards from the barrier, water stopped me. Eight inches deep, it flowed over the road. I could see dry pavement beyond the washed-out segment, but knew fifteen miles of bottomland separated us from the next hills. Who knew how high the flood waters ran further ahead?

My grim expression told Sue the bad news. "Looks like it's a third night in Hermann." We again crossed the bridge and reclaimed our motel room. After shucking our loads, we took off for the Stone Hill Winery, Hermann's one tourist attraction we'd yet to visit.

The rising water had scared off out-of-town tourists, so we got a private tour of the winery. "In 1900, Stone Hill was the third largest winery in the world," our guide said, "second in the U.S. behind an Ohio vintner. They produced 1.25 million bottles annually before prohibition."

She led us underground, past the modern winery equipment, into a large cellar. On either side, arches reminded me of Roman catacombs. "These are the largest arched underground cellars in North America," she explained. "When prohibition came, the feds made sure all the casks and presses were disassembled. With alcohol banned, they used the cellars to grow mushrooms."

She told us all about wine making, showing us new stainless steel vats. "Our production is back up to one hundred thousand bottles a year. Not as large as before, but we're growing. We've won more awards than almost any other winery in the country." She led us back to the main shop, and handed us a wine list. "Now for everyone's favorite part of the tour — the wine sampling!"

As we sipped some house favorites, she told us about special events. "It's too bad you didn't come through in two weeks. That's when we hold our grape stomping contest. Contestants get two minutes to stomp. They get points for how much juice they make, and for their stomping style. Don't worry," she added, "you're not tasting *that* wine."

The bottomland remained flooded. The scene as we crossed the bridge awed me — land which yesterday was only muddy now lay hidden under a shallow lake. Lines of utility poles marched into the watery distance, disappearing in a swamp of trees. Water coursed over MO94, forming small waterfalls as it dropped off the road's shoulders. The Loutre River ran smoothly and strongly through several breeches in the levee. Farm houses and barns stood isolated, floating on the glassy surface. Overhead, ridges of cumulus clouds stretched into the distance.
                                                           -journal entry, May 1

THE GOLDEN RULE OF Cross-Country Walking: 'go with the flow.' Here, that meant going away from the flowing flood waters.

I glared at the water lapping against the barricades. "I don't think Highway 94 will open for days. Guess it's time to rethink our route." Unfolding the Missouri map, I checked for a road out of the bottomland. "If we head north on State 19, we'll reach I-70, and can parallel that into Columbia."

The road north gained elevation gradually, dishing up gentle hills mixed in with large dollops of flat terrain. Around us white flowers graced dogwood trees, crystal ponds reflected ranch houses and emerald fields, and forests alternately hugged and shunned the curving road. Traffic was light for a sunny Sunday.

In Bigspring, a village too small for a post office, my stomach demanded lunch. In Bigspring, that meant the Dusty Rose Cafe. Housed in a large square gray building, it looked like the best — or worst — of food, the type of place truckers told you to hit — or to avoid.

Inside, we noticed concrete floors, a handful of tables near the front window, and a grill and sink near the back. Shelves lined a far corner, filled with aged canned goods and abandoned displays. An elderly couple sat at one table, and a young woman stood talking to them. When we walked in, she greeted us cheerfully. "Hi, I'm Dusty Rose. Are you two hungry?"

I nodded. "What do you have for lunch?"

"How about a hamburger or cheeseburger? We should have potato salad, too, and I think there's soup left."

"What kind of soup?" Sue asked.

"Let me check." She strode to the back and ducked behind the grill. "Looks like chicken vegetable or something."

So Dusty Rose's would never make the Michelin Guide. For two hungry walkers, it was an oasis. My burger came thick and juicy, propped on a homemade bun. Pineapple upside-down cake topped off lunch, a hearty slice jammed with fruit. Dusty Rose's got four stars in our Road Food Review!

The next day we walked the service road next to I-70, waving at the passing trucks. We took turns waving, seeing who could get the most truckers to honk. "We should have brought the CB," lamented Sue. "Can you imagine the stories bouncing around the airways right now?"

Too soon the road dipped away from the freeway. As the midmorning sun broke through the curtain of clouds, we plopped ourselves down for a juice break next to a pasture. We sat there, enjoying the juice and idly chatting with the curious cows, when a pickup truck pulled up. A woman wearing jeans and a western blouse popped out, nodding at us from under a wide-brimmed hat as she headed to the fence.

"Howdy," I called. "We're just taking a quick break, and will be moving on in a moment." This seemed to satisfy her, and after scanning the cows in the pasture, she climbed back into the truck. Instead of leaving, she honked the horn.

"That attracts the cows," she explained. In the pasture, the herd left the barn and ambled toward the gate. She stood on the truck's bumper and counted the cows, then shook her head. "I have thirty-five cows, but I only count thirty-three. How many do you see?" I counted, and got the same answer.

Finally she spotted a Brahma on the wrong side of the fence, and went to retrieve it. By the time she returned, we had finished our break. "Thanks for your help," she said. "By the way, my name's Rita Rees." We exchanged names before parting.

Old U.S. 40 gave us tranquil walking, free from the traffic barreling down the interstate. Old farms and barns instilled a mood of times long past. The mood followed us into Williamsburg, where we wandered into Crane's General Store. A relic from days when the town bustled (the sign stated, 'founded 1920'), the founder's sons still ran it.

Walking into the dimly-lit store took us back to those days, when general stores kept towns supplied with all the basics of life. Staples crowded the narrow aisles and wooden floors. Brakemen's lanterns hung from the ceiling. Along one wall, porcelain dolls from three inches to two feet tall lined a shelf. Doll carriages, arrowheads and sleigh bells shared display space. An old Coke machine sat against one wall, surrounded by Tiffany lamps.

The Cranes had set one corner of the store aside for clothing — jeans, shirts, hats, boots. A neighboring aisle featured stuffed rodent 'statues,' set in rock band or family poses. Across the store I noticed several pieces of antique machinery and farm tools, a potato cutter catching my eye. In the center of the store, a cast iron pot-bellied stove radiated heat, taking the nip off the cool evening. A few customers sat around it, warming their hands.

WalMart it wasn't!

We were sitting on the side of old U.S. 40, having a biscuit break, when who should drive up but Rita Rees. This time she stopped and visited, asking about our trip.   -journal entry, May 3

As we neared the day's goal, the first church west of Fulton, an ambulance raced by. A minute later, three police cars followed, sirens howling. Once we crested the hill, the church entered our view. There sat all the official vehicles, clustered around a pickup truck in the parking lot.

"When I returned from lunch," the church caretaker told us, "I recognized the truck, but I thought the driver was sleeping. After a couple hours, I checked to see if he was okay. The guy had shot himself."
                                                              -journal entry, May 4

THE SUICIDE TOOK THE shine off a fine day. We cooked dinner on the church steps, talking in hushed tones. Camping there that night no longer seemed a good idea. After eating we again loaded up, putting a mile between us and the tragedy.

Otherwise, the walk had settled into a comfortable pattern. Temperatures climbed into the 70s, and the land dried under sunny skies. Sue had grown used to the bike, chugging up the few hills the terrain threw at us. For me, leaving the bottomland had finally given me litter to bag. No longer was everything hidden under layers of mud and sand.

On old U.S. 40 I found the new year's first two pairs of BVDs, one dirty, one clean. A lint trap was nestled next to a highway worker's orange vest, liberated from its dryer. A tee shirt lay sodden on top of one hill; the logo showed two condoms lying in bed, one reading a newspaper, the other remarking, "Boy, do I feel used!" I glanced at a *Greatest Hits of 1956* cassette before bagging it, and one song struck a chord: Clarence 'Frogman' Henry's "Ain't Got a Home."

We averaged thirteen miles a day, rarely going over fifteen. The day after the suicide, though, we set our sites on Columbia, anxious for a motel after five days with no shower. The temperature broke 80° for the first time, and the miles dragged. Twelve. Fifteen. Seventeen to reach the city limits. Thoughts of a long soak in a hot tub drove us forward that eighteenth mile.

We lolled in the room the next morning, waiting for the rain to abate. Once we left, we strolled through Columbia. The city charmed us: downtown was clean, without empty storefronts and graffiti-tagged walls. Beautiful brick houses anchored quiet residential streets, and trees provided a leafy canopy. Friendly natives waved, and store clerks showed real service.

We left town on the service road paralleling I-70. At the top of the first rise, Sue spotted two five-pound bass, resting on the wet grass collecting maggots. "Now where did they come from?!" she asked. "There's no lake here, and we're miles from the river. It hasn't been raining THAT much!"

NOTES FROM SUE'S JOURNAL:
Spent afternoon lazing and eyeing cows. <u>Gorgeous</u> sunset over hills!
That's why we're here.   *- May 3*
Love being out with cows, birds, pastures, etc. Not even thinking of
California or work.   *- May 5*
Can't keep track of days. Oh, well, doesn't matter — we're having fun.
         - May 6

PERHAPS THIS WASN'T THE night to camp next to a cemetery.

The storm began in earnest when we bedded down. Thunder provided percussion for the symphony the rain played on our tent. Lightning regularly lit the forest of gravestones surrounding us. Wind howled all around, the voice of the storm — or were they voices of the spirits we'd disturbed?

We slept little that night.

The next day we finished flanking the interstate with a stroll along Old Rocheport Road. The country lane lay separated from the highway by only a thick line of forest. We welcomed the change from the blacktop, accompanied by gurgling brooks and the scent of rain-scrubbed air. Only the constant roar of unseen trucks reminded us where we were.

As we approached the Missouri River, valleys cut deeply into the hills. We found ourselves on a ridge, with views miles to the west. The world was so GREEN! Green fields, green hills, green valleys. Forests covered the hills, interrupted by only a road and an occasional mansion.

We descended from the ridge into Rocheport. *The town of 2500 had a one-block-long downtown consisting of a post office in the old bank building, a craft store, an antique dealer, and a store with an old 'Drug Store/Coca-Cola' sign above. They were having their Second Annual Chocolate Festival (leave it to Sue to find a town celebrating chocolate!), complete with live Dixieland jazz band and square dancing. The town cried out for pictures, with historic churches and well-kept B&Bs (including one in the old school house).*
         -journal entry, May 7

A policeman had parked on the main street, so we asked him about the town. He urged us to check out the Chocolate Festival. "Last year's celebration went nowhere. The floods scared everyone away. They're hoping to make up for it this year."

"Where can we eat?" I asked.

"There's a really nice restaurant downtown, but it might be pricey. I'd recommend the Trailside Cafe, right on the Katy Trail. Roger Slate'll take good care of you."

The policeman beat us to the Trailside. When we pulled in, Roger Slate was waiting. He took me to his shop and loaned me tools to clean two weeks of grime from the bike. We bought lunch, then ordered sandwiches for a picnic dinner, to which he chipped in two bananas. He warned us of trail conditions ahead, and urged us to ride back and see a scenic Katy Trail stretch a mile east of there. He also surprised us with news of our 'friends'.

"Three other backpackers came through here two weeks ago. They said they were going to the Pacific, too."

"Three?" I asked. "A lady in Defiance told us a backpacking couple had passed through there."

"That might be. This group had two men and a woman, but one of the men complained about not having much time off. Maybe he hooked up with them later."

While Sue rested, I rode the bike east on the Katy. As Roger promised, *the trail around Rocheport is stunning. Limestone bluffs south of town squeeze the trail against the river. Caves burrow into the cliffs and waterfalls leap from the heights. Park benches offer a chance to sit and watch the river roll by.*   - journal entry, May 7

That afternoon we followed the Katy west to U.S. 40. Last year's flood had hit this area hard, and the land had not yet recovered. Silt washed up to the road's edge, looking like an ocean beach after high tide has receded.

"This whole area got covered in sand last year," said the owner at Grotjahn's Service Station a few miles further on. "If the sand laid down less than an inch thick, the farmers can plow it under and try to plant. If it's thicker — which many places are — there's nothing they can do. That land will be useless for years to come."

U.S. 40 was barren — no towns, little traffic. The few farmhouses showed no signs of life, just empty shells anchoring barren fields. Pushing on to Boonville, six miles ahead, was not an option — little time and even less energy insured we'd spend the night in the bottomland. We chose the yard of a beautiful white mansion to pitch our tent. As we drew close, we noticed a five-foot high waterline ringing the home and debris strewn about the yard.

An old tennis shoe. An unopened tin of sardines. A child's action figure. Mud-caked lawn chairs. A plastic coffee cup.

On the front lawn lay a pile of ruined furniture: an easy chair, an overturned table, file cabinets. A bicycle. Looking inside through a window, we saw dresses and a kitchen radio, and a wall where kids' heights were marked.

A rocking horse was upended outside the barn; inside, a boy's bike stood buried eight inches deep in silt. A swingset by the road waited for children that never returned.

We found no name on the mailbox, just "Rte 1 Box 83." An anonymous life, uprooted at the whim of Mother Nature.

                                      -journal entry, May 8

** CEMETERIES AND SCHOOLS **

* MISSOURI *

May 8 - May 21, 1994
158 miles -- 27 bags
TOTAL, 2069 miles -- 807 bags

Wealth I ask not, hope nor love,
        Nor a friend to know me;
All I ask, the heavens above,
        And the road below me.
                -- Robert Louis Stevenson, "The Vagabond"

────────►◆◄────────

BOONVILLE HAD FREEWAYITIS.

The blight we'd seen in so many towns had infected Boonville, too. The downtown, perched on a bluff above the river, harbored little activity on a Sunday afternoon. We spotted one cafe open, along with a small handful of other businesses. Thespian Hall, the oldest operating theatre west of the Mississippi, headed the list of historic buildings, but many had fallen vacant as stores moved toward the interstate. The empty streets gave it the feel of a modern ghost town.

We reached the town of 7000 late in the morning, looking forward to an afternoon off. Our first item of business was to get rid of the packs and panniers. Flagging down a policeman, I asked about campgrounds in town. "Sure," he said. "Take this road two miles to I-70, then east one exit."

Another Golden Rule of Trekking: 'If you don't like the answer, rephrase the question.' "That's out of our way," I said. "Is there anyplace in town — a park, a church — we could tent for a night?"

He thought for a few seconds. "You could try the city park. It's closed at night, so no one will bother you." He gave us directions, and we went to check it.

The park covered several rolling hills overlooking the Missouri River. Families picnicked on the grass, and kids played Frisbee near the restrooms. We found a flat spot hidden from the road and set the tent, then threw our goods inside. "Are you sure they'll be safe?" Sue asked.

"I hope so. I'm not going to sit here all day watching them." With a last nervous look back, we returned downtown.

After lunch we visited the town's cinema. An elderly couple staffed the box office, she at the cash register, he sweeping the lobby. Two young children ran underfoot, and I heard the boy call the man 'Grandpa.' When Grandma saw Sue ride up on the bike, she waved her to bring it in. "You can park it by the video games."

The granddaughter, a six-year-old bundle of energy under a mop of blonde hair, came skipping up front. Noticing Sue's bike, she asked me, "Where's yours?" When she heard my answer, her mouth dropped open. "WOW! Grandpa! Did you hear that!?"

He had. With the movie starting, he didn't keep us, but after the show he waited with questions. The kids gathered around, eager to hear about our adventure. With laundry and shopping still on our 'to do' list, we couldn't stay long, but we did chat for a time.

The hours flew by, and the sun had begun its goodbyes by the time we returned to the park. Eight o'clock — and we'd left our gear unattended since noon. _Had we made a mistake? Would our tent still be there?_ Of course, we found everything untouched.

And why not, I thought. _There must be a reason they call this the heartland!_

I knew we'd found a winner when I saw the fifteen-foot-tall jean-clad statue next to the Phillips 66 sign. In the yard of the Big Man Service Station, a van emblazoned with 'Missourians for a Republican Congress' gave clear notice of the owner's political leanings. We noticed him standing out front as we pulled up. With a white beard hanging low from his wizened face, he reminded me of a slimmed-down Santa Claus.

Inside the small shop, the walls were lined with signed portraits of Republican presidents from Nixon on, bracketed with "Bush '92" and "Quayle" license plates. One display case overflowed with buttons touting "Clinton/Gore — Gone in Four" and "Rush Limbaugh for President."   -journal entry, May 9

"HAS EVERYONE GONE MAD?" muttered the Big Man customer when he heard WhiteBeard tell us of the other hikers. "What's wrong with driving cross-country? At least you don't spend your life getting there."

Maybe we were mad, but we had partners in our dementia. From WhiteBeard, we now also had a description of the trio, letting us picture the people we chased. "They were quite a bit younger than you," he said. "The girl could turn heads with her long blonde hair and long legs. One guy was really dark, and I'm not talking suntan."

"They came through here, huh?" That surprised me; I'd figured they'd stay on the Katy Trail.

"Two weeks ago, yep. They said they'd walked from Delaware to St. Louis last year, and took the winter off." Who knows? Maybe they'd dogged our steps in 1993, hearing about the crazy couple cleaning roads ahead of them. Maybe they'd wondered about us, who we were, what we looked like, why we walked. Maybe, like us, they'd pieced together clues at every stop, playing detectives hot on the trail of their suspects.

These detectives chanced losing their prey's trail, leaving the main roads. The interstate cut west; the tourist track headed northwest. We struck off between the two, heading into an area where the towns were small and the gaps between large. "This is the life," Sue said. "There's no stress out here, only bugs and bovines."

For three days we enjoyed the 'wilderness.' Temperatures settled into the 80s, and the sun kept the rain at bay. Friendly locals kept us supplied with water and showers. The rib that had pained Sue in the bottomlands (with her, body parts needed no reason to hurt) had healed, and she now suffered only from swollen ankles.

The friendliness carried over into Marshall. As we traipsed through town, we attracted stares. One fellow in a pickup did a double-take, then raced around the block to catch us at the next corner. "Looks like you got the harder job," he said to me. "What happened to your bike?"

"If I make it to California, my wife will buy me one!"

A few blocks later, another motorist blocked traffic when he stopped to ask about our trek. Closer to downtown, a businessman questioned us, then a well-dressed woman stopped to thank us. "I think more people should get involved," she said, "and take responsibility for fixing our problems."

"That's why we're out here," Sue said. "It may not be much, but we're doing something."

The woman nodded knowingly. "It's the government, you know?

People are so used to the government trying to fix everything, they don't take care of themselves. The government should get out of the business of fixing social problems. Let the community and the churches take care of the homeless — they used to, you know. They have a stake in helping people."

She opened her purse and rifled through it. "It's simple, really. If your neighbor gives you a hand, you'll probably return the favor. If the government gives you a hand, who do you pay back? Too many people figure they've got it coming to them, and they take, take, take." She pulled her hand from the purse, clutching a pair of one-dollar bills. "I didn't mean to keep you. Here's two dollars — it's all the money I can find. You're doing a great thing. Have a cold drink on me."

After lunch we hit the library, researching routes west. Did the towns ahead have cafes? Was this road flat or hilly? Which one had less traffic? After our questions, the librarian had one for us: "Are you with those other three backpackers?"

Mark up one more piece to the puzzle. She identified one man as Indian, which explained the dark skin. "They looked college-aged," she said. "Maybe they were on a long summer break."

How long would we follow them?

Some restaurants you can rate by calendars, some by clocks. Others specialize in being nondescript, memorable only for the food.

Several people in Marshall recommended a truck stop cafe on the way out of town. All we saw was the '4-T Truck Wash,' an industrial-type business with gray aluminum-sided walls and no indication they served food. When we used the restrooms, we noticed one end of the concrete-floored building had been partitioned off for a cafe. Plastic bench seats surrounded the tables in the style of the best fast food outlets. Two pinball machines in the corner kept company with a jukebox belting out country-western tunes. Polaroids of truckers, labeled with their CB handles, adorned the walls.

We ordered a breakfast a trucker would drive half the country for — a plate heaped with food, tasty and down-home without floating in grease. The price impressed us as much as the taste — two thirds what we'd pay for less food in southern California.

-journal entry, May 12

"ARE YOU SURE WE'RE not in Kansas?" asked Sue.

I understood her confusion. The Ozark hills had disappeared, and farms stretched to the horizon. After one long curve outside Marshall, the road ran straight as a ruler, cutting through a land as lonely as any we'd seen. All trees had been cut down within the highway's one-hundred foot easement, leaving us no shade.

We'd packed sandwiches before starting, but despaired of finding a picnic spot. Finally I saw it — a yard perched above the road, with trees that overhung the berm. Who cared if the owner was mowing the yard? If we stayed low on the berm, she'd never see us.

While eating, we waved at the passing trucks, most of whom honked back. "Do you think the person mowing," I asked Sue, "is wondering why all these trucks are honking at her?"

I waved at the farmer on one slow-moving tractor, who gave us a quizzical look. He slowed and turned into the driveway. A minute later, we heard a call from behind us. "Do you want something cold to drink?"

In moments Jack Harriman delivered two large tumblers of ice-choked tea. As we drank, he told us about the area. "Most farmers here grow corn and beans," he told us. "At least they do when the weather lets them. Normally they'd have finished planting two weeks ago, but only half of it's in the ground today. The rains have made it too wet to plant."

By now we'd gotten used to sightings of the trio we'd dubbed Blondie, Gandhi, and Friend, and Jack gave us our latest. "I saw them two weeks ago," he said. "They were straggling along, going pretty slow. Looked like they were tired of each other's company, too. Each of 'em walked about a half mile apart."

I could understand that. Without litter to divert us, we'd probably fight too. Not that the area had much. A dollar bill and a steak knife highlighted two days' pickings as we pushed west. Maybe the whole county had adopted Alma's town motto: 'the Cleanest Little City.'

For a town of under five hundred people, Alma bustled. The streets were clean, and flowers hung outside the cafe. We shopped in the well-stocked grocers, heeding warnings that little awaited us in Corder. On the way out of town, I noticed the Trinity Lutheran School. "We haven't talked to any schools yet this year," I said. "They'll be letting out for summer soon. Should we try here?"

Sue hesitated. I could read her thoughts: we couldn't get into schools with advance notice last year. What were the odds with NO notice? Did we really want the rejection? Finally she shrugged. "Well, I suppose we're here. Can't hurt to try."

We walked in and asked for the principal. He looked at us warily at first, obviously unused to backpackers invading his domain. He nodded as we offered to speak, then said, "Hold on a second, let me check."

When he came back, he looked apologetic. "It's bad timing," he explained. "We let out at noon today. Most classes are busy. Only one has time to see you, the combined seventh and eighth grade."

Spontaneity pays! I had no time to rehearse, but also no time to get nervous. As in Iuka, I talked little, asking the kids questions and getting them involved. My thirty minutes sped by.

By 1:00 we'd reached Corder, Alma's 'homely sister' — or so people had told us. To our pleasure, the dire descriptions fell short of the truth. Corder, though grittier than Alma, lacked none of its hospitality. The town had all the amenities we needed: a cafe for lunch, a tavern for dinner, a library to pass the day.

After lunch we headed for city hall, eager to get camping settled. The city clerk called the police chief, who hurried over to interview us. He asked about our trip, satisfying himself we posed no threat. "Three hikers came through here two weeks ago and camped at the park, too. I was more leery of them. They looked pretty seedy. I doubt they'd showered for a month."

With nothing but the library to lure us away, we sat and talked with the chief. "My dad was a policeman in Colorado for years, in a college town," I said. "What's it like fighting crime in a town of three hundred people?"

"Not very exciting," he admitted. "Which is fine with me. Most of our calls are for dead dogs or cats on the road, or people racing riding mowers. I read the police reports coming out of Kansas City and know I'm in the right place."

He leaned back in his chair. "Anything can happen in the city. Just yesterday in KC, a man mowing his lawn ran inside to answer his phone. When he came back out, his mower was gone."

I remembered his story that night, lying in the tent listening to the Kansas City news. Earlier, thieves had stolen 2500 square feet of sod from a construction site.

Were the two thefts related?

West Virginia has no monopoly on amusing signs. Higginsville checked in with the Church of the Living Waters and (my favorite) Barnhart's Sewing Machines and Fish. Talk about one-stop shopping!
                                                    -journal entry, May 14

"LOOK! A TANDEM WITH panniers!" Sue pointed at the bike propped outside the restaurant door. "It's our first bike tourers!"

Inside the restaurant, we looked around. *Hmmm. Would they be the ones with the matching, brightly-colored Lycra outfits?* We took the adjacent table, and after ordering, leaned over to chat. "How far are you going?"

"We're on a four-day trip, KC to Marshall to Sedalia." Eyeing my pack, he said, "You've got quite a load. Where are you headed?"

We talked while they ate, trading clues about the road ahead. When our food came, they left, hoping to make miles before the rains fell. Our plans called for more time in Higginsville, doing laundry and getting supplies.

Sue left me in charge of the clothes while she went for a hair cut. She returned an hour later, with shorter hair and a long smile. "The people here are so friendly! I had a great chat with the stylists. The owner asked where we stayed at night, and said we could camp in her yard!"

"Do you want to?" I asked. "We don't have to walk this afternoon."

"I already told her 'no.' We've only done six miles today. At that rate, we'll never get anywhere."

A young man walked in with a tall basket of laundry as Sue stuffed her clean clothes in the panniers. Looking us over, he asked, "Taking a trip?"

"All the way across the country!"

"No kidding! I met three other people here two weeks ago, and that's what they were doing!"

"We've been chasing them for weeks. We hear more about them almost every stop."

He frowned. "I should have brought the picture I took of them."

Drat! What other chance would we get to see them? "Did they say where they were headed next?"

"They talked about going straight west, toward Kansas City."

So our paths would diverge, as we planned to angle north. This time, we lost their trail for good. We would hear no more tales of Blondie, Gandhi, and Friend, though we often thought of them as we plodded west. Did they also reach the Pacific?

We said goodbye and headed for the city limits. At the edge of town the clouds closed rank, and lazy raindrops fell. "Maybe it's just a sprinkle," I said. "Let's duck inside McDonald's, and let it pass."

Two hours later, the drops still fell, and darker clouds loomed to the northwest. I knew we'd never reach Lexington by nightfall, and weathering the storm in the open had no appeal. Staying in Higginsville started looking good. "Maybe you should call your hairdresser," I suggested, "and see if her offer still holds."

It did. Barb Edwards gave Sue directions to her house on the other edge of town. We waited for the first storm to end, then hurried across town before the second started.

We found their house on the 'estates' side of town. On a wide lot, it neighbored open fields. Raindrops sparkled on the emerald-green lawn, with bushes and trees flanking the immaculate house. Barb and her husband Hank sat on the patio with Hank's brother and sister-in-law, and they offered us drinks as we walked up.

The six of us sat on the patio, watching the next storm begin. When the wind started

Barb Edwards and Wrinkles

blowing the rain sideways, Barb insisted we spend the night inside. "You'd never stay dry out there!"

The night passed quickly, as nights with good friends do. I remember Barb, looking relaxed yet elegant with her trim figure and perfectly coifed (of course) blonde hair; a showcase home filled with cabinets, bookcases, and woodwork; their Sharpei dog Wrinkles, who sloshed like a flat tire, or galoshes being shaken; easy conversation about everything and nothing.

Early the next morning, after promising Barb we'd write, we set off. Lingering memories of 1994's first Instant Family helped the miles float by. By lunch we'd reached Lexington, site of one of the state's biggest Civil War battles.

With the afternoon free, we toured the battle grounds. The fight had seesawed back and forth, with first the Yankees, then Johnny Reb winning. In the heat of the battle, a cannonball fired from the Union entrenchment flew a quarter mile and lodged high in a pillar of the courthouse. One hundred and thirty years later, it still sat there, a smudge of black against the gleaming white of the courthouse.

At least, so said the postcards we bought. "The Civil War part is correct," an old man told us as we ate dinner at Hardy's. "Several years ago, though, a city lawyer got worried about liability. What if the cannonball fell out and hit somebody? They couldn't take it out, since it's a town landmark. Finally they hatched a plan: remove the cannonball and put it in the museum. Then paint a croquet ball flat black, and stick it back in the pillar. Voila! No more problem!" He looked around, then leaned forward conspiratorially. In a low voice, he said, "I know, because a friend of mine worked for the city. He told me."

As I gazed at the ball later, I wondered, *cannon or croquet?* I couldn't tell . . .

THE HAND-LETTERED SIGN IN Joyce's Cafe listed their prices:

Coffee Rates:

1 cup	*50 ¢*
1 hour	*1.00*
½ morning	*2.00*
all morning	*2.50*
all day	*3.00*

*Spoonknockers, cup wavers, thumbsnappers,
whistlers, and liars pay double.*
ASK ABOUT OUR WEEKLY RATES!

-journal entry, May 16

THAT'S THE FIFTH PERSON to wave or give me thumbs up, I noted as I waited outside the Richmond WalMart, babysitting the bike. *Did we hit the news? Had someone stuck a sign on my back saying, "Wave at the poor tourist?"*

I got my answer when the next car pulled up. The people inside smiled, then the passenger rolled down her window. "Are you the man we heard about on the radio? The one bicycling from San Francisco to Boston for AIDS?"

This area, I concluded, must be the Mecca for offbeat travel. Lewis and Clark set the tone in 1804, and it hadn't died in 190 years. Us. Blondie, Gandhi, and Friend. The AIDS biker. We even read in the *Kansas City Star* about a group of Native Americans, walking coast-to-coast protesting something or other.

As we headed into the heart of Richmond, we saw two bicyclists with bulging panniers. When they noticed us, they pulled over. "We've heard about you!" one said.

"About us?"

"Yes! We were at a rest stop, and a motorist mentioned seeing a couple, one on bike, one on foot. They must have meant you!" They were bicycling to Jefferson City to attend a convention. "Why take three hours to drive there when you can take three days and enjoy yourself?"

Our 'fame' also beat us to the *Richmond Daily News* offices. The reporter was on an assignment, so we waited for him. When he returned, he looked at the bike outside, glanced at my backpack, and asked, "Are you the people I heard about?"

As Pete Maher interviewed us, I sized him up. He was our age, fighting a holding battle with middle-aged spread. Though easygoing, he didn't strike me as a local — the earring he wore gave him away. Sure enough, he had moved from Los Angeles one year earlier.

After the interview, we began our daily 'permission to camp' dance. Waltz to the library — they suggested asking the mayor. Jitterbug to city hall — they referred us to the police. Two-step it to the PD before they close the doors at 5:00.

The Richmond Police Station occupied a converted double-wide mobile home. The public entry led to a tiny foyer barely large enough for the couch and chair stuffed into it. Three teenage girls waited inside, occasionally ducking out for a smoke, and behind the glass-walled front desk a matronly woman scowled at them. Her badge identified her as Eileen Wright, and she looked as if she'd enjoyed fifty-plus years of making people's lives miserable.

We described our problem, which she listened to with nary a smile. "The laws don't provide for camping in the parks," she said. "I'll have to ask the chief."

She retired to the radio room, where she spent several minutes out of our earshot. When she returned, she wore the same scowl. "I radioed an officer, and he's going to check with the parks director. He'll call back."

The next half-hour crept by. Cigarette smoke from the girls drove us from the foyer; the late-afternoon heat rippling up from the pavement drove us back inside. Finally the girls finished their unknown business and left, and we propped the door open to let in fresh air.

With the girls gone, Eileen relaxed. She lost her battle with curiosity, and asked about our walk. After another twenty minutes with no word from the park director, she dispatched a second officer to find the first one. Finally the answer came back: "He says you can camp in the main park. That's back a mile on the highway. I just need a reference phone number and address."

Before we left, she flashed us a big smile. "The trip sounds great. Stay safe and have fun! And I'll forward the _Daily News_ article to this address!"

After all that, we didn't even camp. From the PD we headed to dinner at the restaurant Pete Maher recommended. Minutes after the waitress sat us, she showed Pete to the next table. "You mean, you believed my line about the good food here?!" he joked.

He joined us, and we chatted over hamburgers and chili. "Anything we just HAVE to see before we leave town tomorrow?" I asked.

"What are you doing tonight?"

"Maybe a hot game of cards, or answering our mail," I said. "Most nights on the road are oh so thrilling."

"Why don't I give you a tour?" he offered. "Forget camping. You can sleep at my place. It's right around the corner."

We followed him home, and stored the bike on his patio. "Don't worry about locking it," he said. "When I moved from L.A., it took me a while to 'unlearn' locking everything. That first winter amazed me. I saw people drive to the grocery store and leave their cars running while they went in and shopped. Nobody ever bothered them."

As we piled into his truck, he gave us a word of warning. "Don't think I'm being morbid, but this is the same tour my boss gave me when I moved here. Back then, I thought it strange that 'showing me the area' meant driving from cemetery to cemetery. Once I saw how tuned in people are to their past, how important family is, it made sense."

He first drove east, ten minutes outside town. "The Hardin cemetery became world-famous last year during the flood. When a nearby levee broke, the flood cut through the center of the cemetery, washing away skeletons and coffins. Pictures of caskets floating fifty miles downstream got beamed across the world."

It still sat much as it had when the floodwaters receded. Halfway across the land dropped a dozen feet to a collage of thick mud, water, and broken gravestones. The water in one pool went down a hundred feet. Across from this gash, erect gravestones spread through the lush grass, a reminder of pre-deluge days.

"Some graves dated to the mid-1850s," Pete explained, "and the wooden coffins had long since rotted away. Skeletons that turned up downstream were impossible to identify. Over here, they've reinterred all those anonymous remains, with blank headstones." Row upon row of closely spaced graves fringed the cemetery, with one whole area (over a hundred graves) reserved for unidentified children. Newly-planted grass battled for a foothold, and several anonymous markers were covered with flowers. People wandered about in small groups, searching for a grave or engaged in quiet reflection.

Heading back to Richmond, Pete detoured through a small river town. A couple of turns later, we'd left Missouri and landed in Saudi Arabia. Sand covered the land. Tiny ridge lines crisscrossed the field, sculpted by the wind. Fence posts marched off into the sandy expanse, marking land claims overruled by Mother Nature. Pete walked out onto the barren land, water seeping into his footprints. "This used to be a farm. Now it's useless."

The tour took a lighter tone when we reached Richmond's main cemetery. It was as big as any we'd seen this trip, with at least a thousand gravestones sprinkled amidst the tall grass. Pete led us atop a knoll, past headstones dated in the 1800s, past others (for members of a group called the Woodsmen) sculpted to resemble tree stumps. "It should be around here," he said, scanning the markers. "Ahhh, there it is."

He pointed to an obelisk which looked far newer than the 1882 date carved on it. At the top, pieces had been chipped from the marker, marring its smooth finish. "This is the grave of Bob Ford, who killed Jesse James. They have to replace the gravestone every few years, because tourists break away pieces for souvenirs until nothing's left."

Pete Maher and the sandscape

We had one last stop on the tour: a three-grave island in the middle of a dead-end street. The road split as it hit the family plot, then rejoined to run another hundred yards. "This illustrates how involved people are with the past. General Israel Hendley died in 1847 while fighting in the Mexican-American War. At the time, they buried him in New Mexico. A couple years back, they built a superhighway over his grave, and his descendants had him exhumed and reinterred here. Relatives from across the country came for the dedication."

He chuckled as we walked to the other end of the green swath. "These graves always make me wonder. Here lies Judge William Martin, died 1856 at age seventy-four. This one is his wife's grave, who died in 1879 aged thirty-six. That would make her thirteen when the judge died. That raises interesting questions about his cause of death."

As he ferried us about, we learned more about him. He had grown up in Townsend, Massachusetts, where the schoolkids so long ago had asked for my autograph. Military service had taken him to California, where he married and had two girls. He stayed there for a year after his wife left him, then gave up everything to move closer to his daughters.

"The first thing that struck me on moving here is how everyone has careers," he said. "You ask someone what they do, and they'll say, 'I'm an electrician,' or 'I'm a waitress,' or 'I'm a clerk.' In L.A., they all have jobs, not careers. It's not, 'I'm a cab driver,' it's 'I'm just doing this until I get my big break acting,' or singing, or writing."

"The weather must have been an adjustment," I noted. "Coming from the dry of out west to the humidity here . . ."

"The humidity is nasty, but at least we get four seasons. Each has its good points. In L.A., the weather bored me. You had six months of wet smog, and six months of dry smog."

He enjoyed the slower pace of life. "Everything's a chore in California, and you're always waiting. In traffic, at the supermarket, at the doctor's. Take DMV, for instance. In L.A. you spend hours in line to renew a license. Here, they have outlets in the grocery stores. I can get a new driver's license and pick up a jar of pickles, too."

"You must have had culture shock," Sue said. "After all, L.A.'s the land of fruits, nuts, and flakes, and this is the heartland."

"Oh, I've shaken people up. My pierced earring, for instance. They're not used to that sort of thing. People here pride themselves on eye contact, but when they first met me, they'd only hold that contact for a few minutes. Soon, I'd see their gaze straying to it.

"It's better now since people are used to me. Some people look forward to my column every week." He laughed as a memory surfaced. "I was only here three weeks before I got my first fan letter. A fan letter! I'd only written two columns, and this lady says she likes my writing style and asks me to critique her writing. I do, and she invites me to dinner. She served salmon lasagna. Let me tell you — *never* mix salmon and lasagna!"

NOTES FROM SUE'S JOURNAL:
So peaceful out here. Such generous people. No stress at all — I will miss all this. The days just melt away.   - May 17

'BLOOD ALLEY' AWAITED US.

The librarian had scared us with tales of carnage on highway 10. "There's very little shoulder and a lot of blind curves. Seems someone wrecks there every other week. I wouldn't recommend it for walking."

Unfortunately, no other road led west. We left Pete's house at 6:30, our earliest start of the whole trip, hoping to miss the traffic. We needn't have worried. The road, though hilly, showed no trace of its 'Blood Alley' persona. 'Trash Alley', maybe, as I filled five bags for the day — a 1994 record that would stand for two months.

Halfway to the next town, we came upon the Elkhorn school. "Should we try again?" I asked Sue. With the heat rising, we were due for a break, so she agreed. We stepped inside, and tracked down the principal.

Patti Smith was a well-dressed woman not much older than us, with a perky smile under a mane of blonde hair. She received our plan with enthusiasm, asking for time to set up some classes. Thirty minutes later we faced eighty-five third graders, three classes stuffed into one room. We followed that with an audience of fifty fourth graders and a reporter from the Excelsior Springs *Daily Standard*.

Our reward was another hot school lunch. This time we ate in the faculty lounge, visiting with the teachers. "Maybe we've found the secret," I told Sue, "for talking at schools. Just show up."

In Excelsior Springs, we tried for number three. Our motel backed up to a middle school, so after a refreshing shower, I called them. Our advance notice worked, and we arranged for a talk the next morning.

I talked to the eighth-grade classes that morning, the oldest kids we saw on the trip. They listened attentively, swamping us with questions. "Do you ever get sick?" (Nothing more serious than a case of diarrhea. Thankfully, road crews had left port-a-potties along the road that day.) "Do you ever get tired of walking?" (Every day, after a dozen miles in the heat.) "Do you recycle?" (We'd love to, but have no way to get the trash to a center.) "Would you recommend this to others?" (For Sue, it would depend on how little she liked them.)

When the questions tapered off, one teacher addressed the kids. "Class, did you enjoy their talk?" A chorus of yeses erupted. "Do you think we could thank them by going home tonight and picking up a bag of garbage from around your house? Who would like to do that?" Hands shot up across the room.

It's so great to feel we're making a difference.

Kearney, Missouri gained fame as the boyhood home of Frank and Jesse James. Today its downtown, both blocks of it, still lives despite the freeway a half-mile to the west. In a prominent location stands 'The Old Drug Store,' a card store and antique shop which occupies the old pharmacy and grocery buildings. We stepped inside to check out the soda fountain.

What we saw impressed us. Though the owners had replaced the fountain bar in the 1940s, the cherrywood back bar dated from 1895. They had stained cabinets lining the wall to match the back bar, and used the original glass doors. Though repainted, the metal ceiling had also made it through. You could recognize it in an old picture hanging on the wall.   -journal entry, May 18

"IF WE'RE SO CLOSE to Kansas," Sue asked as she puffed up another hill, "then where's all the flat land?"

Where, indeed. State highway 92 resembled a roller coaster with its ups and downs. The previous day I'd counted twenty-three hills, one every half-mile, and today continued the trend. Thankfully they weren't steep or long.

We passed north of Kansas City, through upscale enclaves of the well-to-do. Some mansions bespoke a genteel southern flair, with white columns on the house and gazebos anchoring lawns graced with massive shade trees. Others simulated the Kentucky horse country, with fine trimmed lawns and whitewashed fences. Most, however, fit the anonymous (read mass-produced), characterless style invading cities across the country, a 90's image of how modern, homogenous America should look.

We reached Platte City early, our final stop in the state. When we checked for a newspaper, we found the town had two. We chose the _Landmark_ for an exclusive interview, since their office was a few blocks closer. Only when they hadn't returned from Friday lunch by 3:00 did we wander to the _Platte County Citizen_ offices.

Inside a skeleton crew attended to business. The whole office gathered as we introduced ourselves. When the reporter left to grab paper and pen, one woman stepped forward. "My name is Jerina. How would you like to spend the night with my kids and me at my farmhouse?" We accepted, and she made quick plans to meet us later. The returning reporter shot her a dirty glance, and she returned to her desk.

We rendezvoused with her at 5:00, and she told us the rest of the story. "Today's my last day there. Monday, I start reporting for the _Landmark_. The atmosphere was a little tense, and I didn't want to involve you. This way, I can interview you too, for 'the competition'."

She drove us into the boondocks, to a farmhouse and barn off a dirt road that she shared with a soon-to-be-ex-husband, three daughters, two dogs, two house cats, five barn cats, and three ponies. Two daughters had plans for the night (LitterWalkers couldn't compete with slumber parties), which left eight-year-old Gwyn with no competition for our attention. She had more questions than TV has commercials, and insisted on giving us grand tours of every part of the property.

After a wonderful home-cooked meal, Gwyn settled down, giving Jerina a chance for her pirate interview. We ended up talking of trips good and bad, those shining in the memory and those we'd rather forget.

"I had my trip from hell when I was twenty-eight," she said, "years before marriage and kids. I was living in Atlanta, and wanted to visit the west coast. Then, AAA had a DriveAway program, where people could pay someone to drive their cars across the country. They hooked me up with a woman who wanted her car in Seattle so she could take it on the Alaska ferry.

"For a week my friend, my Great Dane, and I would see the country. We set out in high spirits. On our second stop, about four hours after we'd started, I took the dog for a walk, tripped and broke my foot. Maybe I should have taken that as an omen."

She settled deeper in the couch. "On our second day, we grabbed ham sandwiches for lunch and ate them in the car. I only finished half of mine, so I stuck the other half in the glove compartment. Of course, I forgot it. The next morning, we left the dog in the car when we went to breakfast. When the car got warm, the sandwich started smelling. By the time we came back out, the dog had chewed halfway through the dashboard trying to get to it.

"In Idaho, the car overheated and started belching black smoke. We had to sit for hours, waiting for it to cool down. We reached Seattle late at night, and stayed in a seedy motel because we didn't know how to get to a better part of town. I lay awake all night, hoping somebody would steal the car so I wouldn't have to deal with it."

And we thought walking was tough!

** THE LAND OF OZ **

* KANSAS *

May 22 - June 7, 1994
226 miles -- 22 bags
TOTAL, 2295 miles -- 829 bags

One day in the country is worth a month in town.
- Christina Rossetti

"SO WHEN DO WE see Dorothy and Toto?"

Sue asked that as we lost our last view of the Missouri River. Leavenworth, Kansas spread out behind us, the federal pen — a massive granite block surrounded by green fields and razor-wired fences — lay to our side, and the Great Unknown stretched before us.

"They're probably visiting with the Scarecrow. Lord knows, we'll probably see more of them than people in the next month." Last night we'd celebrated in Leavenworth, our last city before the wide-open expanses of the Great Plains. Our next town over four thousand people lay 370 miles away, a good month's walk.

"You mean I've got nothing but wheat fields to look forward to?" she teased. "Maybe I'll take my ruby sneakers, click my heels three times, and say, 'There's no place like Colorado, there's no place like Colorado . . .'"

We continued to joke about Oz as we rolled out of town. "You wanted rural, you got rural," I told her. "I just hope the bike doesn't break down. Would Auntie Em or Uncle Henry know how to fix a Nishiki?"

Despite worries of boredom, I enjoyed the passing scenery. Far from flat, the road danced over rolling glacial hills. Spring had worked its magic on the land, coloring fields with wildflowers, crowning the trees with lush green coats. The sun chased away the morning fog, bringing on short-sleeve temperatures.

No cares, no worries, no reason to hurry. We reached the Hilltop Market early that Sunday afternoon, and took a long break with the *Kansas City Star* mega-paper. *After an early dinner, we covered the last few miles into Easton. Crossing the bridge into town was like entering a*

1950's TV series. Trees shaded the highway. Houses lifted from Ozzie and Harriett's neighborhood lined the streets, and smoke curled up from backyard incinerators. Kids played on swing sets in fenced yards. At the local ballfields, throngs of people watched their children compete in a regional peewee ball tournament.   -journal entry, May 22

The park bustled with activity as one team after another battled on the diamonds. We grabbed seats on the bleacher's edge, rooting for the home team, cheering each hit the tykes made. They gave it all their heart, living and dying with each pitch.

At inning's end I wandered to the concession stand. "Who would I ask for permission to camp here?" I asked the teenagers working the booth.

They looked at each other when I explained why, surprise on their faces. "I'll ask my dad," the girl said. "He's the mayor. I don't think he'll mind."

News of the Litterpickers soon spread. Several parents asked about our trip. Others told us of the towns ahead. As the last game started, the concession stand closed, and the mayor's daughter brought us leftover hotdogs and Cokes. "My dad said no problem with camping. Here — this food's on the house."

Midway through the championship game, a stocky boy stepped to the plate. His first swing grazed the ball, arcing it over the backstop high into the air. I watched it start its downward trip, well past us but aiming toward Sue's bike. She looked in alarm as it hurtled down, missing by two feet.

She shot me a withering glance. "That bike BETTER not get hit . . ."

"JESSE JAMES LIVES IN Valley Falls."

Frank Shrimplin smiled as he dropped that bon mot. "Of course, he's not the famous outlaw. This Jesse James used to be a prison guard. However, the real Buffalo Bill did live here as a boy. Back then, they called the town Grasshopper Falls."

Frank's Pharmacy anchored one end of a lazy Main Street in Valley Falls. With time to kill before lunch, we had wandered inside for a limeade float and a sundae at the soda fountain. Frank, with his short hair and spectacles a picture of an old-time druggist, had come right over to greet us. "You must be the people my clerk was talking about. She said she'd seen someone walking toward town."

Besides the ice cream treats, he gave us a running commentary on the town and his drug store. "This half of the store houses a pharmacy museum," he said, leading us through the doorway in back. "I've run it for thirty-one years. Much of this stuff came when I bought the store, the rest I acquired in the course of business."

Display cases lined one wall. On the shelves sat dozens of bottles filled with tonics, ointments, and powders. I looked through labels dating back a hundred years or more. "Those are the original contents," Frank said, "from days when the local druggist mixed his own medicines."

Antique cash registers, typewriters, and other devices vied for counter space. Along one wall, several newspaper articles yellowed. "This place has been featured in papers and magazines," he proudly stated, "and shown on CNN. They've filmed commercials here, and it's appeared in movies."

Before we bade Frank and his pharmacy goodbye, he gave me a baseball cap with 'Frank's Pharmacy' printed on the front. "If anyone asks you about it, tell them to visit us. Main Street, Valley Falls!" The hat would last over two months, until an inadvertent spray of DEET bug repellent dissolved the logo.

For lunch, Cozy Corners cornered the sit-down market (a deli and a fast-food booth provided competition down the street). The food was down-home, the service unhurried, and locals packed the place. As we waited for our food, one patron stopped by our table. "I wish you the best of luck. I saw you on the road last night, looking pretty tired. Didn't think you'd make it this far."

We passed the afternoon in the library, reading old Reader's Digests in air-conditioned comfort. Kay Lassiter, the middle-aged woman serving as town librarian, relished our company. Between asking questions about the walk, she introduced us to everyone who came in. "Warren," she addressed one lanky man who had stepped out of a Marlboro ad, "these folks are walking across the country picking up litter!"

He eyed us from under his cowboy hat. "You the ones who left the bag of trash by my field?"

"We're sorry," I apologized. "The state should send a crew to pick it up soon."

He nodded. "Thought it might be you. Bag wasn't there yesterday when I drove by. I picked it up, like I do for anything big."

Kay suggested a saddle club six miles past town for camping, and called the owners for permission. In the cool of the late afternoon, we knocked off the last miles, arriving well before dusk. After pitching the tent, we looked for a place to fill our water bottles. The saddle club had no faucets. "I'll ask the people across the street," I said.

I returned with more than water: two giant tumblers of iced tea, a bowl heaped with garden-fresh strawberries, and three kids. "They just picked these an hour ago," I explained. "The berries, not the kids. They have even more at home, and insisted they'd never eat them all." Brian, Pam, and Siana Miller kept us company until bedtime as we sipped and snacked, asking about our adventure, telling us of their plans for summer vacation.

Our summer vacation stayed dry as the skies dished up perfect weather. The terrain surprised us: thick woods, rolling hills, verdant valleys. Not at all the boring string of endless farm fields I'd feared. The scenery helped speed the miles along, and we soon found ourselves ahead of schedule.

Two miles outside Holton, as we ambled along a country lane, a junker car stopped ahead of us. The driver jumped out and hurried back. "Do you know what you're doing?!"

The abrupt question surprised me. "Picking up roadside litter," I said defensively.

"Oh." His face fell. "I thought maybe you were collecting cans. I've been throwing them in my back seat for a year, and thought you might want them." Alas, if only we could recycle.

We chuckled over the encounter as we entered town. Holton, with 3200 people, almost qualified as a city, complete with a downtown, fast food, and a WalMart. Eager to shower off five days of grime, we headed for downtown's only inn.

The Josephine Hotel, a city landmark, had first opened in 1890 to cater to the railroad trade. It held a turn-of-the-century elegance, with a 100-year-old box piano in the lobby, a guest register from the last century, and a portrait of Josephine (the original owner's daughter) overseeing it all. "This hotel has hosted celebrities from President Grover Cleveland to actress Kirstie Alley," said the owner, Judy Tiner.

"Now you've got the LitterWalkers," I joked. "How much for a room?"

She glanced at the reservation sheet. "Nineteen of our rooms are taken. The only thing left is our three-room suite." I started to shake my head, unwilling to blow the month's lodging budget on one night, when she quoted the price: "Forty-five dollars."

I kept forgetting: _dollars go further away from the city._

On our way to dinner later, I noticed a van outside the hotel. The banner on the side read, 'Rich Becker for Governor: Grass Roots Tour of 627 Towns in Kansas.' "I didn't know they had that many," I told Sue.

They had exactly that many, we found out. As we ate our salads, watching the traffic outside, who should pull up but Rich Becker in his van. Once in the restaurant he visited every table, introducing himself and asking for votes. When he hit our table, we told him about our own grass-roots tour. "Of course we're only hitting twenty-three towns in Kansas. Do they really have 627?"

The gray-haired candidate nodded. "That's what the map shows. Some are small — no mayor, no post office, not even a store. I'll still stop and try to find someone to talk to."

The next morning, as we prepared for another day's adventure, a sleepy-eyed Rich Becker caught us on the stairs. "Sorry I didn't have time to chat last night. I know how it is to be on the road. How do you plan your route?"

"We try to stay off the busier roads," I replied, "and find a path with towns close together. That'll get tough to do as we get further west."

He nodded knowingly. "I let my wife choose our route. She's better at maps than I am." He sipped his coffee and slowly shook his head. "I sure admire you for your ambition. I've always said, if you have a dream, you should pursue it with all you've got."

Our first taste of Kansas wind did little to dampen our enthusiasm for another postcard-perfect day. Forsaking U.S. 75, the characterless mega-highway that obliterates hills with 'cut and fill' and denudes the land of trees in its one-hundred-foot right-of-way, we strolled up the old highway. Here, the road flowed with the countryside, sliding over the rolling hills, slipping out of sight around forested bends. Houses and pastures squeezed the lane, giving it a sense of life not isolation. We chatted with one fifty-year resident hand-weeding his front lawn. He looked forward to his coming 60th high-school reunion. "There's still thirty-five of us up and kicking," he marveled. "We're all pushing eighty!"   -journal entry, May 26

GOFF SURELY RANKED AMONG the smallest of the 627 towns. A cluster of houses at a bend in the road signaled the start of town. A large stone bank building and a post office marked 'downtown,' joined by a small market and a building undistinguished but for a coke machine. The town park was deserted, as were the streets when we strolled into town at noon.

When asked about a cafe, the postal clerk pointed to the Coke machine building. We walked back and pushed through the screen door into a small room with a half dozen tables and a 'Roadkill Cafe' poster on the near wall. The woman behind the counter looked up from reading the morning's Topeka _Capitol-Journal_, eyed my wife, and said, "You must be Sue." Turning to me, she observed, "Obviously, you're Glen."

Of course, the Capitol-Journal, I thought. _I guess we're 'famous' now._ The small-town papers we'd hit so far this year always came out days after we'd left, but the Topeka paper covered most of Kansas. They'd photographed us yesterday, and rushed the story to print.

With other customers to serve, she left us to eat in privacy. After we finished, she came to the table, not with a bill, but with our front-page article. "You must do this all the time, but could you autograph this?"

An hour later, as we traversed more lush farmland, we passed a ranch house with an antique railroad crossing sign in front. Two minutes later, a young man on a small tractor raced up behind us. Jared Dobbins, clad in blue-and-white-striped overalls, was in his early 20s, and wore a smile beneath his engineer's cap. "You just passed our farmhouse," he greeted us. "Would you care to come back for a cold drink?"

He led us back to the ranch house, where his father James — also decked out in railroad coveralls and hat — waited with lemonade. "We saw you in today's paper," James said, "and then saw you walk by. We couldn't let you leave without meeting you."

Inside, railroad memorabilia decorated the house. "We're getting ready for a weekend trip with our railroad wagon," Jared said. "Every year we get together with twenty people and three other railcars, and ride a hundred-mile stretch of track. This year's trip runs from Osage to Emporia."

The conversation quickly turned to litter. "We clean the highway a mile either side of our house," said James. "We've found a lot of unique junk in years of doing this; I'm sure you have too. Here's one thing I've saved." He handed me an all-wood clipboard, vintage 1950s.

"We haven't really seen much litter in Kansas," I said. "People here seem more concerned about it. Or maybe it's because there's fewer people. What's it going to be like when we get in the middle of nowhere?"

"That's funny," said Jared. "I thought we WERE in the middle of nowhere."

We laughed. "Not even close. The suburbs of nowhere, maybe, but not the middle."

"I read one thing in the paper that I wondered about," said James. "Do you really find underwear by the roadside?"

"Every few days, normally," said Sue. "For the past week, though, we haven't seen any."

He shook his head slowly. "We don't throw away our underwear in Kansas. We wear 'em until there's holes in 'em, then we use 'em for rags."

The short visit primed us for the final miles into Corning. The town could have passed for Goff's younger sister: Its population hovered at 150 souls. A dirt road Main Street featured a carbon copy of Goff's bank (though this one had no sign). The post office looked abandoned. A single store identified by a Coke machine guarded the exit from town. To one side of the post office, a massive stone building flew a U.S. flag; the scant markings on it (a 'WPA' inscription and a date in the 1930s) gave no clue to its function. On the other side, Michelob and Bud Light signs in the shop's window identified our entertainment for the night.

After dinner we spent an hour in the bar, nursing a beer, playing pool, and reflecting on small-town life. Before leaving, Sue used the ladies' room, and came out laughing so hard that tears streamed down her face. Once her hysteria died down, I asked what the joke was.

"Remember in the Goff cafe," she said, "when you couldn't find the light switch in the men's room?"

"There WASN'T any switch there, is why I couldn't find it."

"The woman's room here has no switch, either. I had to screw the bulb in!" I could read her thoughts: *Only in the land of Oz could electricity be a novelty.*

As we ventured deeper into Oz — er, Kansas — we grew used to the lack of signs. In small towns, everybody *knew* the shack on the corner sold food. Why bother with neon? Even Centralia, with five hundred people, had a bit of that attitude. When we asked about the best place for lunch, locals sent us to Sixth Street Station. "It's right on the highway. Go down the hill and cross the street. You can't miss it."

The only building at the bottom of the hill had a big sign stating 'J K Bus Service', and gas pumps stood outside. We nearly turned back before I noticed someone had covered the pumps. Looking closer, I saw people sitting inside the storefront. The aroma of Mexican food told us we'd found the right spot.

"It's the people from the paper!" The family seated around the large table recognized us as we walked in, and the matriarch of the clan got up to greet us. "We'd like to treat you to lunch. Please — will you join us?"

We ate our meal with three generations of Woolsoncrofts. Ivan and Margaret headed the clan, their days of farming behind them. Their son Jim bridged the gap, still working the fields (sunflowers were his specialty) but getting on in years. Jim's son Greg and his wife had barely started their years together.

We talked about how friendly we'd found the people in Kansas. "Yesterday outside Goff," Sue said, "an older man with no arms drove up and asked if we needed a ride."

"That's Ed," Jim said. "He's always ready to help. He had his arms pulled off in an accident with a hay baler."

"We also visited with the Dobbinses," I said. "They'd seen us in the paper too."

Greg nodded. "I know Jared. I've helped him stack beans a few times."

And now, the Woolsoncrofts. They joined a list of names and addresses which grew nearly every day. The kindness shown by strangers still amazed us whenever it happened.

Our list grew the next morning as we headed for Frankfort. The humidity rose under overcast skies, making for a muggy walk. Five miles from town, a Jeep with 'U.S. Mail' on it pulled up behind us. "I saw you walking two days ago," said the driver. "How far are you going?"

Moments after he drove away, another car stopped. The elderly couple had seen the Topeka article, and wanted to thank us. Before they left a third car pulled behind them, asking us how far we had come. Fifteen minutes later I noticed the postman returning from Frankfort. He slowed as he approached, rolling down his window. "You look ready for a break," he said, handing us a brown paper bag without stopping. Inside, we found chocolate bars and two cold bottles of peach-flavored mineral water. Wonderful!

We reached Frankfort late in the morning, ready to escape the growing heat. We must have been a sight, me trudging along under the weight of a bulging backpack, Sue coasting beside me. As we crossed town, I heard a call from behind. I turned and saw a bare-chested man running after us, pushing a bicycle. "Do you want my bike?" he asked. "I can give you this bike!"

"GO AHEAD, LAUGH ABOUT KANSAS," I said in mock affront as we dined on pizza. "This area is vintage Vacationland. If we had a car, we could zip up to Marysville to see America's only black squirrels. We saw the white variety in Illinois, so that's only fair."

Sue glanced at the tourist brochure between bites. "We could also stop in Hanover to see the original Pony Express station."

"Here's another must-see." I pointed to the listing for Morrowville. "How could we live with ourselves if we didn't see where someone first invented the bulldozer?"

Despite our joking, we did walk in the tracks of history. For the first time, our path crossed the Oregon Trail, that westward migration we mimicked. Alcove Springs hosted our first Historical Marker of the trail.

In 1841, the first group of emigrants had headed west on routes defined by mountain men and fur traders. They followed rivers through Kansas, crossing the Big Blue River at Alcove Springs. The Donner-Reed party camped there on May 26-30, 1843, waiting for low water so they could cross the Big Blue. Later, the group tried an untried cutoff across the Utah desert, suffering critical delays. When a blizzard stranded them near Lake Tahoe in the pass now bearing Donner's name, thirty-six of the eighty-one emigrants died, and the others ate the dead to survive.

We're a day behind them on the calendar. Will _we_ finish before the snows hit?

I couldn't help but worry over things like that — the curse of the engineering mind. Still, our numbers in May looked good. "Taking Memorial Day off in Franklin didn't hurt us," I reported. "We made 376 miles this month. That's ninety more than we averaged last year!"

"I'm so happy for you, husbandly one," Sue replied, humoring my numbers fetish. "I had so much fun that day, watching the farmers run their John Deeres through the car wash and listening to teenagers roar around in cars with no mufflers."

"Be thankful they had a well-kept park, and that they opened the swimming pool."

Our break there kicked off a lifestyle we'd enjoy for four hundred miles. We grew so used to camping in city parks that we ceased asking for permission. Most towns over 350 people also boasted a swimming pool, which meant free showers nearly every day. And who needed a watch? In every town sirens went off at seven or eight in the morning; noon or one o'clock; and again at five. We basked in this simple life until we neared Denver, where the wide-open plains closed again.

We also got used to laughing about some oddity — or 'Ozz'ity — in most every small town we visited. In Blue Rapids for instance, the pizza parlor had a shower stall in the ladies' room. "If thinking about pepperoni gets you too excited," I chided Sue, "you can take a cold shower!"

After pizza we returned to Blue Rapid's city park to find four elderly men playing under the lights. "Croquet!" I said. "Who's winning?"

"Not quite," one man said. With his riding cap, he looked very British. "It's roque."

I looked closer at the court. "I see you're playing on sand. Are there other differences?"

He nodded, his riding cap bobbing. "Our mallets are smaller and heavier than croquet mallets, and are handmade. The big change, though, is having borders around the court." For emphasis, he tapped a board at court's edge. "You can ricochet off them."

He told me more between turns. "We've played here for ten, fifteen years every Tuesday night from snowmelt to snowfall. We maintain the court, and help the city pay for the lights." I watched them play for a half hour before joining Sue in the tent.

The next day we covered nineteen miles to Greenleaf. Around us, the land slowly changed. Gone were the wooded valleys and gentle hills. The slopes cut more sharply from the flat tablelands, hinting at the buttes soon to come. The farmers' fields stretched for miles, replacing the lush green with shades of tan. Towns grew further apart.

In Greenleaf we took our hard-earned showers then lay by the pool, dangling our feet in the water. As we relaxed, the pool cashier came over. "I know you've planned on tenting in the park," she said, "but you might change your mind. On the radio, they just announced a tornado watch."

I looked at the sky, where black clouds invaded the last patches of blue. "Thanks for the warning, but it's okay. We've survived quite a few storms."

We did need to get the tent up, though. A quick scan of the park convinced us the best spot bordered the restrooms. We took extra care to drive the stakes deep, anxious to keep everything secured. As I finished the last corner, I saw an officer approach us. Were we in trouble for not getting a permit? Would he chase us off because of the storm?

"Are you Glen and Susan Hanket, the couple walking through picking up trash?" We nodded. "The newspaper reporter from Washington — that's fifteen miles from here — asked us to track you down. She wants to know when you'll hit town tomorrow."

We said about noon, which he radioed back to the dispatcher. When he finished, I asked, "What about this tornado watch? Will we be safe here?"

"It's only a watch, not a warning," he said. "You can check the clouds if you're concerned. What you're looking for is a really dark line, darker than the surrounding area." He pointed to the northwest sky. "Like over there. If that developed a bit, got even darker, then you should worry. If it does, there's a tornado shelter in the church across the parking lot. Get there quick if you see a funnel."

We thanked the young officer. As he got back in his car, he promised, "I'll tell my replacement on the night shift you're here. If they call a tornado warning, he'll notify you."

Thus forewarned, we headed downtown for dinner. Most of the town was buttoned down tight, as if everyone waited out the storm in their cellars. Only the American Legion Hall stayed open. Two other customers shared the lounge with us, and we chatted idly with them. I paid no heed when the phone behind the bar rang.

The bartender answered it, then looked straight at us. "Glen or Sue? It's for you." It was the Washington reporter, getting a leg up on tomorrow's scoop.

It was our first and only phone call of the trip. Where else but in the land of Oz?

Last night was the fiercest of our 'dark and stormy nights' in the tent. Rain came down from 9:00 p.m. until 5:00 a.m., alternating between gentle drizzle and batten-down-the-hatches pelting. The sky provided an all-night fireworks show, scattering lightning in every direction, and belching out thunder guaranteed to drive thoughts of sleep from our minds. The blasts of northern wind threatened to uproot the tent and us

with it, forcing us to consider abandoning the tent and cowering in the
restroom.   -journal entry, June 2

"WELCOME TO THE GREAT Midwest America puppy mill."

The greeting came from Bill Acree, founder and owner of Kansas Specialty Dog Services. In Washington, it topped the list of tourist sites, and the reporter encouraged us to visit. Bill himself, an energetic man bouncing from place to place, took a few minutes to brief us on the company.

"I started in this business raising puppies for other services," he continued. "When I finally realized they weren't doing anything I couldn't do, I opened this place. People would ask me how I hoped to make a go of it in rural America. I said it wasn't rural America. It was real America."

He handed us off to an assistant while he hurried to other chores. Karen started the tour by describing the different 'doggie majors.' "We train three types of dogs. The best-known, of course, are seeing-eye dogs. We also train service dogs to help the handicapped. This includes dogs that cue deaf people when a phone rings or a timer goes off, or to grab things that partners in wheelchairs can't reach. The final course is for social dogs, which we send to nursing homes."

She showed us where the dogs train with their human mates, several rooms patterned after an apartment or small house. "We train the dog for four-to-twelve months, depending on the course. We then bring in the recipients and train them with the dogs, both here and around Washington. It takes twenty-four days to get a blind person working with their seeing-eye dog. People getting service dogs need fourteen days, and social dogs take seven. Our recipients range from the elderly to children; most services won't give a dog to anyone under eighteen."

I noticed a Siamese cat slinking through the mock dining room. "You have seeing-eye cats, too?"

"Oh, no," she laughed. "Snowball and one other cat were strays which adopted us. They help with training. They'll harass the poor dogs to no end, batting them on the snout, daring them to respond. We train the dogs not to let anything — including cats — distract them."

As we stepped outside, our next stop announced itself: the nursery. A symphony of barks erupted as we approached the puppy enclosure. "We have our own breeding stock, which we cultivate for intelligence and temperament. Some of our puppies are fourth-generation offspring of our original dames."

"How young do you start training them?" Sue asked.

"We don't keep the puppies on site. After we wean them, we farm them out to families that raise them for a year, under our guidelines. We then take them back and train them."

"It must be hard on the families, giving up a dog they've raised."

"That is the hardest part. If the dog washes out of training, those families have the option of taking it back. However, we only have a 26% release rate on the returned dogs, while most services hit 60-70%. We're low because we have our own breeders and know the bloodlines."

We walked through the youngster's kennel, admiring the pups. They yipped excitedly at the intruders, melting our hearts as pups usually to do. Next door was the current class of cadets, a fine looking bunch of Labradors, golden retrievers and German shepherds. In one cage, looking out of place, paced an old greyhound.

"He's a retired racer," the guide said. "We often bring them into the program. They're not as intelligent as our other breeds, but they work well as social dogs. You've got to make them think it's a game, that it's their idea."

Sue winked at her. "Like training husbands, right?"

So that's how she did it! And I'd thought walking mega-miles while she coasted on a bike made sense. As it did the next morning, when we faced our second nineteen-miler in three days. The road slashed straight west, an asphalt monster chewing through hills and swallowing farmland. Late in the day, we saw the monster eating: road crews widening the highway, gnawing away ever-larger chunks of land.

The flagwoman eyed us with surprise as we rolled up. "The road's all cut up. I don't think you'll want to ride that bike through here." Some sections were grooved, others dirt — not prime conditions for a touring bike. "If you want," she offered, "I'll throw the bike in my pickup when we quit, and drive you into Cuba. It's 5:30 now. We'll call it a day by seven."

She gave her name as Lavonne, "but everyone calls me Shorty." As cars stacked up behind her 'STOP' sign, she told us stories of life on the road crew. "We get all sorts of people through here. If it's a long wait, people get bored and handle it in different ways. One trucker fell asleep on me. I had to shake him to wake him."

In her 40s and far from dainty, Shorty looked as if she could handle most situations. Still, some people went too far. "One trucker got all upset when he had to stop. He shouted and yelled at me, but I wouldn't let him go. He finally jumped out and started beating me with his hat. A couple of coworkers had to pull him off me."

Our tale of the seeing-eye dogs sparked another memory for Shorty. "One person drove past my station every day with five puppies in the car. I adored one of them, the cutest one, and I always reached in to pet it. One day he asked me, 'Would you like to hold it?' I said yes. He handed it to me, drove off, and I never saw him again."

As the clock ticked past six, I got the walking itch. Unwilling to give up the day's last five miles, I set off on foot, leaving Sue to Shorty's tales. They caught up to me two miles from town, and chauffeured me the rest of the way. To mark our passage through her domain, Shorty treated us to a beer at the local tavern. We swapped more stories for an hour, until we left to grab some shuteye.

That night howls of coyotes laced the air, leading a parade of night noises. We snuggled close in our canvas home on the range.

The land is finally getting flat, and trees are thinning out. Grasslands and wheat fields take over, and plateaus replace the rolling hills. As the scenery changes, I wonder how the pioneers on the Oregon Trail must have felt, entering a land unlike any they'd seen before . . .

Nothing can beat a hot shower after a sweaty day of walking. When that shower comes with no roof to shut out the rosy glow of a beautiful sunset — well, sometimes life can't get any better. Ahhh, Courtland — home of the world's best pool showers.   -journal entry, June 5

AS THE RAILROADS SPREAD west in the 1800s, they had to worry about restocking supplies such as food and fuel. Most importantly, they needed water to refill their boilers at regular intervals. To this end, the railroad companies built large water tanks in towns spaced about forty miles apart. When the train pulled in, the fireman would pull on a rope to start the water flowing to his boiler. Towns which had little but water to offer, railroad workers called 'jerkwaters.'

Not to imply anything about Mankato, of course. We just expected more from our last one-thousand-person town in Kansas. We started the day in high spirits in Courtland, after another stranger paid for our breakfast. Eighteen miles in 95° temperatures quickly dampened that, and by day's end we were snapping at each other. Only the promise of a night in town kept us going.

The town, double the size of any other within twenty-five miles, disappointed us. The 'Heartland of the West' (or so the city limit sign called it) was in deep cardiac arrest. It lacked a bar or tavern, and the grocery store closed by 7:00. The Laundromat had locked its doors the previous year after college kids had stuck a child in the dryer, which left the entire county with no place to wash clothes. Since we hadn't hit one of the four nights each week the Pizza Hut opened, our dinner choice ran between a deli and the Do Drop In Cafe. We chose the cafe, only to discover that in Mankato, Monday night was Pancake Night. After eighteen miles, I'd hoped for more than flapjacks!

By the time we'd settled in the park, the newspaper had closed. However, someone had tipped them off, and the reporter tracked us down. She listened to our story, then mentioned we weren't the only travelers in town. "I came by earlier, and thought that might be you camped over there." Pointing to a camper parked near the pavilion, she continued, "I found out they're bicycling across Kansas."

After our interview, I wandered over to introduce myself. Gary Goodwin and his cousin sat in the camper, nursing sore muscles. "We both grew up in this state," Gary said, "and wanted to see it close up." He drove their support truck, pulling ahead and then biking back. I stayed for only a few minutes, long enough to get his address in Laramie, Wyoming, and promise to look him up when we walked through. (Unfortunately, our route changed, and we never did hit Laramie.)

We made good time leaving town the next morning, strolling under bright blue skies. Within an hour those bright skies filled with clouds, and a bank to the north grew ominously dark. When a silver line formed between the light clouds above and the black ones at the horizon, we began worrying about a storm. *Time to check the Walkman.*

The radio squawked reports of a severe storm warning, covering one-quarter of Kansas and most of southern Nebraska. Five miles to the north, directly over our destination, the storm cell churned out its worst weather. As the radio spewed out warnings of one hundred mile-per-hour winds, the silver line advanced, and the clouds took the sun prisoner. "We're miles from any town," Sue said. "What do we do?"

A farmhouse lay ahead, the name Pearson on the mailbox. We knocked on the door, but received no reply. With a black curtain now covering half the sky, I saw no options. "The garage is open. We'd better take shelter there."

We barely reached cover before the drops began falling. The rain beat on the garage roof, reaching a crescendo in no time. For ten minutes, the skies opened, pouring down around us. With its fury spent, the storm settled in for a soak, drizzling for another hour. Finally, ninety minutes after we'd ducked inside, the clouds left, flying south to terrorize another county.

"Time to move on," I said, packing away the Walkman. I hoisted my pack and turned in time to see Farmer Pearson pull his tractor into the driveway, a surprised look on his face.

I explained why we had used his garage, and he smiled and nodded. "Typical Kansas weather," he said. "I was plowing my fields five miles to the west, and could see it coming down. Over there, we didn't get a drop."

Sounds about right for the land of Oz.

Today has been a tale of two towns, both near 300 people, separated by fifteen miles and a state line, but worlds apart.

Burr Oak, our final Kansas stop, 'Rust Capital of the Great Plains,' epitomized the worst of the decaying Midwest towns we've passed through. The downtown consisted of a cafe (open until 2:00 p.m.) next door to a tavern (serving dinner), a hardware/grocery store with limited food across from a hardware/cold pop store, a crafts shop, a garage, a post office, and a paint store in dire need of repainting. The cafe specialized in dinginess — the standard hamburger-and-fries menu was augmented by hamburger and gravy served over the morning's leftover biscuits.

The city park, small as it was, had restrooms not maintained — the women's toilet was stopped up, and someone had defecated in the men's urinal. The townspeople, with one exception, showed singular disinterest in us, never asking who we were or why we were in town. If not for a well-kept school and a tavern with a creative menu, we would have written the town off as a big mistake — especially compared to its Nebraska neighbor.   -journal entry, June 8

** FENCE BOOTS AND FOREIGN PORNO **

* NEBRASKA *

June 8 - June 26, 1994
216 miles -- 25 bags
TOTAL, 2511 miles -- 854 bags

One of the purposes of travel is to avoid your destination at all costs (once you're there, you're there, and you'll never be permitted that long bated breath of anticipation again).
-- Lawrence Millman, "Last Places"

Fifteen miles north of Burr Oak lies Guide Rock. Our introduction to Nebraska filled us with high hopes for the rest of the state. Despite several boarded-up buildings, downtown offered far more than Burr Oak: a bank, two restaurants (one with a lounge), a well-stocked grocery store, a hardware cum gift shop, a TV/stereo outlet, an ice cream parlor, and the obligatory post office. The city park, four times the size of B.O.'s, had well-kept grounds and spotless restrooms.
-journal entry, June 8

"RANGE WARS!" PAM FRANK hissed those words. "This area erupted in them one hundred years ago. Cattlemen hated sheep ranchers, and vice versa. The moods were so tense the foes wouldn't even stay in the same hotel. Guide Rock had two, one for each side. You saw the hotel down the street, getting restored? Cattlemen stayed there."

The hotel was only one sign of the revival sweeping the town. Elsewhere, workers squeegeed the windows of the lounge. Foot traffic plied the sidewalks, ducking in and out of shops. "In the last sixty years, hardly anyone stayed here. Five years ago you could barely tell us apart from Burr Oak. Now the town is coming back."

We had wandered into the Tin Roof Sundae Shop, where we'd met the owners. Newcomers to town, Pam and Henry Frank had jumped into the revival. "Take our shop here," Henry said. "We opened two weeks ago, after a lot of work. When we redid the false front, we found the whole building leaned. We hired a bulldozer to push it upright, and a lot of folks came to watch, expecting the whole thing to topple. I'm sure they walked away disappointed when one good shove righted it."

"We've met people who come for ice cream all the way from Red Cloud," Pam said. "A few said they grew up in Guide Rock, and want to move back. Maybe people are finally getting tired of the stresses of city life, and miss having roots." She smiled at her husband and laid her hand on his arm. "We came from the east coast, and would never go back. People are *so* friendly here!"

Again, we'd found the heart of the country in the rural landscape. Guide Rock set the tone for the area, and Red Cloud expanded on it. At 1200 people, it qualified as a major town, with all the amenities — such as laundromats. After so long on the road, we had become connoisseurs of coin-ops, and Hometown Laundry got our highest rankings. The TV didn't surprise us, but the exercise bike did. We got the biggest kick from the name-tags stuck to each washer, saying, "Hello. My name is Betty," or Susan, Mary Lou, Mom, etc. The dryers went further, with labels stating, "Lotty does well with fluffy things (curtains, panties)," or "Agnes handles heavy clothes best (like overalls)," or "Hilda likes the general run of clothes."

Sue chatted with the woman using the adjacent washer. "I ate at the cafe across the street," she said, "and mentioned to the waitress I was moving here. 'What day?' she asked. 'I'll help you unpack!' I hope everyone's that friendly here!"

As we rolled along we learned about history, Great Plains style. Willa Cather, born in Red Cloud, had won the Pulitzer Prize for her stories of Great Plains life in *O Pioneers!* and *My Antonia*. Pierce Lyden, the original black-hat-and-moustache villain from the dime-a-dozen Western movies, still lived in Naponee. Naponee also claimed fame as the birthplace of David Janssen, TV's 'The Fugitive.'

Outside Red Cloud we saw the Starke barn, the largest round barn in Nebraska and one of the largest in the country: 65' high, 130' in diameter, a center silo 28' across. "Not one nail in it," a neighboring farmer told us. "The 12x12 timbers in the frame are held together by pressure. The weight of the upper part 'cements' it into place. Experts say it can hold more'n a thousand tons."

The miles passed quickly, long stretches of wide-open fields. Several ranches sported the feature of which Steven Newman had warned us: fence boots. The owners had nailed worn-out cowboy boots onto their fence posts, the weathered toes ofttimes drooping straight down. "No one could ever explain why they did it," he had said. "They just shrugged and said something about tradition." We later bought a postcard picturing the fence

boots above the caption, "Cowboy's souls (soles?) go to heaven." Maybe that was their first step?

As the land grew flatter, the scenery petered out. To occupy the time, Sue hummed old songs, and I made up new ones. Passing though Franklin, I gained inspiration from an edge-of-town motel ('Plank's Plunk and Bunk'), and soon I had rewritten 'King of the Road'. "Let me sing it for you," I told Sue on a hot, treeless stretch. "Pretend I'm Roger Miller."

typical Nebraska scenery

"D.Q. and Casey's cups,
              Beer cans and ice-cream pushups,
Picking litter on the fly,
              Adopt-A-Highway has been by,
Ah, but two hours of walking west,
              Brings us to what we like the best
'Nother city park to set up camp in,
              King of the Road!

"Bovines watch as we pass,
              Chewin' on their cud and grass
We talk to them, get them up
              As we march by, Hup! Hup! Hup!
Cornfields spreading far
              Ten minutes, we'll see another car
Nebraska's the place to be,
              Don't you believe me?

"Another day, another town
              Friendly people all around.
Fluffy clouds, a little sun,
              Oh, aren't we having fun?
But two miles of walking west
              Brings us to what we like the best
A swimming pool with showers to clean in
              King of the Road!

"McDonalds and Wendy's bags
              Underwear and dirty rags
Just another freedom day
              Litterwalking away!"

Sue rolled her eyes and groaned. "Hey," I cried, "the cows liked it!"
Either that, or those Angus grins came from reading the girlie magazines. In an episode fit for _The Far Side_, we noticed magazine pages lying in a ditch twenty yards from grazing cattle, five miles outside Red Cloud. A closer look revealed, not _Playboy_ or _Hustler_, but _foreign_ porno rags. High class cows here!

I had to read further. "Listen to this," I said, opening *Starman*. "It says, 'Ich warte immer noch auf meinem Partner! Ich suche die Herausforderung! Beruf äußerst erfolgreich!' Or else!"

Sue peered over my shoulder. "How about, 'Nicole jung, schön und klug — stellt sich dem Leben frontal, furchtlos, und ungestüm.' What does that mean? Young, pretty Nicole likes her love forwards, backwards, and sideways?"

I glanced at the other rag Sue had picked up, *CATS Magazyn Protyczny*. The headlines looked Polish: NAJPIĘKNIEJSZE MIKOŁAJKI. KRAINA SEKSU I MUZYKI. "Drugs, sex, and rock'n'roll?" I guessed. Inside, we read the ad for the Jessica video: "Ta ślizena, jasnowtosa dziewczyna, która wyssie z ciebie wszystkie soke, ma trzy nęcące dziurki do zabawy."

Sue grabbed the *CATS* and waved it at the nearby bovines. "How dare you waste your time reading this! And how could you even think of doing zabawy with poor Jessica!"

The Highway Cafe in Riverton was a relic from the '40s. The cash register, an old plastic radio, a candlestick telephone, rusted metal barstools — even an ancient EAT/GAS crosswords sign in front. The owner, eighty-five years old and suffering from cancer, shuffled back and forth cooking breakfast (our choices: eggs, or ham and eggs) and pouring coffee. Though she greeted us warmly, she never stopped scurrying, and she took our orders with no-nonsense haste. Thus, when I asked for eggs sunny side up and they came back scrambled, I didn't say a word. Good thing, too — a customer whispered to us how years ago, Vi had pancakes on the menu, and one regular always complained they were too tough. One day she cooked a rag in his short stack and served them to him.   -journal entry, June 11*

What still surprises me is the region's friendliness. People say hello, ask where we're from, offer us help. Maybe the slower pace of life gives them a chance to care about more than getting that close parking space at the mall, or making three more sales calls before rush hour clogs the freeway.   -journal entry, June 13*

THROUGH NEBRASKA WE FOLLOWED the Manure River.

That's what the Republican Pawnee Indians called it, a result of the throngs of buffalo which lived along its banks. When the government began surveying the state in 1855, they thought the name a tad too descriptive, and renamed it the Republican River after the Pawnees that lived there.

After President Lincoln signed an 1863 law allowing free homesteads in the territory, settlers streamed in. Frontier towns which sprung up struggled to survive, competing with nearby settlements for stores, schools, and roads. People quickly found they could help their town most by having it named the county seat.

In Harlan County, two towns fought for that title. Settlers called five elections in ten years, with Alma winning the final two. Citizens of Orleans, angered over purported voter fraud, appealed the results. The Supreme Court found irregularities (they used much stronger terms) with voting in Alma and threw out their votes, naming Orleans the winner. However, the court then ruled the entire election invalid, resulting in no change. Tired of the legal runaround, a band of Orleans men stole the county records from Alma late one night during a drenching rainstorm. On the way back to Orleans they lost the papers in the flooding Republican River.

Back then, the towns fought for their lives, the loser often sentenced to a steady decline. Now both Alma and Orleans, along with most other towns we visited, drifted lazily, far from the frenzied pace of the big city. We could predict what coming towns would offer: A library branch, open between two and five hours, two-to-six days a week. One or more cafes which closed at two p.m., and a tavern where we could get dinner. A granary/feed co-op guarding the railroad tracks. A general store stocked with goodies to get us through another day. For villages over three hundred people, add a swimming pool. At nine hundred, they supported a weekly newspaper. A few larger towns featured banks, hardware stores, grocers, and restaurants — everything a walker could need and more. Of course, we couldn't forget the sirens three times daily!

Along the river, we hit one or two towns every day.

They never snuck up on us. Visible for miles, the water towers announced the presence of each village. After a while, the towers took on personalities. Unadorned cylinders looked like giant cans of Pringle's potato chips. Spherical ones reminded us of golf balls teed up, waiting for

Goliath to drive them. The most popular style resembled the head of Oz's tin man welded to a bar stool. Though many were unpainted, others wore coats of azure, green, yellow, or (in one case) orange and blue school colors.

Deep in the 'Meat and Potatoes' Belt, our diet grew boring. "I'm sick of hamburgers and microwaved pizzas," Sue lamented, "and chicken-fried steaks — how can you eat that?! What does it take to find vegetables in this state? Oh, sure, they've got salads, but they drown them in Dorothy Lynch dressing." This mixture of tomato soup and sugar, Nebraska's State Dressing, appeared on every menu across the state — but we found it nowhere else.

What our meals lacked in variety, they matched in atmosphere. We ate most dinners serenaded by country music, courtesy of the record machine in some far corner. "By the time we leave the state," I joked, "I'll know the words to 'Bubba Shot the Jukebox' by heart."

Every day the flat land grew even flatter. June 15 marked the first day we climbed no hills. To the south, a line of trees paralleled our path, marking the course of the river. To the north, farm fields spread to the horizon. The temperatures settled into the mid-80s with an occasional foray to 90°. Clouds came and clouds went, some nights treating us to a pageant of lightning, but no rain came our way. Wind became our constant companion, boredom our constant enemy.

"Now there's a unique one!" I pointed out the latest in an intermittent parade of original mailboxes. We had seen several painted like cows, with black spots on a white background and wooden feet tacked to the sides. Earlier that day Sue noticed a pig, painted pink and white. Now I'd logged a winner.

"Where?" she asked as she rode by it. "Oh! Talk about blending in." Standing in front of the field of corn, a metal cornstalk rose, the ripe 'ear' ready to accept the day's mail.

An hour later, we approached a crew of three repairing the train tracks next to the road. "How's your singing voice?" I asked Sue. She looked at me with a question in her eyes, but my smile clued her in. "Wait 'til we get closer."

As we passed them, we broke into song. ♪"I've been workin' on the railroad, all the live long day . . ."♫ They looked up, startled, then smiled and waved. (Thrills were thrills, cheap or not!)

Each town we hit had a story. Oxford, for example, we reached on the eve of their big Turkey Days festival. By 6:00, the police had blocked Main Street, and the carnies had taken over. The crowds, the "Try your luck! Easy to win!" calls of the hawkers, the smell of cotton candy, the screams of kids rocking on the Ferris wheel, would come after we'd moved on. This night, I watched it take seed, saw the horses bolted to the carousel, the power hooked to the roller coasters. Saw "carpenter's crack" above the worker's sagging pants. (Some things are universal.)

Arapahoe showed us how the city parks stayed so lush. Our peaceful night suddenly ended at half past midnight, when a barrage of water drummed against the tent. Jolted awake, Sue peered out the flap. "Oh, great, sprinklers!" Timing our exit for the next cycle, we jumped out, pulled up stakes, and dragged the tent to dry safety. An hour later we repeated the exercise, when the next bank of sprinklers sprang to life.

Cambridge teased us with memories of last year. We took in the local baseball games to pass the evening, and one foul ball landed four feet from Sue. She promptly left.

In Indianola, site of a World War II German POW camp, the bartender told us how the town got its name. "Some people say the first settlers came from Indianola, Iowa, but that story's too pat. Others say that when whites first settled the town, a big battle between rival Indian tribes took place nearby. One wounded squaw made her way into town, where she died days later. They buried her in the town park. Her name was Ola." He paused, then added, "However, a few people insist that back in the 1800s, the settlers here forgot how to make butter. They got a recipe from the Indians, and made so much they had to give it away. The town's name, they swear, is a contraction of the original 'Indianoleo'."

As we sat at the counter listening to his tales, a news flash on the television caught our eyes. Assembled for the TV cameras, a lawyer and family friends issued their plea: "OJ, turn yourself in. Don't do anything drastic." In the heartland, as it had across the country, the 'OJ Show' had begun.

We watched for a few minutes, discussing the case we'd seen in the papers. When the excitement on the screen died away, we picked up our tired bodies and headed back to camp. On the way, we stopped at the co-op/mini-mart for a cup of java. I browsed while Sue waited to pay, noticing several items I'd never seen on the shelves of a 7-11. "What's this, Bovine Rota-Corona vaccine?" I asked myself. "Sounds like a big seller. Oh, I've got to have a J-99 Hercules Fetal Extractor! How could I cross the state without one?" A book giving hints for successful feedlot management provided gems of wisdom. "For healthy operation, get cows that are healthy and have not been subjected to stress. Process cows immediately off the truck or depression will set in and last forty-eight hours."

That's what Nebraska needs, I thought, *depressed overstressed cows!*

As we walked to the tent under cloudless skies, televisions from coast to coast again focused on Los Angeles. Millions of eyes across the country watched the Slow Freeway Chase of the White Bronco. Our eyes searched the heavens for constellations and shooting stars.

I think we had the better show.

"DO YOU THINK THEY charge extra for the cold running water?" I asked Sue.

Our motel room in McCook ended up as no bargain. Unwilling to pay $60 at the chain motel next door, we settled for the $20 special at the motel with no sign. Now battered by torrential rains, the room sprung a waterfall over the bed.

We'd taken an extra day off as a sanity stop, a break after four weeks of tiny towns. Though we'd continued to knock off the miles at a record pace, the month of rural life had tested our endurance. We needed a taste of city life. At eight thousand people, McCook ('City Without Limits') had amenities we'd forgotten about — movie theaters, ethnic food, a daily paper.

"You know, I'd planned on refinishing the roof next week," the owner said when we notified him. "I'll move you to the room next door."

We'd hoped the break would rest bodies weary from our unrelenting pace. Sue's, in particular, showed the stress. Her feet hurt from pushing the bike when her seat was too sore to ride it. The second McCook room provided a less-than-perfect antidote, since the bed springs gave out an hour after we'd switched. Still, a lazy morning, shopping, an afternoon nap, and Chinese food recharged us for two more weeks in the hinterlands.

On the road the next day, we met our first bike tourer since Missouri. "Heading for Chicago," he told us. "My wife's driving a support car so I can ride without panniers."

"How are the roads to the west?" Sue asked. "I love biking U.S. 34, with its wide shoulders."

"It's like that most of the way to Brush, Colorado. You'll be fine if it cools down. If not . . ." He slowly shook his head. "My first couple days out of Boulder, the pavement was so hot it melted my tires."

With us well rested, the miles came easy, and we finished walking by noon. Our hometown *du jour* was Culbertson ('Small Town, Big Heart'), another town falling victim to decay. After lunch and a shower, we lodged ourselves at the park next to the pool. The bike and pack quickly attracted notice, and three thirteen-year-old girls came to visit. They chatted with us about schoolgirl stuff until a precocious seven-year-old girl wandered by and demanded our attention. She climbed on Sue's bike, danced on the picnic tables, pestered us with questions, and generally made a nuisance of herself. After a long string of boring afternoons, we welcomed the diversion.

"So this is the Great Plains," Sue remarked as we crested our first rise the next morning. The view stretched for miles, overseeing thousands of acres of ripening wheat rippling in the breezes. To the south, a line of green marked the rapidly dwindling Republican River. Elsewhere, rare clumps of trees dotted the landscape, like emerald islands in an ocean of gold.

At 8:30, a voice from behind surprised us. "You must be the people we heard about in McCook!"

We turned to see a couple astride two fully-loaded bikes. "Hi. I'm Kirk Maharry," said a man who confessed to an age in his fifties. "This is my wife Diana. We're bicycling from Iowa to Greeley, Colorado."

Diana nodded as Kirk introduced them. She looked ten years younger than her husband, but much wearier as she straddled her bike. "It's my first bike tour," she explained. "Kirk's done several, and he finally talked me into joining him."

Kirk, a teacher in Iowa, liked the long school breaks for outings such as this. "We're setting a medium pace," he said. "We had a couple of sixty-mile days, and today we're shooting for eighty."

We exchanged addresses before they rode on. Within minutes they had vanished from view, hidden by a wide turn in the road. For half an hour, I pondered on their trip, envying them their 'rapid' transit — until another call from behind ended my reverie. "You must be the couple they talked about in McCook!"

This time, the bicyclist rode alone. Mike looked twentyish, with an athletic build and muscular legs. "I left Lincoln two days ago, on my way to Denver."

"You left Lincoln Monday?" I asked. "That's quite a distance."

He nodded, his bike helmet reflecting the sun. "I'm riding 110 to 120 miles a day."

"At that speed," Sue said, "you'll probably catch Kirk and Diana by lunchtime."

NOTES FROM SUE'S JOURNAL:
Storm moved in at 6:30 when we started to walk four miles to the lake. Foot pain so bad I cried. Pushed bike up hill 'til tire went flat. Glen changed it, but pump won't work. Walked to lake, camped in rain fifty yards from train tracks. Pain excruciating — butt aches — ankle itchy and swollen from bug bites. WANT TO GO HOME.
- June 22

MURPHY FINALLY CAUGHT US, enforcing his law on a lonely hill miles from anywhere. The flat didn't faze me; I knew we'd suffer at least one this trip. The drizzle ranked as only a slight discomfort. When the bike pump failed, though, my mood sunk. Frustrated, I remounted the wheel and helped Sue push the bike the last mile.

Early the next morning we thumbed our way into Stratton. After filling the tire with air and the panniers with food, we set out for the day's goal — the blip on the map labeled 'Max.' The previous night's rain had cooled the air, giving it a fresh taste. We set a brisk pace for two miles, until the tire went flat again.

No point in trying to fix it out here. Our extended thumbs promptly stopped a Cadillac — great for a luxury ride, but no help when you're hauling a bike. The laundry truck that stopped next was less cozy, but it had room for Sue and the Nishiki. I waved goodbye and tackled the ten miles into town.

Max was — well, it was Max. (No official nickname, though I would propose 'Huh?') According to the map, one hundred people called it home. Five or six may have also called it work, between the gas station, post office, and granary. It stretched along a half-mile of highway, with homes to the north and the rail line to the south.

Sue waited for me at the gas station. "It's a good thing we got groceries," she said, "unless you had your heart set on microwaved Beanie Weenies. The selection's pretty poor."

The selection did include ice cream, which I knew would taste good in the late afternoon heat. Inside, I asked the owner how late she stayed open. "Oh, five o'clock. Or maybe four, or three, depending how I feel."

We retired to the Max park for a picnic lunch. The park looked little used: Uncut grass grew up the legs of two picnic tables. Swings on the swing set hung half-attached. Dirty windows on the locked clubhouse revealed a near-empty room inside. The nearest restrooms were back at the gas station — we hoped Mother Nature wouldn't call after five o'clock (or four, or three). For one night, we would survive.

"So what now?" Sue asked as she made her sandwich. Frustration filled her voice. "I can't go much further. I thought my feet had toughened, but now I have blisters under my calluses. Last night it took everything I had to push the bike up that hill."

I shook my head, gazing into the neighboring fields. My mind raced over our options, but it turned up no easy answers. "I guess we have no choice. I'll have to call Dad and see if he can come get you. What is it, about two hundred miles? Then you can come back with the car."

Her face fell, but she didn't argue. "Please don't make him come today," she asked. "It's too late. Maybe he can meet us in Benkelman tomorrow."

I returned to the station after lunch to call my father and repair the tire. Four men sat inside mixing and kneading the latest gossip, forming it, watching it rise. I listened to them as I surveyed the selection of ice cream. The one doing the most talking caught my attention: older, balding, and with a knot the size and shape of a golf ball growing from his forehead.

After staying long enough to insure I'd be the next topic of discussion, I stepped outside to fix the tire. The brand new tube had sprung three leaks. This time, I hoped my patches would hold air.

Then it was back to the park for another endless afternoon playing cards, reading, and watching weeds grow. Two eight-year-old girls interrupted one spirited game of rummy when they walked their dog through the park. We asked them several questions, trying to start a conversation, but they kept their distance and answered us with nods and shrugs.

Shortly after they left, a gunshot echoed through the air. An eerie silence fell over the park, punctuated by a second shot, then a third. "It's coming from the highway," Sue noted. A fourth shot. We moved to our tent, trying to see past the trees in the next field. A fifth shot sounded before sounds of life returned to the day.

Within minutes, we heard the squawk of a police radio. Sue imagined the worst. "Maybe someone got shot! Geez, I hope they don't suspect us. I can see it now: 'Drifters Enter Max, Go On Killing Spree!' What a headline!" The headlines grew ever more absurd as our imaginations ran wild, until hunger for ice cream ended the game.

That evening, as the setting sun painted the western skies orange, I spied a couple entering the park, heading our way. She was petite, a marked contrast to the large man at her side. With a brawny chest and athletic legs, he could have played football. In the fading light, I pegged them as our age.

"How're you doing," the burly 'Max'ite said. "My name's Moose, and this is Kim." We introduced ourselves, and offered them a seat at our picnic table.

"You two have really got the phone lines burning up," Kim said. "Some folks said they saw a strange man alone on a bicycle, riding back and forth to the store. Someone else said, no, he had a woman in the park." She flashed a winning smile. "We figured we'd better check it ourselves."

"Yeah, I bet a lot of news gets spread at the station," I said. "I heard a group of them going at it today. The guy with the growth really talks up a storm."

Moose chuckled. "Oh, you met him? He's a real character — we call him Pumpkinhead. He had it removed once, but it grew right back. Last Halloween, he painted it orange!"

We talked about the excitement of life in Max. "It must get so boring," Sue guessed. "However, they did have the shooting today. We're dying to know what happened."

"Oh, that," Moose said. "We heard it was the police. The officer hit a deer, and had to kill it."

"Can you believe," Kim added, "he hit it with a brand new police car? Less than a hundred miles on it."

Kim and Moose from Max

Otherwise, they agreed. "It's boring, but it's cheap," Moose admitted. "Our house cost under $20,000, and we don't worry about crime. The closest we got to a 'criminal element' in town was the time the hobos hopped off the train, thinking they'd reached Benkelman. Boy, were they surprised!"

They kept us company until 10:00, breaking our long string of lonely nights. Before leaving, they invited us to go fishing with them Saturday. "Sue won't be here," I explained, "but I'd love to!"

As we lay in the tent later, tossing and turning in the lingering heat, Sue gave my hand a squeeze. "I'm sorry about 'quitting' again," she said. "Especially so close to our July 4th break."

I snuggled close and hugged her. "You're not quitting, you're taking care of your health. If you don't get off your feet, they'll never heal."

She shook her head, her hair brushing my face. "I AM quitting," she insisted. "Whether I want to or I have to, it works out the same. I'm an easily bored person, I know, but I could handle the boredom by itself. It's only when I'm in pain and I have nothing to take my mind off it that drives me crazy."

She struggled to keep her voice from cracking. "If I try to walk, my feet blister. Then I get on the bike, and my hips hurt from pedaling and my ass hurts from sitting. If I favor one part of my body, something else kicks in. I just can't handle fifteen miles every day.

"I would be fine if I could cross the country at five miles a day. I know, I know. We can't do that, because we have nowhere to stop or eat until the next city."

I brushed away a tear trickling down her cheek. "I wish I could arrange that."

She squeezed my hand tighter. "I've given it all I can. I try to psyche myself up, to tell myself, 'Susan, you won't be in pain tomorrow.' Then I go to bed, and I can't sleep because my heels hurt too much to lay them down.

"I'm not a quitter; you know that. I want to do this trip. I want to find a solution, short of a car, which will let us do that. With a car, people look at us and think I drive you ahead, that we cheat. We've seen how it keeps us from meeting people."

She stopped and fixed her brown eyes on me. "Tell me the truth. Are you having fun?"

I laid back and stared at the stars through the tent window, as if they could give me words I needed. "I feel guilty that you're going through this much pain because of me. Yes, it's my fault," I cut off her protests, "because if I said I'm tired of this trip, we'd quit today, and you could get back to a normal life. But I'm too stubborn to quit. I've started this thing, and my past is littered with projects I never finished. For once, just once, I want to finish something that's hard, that I couldn't coast through."

"So you're enjoying this?"

"I didn't say I'm not bored. I am. And it will get worse through Wyoming and Idaho, count on it." I rolled on my side to face her.

She nodded. "I'm worried about it, too. Right now I'm looking forward to July 4th with your family, picnics and fireworks and all. Then we've got Fort Collins, where you went to college, seeing your friends and my aunt and uncle. After that, though, there's nothing — no family, no friends, not even many towns — for three months. Nothing but scrub brush and summer heat until we're almost done. How will we get through it?"

We lapsed into silence, thinking about the task ahead. Was the car our only option? How else could we get through the desolation of Wyoming, a problem we must soon face? After a moment, she asked, "You don't like having the car, do you?"

"It wasn't what we planned," I said. "Forget that it makes meeting people harder. Forget the added expense. I know you're not happy sitting in the car. You deserve to be out there too, getting your exercise, doing what you dreamed of. Why should you be sentenced to the sag wagon?"

"Because my body says so!" she said, her voice a mixture of bitterness and resignation. "This whole trip has been one long case of 'let's fix Sue,' of how can we get Sue through the next week, or the next month. How do you think that makes me feel?"

No doubt about it, we've reached the area early settlers dubbed the 'Great American Desert.' Flat, treeless (except for watering holes and streams), and hot sums it up. With nothing to stop it, the wind races by all day. Ranch houses are growing rare, and cattle provide the only scenery. -journal entry, June 25

BENKELMAN, WITH 1200 PEOPLE, looked ordinary enough when we rolled in late in the morning. The bike had worked fine, the tire leaking no air. We crossed town to the city park, meeting my father there. As we tossed the bike in the back of the pickup, Moose and Kim drove up with their picnic lunch. "We wondered if you'd be here," Kim said. "You really go for the parks, don't you?"

Our lunch passed quickly. I relished seeing Dad again, and babbled about our adventures in Max. Too soon, though, the food was gone, followed by Dad and Sue. With the pickup disappearing down the road, I busied myself pitching camp, trying to ignore the loneliness I felt. Voices from behind startled me as I unrolled my sleeping bag.

"When did you get here?"

I turned to see the two girls we'd met in Max, walking their dog through the park. Yesterday they'd been too shy to talk. Today they bubbled as they asked about my day's walk, and told me about themselves. Vanessa had finished second grade and Lindsay third, and both looked forward to a long summer break. They found me again an hour later, as I hit the pool for my shower. I enjoyed the unexpected attention.

I passed the afternoon writing and visiting with RV campers parked nearby, setting up for a family reunion. As evening tiptoed in, I wandered downtown for dinner and to call Sue. Crossing the street, I heard a call from a second floor landing. "Glen! Hi!" Vanessa and Lindsay again.

Minutes later, a car cruising the main drag speared me in its headlights. Moose's voice boomed from the car. "Are we still set for tomorrow? We'll meet you at the junction about 2:00."

Who will find me at the softball tournament? I wondered. *Rod Serling, perhaps? I could almost hear him: "He expected to hide in a small Nebraska town, but instead wandered into . . . the Twilight Zone!"*

I had barely grabbed a seat on the bleachers when I heard my name again. "Came for some excitement, huh?" asked the reporter we'd talked to that morning. "Where's Sue?"

Someplace far less interesting than the town with no strangers!

The loneliness I dreaded came calling the next day as I struck out onto the prairie. A hundred yards to the north the Republican River had shrunk to a mangy stream, marked only by an intermittent line of trees. The grasses grew brown in the summer heat, and I saw my first cactus. A few cars passed by, as did a bicyclist with his dog perched on the panniers. "I'm just traveling around," he said as he passed without slowing.

Shortly after two, Moose and Kim found me at the road leading to the lake. I climbed into the back of the truck with Moose's sons Mitch and Josh, and we bumped up the dirt road to Rock Creek Lake. His boys, aged ten and twelve, were avid fishermen, and we four men spent an hour that evening floating in the canoe. The fish didn't bite, but it made no difference. For another moment, life was perfect.

In the morning, Moose donned his chef hat and whipped up a breakfast of bacon, eggs, and cobbler with fresh blueberries. "I've got to give you credit, Moose," I commended him. "This is the second best breakfast I've had this trip."

"Only the second?" He curled his lips downward, pretending to pout.

"Well, what can you expect when first place was waffles with fresh maple syrup!"

The empty miles dragged by on my way to Haigler ('Cornerstone of Nebraska'). Sue met me there late that afternoon, beaming. "I've got good news!" she said. "A friend of your mother gave me a cream to help my calluses. They're already better!"

"Oh? What is it?"

"Promise not to laugh? It's Bag Balm."

I choked back a chuckle. "The stuff farmers put on cows' udders to keep them from drying out?" I kissed her on the cheek. "Leave it to my wiffums to use moo moisturizer!"

She put her hands on her hips and shot me a playful look of disdain. "Hey! There're more cows out here than humans. If it's good enough for them, who am I to argue?"

** WHAT'S IN A NAME? **

* COLORADO *

June 27 - July 21, 1994
212 miles -- 51 bags
TOTAL, 2723 miles -- 905 bags

It is always oneself that one encounters in traveling.
- Lance Morrow

The blue Trans-Am tooted its horn as it passed, then pulled over in front of me. As I approached it, the driver cleared off the passenger seat for me. He looked up, surprised, when I walked up the driver's side instead. "Thanks for offering the ride," I said, "but I'm walking across the country."

He stared at me in disbelief. "What country?"

-journal entry, June 27

THE PLAN SOUNDED FOOLPROOF.

"What can we do for our folks?" I'd asked Sue in Kansas. "Your dad's spent a lot of time chronicling the trip, logging all the articles we send him. My mom's handled all our bills and our mail. How can we repay them?"

The answer eluded us that day, but slowly a plan formed. "If only we could dedicate the trip to them," Sue mused. "I know they're with us in spirit. If only they could join us on the road . . ."

"Maybe they could, in a way." I drew out an idea which had just formed. What if, in some small town, Jim and Dorothy Armstead told the newspaper about their epic walk? Her parents could have a gift — 'instant fame' — no one else could give them. If we pulled it off, then Joe and Pat Hanket, LitterWalkers, could stroll into another town.

We'd put off trying it in Kansas, since reporters had already seen us in the Topeka paper. The *Omaha World-Herald* featured us our first day in Nebraska, spreading our names across the state and postponing our plan again. In Colorado, though, the daily papers came out of Denver. "We could appear in the small town weeklies," I figured, "and be forgotten by the time we hit the *Denver Post*."

We targeted Wray ('All-American City') for the switch. Before approaching the *Gazette* offices, we rehearsed our stories. "Remember," Sue coached, "we live in Connecticut, we met in New York. You work as a sales manager at Lever. We have one daughter Sue, who's in college. Got it?"

I hoped my nervousness didn't show. With ninety interviews behind us, we had no trouble talking about the walk. The personal questions tested us, but our memorized answers came easily. As the questions ran out, I relaxed — and stumbled over the final query. "I think this is so great," the reporter said. "How long have you been married?"

Never the quickest person, I froze. I stole a glance at Sue, who hesitated for only a second. "Nineteen glorious years," she answered, patting my hand with affection.

The next morning the buttes outside town inspired thoughts of John Wayne movies. *Here come the Litter Wranglers, ready to lasso those rogue beer cans!* By 10:00 the buttes had fallen behind, leaving a land shorn clear of landmarks. We could see six or seven miles across the flat earth, no trees or hills blocking our view. Far ahead, the water tower for Eckley beckoned.

Eckley ('For Sale By Owner') held little more than a tavern right on the highway. Signs on U.S. 34 mentioned a grocery/deli downtown, but the one-block strip was deserted. In one window of a boarded-up building, I could see faded ads hawking the deli specials. "Last year, they opened a general store here," the librarian told us. "Three months later the deli moved in and siphoned off half the business. With the competition, both went bankrupt."

So Eckley survived with a tavern and a library. We camped at the base of the water tower, next to the library. The next morning we stayed for story hour, a weekly event for the area kids. This week, they were surprised by a guest speaker.

As the temperatures climbed back into the nineties, the walking grew tedious — and lonely. Little traffic traveled U.S. 34, and no one honked or waved. I covered most miles by myself, though Sue did walk a little each day. Her infected heel slowly healed, thanks to regular applications of Bag

". . .'L', as in 'Litter'. . ."

Balm. "I'm glad it's better," I told her, "but if you sprout a nipple down there, I'm throwing the stuff away."

As in Kansas and Nebraska, the lack of traffic kept the litter down. Each day I filled only two bags with beer cans, cigarette wrappers, oil cans, and — of course — underwear. Black lace panties topped our prize list for the region, and we saved them for my youngest sister. (She disposed of them properly.)

After Eckley, Yuma (2700 people) felt like New York City. We even found ethnic food! At the Mexican restaurant, the owners struck up a conversation. "We moved here from California a year ago," he said. "We love the small town atmosphere, and don't miss Los Angeles a bit." The four of us played the name game — "You lived where? Did you know so-and-so?" — and actually won a round: he used to work with a good friend of ours.

After lunch we girded ourselves for another interview. This time Joe and Pat Hanket related their litter crusade to the *Pioneer* reporter. We breezed through the interview, though inside I hated the charade. Afterwards we agreed: enough! "I know we're bored with interviewing," I said, "but I can't stand lying. From now on, let's be ourselves."

Hot, dry and flat. Relentless, parching wind — air mass on a mission, gotta get there. Sky so blue my eyes water, punctuated by a solitary cloud. Miles of golden grain, stretching to the horizon. Town limits signs which list elevation, not population. Legions of grasshoppers swarming about my feet. And eighteen-wheelers blowing by all morning long.

Just another day in eastern Colorado.

-journal entry, June 30

"MY WIFE AND I are walking across the country picking up litter," I told the reporter at Akron's *News Reporter*.

She nodded. "So which names are you using today?"

My heart fell to my feet, rattling somewhere around my toes. My smile fled as I stammered out an apology. Sheepishly I explained why we'd misled her fellow reporters. "So we thought it was a harmless way to give our parents a thrill. If you don't mind my asking, how did you find out about us?"

As she listened, she betrayed no emotion. Her impassive face gave no clue whether she condemned our mischief or dismissed it. Finally she smiled slightly. "Here on the plains newspaper people stay pretty tight. The editor in Yuma caught your story in the Benkelman paper Wednesday, and noticed the different names. He called the reporter in Wray, whom you had given a third set of names. Then he called me."

After giving her the whole story, we slunk off to the library. Ten weeks of travel with no real break had let the stresses inundate me. Worries about Wyoming. Slogging through the heat. Battling boredom. Now, the embarrassment with the papers. Under these weights, my mood plummeted.

I needed a break.

The next morning temperatures dropped ten degrees, promising us an easy final day. We raced through the fifteen miles, dropping into the barren reaches of the South Platte River valley. The coming holiday brought out another songwriting mood, and I composed a ballad to the tune of *Jingle Bells*:

Pepsi cans, Millers cans,
                    Jingle all the way
Oh what fun to pick up trash

On 34 Highway!

Across the land we go
                With hiking boots and bike,
Picking up litter
                As we take our hike.
Trucks go whizzing by,
                Blowing us away.
Oh what fun to litter walk
                Every single day!
Mountain Dew and Coors cans
                Jingle . . .

Sun comes peeking out
                As we make our rounds,
Wind will soon pick up
                Trying to cool us down.
Cows watch as we pass
                With the same blank stare
We always wave and talk to them
                As if they really care!
Sam's Club cans, Keystone cans
                Jingle . . .

"I remember when I met you," Sue interrupted my recital. "Back then,
you seemed so normal . . ."

*In the 1920s, With the increasing popularity of the automobile, a
national network of roads sprung up to connect the nation's cities.
Before the federal government standardized the growing highway system
with route numbers, civic groups named the roads. Many names were
prosaic, lending glamour to a strip of asphalt — Rocky Mountain
Highway, Sunrose Highway. Others leaned to the pedantic, mentioning
the cities linked. Thus, when we asked the librarian about county road
Q to Wiggins, she replied, "That's the old DLD, or Detroit-Lincoln-
Denver Road."*   -journal entry, July 13

OUR THREE-DAY BREAK TURNED into five, then eight days as we forsook the road for family events. The parching weather reported from the plains did little to rekindle our fire, and the dark cloud of the newspaper fiasco kept us subdued. Maybe, I dreamed, the furor would die if we gave it an extra week.

Yeah, and maybe we'd win the lottery, too. My hopes were dashed our first afternoon back on the road, hiking and biking again. We stopped at the weekly paper in Brush, introducing ourselves to the clerk at the desk. As he fetched the editor, I picked up a copy of Akron's *News Reporter* from the counter. Our front page article — "Unique Couple Spending an Unusual Summer" — left me with mixed emotions: pleased to see she focused on our litter war; disappointed she used the name game as her lead. The disappointment turned to dread when the clerk returned from the back room. "Thanks, but he says we'll pass."

Fort Morgan, our next town, had a daily paper — the first since McCook. At ten thousand people, the city struck me as cosmopolitan. *Surely their newspaper will cover us.* I entered their offices with confidence, and Sue hesitantly followed. To a reporter, I explained our visit. "We're walking coast-to-coast cleaning up trash, and always stop at the local papers to tell our story."

An editor heard me and came to the desk. "Picking up litter, huh? I read something on my wire about two walkers who weren't who they said they were. I don't think we'll cover you." He turned to walk away.

Something inside me snapped. "Now wait a minute!" I demanded, stopping him. "You're a community newspaper, and you're supposed to report the news, right? Well, we've walked 2700 miles and picked up 4500 pounds of trash. People in seventeen states have followed our trek from articles in over one hundred newspapers. Are you telling me *that's* not news?"

He stood silently as I pounded out my statistics. When my tirade finished, he hesitated as if ready to argue, then thought better of it. To the reporter, he said, "Why don't you take his information, and find out which roads they're walking. We'll send a photographer to catch them in action."

I left the paper hopeful we'd broken the curse. However, Sue's spirits had sunk. "I can't take this, getting embarrassed in every town. Who knows how many papers that editor in Yuma called? He's probably notified every stop along our route."

"That's impossible, because he doesn't know our route. Sometimes, *I* don't even know it until we're walking it, it changes so often." Still, the fear remained. That gnawing worry followed us for weeks.

Despite that setback, I quickly regained the thrill of the road. Breathing the fresh air, feeling free, knowing every step brought us closer to our goal — these things drove me forward. Sue cruised on her bike, happy to be free of the car.

Every afternoon we watched billowing cumulus clouds thicken. The setting sun splashed deep pinks and purples as it dove for the horizon, painting the underside of the storms. Rain often pelted down at dusk in haphazard fashion, sometimes drenching us, usually staying in the distance. Later, cascades of lightning rolled across the sky, fighting the growing darkness. I knew we weren't the first to marvel at Nature's stage show. Oregon Trail diaries described the awe the pioneers had held for the ferocity of the plains storms.

The open land encouraged fast travel. Few houses filled the empty miles, a mixture of irrigated fields and parched prairie. As the population dipped, so did our choice of side roads, until we faced a seventeen-mile day hiking I-76 from Wiggins to Roggen.

East or West, trash is still trash

A light cloud cover kept us cool, changing the day from an endurance contest into a pleasant stroll. We limbered up the litter sticks as we found the first substantial trash of the year. "That must have been quite a party," I remarked as I discovered four bottles of Bud Lite next to an empty gallon of antifreeze. "Somehow, I can't imagine beer with a Prestone chaser."

Near Roggen the freeway turned into a treasure trove of grabbable garbage. After a well-worn teddy bear hitched a ride on Sue's bike, we outfitted him with pink undies and a sun visor. I collected an unused stuffed toy ambulance (we saved it for a present), and added a pillow to our sleeping gear. To cap the haul, Sue unearthed a faux-diamond-studded watch (it had taken a licking, but was still ticking). "This is like shopping at the mall," she said, "only cheaper."

We finished the day with an afternoon of people-watching at Stuckey's. They had run out of pecan logs — "I'm crushed," Sue said. "What's a road trip without a Stuckey's pecan log?" — but had no shortage of travelers wandering through. I talked with two men who had rolled in on a motorcycle.

They were carpenters, riding from Minneapolis to Las Vegas. "I had gone east to pick up my friend," said the driver. "He needed a job, and the contractor I work for has a four-year backlog on casinos. He builds two a year."

"You work construction in Las Vegas?" I asked, amazed. "How do you stand the heat?"

"We do inside jobs, building rooms. We hope to whip them up — bang — bang — bang." He described the Vegas building boom, of casinos sprouting from the desert with replicas of the Eiffel Tower or the New York skyline.

"What about you?" he asked. "Isn't walking a slow way to get anywhere, much less across the country?"

I nodded. "We did seventeen miles today, and that was a long day."

"Shoot, we get upset if we don't get that far in fourteen minutes."

As we talked, a car with Minnesota plates arrived. While the man pumped gas, the woman came over to the cyclers. "I thought it was hard crossing the country in a car," she said. "I can't imagine doing it on a motorcycle."

He smiled and pointed in my direction. "If you think we have it bad . . ."

Keenesburg wins the prize for the best town slogan: "Home of 500 happy people and a few soreheads." The soreheads must include the person in charge of the city park — for the first time in two months and over forty towns, we can't camp there. Worse, they never unlocked the restrooms. Why even have them?

One of the happy people ran the New News. We entered the offices with trepidation, and our hearts sank when the owner/editor/reporter said someone had called. However, she recalled the caller as a "public relations director" for a pair of cross-country walkers. She interviewed us, paid for our dinners that night, and helped us find a tent site.

-journal entry, July 15

THE 'WYOMING QUESTION' HAD worried us since Nebraska. How could we cross the Rockies and Wyoming, with services spaced twenty to fifty miles apart?

"I can't ride that far each day," Sue declared. "And don't tell me you can walk it, either. Remember last year, when you started limping in New Hampshire?"

In the congested sprawl of the Front Range, the desolation of Wyoming felt a thousand miles away. However, it loomed only ten days ahead, and we had to decide how to traverse it. "Not to mention the boredom aspect," I said. "If you struggled to cross the Great Plains, you'll never survive the Cowboy State."

"Maybe you should ride my bike for a week, as far as Utah. I could drive the car, and then store it somewhere in Idaho."

I shook my head slowly, unhappy at the prospect. "That feels like a sellout, like I gave up when the going got rough. 'I walked across most of the country, all but the hard part.'"

I tied off another trash bag, dropping it on the shoulder. Our collection rate had more than doubled in July, up to four bags a day. The previous day we'd hit six bags, a high for the year — but far short of last July's ten-bag average. More people, more trash.

"It boils down to why we're out here," she argued. "We're not trying to set any records, to be the first or the fastest, right? We're doing this to clean the country, if only a little bit."

"Yes, and to meet the people," I reminded her. "I know, how many people will we meet in the middle of the desert?"

We traded positions, and I pushed the bike as Sue picked trash. "This year I've been a burden," she continued. "Except when we switch, you do the picking, and I just slow you down. I feel guilty! This way, I could pull ahead and bag litter while you're riding. It's MY turn to work." She plunged the litter stick into the weeds and came out with the burner coil from an electric range. "No matter how strange the trash gets."

I couldn't argue her points. Guilt pangs struck me, too, when I realized we'd only picked half as much litter as we'd picked last year by this time. Biking, I knew, wouldn't solve the problem. _Isn't there a better solution?_ I still had seven days to find one.

That week promised a different challenge for us: readjusting to semi-urban life. Gone were the water towers that heralded new towns. Gone were the pools in the villages, and with them our chances to shower. Libraries, our favorite tool in the fight against boredom, grew scarce. I began missing our simple, Great Plains life.

We specially missed the 'no-hassle' camping. No longer could we count on spending nights in city parks. In Fort Lupton, as in Keenesburg, the city banned our tent. Soon we found that Fort Lupton kept their pool closed on weekends, and that we missed the library by ten minutes. When the bike sprang another flat, I gave up. We holed up in a motel and tried to put the day behind us.

In the morning we turned north on U.S. 85. Another party midden kicked off the day: eleven bottles of Coors and a gallon of milk. ("Get down and get crazy in Ulcerville, I guess.") We filled bags quickly with pop cans, hamburger wrappers, milk cartons, and fifty-two gardener's gloves. The day's prizes consisted of a plastic sword and a baseball signed by the Colorado Rockies, both of which we saved.

We reached Platteville by one o'clock, and found the town's sole officer driving his rounds. Our request brought a smile to his face. "No one's ever camped in our park before! I see no problem with that."

I saw the problem when I noticed the puddles in the park. Severe storms had hit the area the day before, but hot weather should have dried everything. No, these puddles had to come from sprinkling. "We should be safe," I reasoned. "They overwatered last night, so they surely won't sprinkle tonight. Would they?" (Yes, we found out at five-thirty a.m.)

The tent sprouting in his park attracted Desmond, a ten-year-old boy with Hispanic features. His eyes opened wide with delight when I gave him the Rockies baseball, and he ran to take it and the sword home. Moments later, he returned with another ball and a bat. "Do you want to play?" he asked.

I shagged flies with for him half an hour, taking turns batting and splashing through the swampy outfield. When I took a pratfall running for one high fly, I decided I'd better save myself for walking. Desmond hung around as we relaxed, asking about the trip, checking the tent. When we left to find dinner, we put him in charge of the camp.

We returned to find the tent sagging. In moments Desmond came running up. "Some kids came by and pulled up the tent stakes," he said. "I chased them off."

That would stand as the only time the whole trip anyone disturbed our tent.

The 'Twin Cities' of Colorado, Milliken and Johnstown (1600 people apiece) lay only three miles apart on the map, but worlds apart in friendliness.

In Milliken, city hall congratulated us on our trek. The police not only showed us the best spot to camp, but promised to watch over us.

When we found out Johnstown had a library and pool (Milliken had neither), Sue called their town hall to verify the hours, and ask about camping. The clerk forwarded us to the police department, and we asked the woman in charge.

"Do you have money?" she asked brusquely.

"Yes, of course."

"Good. Then go to the KOA. It's four miles west of town."

"Oh. Well, we heard you have a swimming pool. How late —"

"We do, but you can't camp there either."

"We ARE on foot, and four extra miles are a lot," Sue said. "Aren't there even any open lots?"

"Lady, you can't camp anywhere in town. I'm on duty, and if I find you, I'll roust you."   — journal entry, July 18

THERE THEY WERE — THE ROCKIES. From the distance, they appeared as a slate-gray fence of peaks interrupting the western horizon. Despite the July heat, scattered patches of white still clung to the higher mountains, mocking the searing sun. In the afternoons clouds blew in, softening the jagged edges of the range.

I had long anticipated this stretch. The monotony of endless plains finally lay behind us. Now every glance to the west found the towering mountains a bit closer, the scenery a bit grander. Later I'd worry about crossing them; for now, I thrilled in their presence.

My mood soared as I crossed the region, so close to where I grew up. Ahead of us beckoned Fort Collins, home of my alma mater, Colorado State University. I looked forward to returning, walking down familiar streets, visiting friends.

Our fear of the media eased, too. No longer did we worry whether someone had 'warned' the next editor about us. The reporter for the Johnstown/Milliken *Breeze* rushed our story to print, getting a dig at the hostile Johnstown police. Likewise, the Windsor newswoman gushed with enthusiasm. "I can't believe this," she kept repeating, shaking her head. "This is really wonderful!"

Such support kept my spirits flying as I walked through the changed countryside. Despite the looming mountains, this was not the Colorado I remembered from sixteen years before. The urban sprawl had rocketed north of Denver, chewing up the green-and-gold fields, spitting out subdivisions of characterless boxes and mega-houses on mini-lots. "I can't decide if it's a cancer," Sue declared, "or if Mother Earth has a whopping case of dandruff!"

As we inched west, the hills grew larger and steeper. For Sue, the rises challenged muscles left unexercised by six hundred miles of plains. We found the worst hills south of Windsor, on a day when sharp headwinds doubled her misery. While I fought the breezes trying to bag trash, she struggled to push the bike uphill into the wind. When I caught her at the top, she had no kind words for me, and soon neither of us had any words for each other.

I stomped off, fuming. My irritation smoldered the rest of the morning, all the way into Windsor. As noon approached, we walked silently through downtown looking for a cafe. Instead, Sue found the *Windsor Beacon* offices and detoured inside. The reporter's enthusiasm quickly doused my lingering anger, reminding me again of how lucky I was to be living our dream — and to have a partner who shared it. The reporter sent us to city hall, where they bent the rules to let us camp. With the outpouring of good will, I logged the town as Colorado's friendliest.

Our good mood spilled over into the next day, our last before tackling the Rockies. As we crossed the Cache La Poudre River outside Fort Collins, a metal structure caught my eye. "What in the world!" I stopped suddenly, and Sue nearly ran into me. "Is that a dinosaur?"

Maybe, but not a dinosaur that any scientist would recognize. Someone had welded together rusty parts from tractors, combines, threshers and other farm equipment. Eyes made from faucet handles stared at the traffic passing by. Brake-drum claws scissored the air in a show of might. Next to it, a sign read 'Swetsville Zoo.'

The litter could wait. We hurried down the driveway, curious about this pop paleontology. Amidst the farm houses, we found a 'gallery,' a small gift shop, and the zoo. At the zoo entrance, the Tin Man's cousin welcomed all visitors, holding a can for donations.

Inside, over one hundred creatures both familiar and whimsical lined the walkways. I identified a triceratops, a scaled-down brontosaurus, and a menacing tyrannosaurus Rex, all made from unlikely combinations of spare parts. The cowboysaurus, a dinosaur with a lasso, stood waiting for the roundup a few paces away from the autosaurus, a thunder lizard which had evolved from legs to wheels.

The dinosaurs mingled with a wide range of beasts and other sculptures: Spiders larger than dogs. Metal flowers blooming in the yard. A trumpeter swan, made with a trumpet. Turtles. Space aliens. Even Mr. Badwrench, working on his car. Every turn produced another surprise.

The raw material used varied as much as the works themselves. Golf balls served as eyes for a grounded mosquito. Half-tires topped with chain gear formed a serpent. A shovel blade found use as a tail. Flexible tubing became tentacles, and propane tanks became eggs. Gas tanks graduated from motorcycles to bodies of swans.

I had to meet the person behind the zoo. An inquiry at the gift shop sent us to the side yard in search of Bill Swets, resident tinker. We found him stepping out of a stripped-down bus. A wide smile spread on his face, shaded by an old straw hat. His greying hair betrayed his fifty-plus years, but his face refused to grow old. It had a boyish charm, the look of someone playing with life.

He looked up as we came over, and I started to introduce us. "I'm sorry," he stopped me. "You'll have to shout a little. I don't hear as well as I used to."

I started over, telling him about our trip. "So I'm walking, and Sue is riding a bike."

A gleam stole into his eyes. "I've got something I'm sure you'll enjoy," he said, leading us to a garage. Inside, surrounded by mounds of other junk, stood a bicycle built for — I had to count the seats. Three — five — seven — ten seats! "It's the most-seater bicycle in the country," he stated.

"You made this?" Sue asked.

He nodded. "I built it when my kids were small, so my wife and I could take them and friends on bike rides. I don't use it much these days, though I did ride it in a July Fourth parade this year. Last time I'll ever do that!"

It was my turn to ask. "Why?"

"A friend of mine took the front seat, I sat in back, and we had eight kids in the middle. Well, none of the kids pedaled. I'm not young enough to handle that anymore!"

Like a child showing off his toys, he took us out back to a converted RTD bus. "The bus out front? I'm making it into an RV like I did with this one. Can you believe I bought it at an auction for $700? The engine only has 1800 miles on it! It didn't have any tires, or I could have driven it home."

Bill opened the bus door and led us into the ultimate motor home. The pink-and-gray-carpeted steps gave way to a tile floor. Inside, the furnishings beat those of most motels we'd stayed in: upholstered chairs; closets; a three-quarter bath; a kitchen; a bedroom with queen-size bed. He pointed out all the details, those we could see and those we couldn't. "To power everything, I put in four electric systems — two 110V, two 220V— and a 6.5 kilowatt water-cooled generator. A 110-gallon tank gives us water for everything from cooking to showers. And over here," he pointed to a control panel, "is an automatic leveling system to use when we can't find a flat parking spot."

Everywhere we looked, quality shined through. "Where did you learn to do all this?" Sue asked. "Are you a mechanic?"

He gave us an 'aw-shucks-it's-really-nothing' look. "Shoot, no, I'm just a farmer. You learn to do things when you own a farm. Tractors or plows are always breaking down, and you're always fixing it with what you've got, making do."

"How long did it take you to convert this?"

"Eighteen months, but I hurried. I figured my wife and I would tour the country in this once we retired — we had great plans. We've been married thirty-six years, and looked forward to many more. Then last fall she went to the doctor, who did a liver biopsy and found cancer. They only gave her five more years." He fell silent for the briefest moment, his ever-present smile wavering. "Sometimes life doesn't seem fair, does it? Hey! I'm spending all your time. Let me walk you back to the zoo."

His smile returned as I asked about his sculptures. "How long have you been doing this?"

"I started in 1980, doodling in my spare time. Friends and neighbors loved what I made, and they encouraged me to open it to the public. Now, I try to build five or six every year. I have more time to work on them in the winter, when there's less to do on the farm."

"Where do you get all the parts?"

He chuckled. "Every farm has a junk heap, where parts and machines end up. Also, I'm lucky to have friends who give me a free hand with their trash."

"Do you ever do sculptures on commission?" Sue asked.

"I did, once. Never wanted to, but this one woman kept asking me and asking me until I finally said, 'Okay.' You know, that's the one sculpture I never really cared for. Not that there was anything wrong with it, I just couldn't get *close* to it. All the other statues have a personality. About halfway through making one, I'll give it a name. With a face, it gets a character. That one, though, never got a name or a character. I wasn't doing it because I wanted to. I never got beyond a business relationship with it."

We thanked him for the tour and returned to the road. I barely had time to loosen up the litter stick before another roadside surprise attracted me. This time, old-time gasoline pumps lured me to drop my pack.

The museum resembled an old country gas station waiting for its next Duesenberg or Pierce-Arrow to pull up. A gas pump topped with a glass tank stood on the service island in front of the station, and a postwar Chevy nosed out of the garage in back. Inside the shop, Bill Vos talked on the phone. With graying hair and a grandfatherly smile, I pegged him as slightly older than Bill Swets.

While waiting for Bill to finish his call, I looked around. Signs from old petrol pumps advertised gas companies — Magnolia, Indian, White Rose, Fire Chief, Handy Dandy — which had long since vanished. Shelves of oil cans, both quart and gallon size, also named companies (Tidex, Rocor, Veedol) I didn't recognize. A poster hailing the 'new' 1939 Chevy trucks hung on one wall. Several antique road maps crowded the counters, the oldest one dating to the early 1920s. Bins in the center of the shop offered yesteryear's magazines for sale, including a large collection of *Car and Driver.*

When he finished his call, Bill Vos gave us a rundown on the museum. "This place was a working station for many, many years. I even helped here as a kid. When the owner died in 1980, it went up for sale, and the buyers turned it into a bike shop. When it came on the market again two years ago, I bought it and turned it into a museum."

"Did all this come with the station?" I waved at the automobilia and petroliana.

"Some did; the rest I've picked up in odd places. A lot comes from people who find things sitting in an attic or a garage, and decide to get rid of them. Last week, for instance, someone called and offered me an antique Coke machine. I asked them how much they wanted for it, and they shrugged. 'You mean you won't charge us to haul it off?'"

After getting our fill of history, we finished the miles into Fort Collins. The city had changed (read *grown*) in the sixteen years since I'd graduated college. Urban sprawl had cast its tentacles miles down Harmony Road, flanking it with industrial parks and condo villages. The *Coloradan* reporter met us as we hit College Avenue, catching us lunching on fast food row. Later the photographer followed us for two miles as we cleaned the streets around CSU.

I took off my pack that afternoon with a sense of accomplishment — and a little guilt. Behind me lay 2,723 miles of walking, from the Atlantic to the Rockies, over mountains and across plains, through blizzards and heat waves. In three days, I would mount a bike, hurrying over hostile terrain. By the time I donned the pack again, we'd be in Utah. *Was I cheating?*

It boiled down to one simple question: why was I doing this? For personal glory, to do something no one else had done? Several people *had* crossed the country on foot, and we wouldn't set any records. To prove my mettle, that I could endure? After two-thousand-plus miles, I had no doubts I could handle the next five hundred. To show I wouldn't quit when the going got tough?

The third concern still bothered me. Walking the desert would prove a challenge, both physical and mental. Would I enjoy it? Probably not, and Sue would like it less. If she rode the bike, we'd have to impose on someone to supply us, to deliver food and water while we trekked for days between towns. If I walked while Sue drove, she'd face five weeks of desolation and boredom. That option might work if this trip was our punishment for having a dream.

But none of the above answered the simple question. Yes, we walked to see the country — my riding wouldn't stop that. We walked to meet the people, and few lived along our I-80 route. Most importantly, we walked to clean the land, to take our anti-litter message to the coast. Sue could collect as much trash as I could (maybe more), and shorten the time we spent out of the public eye. As she said, "You've done your good deeds. Now let me earn my keep."

THE _COLORADAN_ ARTICLE HIT Saturday, giving us a boost as I struck off on two wheels. They printed a glowing article — and gave us publicity we could have done without.

As we worked our way over the Rockies, the Associated Press put the article on the wire. The story again spread across the country, all the way to the distant corners of eastern Colorado. There, our enemy in Yuma took note of our progress, and moved to humiliate us again.

"You'd better call your Uncle Steve," Sue's father told us when we checked in. "He got an angry call from the editor of the Fort Collins paper, asking about you."

Angry understated it. We had left Steve's number with the reporter. When the editor got a call labeling us a fraud, she called him demanding an explanation. "I'm calling as a courtesy before I print a retraction," she said, "and send _that_ over the AP."

Luckily, both branches of the Armstead family shared the same sense of humor, and Steve quickly pieced together what happened. He calmed the editor, assuring her the story we gave them was true. "I finally convinced her," he told us. "Though I wish you had clued us in."

His defense saved our AP story. However, the _Coloradan_ editor called the _Windsor Beacon_ before reaching Steve, questioning the reporter there. That reporter, so enthusiastic a week earlier, joined the ranks of our foes. She tracked down my parents' phone number, and interrogated them as if their son had shot the president. My mother's explanations got nowhere with her, and the _Beacon_ ridiculed our 'supposed' exploits.

We'll never make that mistake again.

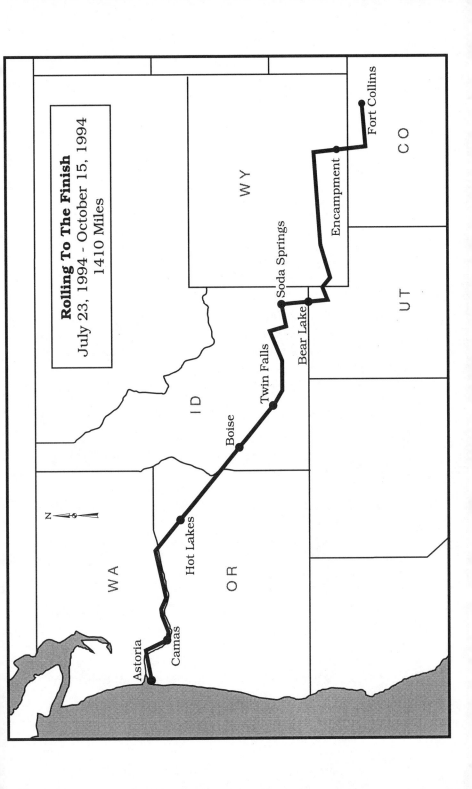

Rolling To The Finish
July 23, 1994 - October 15, 1994
1410 Miles

N

WA

OR

ID

WY

UT

CO

Astoria
Camas
Hot Lakes
Boise
Twin Falls
Bear Lake
Soda Springs
Encampment
Fort Collins

** MAIN STREET U.S.A. **

* COLORADO - WYOMING - UTAH *

July 23 - August 1, 1994
451 miles -- 22 bags
TOTAL, 3174 miles -- 927 bags

The world is a book, and those who do not travel read only
one page.   - St. Augustine

————➤ ◆ ◄————

*Today was our hard-earned reward for enduring the plains. The road
over Cameron Pass awed us — pristine mountain lakes, patches of snow
looming above emerald slopes, fluffy clouds like dollops of whipped
cream floating in a baby-blue sky.*

*After soaking in the scenery, we started down the other side — and
stopped on the first turn. Nakhu Crag soared above us, shooting three
thousand feet straight up from the valley floor. The snow-tipped peak of
"Eagle's Aerie" dominated the Never-Summer Range behind it.*
                                        -journal entry, July 24

"TELL ME AGAIN," I asked, trying hard not to laugh. "How did you
hurt your hand?"

"It's not funny," she said, a playful tone in her voice. "It really hurts.
All I did was stuff the sleeping bag into its sack."

I threw my hands in the air and rolled my eyes. "See what I have to deal
with, Bill? Every day, life's such an adventure."

Bill Padilla had joined us for four days as we tackled the Rockies. Best
friends since our college days, we'd spent countless hours hiking the hills
and biking the beaches. In 1989 his ill-timed shoulder injury had sent me
to Europe by myself. A year later we spent three weeks bicycling New
Zealand, exploring the mountains and shorelines of Down Under. Now we
linked up as the Litterwalk took to wheels.

He grinned as he loaded his panniers. As disasters went, we knew this
was minor. Sue's hand would quickly heal. Besides, how could we worry

when a perfect day surrounded us? The scenery unrolled as we steadily moved up the Poudre. Rafters blasted through churning rapids. Snowcapped ridges looked down on forested canyons. Fishermen waded through the river, casting their lines under clear skies.

One thousand walking miles hadn't prepared me to bike over mountains. I struggled up the steeper hills, inching along in first gear as Bill pulled ahead. Watching the shoulder pass underneath yard by yard, I noticed little trash and many 'This Section of Road Adopted' signs.

We stopped atop the pass — at 10,276', the trip's 'high point' — to toast our success. Soon we sped downhill, losing most of the five thousand feet I'd worked so hard to gain. We quickly found ourselves surrounded again by sagebrush and cattle ranches. If not for the glorious mountains ringing the high valley, I'd have sworn we'd blundered back onto the Great Plains. Even the towering thunderheads reminded us of Nebraska. When the lightning started, though, I stopped daydreaming and started sprinting. Bill and I raced the approaching storm the last four miles into Walden, winning the shelter of a gas station as the drops began falling.

a real Rocky Mountain high

The next day we wheeled through more wide-open ranch land, aiming for our nineteenth state. We crossed into Wyoming at 10:15; at 10:16, the headwind started. "Get used to it," Bill said. "Wyoming is known for its winds."

We'd soon know it for its trash. I watched the road shoulder as we neared the border, and counted only two candy wrappers and one Coke can in two miles. Just over the state line, leaning against the 'Welcome to Wyoming' sign, three beer cans marked the new territory. I stopped in the first few miles to bag larger items, but tried to ignore the rest — predominantly beer cans. "I'd almost forgotten," I told Bill. "Motorists in Wyoming measure distances by six-packs."

Between the wind and the trash, it took all day to reach Encampment, Wyoming. We first stopped for a cold drink, and then to ask about the town's most noted attraction. "Where's this two-story in-line outhouse I read about?"

We followed the clerk's directions to the park/museum, where we learned about the town. In 1897, miners struck a copper vein in the surrounding hills, bringing the town to life. Soon, tons of copper came out of the mine, carried to the mills by a sixteen-mile-long tram — the longest in the world. After extracting two million dollars of ore, the mining company was indicted for fraud. The town quickly went bust.

In recent years citizens had restored the original village at the open-air museum. In front, a tram tower and car heralded the town's early fame. The village itself curved around a greenbelt; the blacksmith shop, saloon, and an ice cream parlor/bakery populated the strip. Old presses sat idle in the newspaper office. Desks faced forward in the schoolhouse and the day's lesson waited on the blackboard. At the end of the strip of businesses, a path led into the trees . . . and to the outhouse.

"It really *is* in-line," I noted. Stairs led to the second story, where the seat (chained off, of course) perched directly over the seat below. "How did they handle that?"

A sign outside the outhouse explained. When winter snows piled up, drifts would block the lower entrance, and the top seat would find favor. Come spring, they'd forego the stairs again. "I can relate," Sue said. "If nature called during a storm — especially if nature shouted — the last thing I'd want to do is shovel my way to the john."

NOTES FROM SUE'S JOURNAL:
Desolate boring country, and lots more to go through. I wish Glen didn't
have to do this — he'll hate it once Bill leaves. I feel so guilty . . . Not my
choice for a memorable anniversary.   *- July 25*

A MILE AHEAD OF us, a smudge moved on the straight-arrow road. As we pedaled forward it grew to a blip, then a bump, and finally became another bicyclist. When we pulled even with him, all three of us stopped.

"So which of you is Glen?" he asked.

By now, little surprised me. "I am."

"I'm afraid I gave your wife a start," the gray-haired biker said. "She was standing off the road, watching antelope romp through the sagebrush, as I pulled up. She hadn't seen me. When I spoke, she about jumped out of her skin."

"I'd think she'd be used to bicyclists by now." For two days we'd followed the BikeCentennial route, a coast-to-coast string of roads laid out in 1976 to encourage bike touring. "We rode with a retired man yesterday, until the hills slowed him. He biked from South Carolina to Missouri last year, and he's doing Missouri to the coast this year."

"I call it the bicyclist's Main Street," he said, nodding. "I'm riding from Kalispell, Montana, to Denver."

"How long will that take you?" asked Bill. This short stretch of the BikeCentennial had enticed him, and he already talked of riding a longer piece.

"It's fourteen hundred miles, and I gave myself a month. I take my time, stopping often, talking to people. Have you seen the other bicyclist from Massachusetts?"

I shook my head. "Not unless they were the couple we passed an hour ago. They said 'Hi' as they passed, but with their loads, they didn't stop."

"No, that's not them. In the Pizza Hut in Rawlins last night, I saw these two men in biking clothes. We got talking, and of course I asked where they were from. 'Boston,' one says. Oh? What part? 'Framingham.' No kidding! What street? It turns out we'd lived a block apart ten years ago."

Sue and the antelopes waited for us, so we quickly moved on. We caught her only moments before the next pair of southbound bicyclists approached. When they got close, "Framingham!" and a wave brought them to a halt.

The two men were well into their cross-country journey, having started from Washington state. "We had a supported trip our first two weeks," the Framingham biker said. "Boy, what a mistake! Jerry really slowed our progress, getting campgrounds thirty miles out of our way, or stopping thirty miles short of where we hoped to reach."

His friend chipped in, "And don't forget the nights! They were even worse. Jerry snored louder than a rock band. He could wake up whole KOAs. How would you like to spend a whole night without a second of sleep, then bike ninety miles the next day?"

"Sounds like a disaster," I agreed.

"Can you believe he came out with only ninety dollars and an American Express card? Not Visa or MasterCard, which is all the stores take. We finally had to tell him it wasn't working, and took off on our own. It hasn't held us back at all, though we now have full packs. We can choose where to stop, and we make more miles."

Bill and I didn't keep them long, since we still had a ways to go to Rawlins. The Wyoming headwinds (the reason most bicyclists cross the state west to east) had slackened, but they still slowed us. Five miles to the north, we could see trucks crawling across the desert, marking the course of I-80.

A mile from the interstate, we noticed a sixth bicyclist inching up the hill. As the gap narrowed, I made out a single woman. "Want to stop and chat, Bill?" I asked, with thoughts of playing matchmaker dancing in my head.

He watched as she drew near. "Well . . . She's having a hard time. I don't have the heart to stop her, halfway up the hill."

WE WENT FROM THE bicyclist's Main Street to America's Main Street: the Lincoln Highway. In the 1920s it had become the first road to stretch coast-to-coast. Now I-80 followed the course of that pioneering lane, each year providing an easy passage for millions of cars and trucks — and a few errant bicyclists.

We joined it in mid-afternoon and cruised into Rawlins. To celebrate Bill's last day with us, we splurged on the town's top attraction. The old Wyoming State Penitentiary had opened in 1901, and held convicts until 1981 — "only three years after they first piped hot water to the cell blocks," Sue read as we waited for the next tour. "They sure didn't coddle prisoners back then."

Posters of old prisoners covered one wall, detailing their crimes. Henry Edmundson's picture drew my attention, the only inmate with a beard. "Get this, Bill. Normally they shaved prisoners when they were admitted. This guy, though, stared down the warden and told him, 'If you cut my beard, it'll be your last.' He'd gotten twenty years for murder, but within a year the warden made him a deal. He could go free, as long as he promised to leave Wyoming forever."

The guide arrived, and herded our group through admitting and into the cell block. Three stories of cells looked onto the gray concrete walls, tiny cubicles with barely enough space for a cot, toilet, and washstand. "Cramped quarters, aren't they?" asked the guide. "Many convicts gladly went to work to get out of them."

"What, making license plates?" asked a woman standing near Sue.

He nodded. "After 1949, yes. In the early years, the prison factory made brooms. That only lasted until 1917, when someone set fire to the straw and burned the factory down for the second time. Then they switched to shirts."

He spun tales of the prison's most noted 'guests.' "William Carlisle, the last great train robber, arrived here in 1916. In 1919 he escaped inside a shirt crate. The crate got loaded on a train, so when he climbed out of the box, he did what came natural. He robbed the train."

The tour went through the mess hall and the exercise yard to the gallows. We saw the hangman's noose and the trapdoor from below, a grisly reminder of the old west. "Would you believe they had to hang one prisoner twice?" the guide asked. "The first time they strung Yee Geow up, he was so light he didn't die. They had to cut him down, wait until he was fully conscious, then made him put on lead shoes and hung him again." After pausing to let this sink in, he added, "It took several more years before officials realized the rope was too short. With a longer rope, the fall breaks their neck and kills them instantly."

Upstairs he showed us the gas chamber, letting people sit in it for pictures. "In 1959," he continued, "several death row inmates planned a breakout. They dug a tunnel as far as the west wall. When they hit something hard, one of them lit a match to see what it was. It was the chamber's gas line. BOOM."

The outside never looked so good as it did after leaving the prison.

I struck off alone Wednesday morning as Sue drove Bill back to Fort Collins. I-80 cut through a desolate landscape of dirt hills and dry creeks, twice taking me over the continental divide. For forty miles the only 'settlement' was a trailer at a highway junction selling microwaved food and mixed drinks. Only pronghorn antelopes thrived in the desert, gnawing on the sagebrush as they watched me cycle past.

My mind wandered back to the Russian college student I'd met years ago while camping in Death Valley. When asked what he thought of the surroundings, he'd replied, "It reminds me of Afghanistan." *This area probably would have, too,* I thought, *except for that wonderful American art form, The Billboard.* On the interstate the signs hawked stores and truck stops miles away. From my college days I remembered the long string of Little America signs, but one billboard surprised me. It read, "Rejoice! Jubitz — straight ahead only 1084.2 miles."

As the morning wore on, I noticed ever more trash. With no litter stick and no Heftys (Sue had them in the car), I could do little but feel guilty about leaving it. I hadn't seen an Adopt-A-Highway sign for days, and couldn't imagine anyone driving out here to clean the road. Thus, when I saw the man toting the trash bag in the center median, it shocked me. I pulled onto the inside shoulder as I reached him. "Are you picking up litter?"

He looked up, startled. When he saw my bike, a smile spread across his weathered face. "Lord, no. I'm collecting cans. I've been out of work for three years, and have to do something for money. My wife's job pays most our bills, but every little bit helps."

Though his face was deeply lined, he didn't look old enough to retire. "What work did you do?" I asked.

"I drove a truck for thirty-five years, but had to quit because of high blood pressure. There's a federal law which says your blood pressure can't be above 130, and mine was 148."

"Do you live in Wamsutter?" That little town of 240 — the biggest population center in this 108-mile stretch — lay twelve miles to the west.

"No, Rawlins. You may find this hard to believe, but I've worked the freeway, both sides, all twenty-eight miles to here since May 1."

We exchanged trash tales, finding common ground in the filth of the public. Soon he glanced at his watch, then hefted his bag. "My wife's expecting me at 12:30, so I'd better finish. Hope you have a great trip!"

I stopped in Wamsutter for lunch, sitting on the curb outside the gas station/mini mart. Inside, I asked about the relative merits of the next two stops listed on my map: Red Desert and Table Rock, neither of which listed a population. "Forget Red Desert," the clerk answered. "You're better off biking right by."

"Oh? Nothing there?"

"A store, sure, but the guy who runs it is a real grouch. He even charges you to use the restroom. You're better off going to Table Rock."

With Sue not due for hours, I rode the extra thirteen miles. Like Red Desert, it consisted of a store cum gas station on a strip of pavement left over from the original Lincoln Highway. At least this spot had shade trees and a swatch of grass.

In front of the station, a thirtysomething man repaired a gas pump. Brian Krause watched as I rode up, and followed me inside to sell me a juice. Once he realized I had no plans to leave soon, he wandered back to the dismembered gas pump. After a few minutes, I joined him outside.

I soon found out Table Rock's policy on restrooms differed little from Red Desert's. In Wyoming, I guess, toilets were treasures to guard zealously. Brian joked about customers who tried to steal a visit to his crown jewels. "I have a sign on the front door, a sign in the hall, a sign on the door to the restroom area, and a sign between the restrooms stating you HAVE to buy something before using the restrooms. I still get people who read the first sign, then read the sign in the hall, then read the sign on the door, then the one between the restrooms. They still use them and leave. I asked one gal, 'What's the matter, can't you read?' She said, 'Oh, I didn't think you were serious.'

"A couple weeks ago the plumbing goes out, so I call Roto Rooter. While I'm waiting, one woman asks me, 'The restrooms aren't really out of order, are they? You just don't want me to use them.' 'Yeah, lady,' I tell her, 'I'd like to see you pee your pants.' She gets all in a huff, promises never to come back and storms out. After she leaves, my regular customers just die laughing."

His grin spread as he recited his litany of bad customers. "The Roto Rooter guy had so much equipment out you couldn't even get in the restrooms. I still had a guy look back there and ask, 'Are your restrooms REALLY out of order?'"

We chatted between his infrequent customers, talking about hunting (his favorite sport), customers, and living in Table Rock. "How can you stand it out here?" I asked him. "What do you do all day?"

"When I'm not busy, I catch up with Oprah, and Montel, and Sally Jessy, and Phil. Boy, they really get some wild guests, you know? Some of those people, I just can't believe."

As always, the conversation found its way back to weather. Seeing the parched land surrounding this oasis, I asked, "How long has it been since it rained here?"

He looked thoughtful for a moment, then replied, "I don't know, I'm not that old."

CHARLES E. AND J. FRANK DURYEA debuted America's first horseless carriage in 1893, starting the automotive industry. Soon, the term 'automobile' entered the English language, followed closely by 'road under construction,' 'model-year recall,' and 'free car wash with fill-up.' By 1903 industry pioneers were selling eleven thousand cars annually, mostly in the big cities.

On May 19, 1903, Dr. H. Nelson Jackson of San Francisco made a wager with a friend. "I'll bet you can't drive one of those newfangled automobiles all the way to New York City," the friend challenged him. Four days later Dr. Jackson, accompanied by mechanic Sewell Croker, set off for the Atlantic. In Caldwell, Idaho, they adopted a bulldog named Bud, gave him a set of goggles, put him in the rumble seat, and kept going. They reached New York on July 26 after driving six thousand miles. Of those sixty-five days, they spent twenty-one resting, repairing the vehicle, and waiting for replacement parts. (It is *not* true that, on the forty-four days spent driving, Bud constantly barked, "Are we there yet?")

For years the lack of truck stops and AAA towing discouraged similar adventures. In the big cities cars quickly graduated from novelty to necessity, but still no roads connected the country's far ends. In 1912 Carl Fisher, promoter of the Indianapolis 500 and of the Miami Beach land boom, became the first to propose such a road. As a way to promote autos (and business for his company that made carbide headlamps), he announced plans for a 'Coast-to-Coast Rock Hiway.' His ambitious schedule called for finishing it before 1915's Panama-Pacific Exposition in San Francisco.

Since much of the route he settled on was little more than a mud hole during the rainy season, his dream had no chance of succeeding. 1915 came and went, and slowly the road grew. In the 1920s backers of his road found themselves competing with other coast-to-coast projects. To give their route an edge with the public, the changed the name to 'the Lincoln Highway.' The name stuck, even after the federal government gave most of the route the romantic designation of U.S. 30.

In Wyoming, the planners chose the natural corridor south of the Great Divide Basin. It followed the Overland Trail, which had succeeded the Oregon Trail in 1862. This new trail had veered south to service the Denver gold and silver booms. Federal officials had also grown concerned about Indian attacks on the old trail; the new route was guarded by army forts.

We visited an original Overland Trail stage coach station which still existed outside Point of Rocks, Wyoming. ("What is the point of rocks?" I asked Sue. "Do they have a purpose?" She didn't know.) The stables barely hung on, their walls slowly crumbling. The main adobe building had aged better, still intact with four walls and a roof. Scenery ran true to desert form: dry creeks, buttes, palisades, little vegetation. "No wonder the early travelers called this 'scenically stupid'," noted Sue.

Rock Springs hid among those desert palisades on a bend in Bitter Creek. The state's fourth largest city at 19,000 people, it provided an urban antidote to the barren land we'd crossed. Restaurants! Library! A newspaper! We had skipped the Rawlins paper, still uneasy after our AP fiasco. Nagging fears still dogged us, but I couldn't resist appearing in a paper called the _Rocket-Miner_. They had heard nothing of us, and took our story with nary a doubt. "They didn't even ask to see a litter stick or our bike," I remarked. "We could have told them I was running for President, and they would have written it up."

The next day we passed thirty more miles of arid buttes and hardscrabble plateau to reach Little America, Wyoming's premier truck stop. Billboards had touted it since we'd hit the interstate (along with Jubitz, now only 972.4 miles away). According to legend, in the 1890's S. M. Covey, a shepherd, survived a winter night lost on the high desert. As fifty mph winds howled around him, dropping temperatures to -40°, he dreamed of warming his feet by a roaring fire in a comfortable shelter. Forty years later, he returned to the spot and built a truck stop.

That truck stop soon grew into a truckers paradise. A deli offered fast food, while the restaurant provided for more relaxed dining. A motel spread over the grounds, surrounded by well-watered lawns and trees. Employee housing filled several blocks in back of the complex. Next to the deli, we signed up for a shower stall, free with a fill-up of gas or five bags of litter. A five-dollar deposit got us a key to a private stall which put our motel rooms this trip to shame. "I can't believe this!" Sue gasped. "Marble floor — sunken tub — sink — toilet — and separate shower stall. And it's spotless! Run the water in the tub, I'm going to soak!"

We spent a luxurious half hour, soaking the grime from our pores. After returning the key, we retired to the TV room, watching mindless comedies with the truckers while a summer storm cooled the night.

Leaving I-80 and the Lincoln Highway the next day, we crossed the most barren stretch of the whole trip — forty-nine miles with no business larger than a Coke machine. The trash belied the lack of people. By herself Sue collected eight bags, a new 1994 high. Her haul included twenty-five gardening gloves, three dirty diapers, a bra, and a letter postmarked 1987.

The following day, she filled six more bags, which didn't begin to clean the roads. As I waited for her atop the hill above Bear Lake, I looked around the brake test area in disgust. In twenty yards of road shoulder, I could have collected four to five bags of trash. *Why do people use the top of a hill as a garbage dump?* I wondered. *Are they worried the extra weight might wear out their brakes on the downhill?*

What a difference a state makes. Immediately after crossing into Utah, we found ourselves in a lush green — even swampy — valley, a far cry from the arid, drought-stricken terrain of Wyoming. Climbing away from the Bear River, thick blankets of sage provided contrast to the ocher slopes of the hills. Then after a high-speed four-mile coast down a 7% grade, the turquoise waters of Bear Lake exploded into view.

So now my days of bicycling are finis.

-journal entry, August 1

** DOWNHILL FROM HERE **

* UTAH - IDAHO *

August 2 - August 17, 1994
152 miles -- 101 bags
TOTAL, 3326 miles -- 1028 bags

For my part, I travel not to go anywhere, but to go. I travel
for travel's sake. The great affair is to move.
- Robert Louis Stevenson, "Travels with a Donkey"

————————◆————————

*I try to be optimistic about the human race. I want to believe people
will do the right thing. When I see a pile of dirty diapers ten feet from an
open dumpster, though, I have to wonder.*

-journal entry, August 2

BEAR LAKE REMINDED US of the lakes of New Zealand. Down
Under, glacial sediment gave lakes a beautiful turquoise hue. In Utah the
glaciers had long since departed, but minerals flushed from the local hills
provided the same color. Ringed by forested hills, the lake shone like a
magic jewel, warding off the surrounding desert.

"You're sure this doesn't drain to the Pacific?" asked Sue as we
paralleled the shoreline. "I thought we crossed the Continental Divide."

"We did," I explained, "and the area around Rock Springs drains
through the Colorado River. After Little America, though, we crossed into
the Great Basin. This lake empties into Bear River, which ends in the Great
Salt Lake. From there — pffft!"

"Too bad. I thought maybe we'd inner-tube the rest of the way to
Oregon."

Only through river travel might we have avoided the trash. Bear Lake,
a noted resort, drew crowds from around the region, and with tourists came
litter. Despite open dumpsters in the pullouts every mile or so, the
lakeshore road sported a thick layer of garbage. We filled thirteen bags our
first day of walking, a number we hadn't reached since Kentucky the

previous summer. Along with the diapers, we bagged more toilet paper here than anywhere else. *Is there a moral hidden here somewhere?*

After a morning of wondering why the prettiest places attracted the filthiest people, I wanted to forget about litter. Five hours of watching boaters play in the lake had stirred memories of California beaches, so after lunch we grabbed our sandals and headed to the shore. A dry summer had dropped the lake to its lowest level in years, and we had to hike over a mud flat to reach the water. The shallow bed of the lake encouraged wading, and we found knee-deep water a hundred yards from shore. And warm! It felt like bath water.

One preteen girl wading in the lake pushed a boogie board with a small animal passenger. To me, the pet resembled a large, furry hot dog. Curious, I waded over to her.

"Is that a ferret?" My question got a nod. "How many do you have?"

"Three," she replied. Looking back to shore, she called, "Mom! Watch P-Bear, he's getting away!"

"I've never seen one before," I said. "Does he like the water?"

"No, but he needed a bath. Okay, Tojo, off the raft!" she said, upending the boogie board. Tojo took off toward land, slithering though the water like a dishtowel on a fisherman's line.

The following day we struck north from Garden City, leaving the crowds behind. The decrease in trash and traffic helped the miles fly by, and we followed the lake into Idaho. As we entered Fish Haven, a van rolled to a stop in front of us. The driver, a woman in her twenties, emerged balancing two bags of groceries. Seeing us, she said, "Hot work today, isn't it?" She looked closely at our faces, then asked, "Are you from around here?"

I gave her the short version. When I finished, she said, "You look hungry. Would you care for a cup of fresh raspberries?"

For me, that was akin to offering a chocoholic free Godivas, and I nodded eagerly. The woman took her groceries inside, then led us to the back yard. She handed us each a bucket and pointed to her garden, where vines sagged with ripe berries. "When I said fresh raspberries, I meant fresh."

As we picked our fill, we chatted with our hostess. "I grew up in San Diego," she revealed, "though I've spent every summer here since I can remember. My great-grandmother lived in town — she died last year, ninety-six years old — and I stayed with her."

A wistful look stole across her face. "She used to tell me stories of coming here as a little girl. The trip took two weeks from Ogden to cross the mountains ringing the lake. As she grew up the trips got shorter, and they soon took only three or four days. Now you can drive here in a few hours."

Hammering from the house interrupted her reminiscing. "This is an old house, and my folks are trying to bring it into the 1990s. A Mormon settler had built it. We know because of the polygamy door."

"A polygamy door?" I asked. "What's that?"

"It's an extra entrance. Often, when a man took additional wives, the wives didn't get along. Some would refuse to use the same door as a rival. They made the man build them their own door."

We had to cut our berry-picking short, since I'd arranged to meet the press at noon. The reporter and photographer from the *Herald-Journal* of Logan, Utah, caught us near the town's only store. The interview went as so many others had, until they surprised me with a new question: "How does it feel to be almost done?"

Almost done.

That sounded strange. True, we had nearly one thousand miles left, but we'd covered three times that. Our biggest obstacle, the Wyoming desert, lay behind us. For the first time, success looked likely. How did it feel? "Good, very good."

Before the article came out, we'd left the road for another break, driving two hundred miles north to meet Ron and Joann Schrantz in Yellowstone. While there, another vacationer noticed my 'People Against Litter' tee shirt. "I saw your picture!" he exclaimed. "You were in the Logan paper!"

How does it feel to be almost famous?

"WHO NEEDS A HOT SHOWER?" I said. "No one's around. We can bathe in the stream." With that I shucked my clothes and leapt into the mountain creek, followed closely by Sue.

The ice-cold water made it the shortest bath I ever took.

Ahhh, such were the pleasures as we left Bear Lake behind. Free camps in the national forests treated us to quiet nights lulled to sleep by crickets. Starlight replaced streetlights, and the scent of pine filled the air. The walking turned rural, more ranches than vacation cabins. One morning a cattle drive held us up as cowboys herded their charges down the center of the highway.

After the cattle passed, we proceeded into St. Charles, Idaho. The city limit sign proudly proclaimed it the Birthplace of Gutzon Borglum. "No, it's not the name of a genetic disease," I told Sue, "or a German phrase for what happens if you don't chew your food. Borglum was the sculptor who carved Mount Rushmore."

She looked at me and sadly shook her head. "You've been watching too much *Jeopardy*™."

We stopped for lunch at the Minnetonka Cafe, three tables and a counter attached to a small general store. I quickly settled on the house specialty. "I'll have the breakfast taco."

"Good choice!" the owner — his name tag read 'David' — agreed. Moments later he brought out a taco that covered the plate, with fixings spilling over the side.

"It's a family favorite," David explained. "Our kids always had to be out early to catch the school bus. Do you know how hard it was to get them up in time to eat breakfast too? With tacos, they could wrap it and run."

David and his family had recently moved to St. Charles, and had not yet gotten used to the 'big-town' atmosphere. "St. Charles has 190 people," he said. "At our last house, our nearest neighbor lived five miles away. The kids aren't used to being so close to people."

We chatted with David between his infrequent customers, finding out what made him tick — and what ticked him off. "We had a school board which pushed out an excellent teacher after twenty-two years," he told us, "only three years before she planned to retire. She cared about kids more than rules. The board's rules stated that each kid needed an eight-color crayon pack, but she told each kid to bring a sixty-four-crayon pack instead. She didn't want to limit them. Well, I rose such a stink when they let her go, they had to bring her back."

In St. Charles he turned his wrath on developers and land barons. "Have you seen all the new houses pockmarking the countryside? They're ruining this area, and it's a shame. The people who live here, they played on these hills as kids. Their parents played on these hills as kids. Their kids are playing on these hills now. In twenty years, their grandkids will see houses on these hills and say, 'Our parents and grandparents played on these hills as kids.'"

I nodded in sympathy. "Who's buying all these houses? Workers?"

"Oh, no, there's no work here. It's people from L.A., New York, Las Vegas, rich people with money to burn. They don't care how they affect the area as long as they get their vacation cabin. Most of these houses are lucky if they're occupied two weeks out of the year."

When it comes to littering, western motorists lack imagination. Nothing interesting graces the road shoulders — we rarely even find underwear. Beer cans, cigarette packs, and plastic pop bottles (sixteen today which were half-full) dominate the pickings. The only deviation was the box for the solid oak toilet seat. The seat had long since disappeared.   -journal entry, August 10

Nine more half-full soda bottles. Aren't people here very thirsty? Or is it a new way to cut down on calories? -journal entry, August 11

THE HAWK HOVERED OVER the valley, wings outstretched, floating in the breeze. Its eyes darted as it held position, scanning the field for prey. Suddenly it swooped, diving into the wheat, out of sight. Moments later it reappeared, a mouse clutched in its talons. The raptor carried its not-fast-enough food to a telephone pole and started dining.

"I wish you could have seen it," Sue said when I caught up to her. "The whole thing happened right in front of me. The hawk flew so close, I could hear the mouse squeal."

Wild animals had always enthralled Sue, none more so than birds of prey. As a volunteer at a California zoo, she had taught kids about nature's creatures, often discussing the diet of raptors. "But to *see* the food chain in action . . . Incredible!"

We'd witnessed a parade of wildlife since leaving Colorado. Pronghorn antelopes munched on sagebrush on the Wyoming plains. A fox hunted his morning meal near Little America. Yellowstone teemed with buffalo, and a moose wandered through our campground in Grand Teton National Park. Now we headed north along Bear River as hawks shopped nature's supermarket.

The area provided welcome relief from the deserts, the one we'd crossed and the one soon to come. The river cut through a wide valley, a rural landscape of farms and pastures flanked by low hills. Again we found towns with parks perfect for camping. Our only disappointment came when we looked for a pool with showers. "Sorry," the city clerk in Soda Springs said, "we don't have a pool."

"You're kidding," Sue said. "In a town this size?" At 3100 people, the town was the valley's metropolis.

The clerk nodded. "They tried to build one back in '37. The engineers planned to use thermal energy — we have lots of natural springs here — to heat a pool, so they started drilling. As luck would have it, they bored right into a carbon dioxide vent, and hot water started gushing out. Thinking quickly, they put a cap on it, but they knew the CO_2 would build pressure and blow it. Well, someone had the bright idea to put in a timer to let it erupt every half-hour. It's done that now every day for the past six decades, unless the wind picks up. Then they'll turn it off, so it doesn't spray any businesses. You know, ours is the world's only manmade geyser!"

The clerk also told us about Soda Springs's 'manmade lava.' "On the edge of town, Monsanto runs a phosphate plant. They generate a lot of molten waste, or slag. To get rid of it, they pour it onto this waste pile five times an hour. People go to watch it flow and harden just like real lava."

What's next? I wondered. *Manmade earthquakes? Manmade quicksand?* We thanked the clerk and left before we could find out. After catching the 3:30 show of the geyser, we drove past the slag cliffs to the town's best-known remaining spring. The town once claimed dozens of springs with colorful names such as Steamboat Spring and Antipolygamy Spring. Most of them disappeared under rising waters when a dam formed Alexander reservoir. However, north of town Hooper Spring still bubbled forth with the water which so impressed early Oregon Trail travelers.

Pioneers had dubbed one of the many springs Beer Spring, likening it to the beverage they had been so long without. "Fremont's men were having a high time drinking the soda water . . ." wrote Jesse Applegate in 1843, "enjoying it greatly nearly a whole day." Could Hooper be the long lost Beer Spring?

Sue's luck on this trip had taught her caution, but nothing slowed me. "I have to try it," I said. "If it wasn't safe, they'd have signs posted." I grabbed a cup and filled it from the spring. Tentatively, I sipped it.

"Well?" Sue asked. "How is it?"

"Maybe after months on a dusty trail," I guessed, "I too could pretend soda water got me drunk."

Rather than following the Oregon Trail north to the Snake River, we jogged west with U.S. 30. The small pass taking us to the Portneuf River marked our farewell to the Rockies. Ahead, only Oregon's Blue Mountains stood in the way of a gradual descent to the ocean. With under nine hundred miles left, my mind again wandered to the finish line. *How many more weeks? How much more trash?*

To celebrate our last Rocky Mountain pass, we rented a double inner tube in Lava Hot Springs and 'rafted' the Portneuf. The cool whitewater provided a grand antidote to thermometers reaching for 90°. Fantasies of hijacking the tubes and floating to the Pacific added an excitement to the outing.

Lava Hot Springs put us in a vacation mood. We wandered through town, ducking into gift shops, checking menus at the restaurants, watching other tourists. The resort town attracted visitors from Pocatello to Salt Lake City with its non-sulphur hot springs, natural spas without the rotten-egg stink. This summer Saturday, though, it had not attracted crowds.

Posters around town touted that weekend as the annual 'Lava Crazy Days.' Curious about special events, we stopped at the Chamber of Commerce for more information. However, the clerk provided no help. "We don't have a schedule," she said, shrugging. "It IS today and tomorrow, I know, but I don't know what's planned. I don't even know who you could ask."

The COC doesn't know about a town celebration? I call that 'Lava Crazy'!

We kept the vacation feeling today, ambling along the meandering Portneuf through a scenic canyon. Far from a desert landscape, trees dotted the hillsides, and ranches, a church, and a store broke up the desolation.   -journal entry, August 14

I COULDN'T GET FINISHING out of my head. Every day I scrutinized our last two maps (Idaho and Oregon/Washington), estimating mileage, breaking the route into hundred-mile pieces. Every day I calculated how many weeks remained, refining my guesses, projecting days' goals and days off. Every evening I pictured us at the mouth of the Columbia, walking the last fifty yards over a sandy beach.

Perhaps my focus on October arose less from a longing to end the trek than a reluctance to face the dreary present. As the days plunged deeper into August, the temperatures rose and a drought settled firmly in place. The forested hills of the Bear River Valley were replaced by barren plains crossed by ancient lava flows, with few trees to break the monotony. Only mounting litter kept boredom from overwhelming us.

All summer I'd longed for another Appalachia, a place to sink my litter stick into. Trash on the Great Plains had barely warmed up our picking muscles. After bagging two tons in 1993, we were on target for only one third of that this year. Idaho finally rescued us from our litter malaise, providing an unending stream of litter. We averaged fifty pounds a day to Pocatello, shooting us past one thousand bags and easing our earlier guilt.

Faced with barren, litter-strewn roads, we had only one choice to stave off boredom. We counted trash. We started by logging 168 cigarette packs on one eleven-mile day. Sue grabbed 225 cans in nine miles the next day, which we followed with 263 cans (two-thirds of them beer) in thirteen miles. Ninety-one plastic soda bottles took us the last ten miles into Pocatello.

On the Idaho plains we rediscovered the friendliness we'd grown used to in the Great Plains. In McCammon, the town cop recommended a camp site in the forest above the valley, far from the city noises. The school principal in Inkom called the mayor for us, okaying our night in the city park.

Pocatello came in time for a much-needed motel room. By now we'd perfected our big-city routine: Hit WalMart for supplies, anything from trash bags and batteries to socks and hats. Lose ourselves in a mindless movie. Wake up our taste buds in an ethnic restaurant. Best of all, sleep well in a soft bed.

We enjoyed the simplest pleasures the most.

Across the country, we have seen no sunsets more impressive than those in this corner of Idaho, and I think I know why. In Kansas, the sun sinks to the horizon with nothing to paint its colors upon. In Colorado, the Rockies extinguish it before its most colorful rays are born. Here, though, the west-facing hills provide the canvas for an awesome show.

As the sun sinks below the horizon, it replaces the sky so radiant blue with one orange and then spun gold. Soon the brown mountains change into a wall of flame. The evening clouds burst with hues like a spilled water color palette — red above, purple front, yellow to the side. As the sun sinks lower and the clouds bleed away, the hills glow like the embers of a dying campfire.   -journal entry, August 15

"METHINKS IT'S A BIT of Wyoming in Idaho," I said, folding the map. "Twenty-five miles to American Falls today, then fifty more to the next town. I hate doing it, but I'll have to bike it."

Good thing we hung on to the car. We had hoped to store the car when we reached Utah, but had no place available. Instead we stuck the bike on the rack and reverted to our 1993 pattern. Sue hated driving ahead and walking back, though she now got to help with the litter.

We had hit the Snake River Plain. For 350 miles we would follow it across Idaho, traveling again in the steps (or the wagon ruts) of the old Oregon Trail. The river cut a deep chasm across the southern part of the state, often disappearing beneath the canyon walls. A hundred yards from the water, the land lay parched under the beating sun. Out of sight to the north, forest fires raged, leaving a thin curtain of smoke which obscured the nearby mountains.

Though we'd again decided to 'cheat' on the walk, we didn't cheat on the litter. I walked half the distance to American Falls before mounting the bike, filling our requisite ten bags. Idaho's litter total grew.

Kathy Morris, managing editor of *The Power County Press*, handled the interviewing chores when we hit town. She took our trek to heart, thanking us for our efforts. "If there's anything you need," she said, "please call me. If you can't find camping, need supplies, or whatever, let me know. I'd treat you to dinner tonight, but I've got to cover the city council meeting." She wrinkled her nose at the thought. "A job's a job."

She promised to send us her article, care of Sue's folks. It was waiting for us (along with dozens of others) when we finished the trip, along with a very touching letter. "I respect the journey you've undertaken and wish you much luck in your future," she wrote. "If more people believed in a positive, worthy cause like you both are doing, we'd have a better world."

At the very least, it would be cleaner.

⁂ LITTER GUERILLAS ⁂

⁑ IDAHO ⁑

August 18 – September 4, 1994
277 miles -- 196 bags
TOTAL, 3603 miles -- 1224 bags

You'll learn more about a road by traveling it than by consulting all the maps in the world.
- H. Jackson Browne, "P.S. I Love You"

I've discovered a new natural law: the slower you travel, the better the scenery. On our honeymoon two years ago, we drove through this area en route to Yellowstone and returned with memories of an incredibly boring ride. Today we passed farms like those in the Midwest, saw Oregon Trail wagon ruts, hiked along the Snake River, and watched swans float by. Boring? Not once we left the interstate.
-journal entry, August 18

"GRAB YOUR CAMERA!" I told Sue. "Let's see some ruts."

For a hundred miles we'd followed the track of the Oregon Trail, dutifully stopping at every Historical Marker. Captain X made camp here! Baby Y was born on this spot! Mrs. Z passed a gallstone here! Finally we'd found a marker which promised more: 'well-preserved ruts, 1/4 mile.' "How could we follow the Oregon Trail without seeing at least one set?"

Signs led us on a short hike to a brush-covered hillside. Through the sandy soil, a two-foot wide gully wove its way down the slope. "So where are the ruts?" Sue asked, looking for wheel tracks.

I stepped to the Historical Marker at the path's end and read. "I think you're standing in it." She stepped from the gully as I read further. "It says here that the oxen pulling the wagons did more damage than the wheels. Most of the wheel tracks have faded away, but the paths the oxen trampled remain. Here, for instance, they went single file down the hill, cutting the gully."

The Snake River had provided new challenges to the westbound pioneers. The feared Rocky Mountains and the desert of Wyoming lay behind them, and they welcomed the flatter land. Food and water now became their biggest problems. Though they closely followed the river, it lay in a steep-sided gorge, its precious water out of reach. On the canyon rim, little grew.

In this area, little had changed in 150 years. Old U.S. 30 crossed a featureless land covered with sagebrush, with driveways leading out of sight the only sign of settlement. The river meandered to the north, darting in and out of view. Far to the south a line of big-rig trucks — the 20th century answer to Conestogas — marked the course of the interstate.

The landscape returned to the 1990s as we neared Rupert. The desert suddenly turned into an agricultural Eden, with farms growing sugar beets, beans, melons, and — surprise! — potatoes. We'd entered the 'Magic Valley,' a broad band of land brought alive by a massive irrigation project on the Snake.

With ten percent of the state's population, Magic Valley worried me. More people usually meant more silly laws against camping. Thus when we reached Rupert, we headed straight for City Hall.

"You want to what?!" asked the astonished city clerk. "I'll have to check." After ten minutes running around, searching for an answer, she came back to the counter shaking her head. "I'm sorry, but it's against the rules. You need permission from the city council. They meet here tomorrow night. You're welcome to ask them to pass a special resolution."

Yeah . . . and maybe they could make it retroactive, and attach a rider banning litter, too. Discouraged, we crossed the river to Burley to try our luck. This time we didn't need City Hall to know the answer would be "no." Everywhere we looked, signs advertised the county fair. Traffic crept around the fairgrounds, and throngs of people walked the streets.

Stymied, we stopped for our media fix. The *Times-News* of Twin Falls covered the Magic Valley end-to-end, and they had a satellite bureau in Burley. Handling the beat was Liz Wright, a slight woman in her early twenties. Our story produced a twinkle in her eyes. "Could I get a picture of you in action?"

Before she finished, she solved our lodging problem. "Why don't you stay with me? I've got a small apartment across from the fairgrounds. Once the fair closes, it should be pretty quiet. You can sleep on the couch or throw your bags on the floor."

The apartment was small, cluttered but clean. A well-worn couch and table filled the main room, and books and CDs lay in piles against the wall. Posters lent a touch of home. "I've only lived here a year," she said. "I grew up in Seattle and graduated last spring from Washington University. I'd hoped to stay in Seattle, but it's tough to get big-city jobs right out of college."

She grabbed us blankets from a closet. "The _Times-News_ made me an intriguing offer. 'Work for us,' they said, 'and open a branch office in Burley.' Working as my own boss, tracking down stories — how could I turn that down?"

"How much news occurs in Burley?" I joked. "Besides the occasional LitterWalker?"

"You'd be surprised." She thought for a moment, then said, "My biggest story came last fall in Albion, a village southeast of here. Police had charged a man in his seventies with child abuse. I poked around and found out he'd molested kids for forty years. With only three hundred people in town, most of them knew about it, but no one had done anything." She slowly shook her head.

We sat and talked about her other stories, and she plied us for tales from the road. Outside her window, cars honked and fair goers shouted. As the evening wore down, I asked her a question which had nagged me. "This half of the state is a broad plain. Why do they call it the Magic Valley?"

She paused, and a tired twinkle sparked in her eyes. "No one's ever told me. I should dig into it. Maybe there's a Sunday feature in the story!"

The gnats were gnasty today. Before, they'd always played a zone defense, staying gnear one certain spot, and we could simply walk away from them. Today they switched to a full court press, harassing us endlessly, leaving us gnoplace to hide. Spraying DEET on my hat seemed to help, until I gnoticed the more macho buggers using the bill of the cap for a landing ramp.   -journal entry, August 20

THREE THINGS PEOPLE ASSOCIATE with Idaho are potatoes, white supremacists, and Sun Valley. We'd seen our share of spuds, and had no desire to visit any militia camps. That left Sun Valley.

"Can we take a side trip?" Sue asked. "I've never been there. Besides, we haven't had a day off in two weeks."

At times I wondered if our dedication to the trip was waning. Since July 2, we'd taken one-third of the days off, and we kept looking for excuses to take more. Still, I couldn't fault our new approach. With the dull sameness of the scenery around us, we needed the escapes to keep our spirits high. Last year we'd bickered constantly as the summer wore on, but this year we'd avoided the fights. Maybe the mini-breaks kept tensions from building.

"Did you know Sun Valley was the world's first ski resort?" I said. "When Averell Harriman chose this spot for a resort in the 1930s, chair lifts had not yet been invented. I read last week how one of his engineers, Jack Curran, got the idea for them when he visited Central America. In a port city, he watched dockworkers load bananas on ships using hooks attached to an endless cable. He replaced the hooks with chairs, and voila! Good thing, too," I added. "Hooks would be very uncomfortable."

Sue rolled her eyes. "You've been spending WAY too much time in libraries. Maybe a few days off will help."

So we headed to the mountains. Sun Valley and its neighbor, Ketchum, lay in a lush valley hemmed in by soaring mountains. This summer Sunday the towns teemed with tourists. Bicyclists pedaled down the river trail. Shoppers crowded the downtown sidewalks. We joined the throngs, wandering through upscale shops filled with touristy knickknacks. In the Main Street Bookcafe a flyer caught Sue's attention.

"Glen, look! They're having a slide show tonight on France's Cote d'Azur. I'd like to see that! Unless you had your heart set on sitting in camp, swatting flies . . ."

We returned for a light dinner, and watched the show. As we sat, I noticed people eyeing my 'People Against Litter' tee shirt. After the slides, one woman approached Sue. "Is your husband the one I heard about on the radio?"

"On the radio? Us?" Sue looked at me, and I returned her confused glance. Our story had hit the _Times-News_ that morning, but we'd talked to no one else.   .

"Aren't you the couple picking up trash coast-to-coast?" the woman asked. "I heard it on the Boise NPR station. They talked all about your trip."

(We found out later the story ran nationwide on the Christian News Network. In Ohio it aired while Sue's sister-in-law Melinda gardened in her yard. It sent her screaming inside. "Jim! Jim! They're on the radio!")

As we talked with the woman, the owner of the Bookcafe wandered over. Steve Mitchell started asking about the trip. "Are you going to write a book?"

Steve shared hints about the book business. "I worked in publishing for years before opening this shop, and my wife Erika edits books." I listened raptly, anxious to find out what awaited me. When I finally glanced at the clock, I saw I'd held him up past closing. Adding his name to my journal, I thanked him and left him to close.

We drove back to camp in the Sawtooth National Recreation Area, a primitive area of craggy peaks and thick forests. Shortly after returning we had a campfire burning, which attracted the young couple from the next site. "I'm Kevin Lupton," the man introduced himself. "This is my wife Peggy."

School teachers both, they had just moved from northern California. "There's no work there," he explained, "and we found jobs teaching in Ketchum. Idaho's beautiful — we haven't missed California at all."

Peggy continued, "The big problem here is housing. Nothing, I mean nothing, in Sun Valley or Ketchum is reasonable. We looked for two months, and finally had to settle on Bellevue, twenty miles south. All the houses up here are ritzy. No one builds anything but million-dollar spreads."

Kevin nodded in agreement. "Our place in Bellevue won't be ready for another month, and the school year hasn't started yet — meaning no paychecks. We've stayed in Sawtooth since we arrived, switching campgrounds every two weeks like the rules demand." He spread out his hands and leaned back. "We'll do whatever we can to get by."

I watched them over the campfire, the orange glow lighting their faces. The couple held hands, smiling at each other as they talked about what awaited them. Soon, I knew, that would be us, getting started in a new place. Where would we end up?

The next morning smoke drove us from the park. The worst of the forest fires plaguing Idaho blazed just outside Sawtooth's boundaries, and stiff winds sent clouds of smoke east. By the time we packed the tent, our mouths tasted of ashes, and Sue's eyes stung. "It's not worth it," I declared. "Let's head back to town and enjoy the rest of our break."

So instead of wilderness, we wandered through the town Ernest Hemingway had called home. A hint of cold in the air reminded me that summer's end lay just ahead, and soon the trees here would wear their brightest dress. The words on Hemingway's memorial plaque rang true:
"Best of all he loved the fall
The leaves yellow on the cottonwood
Leaves floating on the trout stream
And above the hills the high blue windless skies.
Now he will be a part of them forever."

I don't think I'll ever get used to being the 'celebrity du jour.' Today, for instance, as we ate lunch at Shoshone's Manhattan Cafe, the waitress came to see how we fared. "By the way," she told us, "management says your lunch is on the house."

What must the owners have thought? To read about two yokels roaming the country, doing something you agree with, is one thing. But to have those same two yokels walk into your cafe?

                               -journal entry, August 21

THE FINAL JEOPARDY™ ANSWER: "Wendell, Paul, Jerome, Rupert, and Kimberly."

What question would fit that? "What are the first names of half the Supreme Court?" "What are the most common names given to babies last year?" "Who plays in the band Hootie and the Blowfish?"

In our case, the winning response was: "What like-sounding towns fill Idaho's Magic Valley?" In this area many settlements had taken Christian names. Were they founders of the respective villages, too humble to allow anything more than first-name informality? Was it an Idaho in-joke, relating back to the Magic Valley moniker? We should have asked Liz Wright to find out.

Towns with first names (we'd already passed Henry, Grace, and Alexander) joined a growing list of things which made Idaho unique. Like washer leagues in Missouri and fence boots in Nebraska, Idaho had their own contributions to culture. Maverik stores, like the Turkey Hill stores of Pennsylvania, gave the 7-11 chain stiff competition. Stinker Stations, with a skunk as the corporate emblem, offered cheap gas every few miles along the interstate. Idaho's answer to Dorothy Lynch dressing was fry sauce, a ketchup/mayo combination in which to dip French fries.

Not that Idaho cuisine stopped at potatoes of various forms. At the Peking Restaurant in Twin Falls, we enjoyed the best eggrolls we'd found on the trip. The Iron Skillet in Wendell served me the best breakfast I'd had since Nebraska: a huge fluffy pancake dominating one plate, with a second plate full of (what else?) hash browns mixed with homemade salsa. Had we discovered a hotbed of hinterland cooking? Or had knowing our trek was winding down sharpened our senses?

It certainly sharpened our distaste for the trash. On our first day in the Magic Valley we filled another thirteen bags, tying our 1994 high. The next day we shattered that mark with eighteen bags, our second highest total of the walk thus far. Our haul included two telephones, cordless and now gutless.

Our bag count soared through the week. After returning from Sun Valley, we logged back-to-back seventeen-bag days. "This is disgusting," Sue stated, pointing at a trash bag overflowing down the road's shoulder. "Look at that. It's full of kitchen trash. Someone must have taken a drive and thrown out their garbage. Detergent boxes, banana peels, coffee grounds, milk cartons." As she snagged it with her picker, a few items fell out. "He even tossed out his mail."

She hesitated and looked at me, her lips curled in a sinister smile. *Sweet justice?* her eyes asked. I slowly nodded.

She speared the two envelopes, then looked at the mailing label. Both bore the address of Jerome Klimes, on East J Street in Jerome. "Oh, great," I groaned. "He's probably the guy they named the town after."

"Jerome's the next town we come to, right?" she asked. "We've got to do something. I've picked up other people's garbage for a year now. I can't let him get away with it." She rebagged his trash in a larger Hefty™, tied it shut, and stowed it in the car.

Thirty minutes later, before breaking for lunch, we drove to East J Street. There, at the address listed on the envelopes, an unassuming house sat behind a white picket fence. The lawn had been recently cut. The garden bloomed with flowers. The yard looked clean — too clean. Taking the bag, I tossed it over the fence.

"Here, Jerome," I called as we drove off. "I think you lost something."

"POTATOES, SHMATOES," THE FARMER had told us. "Lots of states grow 'em. Idaho grows only one-fourth of the nation's crop. You wanna know what market they got cornered? Trout! Eighty per cent of the country's hatchery trout come from right here, along the Snake River. You've gotta check out a fish farm before you leave."

We took his suggestion, and saved an afternoon to visit the Blue Lakes Fish Hatchery. Scores of fish pens stretching toward the river, all teeming with finny food. Behind the pens, two unmarked buildings housed the packing company. A thirtyish woman walking by provided the only sign of human life. I stopped her and asked, "Where do we go for a tour?"

She looked us over before saying, "Follow me." Walking to the second building, she led us into an anteroom devoid of furniture."You'll have to wear these," she said, handing us smocks and hairnets. "I'll find someone to show you around."

She quickly returned with a middle-aged man in tow, telling him we wanted a tour. He nodded, then said, "Go ahead, Kara. Give them one."

"Me?" She looked flustered. "But I've never led a tour. I only started here last month."

"That's no problem. You know the place." He looked at us, smiling as he read our tee shirts. Turning to Sue, he asked, "How are your feet?"

The question surprised her, but then she remembered: the *Times-News* had mentioned her blister problems. "They're getting better. Thanks for asking."

He wished us luck and left. Kara donned her hairnet and ushered us into the main packing room. The L-shaped room resonated with the sound of machinery. Water sloshed on the floor, dripping off tables laden with fish. Through one door men hefted tubs of fish, spilling them onto the tables.

I could see why Kara had not wanted to guide us. A slight woman, she struggled to project her voice above the roar of the machinery. "This first machine slices the fish," she shouted. "The next one sorts them by weight. The third box cuts the backbone out, unless the fish is too large. That's her job —" she pointed to a woman sitting behind the table "— catch the big ones and cut them by hand." We watched as the worker's hands darted to grab an occasional fish. "At my last job," Kara said, "we had to cut all the backbones out by hand."

She moved to her work station. The roar of the machines had lessened, and she dropped her voice. "I fillet the fish, the last step before packing. Here at Blue Lakes, they do things right. At my last job, the fish were still alive when they reached me. I told my boss I couldn't cut them straight because they wiggled, but he said not to worry about it."

With the smell of fish assaulting our noses, we walked past the packing table onto the loading dock. Boxes of fish lay waiting for delivery. "We ship to local restaurants and across the country," she finished. "That's about all. Do you have any questions?"

"What," I asked, "no free sushi samples?"

On the drive back to Twin Falls, I proposed another adventure. "On this trip I've had the chance to do things I'd never gotten to do, growing up in the city — milking cows, making maple syrup. Before we finish, there's something else I'd love to try — and this is a good place for it."

"What's that?" Sue asked hesitantly. "Or do I not want to know?"

"Promise not to laugh? Help in a cattle roundup."

She nodded. "How would you arrange that?"

"The same way Peter Jenkins did, when he walked across the country. He went to the Chamber of Commerce in Twin Falls, and they referred him to a ranching family." I shrugged. "Since Jenkins wrote about it, they've probably been swamped with requests."

Not even close. Kent Just, a jovial man with a full head of red hair, greeted us warmly as we entered the COC office and asked how he could help us. When we made our request, a look of surprise replaced his ready smile. "I don't think anyone's ever asked us that before."

"Maybe not for sixteen years," I replied. I told him how the Jenkinses had stopped in 1978. Back then, someone referred them to a bank president who then introduced them to a ranch family.

"A bank president, huh? Well, I can refer you to David Mead. He retired a few years ago. I'll also give you the number of Jack Ramsay, president of another bank."

"Jack Ramsay? That's the same contact Peter Jenkins used!"

Kent chuckled. "In 1978? No, he would have called Jack Senior. This number is Jack Junior's."

We thanked him and headed for a phone booth. Rather than repeat the Jenkinses' adventure, we started with David Mead. "Do you have to go to a cattle ranch?" he asked. "I can refer you to the Williamses, the son of the rancher Peter Jenkins stayed with. I'm sure they'd like to meet you. If you'd consider a sheep ranch, though, I can give you State Senator Laird Noh's number."

I called the senator, who raised sheep south of Twin Falls. Our request piqued his interest, and he asked to meet us for breakfast the next morning. "I get started early. Is seven o'clock okay?"

We beat him to the restaurant, and waited for a wiry, weathered cowboy (sheepboy?) in jeans, plaid shirt, and a ten-gallon hat. Promptly at seven a thin, fiftysomething man with gray hair and glasses walked in, saw us, and asked, "Glen? Sue?"

He reminded me of a college professor, an image which grew stronger once he started talking about sheep. He discussed the science of ranching, peppering his talk with million-dollar words. "Early each year we graze the animals in desert pastures, then move them into the foothills in the spring, and finally transfer them into the mountains. The progression lets us take advantage of different plants blooming on different cycles.

"The plants the sheep eat have varying nutrition based on their maturity. They have the most value in their early growing stages, and when the plants mature and begin flowering, the nutrients and the vitamin content decline rapidly. When they're young, they're extremely digestible — that is, for a ruminant."

His words flowed smoothly, like a teacher reciting a lesson given time and again. "You can't disparage sheep by saying they're stealing grain which we could use to feed people," he continued. "Sheep eat vegetation humans couldn't eat, and they have the bacterium to metabolize it into useable fuel. They're efficient little factories. In fact, the only animal more efficient in converting food to body mass is the rabbit."

After wrapping up Sheep Ranching 101, he asked if we had any questions. I did. "In Nebraska we heard a lot about range wars. Does that still go on?"

"Not anymore, since it's no longer a situation of first-one-gets-the-land. However, I still run across remnants of the conflict as head of the Resources and Environment Committee in the Idaho Senate. I recently helped overturn an old law which forbade sheep grazing within two miles of any residence. That had given a lot of uncontested acreage to cattle."

"Where do you make your money?" Sue asked. "From wool?"

"Fifteen per cent of our income comes from wool," he said, "and the rest from slaughter. We sell our wool to Pendleton Mills, and shear the sheep in February, right before they lamb. That produces a healthier lamb. Plus," he smiled, "it makes it easier for the lamb to find the spigot."

My turn again. "What type of sheep do you use?"

"We breed a mixture of one-quarter Finnish Landrace and three-quarters Ramboiullet. The Finnish breed mature to pregnancy age earlier, but often do not stay as healthy, and they are much poorer in terms of meat quality. That mix works well for us."

"How many ewes to rams do you have?"

He chuckled. "Well, the Rambouillet rams are quite — how would I put it?"

"Party animals?" I offered.

"Yes, quite the party animals. One ram can service fifty ewes."

The waitress had long since cleared away the breakfast dishes. Laird checked the time and checked his appointment book. "I hope I haven't bored you too much," he said. "If you're interested in learning more, why don't you join us tomorrow? We're taking the flock off their summer pastures in the mountains, trucking some to winter pasture and shipping the others to feedlots." We accepted the invitation, arranging to meet in Hansen the following morning, early.

"Five-thirty," Sue grumbled as the alarm woke us. "You had to say we'd meet him at 5:30. That's not an appointment, that's a sentence." We broke camp in the dark and drove to meet Laird, where we switched to his pickup.

Under starry skies he drove us forty-five minutes into the mountains rising on the Idaho-Nevada border. At the end of a dirt road winding among the mountain meadows, we met his other helpers: Laird's wife Kathleen, Kathleen's sister and husband and two girls, Laird's son, and three truckers. "Our foreman — he's Basque — is out with the shepherd right now," Laird said, "herding the animals toward us."

The minutes ticked away as we waited for the sheep. Slowly the night succumbed to the dawn, and the stars flickered out. A brilliant orange glow bloomed at the horizon. As the growing light added details to the land, I saw a cloud of dust rising to the west. Soon we saw the sheep, prodded forward by two men on horses and a trio of energetic dogs. As the sheep neared, the crew helped herd them into the pens.

The foreman worked in the pens, clapping his hands, yelling, scaring the sheep into the maze. The corridor quickly narrowed to a path only one sheep wide, leading to the loading ramps. Laird manned one gate off the corridor, opening it to shunt off six-year-old ewes; a helper manned another gate to separate their breeding stock. For the rest the gates stayed closed, leaving only . . . THE TRUCK.

Many animals, panicked by the noise and activity, bucked and jumped, some clearing the fence. Most sheep which avoided the truck did a 'victory leap,' jumping four or five feet in the air as they joined their fellow escapees in the holding pen. "That's comical," I said to Sue. "It's like, 'Oh boy! I made the team!'"

Inside the truck the doomed lambs made a racket, talking about their upcoming mystery trip. "Baaa! (Let me look at the) maaap! (Don't push me — you're too) faaat! (I didn't have time to) paaack!"

Finally the last sheep cleared the maze. Loaded full of lamp chops and Pendleton shirts, the first two trucks started down the mountain. The rest of the crew repeated the process with the six-year-old ewes and the breeding stock. This time Sue and I pitched in, standing at the loading chute, grabbing the passing sheep by the tail and shoving them up the ramp.

From my perch, I caught glimpses of the worker inside the truck, directing the sheep forward. When the stream of ovines slowed momentarily, he stuck his head out for fresh air. "Are you having fun?" he asked.

I nodded. "This is great!"

lamb aerobics -- jumping for joy

"Really? Maybe we can sign you up for more work . . ."

"Not your job, I hope. It looks pretty dirty in there."

"Oh, it's not so bad. Usually the sheep are so frightened they just hurtle past. Occasionally they bump into you, and once in a while . . . A ten-year-old ewe once got so worked up, she ran right up and butted me. Then she backed up and went at me again, four or five times. When the dust cleared, though, I won."

The story didn't change on this day, either. By midmorning, the entire crew had won. All the sheep had been loaded, and trucks assigned to either winter grazing or feedlot. We rode back with Laird, learning more about the state of ranching.

"What about grazing on government land?" I asked. "I know your sheep were on national forest land."

"That's quite an issue nowadays," he agreed. "Yes, a lot of people abuse the privilege. With any large group of people, some will always take advantage of the rules. If a rancher simply doesn't know proper grazing techniques, then education is the answer. If he's irresponsible, that's different." He thought for a moment, then added, "Call them the ranching industry's 'litterbugs.'

"Grazing does not have to decimate the land," he continued. "We use responsible grazing practices. For instance, we'll use one meadow two straight years, then let it recover for two years. Other meadows we'll come to later than we could, so they have time to take root or go to seed. You have to pay attention to the different physiological needs of the different plant communities."

"What about sheep herders?" Sue asked. "Why have them but not cattle herders?"

"Sheep require a full time shepherd to protect them from predators like coyotes and cougars. Cows are too large for the predators to target. When sheep are in the high meadows, someone must stay with them. Ranchers used to hire Basque immigrants for the job, but they're not so prevalent anymore. Now, most shepherds come from Mexico, Chile, or Peru."

He had one last word on the sheep-cattle question. "Historically, sheep have held much more importance than cattle. When forced into new lands, man migrated with sheep. That way, they could take their clothing and their meat."

Today was our most pleasant day of walking in Idaho. For the first time in weeks, clouds kept the sun at bay. The road north from the Hagerman Valley rewarded us with views into the Malad River Gorge, of 'melon gravel' dotting the pastures, of irrigated greenery bordered by sere cliffs, and of mountains spiking the northern horizon. Once we climbed out of the canyon and passed Bliss, we strolled another quiet farm road, with long vistas in every direction.

-journal entry, August 27

ACCORDING TO E.P.A. ESTIMATES, the magazine article stated, 80% of the landfills in the United States will fill by the year 2000. One-third of that trash is packaging. Today's throwaway society in America generates two hundred million tons of garbage annually, or 3.6 pounds/day for each person in the country.

Yeah, I thought, *and the roadsides of this state must get half the total!*

"It's official now," I reported. "Idaho wins the litter title. We hit 213 bags today, five more than we logged in West Virginia in the same distance. And we still have a hundred miles to go!"

"I could have told you that yesterday at 'Bottle Gulch'." She referred to the country lane we'd cleaned near Wendell. In fifty yards she'd filled three Hefty bags so full of beer bottles, she couldn't lift them. "Appalachia may have been filthy, but we walked the main highways. How many people ever drive these roads, except to toss their trash?"

I nodded. In Magic Valley, 131 miles from Rupert to Mountain Home, we had set a mark we'd not reached even in Appalachia: 142 bags, or more than a bag for every mile. That included days we got so disgusted that we gave up picking halfway through.

Our last day in the region, trekking from Hammet to Mountain Home, secured the record. Twenty bags in fifteen miles! It ended as our high-litter mark for 1994, our second best of the trip.

To make things worse, the trash had gotten so BORING. Had our jaded eyes seen it all after 3500 miles? Had we stopped cursing the Camel packs, stopped letting the Pepsi cans peeve us, stopped bemoaning the BVDs? The only variety we noticed as we moved through the fertile Hagerman valley was the growing amounts of produce on the road: sweet corn, onion, beets, potatoes.

Still we followed the old Oregon Trail. At Glenns Ferry, we camped at Three Island Crossing, a famous — and feared — landmark. Here, travelers faced a hard choice. Should they follow the Snake River, where water becomes scarce for one hundred miles and the river is difficult to reach? Should they cut overland to the Boise River, risking their life to cross the surging Snake? At Three Island Crossing, though the currents ran strong, three islands divided the Snake River into more manageable stretches. This, then, became the chosen route — with a crossing that claimed many emigrants.

Today, all the traffic flows north of the river. The bluffs on the south side sit undeveloped, much as they appeared 150 years ago. From the park, we could easily make out the wagon (or oxen) ruts as they angled down the steep slopes. After so many miles along the Trail, they no longer seemed a novelty.

As we finished the Magic Valley, the forest fires to the north continued to blaze. In Mountain Home the smoke worsened, dropping visibility below three miles. The sky turned from blue to shades of brown, and the taste of ashes filled our mouths. What would we find in Boise, twice as close to the inferno?

I will remember Eagle, Idaho best for two things: the perpetual traffic jam at the town's only stoplight, and Orville Jackson's Eagle Drug Store. How many other western towns can claim a drug store open since 1906?

Far from an antiseptic, white-tiled chain outlet, Jackson's harkens back to the days of the general store. The shelves stock cures for everything from headaches to hoof-and-mouth disease. A rack of baseball caps leads into a selection of striped railroad engineer hats — I hadn't seen one of those since my grandfather died. Suspenders and washboards hung one crowded aisle over. In the back, offering refuge from the narrow aisles, we found a soda fountain lined with candy.

Surprises greeted us at every turn: Antique reproductions of Coca-Cola trays and oil lamps. Tin boxes with ads for Wheaties, Nabisco, 20 Mule Team Borax, and Lifebuoy Soap. Horseshoes in all sizes. Shelves stocked to the ceiling with trash cans and canning vats, Neatsfoot oil and baby oil, cowboy cookbooks and National Enquirers.

Occupying the entire west wall was a collection of pharmaceuticals dating to the '20s and '30s. Looking through the dust-covered containers provided serendipity: Jars of acetylsalicylic acid, now better known as aspirin. Camphor squares. Precipitated chalk, used for removing grease stains from clothing. In a clear green bottle, pure powdered caffeine.

"I've run this place twenty-one years," said the owner, his black and gray hair topping a frame neither slender nor stocky. "That's been a long time of locking and unlocking the same door, and I'm starting to feel it."

"Have you always offered this much variety?" I asked.

"I've added a few new products," he confessed, "but it looked a lot like this twenty years ago."

I glanced at the line of cars idling outside. "Not this much traffic then, I bet."

"No, it's gotten worse the last two or three years, with people moving to the Boise area. It won't get better, either, until they build the bypass next year."

Maybe then Orville Jackson's can go back to being a quiet country store.   - journal entry, September 2

"THE NEWS ISN'T GOOD for Idaho," the TV reporter intoned.

Our description of the state as "the nation's trashiest" went out to Boise on the six o'clock news. Responding to my phone calls, two stations had sent crews to cover our stroll through the state capitol. ABC caught us near Fairly Reliable Bob's Used Cars; NBC filmed us as we cleaned litter in front of the State Highway Department offices. We'd planned to meet Wally Turk (our Highway Department contact) there, but he canceled when he discovered a meeting on his schedule for this day. Or had I told him once too often how filthy his state was?

The last big city of our trip, Boise tempted us with fine eating. Onati's Restaurant, a Basque restaurant well known in the city, landed on our 'Best Of' list. We enjoyed a feast: a bottomless tureen of spicy bean soup, unlimited salad, chicken croquettes, sauteed sweet peppers, fish baked in butter, and pork marinated in paprika and garlic and sauteed in olive oil. My mouth watered for weeks!

The Earth Food Cafe won our lunch business. For months we'd craved a vegetarian cafe, but no town had come through. When I read a review for

Earth Food, I saved it, taking note of their special offer — 'arrive by bike and get a discount'. "What about people who walked here?" I asked the waitress. "And picked up litter on the way?" For those folks, free.

We needed the good food to fuel our pick-ups. From Boise to the state line the trash did not let up, keeping our minds off the pall of smoke. To complement Wendell's 'bottle gulch', we discovered 'can canyon' on State Highway 44. In sixty yards of eastbound shoulder I collected 101 cans. Across the road Sue bested me, bagging 104.

Variety crept back into the waste. "Here's an interesting letter," I told Sue as I opened a stray envelope. "Looks like old Howard Boyd got himself in trouble. He's supposed to report for genetic testing to resolve a paternity suit." Sue salvaged a flashlight with good batteries. Best of all, our long losing streak ended when I found our first REAL money — a five-dollar bill. "I hope you didn't dream of getting rich this trip," I said.

As we prepared our goodbyes to the Gem State, we also hoped it served as a farewell to attacking insects. Near Notus, biting flies descended on us before we could react. Welts soon covered our legs as we slapped ourselves silly. A local woman agreed that they were bad, giving us her condolences along with a bag of fresh tomatoes.

NOTES FROM SUE'S JOURNAL:
While walking, I thought of an epitaph for when I die:
> *I loved, I learned, I grew,*
> *and left the world a little better*
> *with hope that others will too.   - September 3*

** ON AND OFF THE "O" TRAIL **

* OREGON *

September 4 - September 18, 1994
200 miles -- 37 bags
TOTAL, 3803 miles -- 1261 bags

Thanks to the Interstate Highway System, it is now possible to travel across the country from coast to coast without seeing anything.
- Charles Kuralt, "On the Road With Charles Kuralt"

———————◆————————

It started in Sun Valley.

We felt it the morning we camped north of town. The cold air numbed our hands and chill breezes watered our eyes. Yes, we had tasted autumn.

Now the end-of-summer winds are blowing, easing the day's heat, bringing a taste of change. Mornings start brisk, and the late-rising sun struggles to raise the temperatures above 50°. Again, I feel that difference, that sense of slowing down, of conserving energy for the cooler times ahead. It is a pleasant mixture of deep emotions: a fond remembrance of hot, idyllic days of summer; an eager anticipation of the colors and smells of fall. It's something I lost in southern California's perpetually pleasant climes, racing the rats for my piece of the big cheese. On the road, though, the long-lost feeling comes flooding back.

-journal entry, September 4

FINALLY OREGON!

Four hundred fifteen miles of Idaho lay behind us, leaving us two states to cross. Oregon invited dreams of sandy beaches and waves pounding against cliffs. Was our trip that close to ending?

Of course, we still faced miles of desert. The Snake River may have formed a physical boundary between the states, but little changed. The sun beat down, the bugs bit, our feet ached. The major difference lay in the

agriculture: we'd left the land of potatoes and entered the kingdom of
onions (the Treasure Valley grows 20% of the nation's crop) and sugar
beets.

We entered Oregon at Nyssa, which proudly proclaimed itself the
'Thunderegg Capital of the World'. I looked at Sue with a question in my
eyes. "I can't even try to guess," she answered. "You'll have to ask in
town."

So ask I did, at the grocers while stocking up. "I saw the city limit
sign," I said to the checkout girl. "What IS a thunderegg?"

The clerk, a blonde girl in her late teens, pursed her lips as she pondered
the question. "I think it's this kind of rock that when you cut it in half you
get, like, crystals growing inside. Isn't that right, Sheri?"

Her friend shook her head. "No, that's something else. I think when you
cut a thunderegg open, you get a picture inside."

The clerk in the next aisle threw in his opinion. "No, you're thinking of
a picture rock. This is an egg-shaped rock, and inside, I think it's granite."

Our clerk shrugged as she scanned our purchases. "I don't live here, so
I'm not sure. There's a rock shop a couple of miles out on the highway.
You could ask them."

As we passed the rock shop the next morning, we looked at
thundereggs. The third clerk had gotten it right: a large, lumpy,
undistinguished, egg-shaped rock which, when cut open, revealed a core of
granite. Most rocks had been polished to highlight the core. "So this is
Oregon's official State Rock?" Sue asked. "I'm not impressed. Methinks
some state politicians have too much time on their hands."

What did impress us in Oregon was the abrupt decline in litter. In Idaho
we'd averaged over twelve bags a day. In Oregon we filled less than five.
Eager to spread the good news, I called Sharon Cumbie at the Oregon
Department of Transportation. "Someone here is doing something right.
This really amazes us."

She sounded pleased to hear that. "Our state Ranger Program deserves
a lot of credit," she said. "We hire high-school kids during the summer to
clean the roads. Not only do the roads benefit, it keeps the kids out of
trouble."

The trash they missed kept our interest. Oregon started on the right note
when I spotted another one-dollar bill, bumping our trip total to $11 and
spare change. A sombrero piñata amused us, but its filling of candy had

disappeared. And the kitchen wastebasket and chair — had someone decided to remodel?

The cleaner roads put me in a musical mood. Tunes drifted through my head, and I started composing lyrics. By the time our midmorning break arrived, I'd finished another road ballad. "This one's for you," I told Sue. "I call it 'The Battle Hymn of the LitterPickers':

"Mine eyes have seen the glory of the coming of my wife,
Even as she's picking litter, she's the light of my life.
By now she's throwing glances that could cut me like a knife,
Her truth goes marching on!

Glory, Susan, LitterPicker,	Glory, Susan, LitterPicker,
Glory, Susan, LitterPicker,	My wife goes marching on!"

Her chorus of groans had barely died away when an old pickup truck wheezed by and pulled off the road a hundred yards ahead of us. The driver walked into the neighboring field, then returned to his truck as we approached. From under his S&W Seed baseball cap, he gave us a broad farmer's smile, the type that put us immediately at ease. "Howdy," he said. "My name's Doyle Schuster."

We returned his greeting. "Sure is beautiful weather, isn't it?"

"Wonderful. If it stays this way one more week, I'll have my crop in."

"What are you growing?" asked Sue.

"Alfalfa seed. You're not from here, are you? C'mon, I'll show you."

He led us into the field. Leaning down, he pulled a tiny brown curl off a plant. Once he rubbed it in his palm, only a smudge of particles remained. "You need a combine or harvester to reap this," he said, blowing the seeds out of his hand. "I know it doesn't look like much, but it's a cash crop. I sell it to farmers in Illinois, Iowa, and Nebraska."

"Just the seed?" I asked. "What about the rest of it? Don't ranchers feed alfalfa to cattle or sheep?"

He shook his head. "Unfortunately we can't. Since we use herbicides, we can't feed it to any food chain animal. We have to plow it under. Soon I want to plant disease-resistant plants and quit using chemicals. We've already got bug-resistant plants, thanks to genetic manipulation." He shrugged. "Of course, bugs are pretty smart. Once we develop a new, resistant strain, they adapt to it.

"Everything's so high-tech today, with the genetics. We even use special bees for pollination. They don't make honey, and they hardly ever sting. Isn't science amazing?"

His farming had not only gone high-tech, Doyle admitted, it had also gone global. "Two years ago, after the Soviet Union broke up, I went to Russia to set up a seed company. It really opened my eyes to what went on in eastern Europe. Now understand, I'm not for communism, but the people fared better under the old system. They had jobs. They were taken care of. Some people I met visited here this summer, and the U.S. amazed them. They couldn't believe how well stocked our stores were!"

He led us out of the field. "I think they're headed for a civil war over there," he continued. "That's why I sold my share of the partnership. I'm getting too old to take chances. I can't risk losing my investment now, when I'm getting ready to slow down."

"Are you retiring?" Sue asked. "You don't look that old."

He smiled at the compliment. "Oh, I'll keep my fingers in the business, but I hope my son will help. He moved to California when he turned eighteen, ready to seek his fortune. He's been a roofer for ten years, but he's gotten burned out on city life. He's moving back here, and wants to get into farming."

A far-off look crept into his eyes. "Lately, I've taken up gold panning. In my free time, I head to the Salmon River. Eight hours of work, and I get $300 of gold. That's why I'm glad my son is coming back. If I can get him running the company . . ."

THE PEACE ENDED NEAR Weiser, Idaho.

For two months we had walked in peace. Gone were the bitter fights of 1993, those high-volume affairs which broke out far too often. We had learned valuable lessons from the earlier conflicts: how to share in decisions; when to back off; the art of compromise. The harsh terrain facing us in '94 left us no doubts: we must work together to cross it. Our unspoken pact carried us through the worst of the desert, bringing us to the brink of success.

It was too good to last.

As always, the spark which set off the fight — disagreeing over where to spend Christmas — served less as a reason to argue than an excuse to do so. Testy tempers on both sides escalated the tiff until, late in the day, we barely spoke to each other. As we silently drove along the river looking for campsites, we crossed into Weiser. The sun had already set and the light faded fast, so I quickly decided. "The fairgrounds look good," I declared. "No traffic, no lights. Let's set up."

In the dusk the dirt all looked alike, so we chose a wide patch for the tent. By now, we could set it up blindfolded, so the growing darkness posed no problem. When I woke the next morning with a stiff back, though, I realized something had gone awry. "No wonder I'm stiff. My Thermarest® pad is flat."

Sue checked hers, and reported the same. Feeling along the tent floor, I discovered the culprit. Burrs, undetected in our foul mood the previous night, dotted the fairgrounds. Several had pierced the tent floor and punctured the pads — a dozen holes, I discovered months later.

The Thermarests® had made camping bearable for two hundred nights. My back would never survive our last month on the hard ground. Thus, we had little choice but to backtrack twenty miles to Ontario, Oregon, for new pads. The store there had sold out, but we bought an air mattress for myself and opted to stack the old pads for Sue. For the rest of the trip, I would inflate both her pads at bedtime, and blow them up again at two a.m..

We broke in the air mattress at Farewell Bend State Park, an oasis of green surrounded by treeless mountains. "This is where the Oregon Trail finally left the Snake River," I read from the park sign. "From here, emigrants headed northwest to the Blue Mountains. Many feared those mountains, the highest points left on their journey."

"I'll take any mountains if it means leaving this desert," Sue stated. "I can't stand much more of this."

The road from Farewell Bend led to Huntington, population 540. On the Great Plains, that size would have ranked the 'Catfish Capital of Oregon' as a busy town. Here, we knew that meant no nightlife, and little day life besides. To avoid another boring afternoon, I suggested, "Why don't we talk at the school?"

Gerald Hopkins, principal of Huntington Elementary, welcomed us warmly. After checking the class schedules, he told us we could open with the sixth graders, move to fifth, then visit the combined kindergarten/first grade. "I'll let you finish with the third grade, our wildest class. With eleven boys and one girl, they can get restless."

Who wouldn't be restless cooped up inside while the sun outside beckoned? The kids still paid close attention, asking many questions when

I wound up my speech. Several wanted to know, "Where will you spend the rest of the day?"

By the time we finished, the whole school knew we'd head for the town park. When school let out an hour later, some followed our trail. I recognized a third-grade boy, with blonde hair in a bowl-cut, pointing us out to his older friends. As they crossed the street, he said, "Go ahead, they're the ones. Ask 'em yourself!"

One of his friends asked, "Did you *really* walk here all the way from Maine?"

Their faces reflected shock when we nodded. "That's a long way! Are your feet sore? What do you do when it rains?"

They barraged us with questions, satisfying their curiosities. Soon the queries tapered off, and the boys began fidgeting. As they looked to each other for ideas, Bowl-Cut spoke up. "Hey — you guys want to see a dead Rottweiler? A train hit him yesterday. He's on the tracks right outside town."

Talking about the dog proved more attractive than actually going to see it. They bandied it about until principal Gerald Hopkins came down the street. "Hey, boys," he called to them. "Come on over. I'll treat you to chocolate shakes." That offer needed no further debate.

The second shift arrived half an hour later, as three sixth-grade girls came by walking an Irish Setter. For thirty minutes they visited while the dog ran loose in the park. They listened to our tales of trash and treasure, and told us of growing up in a small town. Finally a dinner bell pulled them away too.

Finally, after hundreds of miles of chocolate mountains — dull, monochromatic piles of dirt and rock — we see promise of change. On nearby hills, single trees stand as lonesome sentinels, green pioneers in a land of brown. A few of the steeper draws feature clusters of pines at their heads. Far to the east arbor outbreaks peppered the slopes, like a two-day stubble on a miner's chin.   -journal entry, September 9

"PROCEEDED ABOUT FIVE MILES over a very dusty road till it became so bad that we could not see our teams or hardly breathe and were obliged to heave to for a season."
    -Cecilia Adams and Parthenia Blank, 1852, present-day Ontario, OR

"Oh, when shall I view, once more, a verdant landscape! One thousand miles of naked rock!"   -Riley Rout, 1848, near Farewell Bend

"We are now traveling through a very mountainous country; the stream running rather in a ravine than a valley . . . The mountains . . . were composed, near the river, of a slaty calcareous rock in a metamorphic condition."   -John C. Fremont, 1843, near present-day Huntington

"At a distance we could see what we supposed to be the Blue Mountains, and they struck us with terror. Their lofty peaks seemed a resting place for the clouds."   -Medoran Crawford, 1842, Flagstaff Hill

"DAMNEDEST WEATHER, ISN'T IT?" the waitress said. "All summer long we've sweltered. Until yesterday, people wore shorts. Now tonight they're predicting frost."

I wondered if we'd walked into winter. Climbing fourteen hundred feet to Baker City had changed more than the scenery — high temperatures suddenly dropped below 50°. Luckily we'd anticipated that, and a box of warmer clothes awaited us at the post office.

Decked out in proper clothing, we toured the grand city. Baker City had begun as a ferry stop on the Oregon Trail, where an industrious settler boated emigrants across the Powder River. In the 1860s gold strikes in the surrounding hills attracted throngs of people. The arrival of the railroad assured the town's success, growing into the finest stop between Portland and Utah.

Today the town showed traces of its former glory. Buildings sprouted granite trim. Ornate arched entrances beckoned. Queen Anne and Victorian-style houses graced the side streets. A magnificent cathedral dominated one block, its walls constructed of volcanic tuff. The Hotel Baker, once the tallest building (nine stories) in eastern Oregon, still towered over Main Street.

In the midst of downtown, nestled among scores of historic buildings, a touch of the modern crept in. "I know espresso is the 'in' thing nowadays," I remarked when I saw it, "and I can understand espresso cafes, but drive-thru espresso bars? Talk about staying awake for that long drive home!"

Though the town impressed us, one thing impressed us more: Trees! To the north and west, mountain slopes climbed into low clouds, and those slopes exploded in green. After enduring a thousand barren miles, my spirits soared to see evergreen forests. Could the end be far away?

Early Oregon Trail travelers welcomed the lush land, too, but their joy was tempered with fear. The desert behind them, however monotonous, had offered 'easy' passage. They now faced not only mountain travel, but hacking a path through the dense woods. With summer fading into autumn, the threat of early snows loomed large.

Their first view of the dreaded mountains came at Flagstaff Hill, several miles east of town. Today, a museum/interpretive center perched on the hill, and huge picture windows framed that view. Inside, dioramas told the story of the trail, revealing the problems and successes the emigrants had faced.

When we visited the center, a more interesting story took place outside. Several covered wagons formed a circle, and volunteers dressed in 1840s garb bustled about. One man looked after a yoke of oxen, and several women tended hot coals in a pit.

"It's our Taste of the Oregon Trail festival," one emigrant told me. "We're cooking the food we've grown used to on the trail, and inviting visitors to join us. They had tickets at the center, but they sold out days ago."

"It must be different to travel with a covered wagon. Where did you come from?"

"We started our journey from Independence, Missouri."

For a moment, I had forgotten I was talking to a Living History woman. "Really? How long did it take you?"

"We started in April 1843. So that makes it — what, 151 years?"

THE DECREPIT LODGE HID at the base of the hill. It popped into view as I rounded the bend, an elegance showing through its decaying facade. The photo bug bit me, hard, and I grabbed my camera.

In the past three days, several people had mentioned Hot Lake. A former Grande Dame of western resorts, its first buildings had sprung up over one hundred years earlier. It fell on hard time in the 1930s, and the last tenant left decades ago.

The main brick building soared three stories tall, towering over the treeless land surrounding it. Deep shadows lurked behind the rows of shattered windows. Holes dimpled the roof. Above it all perched a sign, its letters falling off, advertising HOT LAKE.

After shooting a roll of film, I set off to find Sue. She waited at a pulloff, gazing at the resort. To her side, geese lazily swam on a pond covered with lilies. Steam rose from one end of the pond, wafting up through a forest of white lily flowers.

As we soaked in the scene, a pickup truck pulled onto the gravel behind us. Moments later a young workman stood next to us, looking at the resort with fond eyes. "Impressive, isn't it?" he said. "I never get tired of looking at it."

I nodded. "You come here often?"

"I work here," he answered. "The owners hired me as a watchman, to make sure vandals don't tear the place apart."

"What are they doing with it?" Sue asked. "Will they restore it?"

For Sale, cheap — needs some work

The blue-jeaned worker shrugged. "They haven't decided. Just to patch the roof and shore up the foundation — the minimum needed to keep the place from falling down — would cost two million dollars. The last owners tried to fix it up, and they went bankrupt."

"It looks ancient. How old is it?" I asked.

"The bathhouse came first in 1864, and quickly attracted a following. The hot baths, they said, helped a variety of ailments. In 1907 Walter Pierce, who later served as Oregon governor, built the main building. It cost him half a million bucks, a lot of money back then. Heck, it's a lot of money today!

"Business peaked in the twenties. It ran as a spa until 1934, when a fire destroyed the old wooden buildings like the bathhouse. The owners fixed up the main building and ran it as a sanitorium from 1941-51, then as a nursing home. It closed for good in '74."

He paused, a sparkle in his eyes. "I'm not supposed to, but . . . would you two like a tour?" He took our enthusiastic nods as a 'yes.' "I do have to warn you, though. A lot of people think it's haunted."

He led us through the acres of gardens, once blooming with exotic flowers, now overgrown with weeds. As we neared the building, its solid nature grew obvious. "The walls are twenty-two inches thick. That's one reason it hasn't fallen apart."

We stepped into the main lobby, our footsteps echoing in the empty anteroom. I looked at the floor, a collage of thousands of dime-size tiles. "All imported from France," our guide reported.

"Over here," he moved to where the front desk had stood, "they had their own post office. In that corner, a newsstand carried papers and magazines. Down the hall, a library kept avid readers happy. They had barbers, a confectionery shop, a drug store, and a commissary. People called it 'a city under one roof.' At its peak, Hot Lake employed 175 people — quite a lot for this area."

He led us into the next room. "They used this big ballroom for gala events — the area's high society would show up. Parrots flew around in big cages hung from the ceiling. Boston ferns lent a tropical air. Sometimes I can picture the balls, like a scene out of Great Gatsby. It must have been something, before the fire destroyed it."

He shook his head slowly, a trace of sorrow in his eyes. "The fire should never have happened. They had a firefighting system on the

grounds, but no one had inspected it. When the fire broke out, they found
the hoses had rotted away. They couldn't do anything but watch it burn."

We next stopped in the examining room. In the gray light filtering
through the windows, I saw old furniture and equipment. Near one wall, a
large machine bursting with tubes, wires, and switches caught my eye.
Complete with tesla coil — the type that shoots lightning bolts between
antennae — it could have come from the set of a Frankenstein movie.
"Back in 1932, this was high technology — a brand new x-ray machine.
Even the Smithsonian doesn't own one this old."

"So this was a noted health resort, huh?" I asked.

"Noted? Newspapers called it the 'Mayo Clinic of the West.' People
came here from across the country, even overseas. The place specialized in
treating tuberculosis, arthritis, syphilis, and alcoholism."

He led us across the hall to the dining room. It seemed to stretch
forever. "At its peak, Hot Lake Resort served two to three thousand meals
a day. In this dining hall they could seat a thousand people. They grew
much of the food on the grounds. A twenty-acre garden provided the
vegetables, and they even raised chicken and cattle."

As he led us to the east wing, he walked on the far right of the hallway.
Wood stained with rat droppings sagged in the center, and scattered holes
showed the floor had gone soft. Creaking boards and hazy light combined
to build an aura of spookiness.

He must have read my thoughts. "After the fire, people started
complaining of ghosts," he said. "Residents of the nursing home heard
footfalls upstairs, even though the upper story had remained closed. One
accountant staying here swore he heard parties up there, with the buzz of
people talking, laughing, and clinking glasses."

At the end of the hall, we climbed the stairs to the second story. Our
guide took us into the first room, which had served as the operating room.
Glass from the observation room window covered the floor at one end.

"The clinic was run by Dr. Phy and his son. He had a reputation as an
innovative doctor, doing things unheard of in his day. He pioneered
techniques in the twenties and thirties which doctors still use today. His
death in 1932, followed by his son's in 1933, started the resort's demise.
The fire a year later made it official."

We moved down the hall to the solarium. There, sunlight streaming in
through huge windows dispelled the ghostly atmosphere which had set in.
A quick glance to the doorway, however, brought it back. The doorjambs

sat askew from settling, a reminder we had left the world the living frequented.

"I'll take you to the third floor now. In the nursing home days, when the third floor was closed off, the owners stored a grand piano up there. In the evening, people could hear ghostly melodies coming from it. The owners finally moved it, because it spooked the guests. For several nights afterwards, people heard footsteps shuffling on the third floor, going from room to room. They were looking for the piano!"

On the third floor we passed more guest rooms. "They had 205 rooms, all heated with spring water. If you'll look inside, you'll find they look a lot different from today's hotel rooms. See all the closet space? And there's no private baths. That's because in the early 1900s people only bathed once a week, but they changed clothes two or three times a day. Thus, people brought a lot more with them."

The third floor housed the main solarium, another large room with wide windows letting in the light. Pigeon feathers coated the floor, and we heard them cooing in the rafters like voices from the past. Spiderwebs spread from the far corner to several windows. "This room seemed the most popular with the ghosts. The owners stored chairs here, and they often heard steps in this area. The story has it that although dust settled on the floors and tables, none settled on the chairs. It's as if someone regularly sat on them . . ."

With the pigeons cooing and the wind whistling through the holes in the roof, I could imagine spirits myself. For a moment I let my imagination fly, hearing the piano playing ragtime, seeing the patrons reading in the sunlit room, smelling the odors wafting up from the kitchen.

I wandered to a window overlooking the courtyard. Slowly my vision of the past, of finely tended gardens and people bustling about, faded. The present came back, and I looked out on an overgrown courtyard dominated by two large trees. ". . . imported those trees," I heard from behind me, "from Europe and Asia, and planted them surrounded by ferns and exotic plants. The pictures I've seen showed a lush garden you could get lost in." Now the trees had shed their leaves for the season, heightening the barrenness.

We walked to the rear of the wing, stepping around more soft spots. At the far end, our guide opened the door, revealing — nothing. Nothing but thin air and a two-story drop to the ground. "A catwalk used to connect this floor to a parking lot on the hill," he explained. "It rotted away years ago. Anyone for a fast trip down?"

Our tour of the main building complete, we retraced our steps to the staircase. "This place has generated a lot of controversy," he told us on the way down. "It played such a big part in the area's history, it's tough to let it go. The local Historical Society insists on saving it, but the owners won't sell them the land. On the other hand, many locals won't come near here because of the ghosts. They want it torn down."

On the ground floor, he led us through unused interior rooms. With no windows and no lights, they plunged us into darkness, and we followed the guide's voice. In the back, we emerged in a room lined with turn-of-the-century tubs. "These were in the outbuildings that burned down. Four bath houses let you choose your type of treatment — sweating, soaking, sauna, or mud baths."

To finish, he took us to the original bath house. Inside steam drifted up and disappeared though the rafters, lending an eerie aura to an otherwise sunny day. "The main springs bubbled up at temperatures from 186° to 208°. They still bubble today, but no one uses them."

I thought about the resort the rest of the way into La Grande, wondering what it was like in the mid-twenties, or later when the ghosts had moved into the 'Spirit's Spa.' We spent the afternoon in the city library, and I researched the story further.

The library had a Hot Lake file stuffed with articles and pamphlets, reports of the fire, and descriptions of the attempts to reopen it. The most fascinating appeared in the _La Grande Observer_ of October 27, 1977, when reporter Dick Cockle interviewed Richard Owens, a caretaker who had lived on the second floor. His recollections made me wonder . . .

"Things would get out of locked rooms. I had some wheelchairs get out of a locked room once, and the room was still locked."

"Sometimes it [the piano] would play for five minutes. Sometimes it would play for a while. After you lived out there as long as I did, you don't pay any attention to it. You don't _want_ to pay any attention to it."

"My room was directly under the old surgery room, and you'd never hear it real plain. There's a woman that screams up there. It sounds like somebody's got her tied up or something."

I'm glad we didn't camp there.

WE FOUND OUR GOLD mine in Oregon.

Like the prospectors who flooded the Blue Mountains 130 years before, we too found riches in the northwest. Ours had none of the flash of gold or silver, and it sure didn't pay as well, but it was far more abundant and easier to collect: aluminum, as in pop and beer cans.

Nationwide, aluminum cans set the pace for recycling. The U.S., on the average, reclaims 17% of its waste (Seattle leads the nation at 45%). One-quarter of the paper and of steel cans makes it back into production, as does 20% of the glass. However, 65% of aluminum cans — two out of every three — get recycled.

For the first time since New England, we walked through a state with a bottle bill. In early 1993, the problem of separating cans from other trash and finding places to redeem them discouraged us from trying. Here we found so little 'other trash,' it hardly seemed worthwhile to make state crews come out for one bag every five miles. We could pick up two or three bags of cans a day, though, and throw them in the car. At day's end, we could trade them at the local grocers.

The first day we carefully crushed each can, stuffing each Hefty™ full. That night, the Safeway balked at taking them, since the state reimbursed them based on volume. Have you ever tried uncrushing 140 pop cans? We salvaged three-fourths of them, earning $5.40 — good wages for an itinerant LitterPicker. Now savvy to the recycle rules, we bagged our cans whole, averaging six dollars a day.

As we scoured the roadside for cans, we kept our eyes peeled for other treasure: Camel Cash, cigarette coupons redeemable for prizes. Sue first collected them near Boise, and soon she had me looking for them. "How many do you think we'll need to get a nice prize?" I asked Sue. "Or will we get stuck with an official Joe Camel™ ashtray?"

When the cans and Camel Cash didn't keep us busy enough, real moolah did. Sue snagged another Washington greenback near Huntington, and I hit the big time near Hot Lake. On the outskirts of La Grande I spotted two bills, a single and a sawbuck. With $9.15 in cans, we netted over $20 on the day. "Heck, that's almost real money!" I told Sue. We blew our fortune on a hotel room that night.

Instead we should have splurged on a warm blanket. From La Grande, our route plunged into the Blues. Ahead of us, peaks soared to 9000', and the highway neared half that. With the cold snap, we expected nighttime temperatures near freezing.

But who's complaining? We've been in the desert so long, I'd almost forgotten what trees were. Now the aroma of firs laced the crisp air. Squirrels and rabbits raced through the underbrush. Bushes painted with red and gold hinted at the coming snows.

Perry. Hilgard. Kamela. The names jumped off the map, recalling bustling towns in the days of mining, rail stops when people traveled by rail. Now the towns have disappeared, leaving small collections of houses — and ghosts? — behind.

In Meacham, the only real village in this part of the Blues, we heard more tales of spirits. The Oregon Trail Store became our home for the afternoon, and we chatted with its new owners. One woman's aunt had worked as a nurse at Hot Lake. "She used to tell me about hearing screams in the closed areas," the woman said. "One night, she attended a party there. All evening she saw rocking chairs rock, though no one went near them."

Behind the counter, her partner nodded. "We had one heck of a time opening this store, too," she said, "because of a ghost. Gus, we called him. We would come in and work, and all of sudden, the bar stools would start spinning. Also, he would throw the ashtrays across the room. We figure he was a frustrated smoker who couldn't light up."

I took it in, fascinated with the stories. With the deserted roads we'd walked, spirits were easy to imagine. "It sounds like this region is bursting with ghosts."

Both women enthusiastically nodded. "Did you see the church camp across the street?" asked the one behind the counter. "Years ago, when it was a hotel, a young lady committed suicide."

The other woman led us to the door and pointed across the railroad tracks. "See that window? She jumped from there. Sometimes when it's misty, the fog will part, and you can see her in the window. People have also seen her walking the tracks."

Maybe she was picking up cans . . .

We started our day in a mountain meadow. Slowly the road dropped, heading toward the Columbia plains. Soon pines lined the road, their dark green canopy offset by red and yellow shrubs — a small concession to the changing of the seasons.

At Deadman Pass the plateau gave way to the rim of the Blues. As we crested the pass, a rumpled landscape spread out below us. Deep wrinkles stuffed with evergreens marked the canyons, and on the ridges

the yellow of autumn grass alternated with ocher brushes and thistles. Below our perch, the interstate cut its swath.

As our knoll petered out to a point two thousand feet above the valley, a vast brown-and-yellow checkerboard stretched to the horizon. To the west, sky met land in a string of jagged points — the high peaks of the Cascades, sixty miles or more distant.

-journal entry, September 17

Mr. Litter, in the woods

OREGON'S FOURTH LARGEST CITY wasn't a town, it was a rodeo.

The Pendleton Roundup, to be exact. For most of the year, Pendleton is a sleepy town of fifteen thousand people best known for its woolen mills and fancy houses. One week a year, though, sixty thousand people descend on it for the rodeo and festival of the Roundup.

The town bulged with people. Hotels displayed 'no vacancy' signs. Parking lots for downtown businesses turned into RV parks. Tent City sprang up at the junior high school, with nylon and fabric domes of all shapes and colors crowding the grounds.

"I think we stumbled upon 'Spring Break' for cowboys," I said as we entered town. Traffic choked the streets, backing up light-to-light. Grandmothers with ten-gallon hats rode in pickup beds. Cadillacs sported longhorns as hood ornaments. On the roofs of street-side businesses people sat on beach chairs, watching the activity below.

Four days of championship rodeo highlighted the festival, but those tickets had sold out months earlier. Instead, we settled for the street fair, which hummed with life on this final night of the Roundup. We grabbed corn-on-the-cob, barbecued ribs and Indian tacos from a street vendor, and settled in for people watching.

The passing crowd gave us a fashion show: People young and old sported shirts with Navajo and Hopi patterns. Cowboy hats outnumbered baseball caps. Hiked pant legs revealed ankle tattoos. Women competed for the largest belt buckles. (I heard someone use the term 'bucklebunnies,' and it fit.) Back pockets of faded jeans stood out with imprints of Skoal cans.

Country-and-Western music wafted through all three blocks of the fair, a different band on every block. Strains of "The Devil Went Down to Georgia" followed us as we window-shopped the arts and crafts: Indian turquoise jewelry; leather belts; pictures of pockets drawn on mattes then stuffed with actual combs, pencils, etc.

At one end of the blocked-off street, crowds waited in line for carnival rides. With Sue's encouragement, I plunked down twenty bucks for a go at the bungee jump. 'Jump' was misleading — they hooked me to a bungee tied to a crane, then let it yank me up. The second bounce was the scariest, dropping me within inches of a street lamp before rebounding. Sue, who turned down the bungee, had her own thrill ride in the Port-A-Potty when a train passed by yards away.

The party surrounding us drew us in, melting away my tensions, bringing on a holiday mood. As we sat resting our feet, the parade of revelers continued, shouting, drinking, smiling. Soon a lanky man in his twenties sat on the bench next to us, watching the crowds. Casually dressed in a western shirt and jeans, he had a bushy moustache and a grin with a missing tooth. He studied us with sidelong glances, taking special note of our shirts.

Finally he spoke. "I noticed your tee shirt," he said, pointing to the 'People Against Litter' logo. He paused, then added, "Looking down the street, I'd say litter's winning."

That brought a laugh and introductions. Wendell Stockdale hailed from Longview, Washington, further along our route. Word of our trip struck a responsive chord. "I don't walk much, but I love traveling," he said. "I've visited forty-six states, and have seen an awful lot. Last year at this time I was in Ocean City, New Jersey, riding out a hurricane in a halfway house."

I noticed he was one of the few people on the street not drinking beer. "I had a good friend who dried out in a halfway house in Seattle," I said.

He nodded slowly. "I've seen my share of them, but I've learned a lot about myself in the process. Sometimes you've got to hit rock bottom before you can find where you want to be in life." Where Wendell wanted to be, he told us, was working with horses and rodeos.

Together we watched partyers pass by, celebrating the end of Roundup. By 10:00 the crowd had peaked, but my energy level had plummeted. The lure of a night's sleep grew too strong to resist, so we bade Wendell goodbye. In turn he gave us a parting gift: his phone number in Longview. "When you reach town, call me. You can crash at my place."

Longview lay only three days' walk from Astoria, our final goal. Were we really so close?

** THE HOME STRETCH? **

* OREGON - WASHINGTON *

September 19 - October 4, 1994
212 miles -- 42 bags
TOTAL, 4015 miles -- 1303 bags

One of my superstitions has always been when I started to go
anywhere, or do anything, never to turn back or stop until
the thing intended was accomplished.

- U. S. Grant

————————◆————————

NOTES FROM SUE'S JOURNAL:
Up at four a.m. in severe pain. Laid in car til sunup. Crying — can't
breathe. Want to be home in bed. - *September 19*

I WOKE TO A dark and empty tent. Crawling outside, I found Sue in
the car. Tracks of dried tears striped her cheeks. "What's wrong?"

"My side," she said softly. "It feels like someone's twisting a knife in
my side."

"I don't understand," I said as I squeezed her hand. "When did you hurt
it?"

She shook her head. "I didn't. This body doesn't need a reason to
torture me. Think of it as my 'body lottery.' Which part will hurt today?"

My heart sank. We'd scheduled the day off for R&R in Walla Walla,
a chance to celebrate crossing the Blues. Hold the champagne, pass the
Anacin™! "Let's find a doctor and get you better."

She grimaced as the pain stabbed again. "No, don't. What can a doctor
do? Give me pills and tell me to rest? I went through the same mystery pain
in Missouri five months ago. It'll go away in a few days."

We sat in silence as the sky brightened. When the sun finally peeked
over the treetops, Sue battled her pain to help break down camp. I then
took the driving duties, returning us to Pendleton. Its empty streets
provided stark contrast to crowds of cowboys two days earlier. Fortunately
hotels had relit their 'vacancy' signs, so we found Sue a bed for the day.

Though her pain lingered for a week, she felt well enough the next day to drive the car while I churned out the miles. Again I endured arid, scrubby desert, a letdown after the mountain forests. The cold snap had ended, and hot, dry days returned. Our six-week streak without rain dragged on.

At Echo, Oregon, we bid our final 'goodbye' to the Oregon Trail. Where it continued west over the barren plateau, we struck north for the Columbia River. Our route ran through fertile fields, another monument to the wonders of irrigation. Berry bushes laden with fruit lined the road. The blackberries weighing down the branches tantalized Sue, and she left the car to reap the free harvest.

At Umatilla we finally reached the mighty Columbia. The river, a broad flat ribbon of blue, separated Oregon from the dirty brown hills of Washington. Barges lazily floated upstream, towing their loads. For the first time since we'd left California, the cries of seagulls serenaded us.

The gulls brought back memories of home, of beach rides and visiting friends, of life before the trek. In three weeks, I mused as I sat at the marina, the Litterwalk would be behind us, leaving — what? For two years, all our energy had gone into the trip, planning, cajoling sponsors, arranging publicity, and walking. For two years, we worked with clearly defined goals. What would give our lives a 'new purpose'?

Our 'old purpose' motivated us here. Trash had returned to Oregon! Again I practiced two-bag picking, separating low-quality garbage from the cans and bottles we'd come to love. From Irrigon, Oregon (first cousin to Walla Walla) to Boardman we filled nine bags, our high for the state. The cans netted us $13.80, a minor fortune.

Signs in Boardman led us to the city-owned campground, a welcome sight after a hot, sweaty walk. Our initial pleasure soured, however, once we checked the grounds. "I guess it's the only game in town," I grumbled as I paid the fee. Later, while Sue napped, I fired off a letter to city hall:

TO: Director, Boardman Parks and Recreation Department
RE: Overnight campground
  My wife and I camped on your grounds on Sept. 24, 1994, as our long trip was winding down. We have been walking coast-to-coast picking up litter. From our start in Maine on April 1, 1993, we have come 3900 miles through twenty-two states, bagging three-and-a-quarter tons of roadside filth.

Our journey has taken us to many campgrounds, both commercial and public. We have seen a wide range of services and accommodations. We're proud to report that your park easily takes the prize as both the most expensive AND the least traveler-friendly we have encountered.

Fifteen dollars to pitch a tent? What a great idea: balance the city budget by gouging travelers. They can't vote you out of office! You really should notify all those towns in Kansas and Nebraska which allow tenters to stay free and RVers to hook up on a donation basis. They are missing a golden opportunity!

And you gave such a creative excuse ("our sprinklers are automatic") to keep tenters from harming your grass. So many cities in Idaho and Oregon (including nearby Irrigon) went to the trouble of turning off the sprinklers in their parks so we wouldn't get soaked . . . all the work they went through — why bother for thankless tourists? Give 'em gravel instead. I'm reminded of days at my grandmother's house, with couches covered in plastic — look but don't sit.

Oh, don't forget the Laundromat! Force those pigeons to pay a full dollar to dry their clothes. So what if they don't use the full fifty minutes? You've got their money, and that's what's important! Save on electricity, too — one small light in the restroom ceiling is adequate. No one really wants to see themselves in the mirror. Of course, no one cares if the shower stalls have curtains — it's just another cost item.

Of course, you've found the ultimate cost saver: don't staff the site. I find it hard to believe that KOAs and Good Sam parks can get by charging only fourteen dollars for a tent, less than you. How do they find the money to maintain their playgrounds, pools, and rec rooms, and still pay for the staff the greedy public expects? Could it be because they're not a monopoly?

However, I think you've overlooked something. THE SHOWERS ARE FREE. Just think — if you installed coin meters, you could turn the park from a 90% efficient money machine to a 100% cash grabber. Hmm . . . maybe Guiness could list you as the world's biggest camping ripoff!

Yes, you've really hit upon a growth industry. People traveling always have extra money. Why not take it from them?

If they can afford an RV, they can surely afford whatever you'd charge. Besides, where else can they go?

Please rest assured that we will mention Boardman in all interviews we conduct the remainder of our journey down the Columbia.

Thank you oh so much.

Despite its other faults, Boardman did have a memorable truck stop. With its faux leather bench seats, greasy spoon menu, phones at the tables, and giant neon "EAT" sign blinking outside, Nomad Inn is the type of place you'd expect to see Elvis.

In fact, we did see Elvis — several times. He smiled from a framed print; his face told the time on another wall; in three other clocks his gyrating hips and legs served as pendulums. Marilyn Monroe joined him swinging in three more clocks. The cavalcade of timepieces also featured pairs of billiard clocks, golf clocks, padlocks with key pendulums, and holograms of Jesus; three giant wristwatches; and four pairs of intertwined hearts. I quit counting clocks at forty.

In addition to Elvis, framed prints of Harley motorcycles, unicorns, and cows shared wall space with Laurel and Hardy and a giant Budweiser label. All were tagged for sale, waiting for a buyer with a loose standard of interior decorating. Decals of regional trucking firms and railroads filled the wall behind the counter, with a few major corporations (Albertsons, Pepsi, True Value Hardware) thrown in for good measure.

To complete the scene, I ordered the truck stop favorite, chicken fried steak. I received a heaping platter of food, tastier than expected, and cheaper than our last several dinners. The waitress serving us remained cheerful and helpful, despite covering the entire room by herself.

-journal entry, September 24

We entered the gorge today, though not the scenic part. Haze from farmers burning their fields still hides the Cascades from us. Hills the color of ashes slope from the plateau down to the wide river.

As we sat on the Arlington docks at sunset, splashes in the water caught my eye. Below us, in water tinged with gold, I saw hundreds of smelt — each a couple of inches long — jumping as they swam downstream.   -journal entry, September 25

"HOW DOES THAT GRASS ROOTS song go?" Sue asked, humming a tune. "♬ Nothing good comes easy . . . ♪"

"♪ . . . no matter how that you wish it would ♬," I joined in. "Yeah, maybe they tried walking across Oregon too." I spun the bike tire in frustration, and it quickly ground to a halt.

Okay, okay, so we've had an easy time of it this year, I thought. *Nothing like last year's Crisis of the Week Club. Still, why does our luck have to change so close to the finish?* First it was the pain in Sue's side. Now we discovered that someone had hit the bike while it was mounted on the car, bending the front wheel. "It can't be trued," I reported, "and it'll rub the frame until we replace it."

I glared at the two-wheeled wonder. For seven weeks we'd hassled with it every time we opened the car's hatch. Only three times had I needed it to cross long stretches of desert. Now we needed it one last time, to help me reach The Dalles. With twenty-five miles between each of the next three towns, I'd hoped to walk halfway to each and bike the rest.

"I doubt the Boardman grocery store would carry bicycle wheels," Sue said.

"And Arlington and Rufus will have even less. The Dalles might have a bike shop, but by then I'll be through riding. I'll have to ride it like this." I turned the bike over and mounted it. "Hopefully the tire won't wear through and blow." On a wobble and a prayer, I set off.

The extra drag on the wheel turned the flat runs into hills and the hills into mountains, but the miles still dropped away. The broad shoulder on I-84 buffered me from the traffic whizzing by. I passed one boring, lifeless slope after another, waiting for real scenery, when I rounded a bend and POW! there soared Mt. Hood. Towering over the neighboring peaks with a hat made of clouds, it begged for a picture.

After nursing the bike into Arlington, we spent the afternoon playing tourist. In the midst of this barren land, we'd heard of two attractions: Maryhill and Stonehenge, both legacies of a pioneer named Sam Hill.

Sam Hill had grandiose plans for a self-contained Quaker community. In the early 1900s he bought seven thousand acres of arid land along the shores of the Columbia to found his dream. Up went a hotel, a church, stores, offices, a school. For his own home, he built a mansion of poured concrete high on a bluff overlooking the river. To connect everything he paved ten miles of roads, the first rural roads paved in the state.

The desert of interior Washington proved a hard sell. After a promising start, interest in his community faded. The last settlers left after a fire destroyed the town, leaving Hill with eleven square miles of broken dreams. For years the land languished.

When the Great War (now known as World War I) devastated Europe, Sam Hill saw a new purpose for his land. As a lasting statement against the wastefulness of wars, he planned a monument honoring the war dead. On the bluff which had held the hotel, he constructed a scale model of England's Stonehenge.

His mansion also survived. Named Maryhill after his daughter, it still sits on the bluff, a striking sight from the river below. Today it houses the Maryhill Museum, with an eclectic collection which includes Rodin sculptures and drawings, Native American rock carvings and baskets, furniture and jewelry from Romania's Queen Marie, and one hundred antique chess sets.

We visited both sites, wandering amongst the stone blocks of Stonehenge, admiring the views downriver from Maryhill. The relaxing afternoon got my mind off the bike, worrying if the tire would last.

The second day passed much as the first had, with a growing bare spot on the tire. In Rufus we arranged to talk to the grade school. After seeing the town — a dilapidated cafe and a rundown lounge composed 'downtown' — we expected little from the school. Surprise, surprise — it ranked as the nicest we'd seen, with spotless rooms and a computer lab with seven new PCs. All for only thirty students!

We talked to the fifteen students in the kindergarten-to-third-grade class. They listened attentively, enjoying the break from normal lessons. "This has turned into a real 'Visitor's Day'," the teacher told us afterwards. "When you called, we already had guests in the room. This morning two missionaries on leave from Zaire talked to us."

That evening we stayed at the riverside park run by the Army Corps of Engineers, a broad strip of grass and trees right on the Columbia. Far from the ripoff of Boardman, ACE parks were no-fee, allowing free camping for up to fourteen days in any month. We soon found that the no-fee policy attracted many full-time campers, people who switched parks every two weeks.

The river gypsies were a breed apart. Bo Peep convinced us of that. Her tent blended into the bushes, hidden from the parking lot nearby, and a clothesline strung between adjacent trees sagged with a full load of laundry. The pajamas and bonnet she wore reminded us of the nursery rhyme, but instead of sheep she tended to a pair of cats. We chatted with her while we pitched our own tent, but she struck us as very confused.

Later we cruised to the far end of the park, checking the facilities. One RVer had transformed his stretch of asphalt into a make-do home. A car and an ATV were parked behind his RV, and potted tomato and ficus plants served as his garden. Close by, two campers had set up dome tents, and each had power cords and leads from TV antennae disappearing into the canvas.

Take away my home, make me rough it, but don't mess with my TV!

"I SWEAR, I'M A JINX," Sue declared. "If it's not my body, it's my bike. If it's not my bike, it's my car. Where will it end?"

"Not at The Dalles, I guess." I paced in the lobby of the Mid-Columbia Medical Center. A doctor had prescribed pain pills for Sue's side, and we waited for the drugs. The bike had come through without a hitch, and we had again relegated it to the rack on Sue's Mirage. Ahhh, the car . . .

"I wondered if it would make it up that last hill," she continued. "The sputtering and jerking remind me of when the turbo went out the week of our weddings."

I winced at the memory. "Sure I said for better or worse," I'd told her at the time, "but I never agreed to $1500 repair bills!" On an engineer's salary, the bill had hurt; on a can-picker's income it could break us. "Maybe it's something minor," I said with forced optimism. "We'll check it in Vancouver."

First we had to get there. From The Dalles we crossed the Columbia into Washington, our twenty-third state. Ahead of us, cutting through the Cascade Mountains, lay the Columbia Gorge — and a welcome exit from the hot, dry weather. For the first time in over two months, we walked through a light rain. The legendary gorge wind kept us cool.

The scenery changed more rapidly than anywhere we'd ever seen. In the twenty-two miles from between The Dalles and Hood River, annual precipitation more than doubled. The barren mountains we'd grown to hate donned threadbare coats of spindly trees, and followed that with lush cloaks of pines. Soon the oranges, reds and yellows of fall shone like stars in a sky of dark green. Fog tiptoed off the river into the forests, reminding me of the coastline of Alaska. Cliffs soared to the sky.

State Highway 14 wove through the lush landscape. At points it clung to the cliffs, with a steep rocky embankment dropping to the river. Trucks hurtled by, squeezing me to the edge of the narrow shoulders. Dozens of tunnels provided a new thrill: Could I run through them before traffic caught me inside? Luckily they were all very short.

Cook, Washington, kicked off the trip's 'home' stretch. For October, we looked forward to several nights indoors: longtime friends in Vancouver expected us; I had relatives in Portland; Wendell had offered his home in Longview. First, though, a good friend had insisted we visit his parents in Cook.

"Are you sure we're not imposing?" Sue asked as we followed the directions to Waldo and Phyllis Zaugg's house. "I mean, we've never met them, and now we show up at their door all hot and sweaty. If they look busy, we should just say 'Hi' and move on."

When we rolled up, they greeted us warmly, easing our doubts. "You don't have dinner plans, do you?" Phyllis asked. "I've planned a feast. You will stay the night, won't you?"

After showing us the house — they'd built the log mansion themselves — Waldo visited with us as Phyllis returned to the kitchen. Now retired, he'd spent his working years with the U.S. Department of Fish and Game. "I specialized in salmon, trying to keep the fish population from dying off. We knew the dams caused the biggest problems, but we weren't sure why. Finally we realized the river had no flow to help wash the young fish to sea. Swimming through still water takes them longer — maybe too long. If they don't reach the sea before their bodies change to need salt water, they die. I studied enzymes until I found one which triggers the fish to move downstream. If we could get them to start migrating earlier, we figured, it could save them."

He told us stories of nighttime fishing trips, taking boats on the moonlit river when the fish were most active. We asked about the house he had built, and of the harvest from his garden. He talked of the area and his roots. "It's too bad Steve and Diane hadn't known your route went by Hot Lake. My dad, Steve's grandfather, lives near there, and he would have loved to meet you. They'll show his picture on the *Today* show next week, when Willard Scott gives the birthday greetings. He's turning one-hundred-and-one!"

At dinner that night we met their son-in-law Gary, a New York transplant. He had recently moved to the Gorge because, as he said, "You can't windsurf in New York. This area leads the world in windsurfing, because the winds are so consistent. Most all the time they blow upstream, and on the few days they don't, they blow downstream. If you get a chance, check out 'the Hatch' tomorrow. I hope to get in a few runs."

'The Hatch,' next to a fish hatchery, wasn't hard to find. On the water, over one hundred surfers cavorted. Their colorful sails turned the river into a kaleidoscope of cloth. They turned, they jumped, they flipped. For an hour we watched them.

Once we hit the road, a van with a windsurfing logo drove by and squeezed onto the shoulder ahead of us. The driver did a double-take when he saw our litter sticks and bags, and asked what we were doing. "Yeah, it's dirty around here," he agreed. "Some dudes don't care, and throw their trash on the road. That encourages locals to call us bums and try to kick us out. It's hard enough to find parking here in season. Today is nothing. In the summer twice this many people will come out. Some of us make it a point to pick up the trash left by the losers, so we don't lose access rights."

The ever-present wind gusted, spinning my litter bag. The surfer smiled and turned back to his van, grabbing his gear. "I gotta get to work, man. The waves are calling."

Just when I think I've seen it all, WHAM, here comes another vista. Skamania. Beacon Rock. Cape Horn. Tomorrow, though, we exit the gorge and leave the river for three days.

Passed the four-thousand-mile mark today, only 130 to go. It feels strange, knowing we must soon think about our lives, post-walk. How frightening!   -journal entry, October 3

IS IT JUST COINCIDENCE that the first syllable of 'gorgeous' is Gorge?

During the endless miles crossing Wyoming and Idaho, I kept focusing on the Columbia River Gorge. We had driven through it in 1991, and its beauty stuck in my memory. *Hang in there,* I kept reminding myself. *Your reward for enduring this comes in the Gorge.*

Now that we'd reached it, we took our time passing through it. We stayed an extra night with the Zauggs, and scheduled a rest day two days later. With the car coughing and sputtering, we drove Oregon's famed Columbia Gorge Scenic Highway. The road snaked through the canyon, sometimes high above the river, sometimes at river level passing spectacular waterfalls. Concrete bridges sported scrollwork from the 1920s. Parks above the canyon gave eagle-eye views of the dark furrow below. The road, we found out, had been designed by Sam Hill, the visionary behind Maryhill and Stonehenge.

After a thousand miles of deserts, I couldn't get enough of the forest. We hiked to several waterfalls, enjoying the lush greenery. One person we met couldn't believe I'd spend a 'day off' hiking. "Isn't that like a tow truck driver spending his weekends at demolition derbies?"

The Washington side dealt us another hand of heavenly beauty as we trekked west. At Cape Horn the road clung precariously to the sheer rock face, the Columbia River far below. Beacon Rock towered over the river like a sentry guarding a gate. The Skamania Lodge, a sprawling wood-and-stone inn built in the thirties, perched on a forested bluff above the road. Inside the lodge a fire blazed in the lobby's fireplace, and we spent the evening reading in front of it to avoid the chilly evening temperatures.

We savored the cooler weather and the lush surroundings. Now free of pain, Sue walked twelve miles a day through the rainforests. Traffic had died down, with heavy trucks forsaking the twisting road for the interstate across the river. What little traffic remained showed us courtesy, giving us ample room on the narrow road. One driver, noticing my pack, stopped and offered a ride. When I declined, he grinned and kidded me, "Okay, just walking across America, huh?"

"In fact," I replied, "yes, all the way from Maine." His eyes grew large, and he left without another word.

Our last night in the Gorge we camped at the Mt. Pleasant Grange. While checking the grounds, Sue found a curious pile of trash. Next to the building, someone had carefully placed an empty Bartles and Jaymes™ four-pack on top of an Alcoholics Anonymous blue book. "Did the person fall off the wagon," I wondered aloud, "or did he have one last blast before climbing on?"

As we left the gorge, it felt as if we'd finished the trip. My thoughts turned to decisions past the walk — what route to drive home; who to call when we arrive; where to stay while wrapping up our life in southern California.   -journal entry, October 4

AFTER THE GORGE, CLARK County was anticlimactic. The land flattened and filled with farms and subdivisions. Traffic and trash increased. My sense of discovery, of wonder, had fled. Now thoughts of friends and family filled my mind, and I longed to move on with my life. *Let's get this over with.*

Friends Debbie and Allyn Sayre expected us on October 5. First, though, we had another night of camping to arrange, possibly our last due to cooler temperatures. One last time we had to deal with the hassles of city camping, begging permission of countless town officials, church deacons, or whomever.

In the twin towns of Camas and Washougal, it went as it had in so many mid-size towns. "No, the laws don't permit it. You can apply for an exemption at the city council meeting." The Camas city clerk worked hard to help us, calling around and finally finding space on the grounds of the Lion's Club. By then, we'd arranged a spot on the lawn of the Presbyterian church.

The return to begging a campsite frayed our tempers, and another spat erupted en route to meeting the Vancouver *Columbian* reporter. It fizzled quickly once we met Brett Oppegaard, who treated us to a fine Italian restaurant. He plied us for background, gaining material he would craft into our best article of the trip. Wine, pasta, and good company cast their spell over us, and our tensions melted away.

The next morning came early as we cuddled away the cold in our sleeping bags. Mother Nature's call finally forced us from our cocoon, and we rushed about while breaking camp to fight off the chill.

"Be careful of those hidden stakes," Sue warned me, referring to two wooden stakes stuck in the church yard but cut off at grass level. "Now what route are we taking today? When do we meet Allyn?"

Out of the tent came the sleeping bags. Out came the pads which still deflated every night. Out came the pillows, the blanket, the toiletries, all the goodies that had seen us through so many nights. I pulled our plastic stakes and tent poles, leaving the tent flat as I grabbed the stuff sack. Sue collected our stakes, and rounded the corner of the tent heading full bore for the car.

And hit the hidden stake.

And fell. Hard.

** WHATEVER IT TAKES **

* WASHINGTON - OREGON *

October 5 - October 15, 1994
118 miles -- 24 bags
TOTAL, 4133 miles -- 1327 bags

Never any weary traveler complained that he came too soon
to his journey's end.
- Thomas Fuller, "Good Thoughts in Bad Times"

"OW IT HURTS IT HURTS OH IT HURTS!" Sue rolled on the
ground, her face twisted in pain. Her left arm curled against her body, held
close by her right.

I rushed to her. "Are you all right? Are you okay?"

She shook her head, gritting her teeth. Tears streamed down her face.
"No. I think I broke it."

"Oh, no, no, not again." I squeezed her good hand. "Are you sure?"

She tried to move her left arm. "I can't unbend it. Oh, Glen, I can't
believe it. Why me? Why now?"

"Maybe you just jarred it," I said with an optimism I didn't feel. "Let
me help you to the car." I hurriedly threw the tent into the hatch, then drove
her to downtown Camas. The door next to city hall led to the police/fire
station, where a dispatcher sat sipping her morning coffee. "Where's the
nearest hospital?" I asked.

"In Vancouver. Is something wrong?"

"My wife fell. She's in the car." I pointed outside.

"Hang on. I'll have a paramedic look at her." She buzzed the back
room, and a man in uniform came out. I took him to Sue, and he checked
her arm. Satisfied she could safely travel, he gave us directions to the
hospital.

Twenty minutes later we added to Sue's growing list of emergency
rooms. The doctor ordered x-rays, which verified our worst fears: a broken
humerus where the bone enters the shoulder socket. "I can't believe you
suffered this break," he told her. "Usually I see this in people over sixty."

Due to the swelling, they could do little for it. "You need to see an orthopedist tomorrow," the nurse said as she fitted Sue for a sling. "We recommend Dr. Ragsdale. You'll have to call his office for an appointment."

We left the hospital in a daze, still stunned by the accident. Was it a coincidence that she broke her leg 110 miles into the trip, and her arm with the same distance to go? How could she hope to finish now?

"We can't quit," Sue answered the unasked question. "Not when we're this close."

"But you can't walk," I noted, "and you can't drive a stick-shift with your arm in a cast. You need to be at home in bed, so you can recuperate."

"You forget, we don't have a home. Anaheim? We'll stay in a motel long enough to get your unemployment checks started, and to say 'goodbye' to our friends. Then we're off again, to — where?" She shrugged her right shoulder. "A motel here, a motel there. What's the difference?"

I wanted to argue, to take her from this adventure-turned-living-hell, but I couldn't. We did have no home, no refuge to escape to. Besides, I couldn't leave the trip unfinished. If the fall had happened months earlier, certainly, I would have quit. If I had known in 1992 the terrible price Sue would pay throughout the walk, I would never have considered the venture.

But all the 'ifs' in the world didn't add up to one decent 'now.'

We'd committed two years of our lives to this goal. Though our success, if it happened, would come with a bitter taste, to accept defeat would be even more sour. Giving up would invite a host of 'what ifs' later, an unending game of second-guesses. I knew Sue would do better off the road, and she knew it too, but she wouldn't let that stop us.

By the time we left the drug store with a new set of pain pills, the morning had passed. We met Allyn for a late lunch, then whiled the afternoon away in a park. At six o'clock, Debbie led us to their home in Brush Prairie, where we made Sue as comfortable as possible.

"So what does this do to your plans?" Debbie asked later as we munched on barbecued chicken. "Will you move back your finish date?"

I shook my head. "No, I think I can still make the fifteenth."

Sue looked up in surprise. "How, since you missed walking today? That puts you fifteen miles behind."

"You forget we'd planned on taking tomorrow and Friday off," I reminded her. "If I walk instead of visiting relatives, we'll be back on schedule." _I'll have lots of days off after the 15th. For now, I just want to finish this._

Debbie nodded. "So will you return to Camas tomorrow to start walking where you left off?"

"Yes, I will." Several times, it turned out. I soon learned what Sue endured with the car, driving back and forth, seeing the same scenery time and again. First, drive to Camas — _where can I leave the car? is it too far to walk?_ From Camas, drive west and stow the car. Back to Camas on the bike, wobbling the whole way. Lock it, and walk — finally! — back to the car. Now drive back for the bike, then 'home' to Brush Prairie.

By day's end I'd memorized every inch.

The solitude brought me a sense of _deja vu._ I saw New England in the thick stands of trees and in the varied architecture. Lush lawns quickly dimmed memories of the brown expanses of Idaho and Wyoming. Traffic avoided the back roads, leaving me alone with my thoughts.

I covered seven miles that morning, meeting the _Columbian_ photographer for action photos. After lunch, I drove Sue to Dr. Ragsdale, and left her to his poking and prodding while I knocked off three more miles. Another three Thursday morn returned me to Brush Prairie, almost back on schedule. A short walk that afternoon would pull me even, and then we could rent a car with automatic transmission for Sue to finish the trip.

As we left the Sayres' house to find lunch, traffic was heavy. Rounding a bend, we saw a gravel truck heading north. His full trailer bounced along the uneven road. As he passed us, a pebble flew from his load — right to our windshield. The glass instantly filled with spider webs.

On October 7.

One year to the day since the errant softball met our windshield and sent the trip into an early break.

Those thoughts careened through my head as I quickly pulled the car over. In the rearview mirror, the gravel truck disappeared around the bend. "I can't take this!" cried Sue. "My body — my car — what else will this trip ruin?!"

The traffic finally parted, and I pulled the car into a screeching U-turn. With foot to the floor board, we took off after the truck. Once we caught him, we tailed him, honking, flashing our lights, waving for him to stop. For three miles we chased him, until he finally pulled over. He jumped from the truck, his eyes flaming. "What the hell you trying to pull?" he yelled, waving his arms. "Are you guys nuts?"

"We need your insurance information." I tried to keep cool in the face of his belligerence. "Some gravel flew off your truck and smashed our windshield."

That further irritated him, and he stomped about, loudly denying any fault. Twice he punched the door of his truck, denting it. I backed away and asked a good citizen who had stopped to call the sheriff. While waiting for the gendarmes, I wrote down the truck's license number, and took note of another coincidence. "You know the doctor you saw, Ragsdale?" I asked Sue. "Well, here we have Rags Trucking."

We exchanged insurance info under the watchful eyes of a Clark County Deputy, and much delayed, took off for lunch. For another afternoon I would forfeit walking, forcing me to play catch-up the next week. After lunch we rented a car in Portland, finding one last eerie coincidence. The numbers on Sue's license plate read '071'; those on the rental car mixed them up to get '017'.

The trip was taking on the air of a cheap novel.

What we'd dreamed of as a victory lap through the Pacific Northwest, savoring the last days of our epic trip, is turning into a struggle to finish. We'd both looked forward to Washington after enduring a thousand miles of desert. Thoughts of walking in the shadows of the Cascade peaks, easing our way through lush forests painted with autumn's brilliant colors, had driven us for months.

Instead I walk through the wooded hills alone, unable to share the sights and smells, pushing myself to reach a weekend deadline. Meanwhile Sue sits in a car with burning, stabbing pain that pills won't touch. Our 'victory lap' has suddenly turned into a grudge match.

-journal entry, October 9

DID THE WEATHER REALLY turn overcast, or did it only seem that way?

I had dreamed of this stretch all summer, dancing through the forested basin, enjoying the greenery we missed so sorely. Instead, I found myself plodding past trees cloaked in mists, their colors muted. The trees filled the air with a damp, musty smell. Clouds hid the towering Cascade peaks from view. Only the sound of my boots crunching along the shoulder broke the silence.

The miles stretched endlessly. Our string of disasters had set us behind schedule, and we now faced an extra day to return the rental car and fix our windshield. Meeting our target date now required five straight days of sixteen-to-seventeen miles. The last time I'd tried that — in New Hampshire a lifetime ago — the pace had left me limping.

At Woodland, Washington, old U.S. 99 dumped me onto the interstate. Trucks and cars raced by, their occupants isolated in their steel cocoons, leaving me with little but exhaust gases. The din hurt worse than the silence of the rural lanes, and I gladly left the highway at Kalama.

Each day dragged through the night and into the following day, nothing lightening the gloom which had descended. Few people frequented the streets I walked. I passed schools in session, but the required miles left no time to stop. The *Columbian* article, the best of the trip, passed with no fanfare. We even missed seeing Wendell, our friend from the roundup, when our calls went unanswered.

Every night we sought out a hotel to rest our bodies and souls. The pain kept Sue on edge, and her high-strength pills offered scant relief. Sleep was a struggle, as shifting position would move her arm, jolting her awake with spears of pain. The constant ache wore thin, shortening her temper.

Our disasters kept dogging us. By midweek we found that Mr. Rags Trucking had given us bogus insurance info. Without a valid policy number, the cost of the windshield would land squarely in our lap.

With that dark cloud hanging over us, I crossed the mighty Columbia on the Longview-Rainier bridge. On the Oregon side, our old friend U.S. 30 struck due west, promising us Astoria in three days. *We may finish yet!*

Despite the pain Sue battled, despite the false leads Mr. Rags Trucking gave us, despite the long miles and missed days, despite the rancorous fights Sue and I had, we're almost there. Nine miles separate us from the ocean — three hours of walking to the beach. NBC is paying a stringer to cover us, and we hope CBS News will join them. Associated Press interviewed us today, as did the <u>Daily Astorian</u>. Tomorrow we return the rental car, then Saturday — the finale.

-journal entry, October 13

FINALLY THE PRELIMINARIES HAD ended. It took hoofing ninety-six miles in six days, but we reached Astoria on schedule, mid-afternoon of Thursday the 13th. However, we barely had time for a victory toast. After securing a motel room for Friday night, we drove to the coast to check Saturday's route. We needed a course on which Sue could join me, walking the final mile onto the beach.

With the route chosen, we drove two hours to Portland to return the rental car. That night the Sayres treated us to a victory dinner. Debbie's brother Dave Meisch, with whom I had double-dated years ago in California, asked about our final day's plans. "It's too bad Debbie and Allyn can't make it," he said. "I'll come see you finish."

Friday the 14th was a study in frustration as we tried to get insurance information from the trucker. 'Rags Trucking,' we discovered, was a one-man outfit. The driver/CEO of the firm swore he'd given us a valid policy number. When pressed, he transferred us to his 'accountant.' His wife yelled at us and hung up, and wouldn't answer when we called back.

The new windshield passed inspection, but the choking and gasping had gotten worse. A quick tuneup by Allyn's mechanic provided no help. With a healthy dose of hope and a large dollop of prayers we left for the coast, unsure whether it would make it to Astoria — much less California after that.

At least it reached Astoria. We were met at our motel room by several messages of congratulations, a request for info from the NBC stringer, and an interview request from the *L.A. Times*. How the *Times* tracked us down, we never did find out.

As the evening closed, I repacked my pack for the final day. The previous week I had donned only my fanny pack, traveling light to cover the miles. For the finish, I reloaded the pack to full weight, stowing all the goods which had gotten us this far. With that done, I dropped into a fitful sleep, with one thought echoing through my dreams.

Tomorrow.

WOTTA DAY. It's hard to believe it's all over — I'm sure it hasn't sunk in yet. For now, I'm basking in the glow.
                                        -journal entry, October 15

"YOU MUST BE THE WALKER!"

The compact car pulled into the motel parking lot as I hoisted my pack. Inside sat a middle-aged man surrounded by camera gear and tape recorders. "I'm Dave Pastor, the TV stringer. All set to finish, I see!"

I nodded enthusiastically. "I've waited two years for this day. I'm ready!"

After confirming the route, Dave drove ahead a mile and set up for the opening shots. I crossed Youngs Bay on the U.S. 101 bridge, the trek's last numbered route. I hardly noticed the light traffic, focusing instead on the beautiful morning. After a week of dreary, overcast skies, this day had dawned gorgeous. Low coastal clouds had already dissipated, leaving the sun alone in a gleaming blue sky. It felt grand to be alive.

Dave shot volumes of tape, catching my stroll through rural Warrenton. From eye level, from the trash point-of-view, panning, zooming, from ahead, from behind, he caught the walk I'd practiced so long.

After two miles of filming, Dave drove ahead to chat with Sue. I turned off Harbor Drive onto Galena, foregoing the busy main drag for a quiet dirt lane. For the last time, I had the world to myself, away from people, traffic, and pressures. Emotions raced through my mind, colliding with each other, forming a colorful kaleidoscope of feelings. Despite the fully loaded pack, my steps sprung one after the other.

I rendezvoused with Sue and Dave on Main Street, and led them onto the last side road. Ninth Street/Dump Road cut west through the coastal woods, providing shade from the climbing sun. I walked along, filling my 1,327th and last Hefty™ bag. "You missed a piece," Dave playfully pointed out. "A Camel pack — maybe it has Camel Cash!" It did, our last coupon.

We met Dave Meisch on Ridge Road, the main road paralleling the beach. My arrival halted a soccer game taking place on a city field. The preteen kids swarmed around, asking for autographs, giving me high fives, shaking my hand. True to form, they peppered me with questions: "Did you really walk all the way from Maine?" "Are your legs cramping up?" "Why did you do this?"

By 11:30 we'd reached Fort Stevens State Park. Dave Pastor sat Sue and I at a picnic table, taping the interview which would air on more than a half-dozen TV stations in the next twenty-four hours. First I, then Sue, answered questions for the camera, reducing twelve months of walking to fifteen minutes' worth of words. Then, at 11:50, our time came.

Time for the last stroll.

With Sue's good hand in mine, we walked into the park. A bike path broke off from the parking lot, plunging us into a coastal glade. The surrounding trees muted traffic noises, and we imagined ourselves miles from civilization. Alone together, we strode the last quarter mile.

We hit the beach at noon, right on schedule. Directly above, a Coast Guard helicopter buzzed the beach. When the pilot saw us, he dipped his rotors, then headed south. "I called them this morning," Dave explained. "They had training exercises planned for noon, but wanted to salute your trip. They postponed their exercises for an hour."

That left our long-awaited stroll to the sea. To the south the beach stretched endlessly, a ribbon of yellow fringed by tufts of grass. To the north, the skeleton of the Peter Iredale — a British four-mast bark which

Finish — How sweet it is!

ran aground in 1906 — silently watched the waves. Behind us lay a continent worth of litter, scenery, and wonderful people. Ahead of us, the surf crashed, the drum roll of our finale.

I stepped into the water, Sue by my side, to an indescribable mix of emotions. With the surf foaming about my feet, I reached into my pack and pulled out a small coin. The token advertised an arcade in north-central Massachusetts.

Facing Dave Pastor's camera, I held the coin so it glinted in the Oregon sun. "Eighteen months ago in Townsend, Massachusetts," I said, "a little girl named Caitlin gave me her lucky coin. She said it was her only gold one, and she wanted me to have it."

With a surge of pride, I added, "If you're watching, Caitlin, I made it!"

** EPILOGUE: THE SPEED OF LIFE **

Most people have that fantasy of catching the train that
whistles in the night.   - Willie Nelson

———◆———

"Are you Glen Hanket, the walker?"
I didn't recognize the voice on the other end of the phone. "Yes, I
am."
"You don't know me, but I read about you in <u>Walking</u> magazine a
while back. I'm thinking of walking across the country next summer, and
wondered if you could give me any hints . . ."

-journal entry, December 15

WE LEFT THE ROAD to an avalanche of publicity. TV stations
throughout the region featured us that night. Papers across the country took
the story off the AP wire. Radio shows in Boston and Chicago interviewed
us, and Voice of America ran an extended piece. Eventually our story even
made it to the *National Enquirer.* Friends from all over sent
congratulations, including a giant card signed by everyone from the Iuka,
Illinois, grade school.

The car (without the turbo) did make it back to California, where we
sold it at a bargain price. After reclaiming the truck, we filled it with all our
must-haves and set off to Colorado. I found a job within three weeks, and
we moved the rest of our goods in early January. The condo took us
another year to sell, after spending $5000 repairing the damage left by the
tenants-from-hell.

We've stayed in touch with many of our new 'road' friends, writing
some, visiting others. The Greiners in Maine hosted us when we flew east
on vacation. Steve and Darci Newman officially christened the guest room
of our new house in June 1995, and I drove back for their wedding in late
1996. On that trip I also visited the Gates family (from South Webster,
OH, now moved to Cincinnati) and talked again to the students in Iuka.

My biggest thrill, post-walk, came in the spring of 1996. Months earlier
Sue had sent my name to the Atlanta Committee for the Olympic Games,

and they responded quickly: "Will you be a torch-bearer?" On Mother's Day I joined an impressive roster of Olympians, award-winners, and volunteers in running the Olympic torch through Denver.

It was a dream come true.

Our life otherwise has settled into a comfortable rut. Sue found work in a veterinary hospital, fulfilling a long-term goal of working with animals. I am again working with computers, writing "software no one cares about or understands." On weekends we like to hike — you may even see us on the streets around Denver, toting a Hefty™ bag and a pair of litter sticks . . .

. . . all any of us need is a very light suitcase.   - Oswald Wynd

** ACKNOWLEDGMENTS **

A TRIP SUCH AS the one we undertook demands a lot, both from those taking it, and from the people around them. It took very little time to realize how important the help of others would be to the trip's success. Family and friends were invaluable in our effort to leave the 'real world' behind, and to rejoin it after the trip. Those wonderful souls we befriended over our 4133 miles helped make our trip worthwhile — without them, we would never have lasted. Of course, we may never have made the first step if not for the generous donations of our sponsors.

Specifically, great thanks go to our families:
Glen's parents **Patricia and Joseph Hanket**, for handling our bills, forwarding mail, lending moral support, and for rescuing Sue in Nebraska;
Sue's parents **Jim and Dorothy Armstead**, for chronicling the trip, endless moral support, "launching" us in Maine, and nurturing Sue back to health;
Uncle **Steve Armstead** for running interference with the press;
cousins **Bob and Lola Coyle**, for a much-needed holiday break;
grandparents **Jim and Lila Armstead** and **Frieda Perrett** for emotional support and for proofreading this text;
and our siblings: **Dirk Hanket, Tricia and Howard McCarthy, Donna Hanket, Jim and Melinda Armstead, Kim and Paul Davis, and Tracy and Bart Surrick**, who all followed our trip via papers and radio.

We thank the friends who got us ready for the road, and kept our spirits up via postcards:
Ron and Joann Schrantz, who helped get us in shape and vacationed with us in Yellowstone;
Larry and Kathy Harlan, who edited the first proof of the book;
Tim Klepaczyk, who visited and stored our car for one eventful week;
Dave and Cindy Kurfman, for opening their home to us;
Pat Minshall, who hosted our farewell party and referred us to her brother in Rutland, MA;
Bill Padilla, for keeping us company through the Rockies;
Debbie and Allyn Sayre for rescuing us after Sue's last injury;
Maralys Wills, Margot Palmgren, and the others from my writing class;
Ben MacDonald, for teaching me the book business;

and others for kindnesses too numerous to mention: Jeff and Kyung Bowman, Nick Damato, Christina and Bernie Dawson, Jeff and Kathryn Fielding, Leslie Fouse, John Kehoe, Rick and Melody MacNamee, Steve and Donna Mills, Marty and Olga Mutsch, Carol Partner, "Cannon" George Ramsay, Joan Saario, Lee and Leslie Schulman, Steve and Diane Zaugg, and Bob and Kathy Zurn.

The wonderful folks from the road kept us sane. In addition to those people mentioned in the text, thanks go to Bob and Nancy Gavelick, Mel and Cathy Hanson, Elin Potter, Judy Parker, Robert and Marjorie Lehan, Hamburg's Ritz Deli, the crew at the *New Jersey Herald* (Beth Ambrose, Anna Murphey, Kathy Stevens), Bob Miller, Dennis Mood, John and Mona Gleason, Harry and Jeannie Thomas, Mary Shank, David Wilkinson, Judy Stackpole, Mr. and Mrs. Riley, Andrew Herman, Vicky Albers, Barb Cioni, the folks at Herman's Riverview Motel, Jeanette Cruz, Maggie Sturgeon, Joe and Bill Crane, Terry Wright, Gary and Tere Dewitt, Charles S. Schaeperkoetter, Ann and Doris in Corder, Maggie Anderson and Connie Pound at Lewis Middle School, the folks at the Monterrey Motel, the Mark Miller family, Peggy Collier, Ray of the Washington Water Works, Pat and Jan Cole, Ruth Pelton-Roby, Dave and Randy in Milliken, Lois Landrum, the Wyants at the Manhattan Cafe, Kevin and Peggy Lupton, John Miller of KTVB7, Rich Cason, Janet Dodson, and Marina Swain.

Very special thanks go to all our sponsors:
Fady Sahhar at **Tenneco Packaging**, for supplying us with **Hefty**™ bags and shirts, and for underwriting the cover design for this book;
Ted Dishner and Marilyn Moss at **Moss Tents**, ME;
Steve Gladstone at **Karhu USA**, VT (**Merrell Boots**);
Dave Wren and Michael Pfotenhauer at **Osprey Packs**, CO;
Byron Shutz at **Garuda Mountaineering**, WA (2nd tent);
Leslie Kirchner at **Sierra Designs**, CA (sleeping bags);
Paul Riddenmeyer at **Pikes Peak Industries**, CO (the litter sticks);
Trish Brennan at **Rocky Mountain Sheepskin**, Westminster, CO (padding for the backpack straps).

And finally, thanks to *Mother Nature*, who humbled us;
and *the Boviners* who kept us company and made us laugh!